The notion that history repeats itself has never been better attested than in this account of the long battle of Friedrich Gentz against Napoleon. The new order in Europe that the French established from the Mediterranean to the Baltic and east to Russia presents a series of uncanny parallels to our own time in the vast attack of the armies of the revolution on the balance of power, and the rising against them of the armed forces and the people they had subjugated. Gentz fought this threat to the liberties of Europe with an energy and skill so lively and intelligent that he seems to be speaking for our own coast-to-coast audience, excepting that his knowledge is never superficial or his views uninformed. Gentz was a barbed, farsighted, timeless commentator on the unchanging elements of statecraft; a Prussian by birth who permitted himself to accept subsidies from foreign powers but only to use them to aid the cause to which he had already devoted himself. With Pitt and Metternich he was one of the embattled civilians responsible for the downfall of Napoleon, and his personal life was as irregular and dramatic as his public career.

Golo Mann, youngest son of Thomas Mann, presents the story of Gentz's life and times with great brilliance and insight. It is possible that all accounts of eyewitnesses of the present problems of Europe need constantly to be supplemented with the perspective of books like this history.

Golo Mann took his doctor's degree at the University of Heidelberg, but left Germany after the Nazis came into power. He taught at the University of Rennes, edited *Mass und Wert* in Zurich; and at the time France fell had just enlisted in the French Army. After making a round of French concentration camps he escaped to Spain and the United States, and later went overseas with the United States Army.

PUBLISHED ON THE LOUIS STERN MEMORIAL FUND

GENTZ AT FIFTY

Secretary of Europe

THE LIFE OF
FRIEDRICH GENTZ,
ENEMY OF NAPOLEON

By GOLO MANN

TRANSLATED BY WILLIAM H. WOGLOM

NEW HAVEN
YALE UNIVERSITY PRESS
LONDON · GEOFFREY CUMBERLEGE · OXFORD UNIVERSITY PRESS
1946

Printed in the United States of America

TO J. F.

TRANSLATOR'S PREFACE

THE translator's best friend is his author, but in the present instance this refuge and strength has been denied, for Dr. Mann is serving overseas with the armed forces of the United States and, it may be added, serving with unusual distinction.

Before entering the army he had been teaching in Olivet College, Olivet, Michigan, and before that had pursued an active editorial and teaching career in Switzerland and France after having taken his Ph.D. in history and sociology at Heidelberg.

In his absence it is fortunate indeed that he was able to persuade a friend, Dr. Erich Kahler, himself a historian and an author of note, to assume the responsibility of adviser. Dr. Kahler has faithfully compared every word of the translation with the original manuscript, and his familiarity with the author's habit of thought, with the events of the period under discussion, with its literary style, and even with its minor characters has made easy and pleasant what otherwise might have been a well-nigh impossible task. If errors have crept in despite all his care, the fault is the translator's alone.

The English version is an accurate reproduction of the German original. Almost nothing has been omitted, and nothing added save a date here and there, perhaps, or a footnote or supplementary word or two where they seemed to facilitate the argument.

In some explanatory material that accompanied the manuscript Dr. Mann points out that Friedrich Gentz has been described by an American author as a fascinating personality, a brilliant and unscrupulous man of the world who wielded a tremendous political influence; by an English writer as the sole example of a political aspirant who, by his pen alone, achieved a position of social equality with statesmen and nobles in an aristocratic country and under a despotic government.

That he was far and away the greatest political writer ever produced by Germany all those who know his work will agree. Yet he was not a purely literary man, nor was he purely German. Since no parliamentary career was possible in his native country he had to make a position of his own, as a private correspondent of ministers and kings, as an international adviser, and as a writer of public manifestoes and secret memoirs. For these activities he was paid by the British and Austrian Governments, and at times by other European governments as well, but he never did anything or wrote anything in violation of his convictions.

He was renowned, too, as a ladies' man, though this part of his life cannot well be emphasized in a political biography. To the final chapter the love of the sixty-five-year-old high priest of conservatism for Fanny Elssler, the famous ballerina, gives a touch of tragicomedy.

The documentation is enormous, and most of it has been taken into account. But the works of the "Secretary of Europe," Metternich's right-hand man, have never been assembled and there exist only some fragmentary *Collected Writings*, an edition of his letters that has never been completed, and his diaries; hence most of the material had to be drawn from such sources as lives and letters, and German, French, and English periodicals.

Thus Dr. Mann.

Miss Ella Holliday of the Yale University Press guided the erring feet of the translator through the dismal swamp of technique, Miss Roberta Yerkes edited the manuscript, and Mr. Eugene Davidson presided over the whole with all his accustomed geniality.

To each my heartfelt thanks.

W. H. W.

New York, February, 1946.

CONTENTS

ILLUSTRATIONS

INTRODUCTION

In one of his pamphlets, a most extraordinary mixture of blind rage and deep historical insight, Edmund Burke compared the French Revolution with the Protestant revolution: Luther's Reformation. Burke, a Protestant, compared the political movement that he hated as cordially as ever a great man hated with the old and hallowed event to which he owed his whole cultural background and the pattern of his life. He repudiated the one, while accepting the other. He recognized the chasm between the two, yet insisted, nevertheless, that they had essential features in common.

Both the Revolution and the Reformation, he argued, brought about world-wide civil wars. Universal in their appeal, they gave rise to parties that disregarded all boundaries between states and nations; so that Frenchmen, say, fought together with Germans against other Frenchmen, and Germans with Frenchmen against other Germans. This confusion resulted in new techniques of diplomacy, of conspiracy and attack, against which Burke was able to warn his generation because their danger had been apprehended even in the sixteenth century. De Tocqueville later took up Burke's analogy, and recommended a reading of Schiller's *Thirty Years' War* for a better understanding of the Revolution.

Now while it is true that the study of any historical event furthers the comprehension of any other, and of current events in particular, "comparison" should not be overemphasized, for comparisons are drawn wherever history is pursued. If the past were wholly different from the present it would be unfamiliar and uninteresting; and, conversely, if the past and the present were essentially the same history would be a bore. Its interest lies in the inextricable commingling of similarity and dissimilarity; of the eternally recurring and the unique. A historical event is illustrative, but of itself alone; an example that does not appear twice.

The event itself does not appear twice, but certain relationships that can be abstracted from it may return in other events and in different proportions. Burke made such an abstraction, and had in mind the reappearance of similar relationships, when he compared the religious wars with the wars against revolutionary France. Properly understood, the analogy was pertinent and illuminating, but to forget that it was an abstraction, and clumsily equate unique happenings, would be to fall into absurdity.

In our narrative no comparison is ever explicitly drawn between the present time and the era of Napoleon. We might have played innocent, and denied any intention of so doing; if it intrudes we might say that it was the fault of the original sources, or of the reader upon whom it forces itself, but we concede that it would be the fault, also, of the author, who chose these sources. We admit comparison, just as we admit the chasm between the times and the characters. In the final analysis, astonishment remains that so much similarity should be possible together with such radical differences.

The relationship based on comparison is confused by another, which is based on continuity. I mean by this that we are the heirs, the great-grandchildren, of those with whom we compare ourselves. We derive the antagonisms that stir us from the antagonisms that stirred them; indeed, since we use the same words for both, words like "revolution," "reaction," "conservative," "liberal," and so on, we are tempted to assume that they are identical. Here there is need of caution.

History depends upon continuity amidst change. But this does not imply an identity of variables, as in mathematics, or a smooth progression, as in mechanics. It is idle to ask what this man or that of the eighteenth century would do if he were alive today. He exists no longer. In his own time he had to live and act under conditions characteristic of his era. Ideological fronts as he knew them dissolved after his death, altered without anyone being able to predict in what sense. Ideas shifted from one position to another, merged, separated, and died. No one continues literally the work of the French Revolution today. On the other hand, there may be parties that carry on its work and that of its opponents indirectly and simultaneously; indeed, there may be several parties that do so, and each in a wholly different way. Connections there are, but they are loose and involved. In searching for what is surely our goal—similarity, continuity, cause and effect, permanence—we realize the unique nature of every historical event and the opinions to which it gave rise.

The same discriminating precision that is required in respect to time is required also in respect to space. For example, to oppose democracy in Germany in the year 1815 meant something quite different from opposing it in France in the same year, or in America; so true is this that the same man could have been for democracy in France and against it in Germany at one and the same moment. Contradictory, it will be said. But when contradiction lies in things themselves, how can it be escaped?

Not less is it to be considered that what we lightly regard as an integrated historical epoch turns out upon closer examination to be shot through with mutations and mysterious alternations in conditions and standpoint. No force and no group has a monopoly on the tendency of any era. To the explosion in France, in 1789, of forces that were latent everywhere the monarchist states, after a long and stupid delay, cried Halt! But this Halt! this uncompromising and inflexible No! was not enough, and they suffered one defeat after another in consequence. Under the influence of these very defeats they transformed themselves, whereas the transformation of the great revolutionary state was a result of its overwhelming victories. There came a time when the old monarchies wanted about what the French had wanted in 1792, and when Napoleon wanted what the kings had wanted in 1792.

To go on with comparison for a moment, the Napoleonic era may appear at once more heroic and less disastrous than our own. In the sparsely populated, leisurely, and spacious Europe of the eighteenth century, a unification of the world was something to be brought about by ideas and genius; thanks to technical and economic developments, physical unity is here today, though not by deliberate plan; and it is misused by the powers of darkness. The present crisis, caused by the abuse of enormous accumulated energies, makes the Napoleonic Wars seem mild as far as the number of combatants engaged and the extent of destruction are concerned. But in those days there was more opportunity for masterly achievements in military and political strategy; place for solitary, productive thinking; time for the slow ripening of men, of ideas, of dramatic situations.

The crisis of the French Revolution was the first of its kind, and the very idea underlying it had to be developed from entirely new and unfamiliar concepts. The idea of revolution in general, later carelessly toyed with for so long, had first to be conceived. The consciousness of living in an era fundamentally different from all the past, of approaching the end of history, arose in heads that had never entertained such a notion before. Because it had taken shape for the first time it burst forth as tremendous personal achievements, and led to such things as Hegel's philosophy of history no less than to the Napoleonic Wars.

There can be no doubt that the amount of suffering must have been proportional to the magnitude of such accomplishments and surprises. Those who experienced this crisis were astounded, for they had never suspected that such a fundamental change as they were witnessing could by any possibility occur. We, on the contrary, who have been familiar for generations with the nullification of everything conceivable, are capable of any emotion but surprise.

The central character of our story experienced history but, except in a remote sense, did not make it. His place was between the intellectual and the practical worlds, but he was creative in neither. He was a publicist, an intellectual passionately devoted to politics, but destined only to suffer through them. He was not a great wave, but merely the swimmer who thrashes about in it with his arms to keep his head above water. He reflected his era in his life; in the ceaseless activity of a tortured mind.

The story of Napoleon has been written a thousand times; that of Friedrich Gentz, the political agent, but rarely. Here the attempt is made to tell it; that is to say, to relate once more the story of the earliest crisis of the modern world from the standpoint of a man who passed through it, and was closer to its origins than most of his contemporaries.

The American reader must bear in mind that this is essentially European history, a contribution to an explanation of events that took place in Europe then and afterward: for the present flows out of the past. America really parted from Europe not because of her war with Great Britain, nor yet because of the Monroe Doctrine, but because revolution succeeded in America, and failed in Europe, for fundamental reasons. A man who, like Gentz, saw through these reasons and exemplified them in his own life can hardly be an ideal character.

PART ONE

GENTZ IN PRUSSIA

SECRETARY OF EUROPE

I

YOUTH

FROM childhood on we are what we are, and all that comes later is but an explanation of what has gone before. The more confused is age the more affecting is youth in retrospect, for already implicit in the sanguine, expectant morning of life lay the burden and heat of noonday and the evening calm.

Friedrich Gentz was born in 1764, in Prussian Silesia. His father, Johann Gentz, was a government official who later attained to the directorship of the Royal Mint, in Berlin; his mother, of Huguenot extraction, a granddaughter of Charles Ancillon, judge over all the French in Brandenburg. Young Gentz grew to manhood during the seventh, eighth, and ninth decades of the eighteenth century under the tutelage of the soundest philosophers of his day, and was an earnest, idealistic, sensuous, mercurial, and easily influenced youth of mellifluous voice when he was sent by his father to Königsberg to profit by the wisdom of Professor Kant.

There he fell in love with a girl named Celestine, and with a married woman named Elizabeth. But Elizabeth loved his friend, Le Noble, more than she loved him, and Le Noble had better luck than Gentz with Celestine. In the end Gentz became engaged to Celestine, to be sure, but when he abandoned his studies prematurely in order to marry her the sooner she left him in the lurch again. This wounded him deeply, for he had thought to settle down early in life through a conventional marriage.

He urged virtue on his friends also, and on her birthday wrote to the unhappily married Elizabeth: "For you, my dear friend, all hope of arranging the pattern of your life in such a manner as to attain happiness is as good as lost. I regret having to speak so frankly . . ." but, continued the stripling of twenty-one, there are only two roads to felicity. Either fate must bend itself to our wishes or we must adapt ourselves to fate. He chose the latter course for her; that was, to tread the path of righteousness, to love her husband notwithstanding all his faults, and to treat Le Noble as a young man well worthy of her friendship and esteem but to remain wholly indifferent to him in affairs of the heart.

Elizabeth later wrote a romantic memoir of her little group, a conventionalized account of her courtships and marriages that affords considerable insight into the character of young Gentz. For example: "He seems to be the life of all their [i.e., Celestine's family's] undertakings. What animation a high-spirited man lends to all around him. . . ." Again, she tells how, at an afternoon tea, he recited Gretchen's "My peace is gone, my heart is sore." His voice was the most affecting music as he ran the gamut from the gloom of despair to rapture's heights; none more perfect than his. And she relates, also, how she was warned not to go too far with such an eccentric and unreliable fellow as Gentz. She replied that this would be not to enjoy the glow of a fire because fire might burn. Gentz the warming, Gentz the consuming fire, was later to be known among his friends as the All-Fertilizing, the Nile, because he stimulated them all. The musical voice, the ready tongue, the magnetism, no less than the eccentricity, the self-will, and the obstinacy were all so intensified in after years that Elizabeth must be credited with having sketched the young man to the life in her *Erinnerungsbuch für edle Frauen.*

After the style of her own time, of course. But in those days they not only wrote romantically, they lived so, in accordance with their period, and in remote Königsberg shared the sorrows of the unhappy Werther and were as ardent disciples of Rousseau, as introspective, as precociously argumentative and sentimental, as freely moralizing and highly communicative, as esoteric and indifferent to public affairs as in any of the literary circles of Berlin, south Germany, or Switzerland.

Later, in the 1790's, a more robust mood set in but Gentz, born too soon, remained oblivious to it. Yet within the bounds of conventions set by his most decisive decade there can be traced in his letters all the earmarks of a forceful young character: passion, confidence, naïveté despite all his introspection, and high intelligence. He has a feeling for language, is inquisitive and avid of reading as only one can be who is resolved to understand the world into which he has been born, melancholy, sensuous, in need of love and guidance, yet never acts except on his own initiative. He takes stock of himself and finds that he is not unworthy of affection, and has wholly decorous ideas on life, work, and love, though perhaps they have not yet become stable. His correspondence with Elizabeth Graun gives a touching account of friendship and first love; touching, but entirely devoid of any poetic brilliance, for young Gentz,

GENTZ AT TWENTY-TWO

though he occasionally drops into verse, is no poet. His style runs from the mildly sentimental to the wildly rhetorical, and at times barely escapes the eccentric.

THE youth who is imbued with an interest in public affairs will live in the past rather than in the present, will see history as something essentially completed, almost legendary, in fact, and the present as without historical significance. He will devour old books long before he comes to take any interest in the daily papers; yet his instinct is sound for before him lies, all organized, the kingdom of the past, and from it he acquires the understanding with which later he gradually reduces to order the chaos of the present. Beginning with the intrigues of the Homeric heroes and gods he goes on to the history of the Greeks and the Romans, and finally, perhaps, catches up with his present. But according to all that young Gentz heard this present was replete with vicious folly, and instructive only because of its warning example.

By common consent the old King of Prussia, Frederick II, called the Great, had already lived too long. The early days of his reign had excited admiration on every hand, but now, after almost half a century, his misanthropic autocracy and the offensive manner in which he continued to spread abroad even his good deeds, seemed perverse and laughable. The freethinking of 1740 no longer impressed anyone; how much had happened since then!

Frederick died, and not a soul in his capital mourned the passing of this old tyrant of a baroque and bygone day, for the advanced thinker of the time held that he had been not only less than great, but actually below the average of mediocrity.

Gentz was already in his twenty-second year, yet this man of destiny is mentioned in his diary but once, and then only in passing, and the youth seems to have taken not the slightest interest in him. The significance of the Seven Years' War, the rape of Silesia, the partition of Poland, and Prussian militarism did not become clear to him until much later; or Frederick did not become historically significant for him until much later.

In so far as he watched the drift of political affairs at all, the young man was inclined to feel great confidence in the future. How could it be otherwise? His age was that of Utopia; of optimism and the courage of youth: his age in both senses of the word.

As we make his acquaintance Gentz was between twenty and twenty-six years old; his twentieth year fell in 1784, his twenty-sixth in 1790. It was a period when our civilization looked toward the future with greater expectation than ever before or ever afterward. Fault was found with almost everything in the present, but it was hoped that the future would remove all grounds for discontent. If modernity means to look only to the present and the future, and the Devil take the past; to heed nought but reality, of which the test is utility; then mankind was never and nowhere more modern than in the Europe of 1787. Countless shadowy hopes possessed the masses and the literati alike and sometimes, indeed, even kings and their ministers. Parties there were none, no irreconcilable differences were recognized, and the world was not so divided against itself as it was to be some years later. The American Revolution was held to be the most precious guarantee of the future. Man in the past had been living in Folly's realm; now he was to be governed by reason. The whole residue of medieval madness must disappear, the benumbing authority of the Roman Catholic Church be destroyed. All were to be equal before the law, and no one was to be held as the property of another. Where now there was complete restraint of commerce, and even within frontiers none dared stir without express permission from the sovereign, there was to be unlimited freedom. Above all, wars between the nations were to cease. No one had any but the haziest ideas on how such a radical and definitive change was to be brought about, but it was agreed at least that the rational must be achieved by rational, that is to say by peaceful, means.

In this gratifying sense the events of the time were interpreted, and even in the fact that the rulers of Russia, Austria, and Prussia fell upon Poland one day and carved out huge slices for themselves good was found. It showed that the great powers would no longer make war upon one another but would settle their differences amicably, albeit at the expense of weaker countries; and anyway, Poland was a corrupt and arrantly Catholic state whose peasants would be far better off under foreign kings of enlightened outlook than under their own rulers. Of this Voltaire, the intellectual leader of Europe, was firmly convinced.

But vague fears went hand in hand with these brave hopes. If nothing were to remain as it was, and had been for so long, disagreeable as well as pleasant surprises might well be in store. Perhaps there would be no more wars. Perhaps the worst one of all was still to come. In Central Europe there was a galaxy of arbitrarily created small states that could no longer justify themselves before the bar of reason. Who was to inherit them? Neither of the two mighty dynasties, Hohenzollern and Hapsburg, would have been averse to getting them; Russia was new, sinister, endlessly large, and ready to pick quarrels along her borders; she wanted what was left of Poland, she wanted the Balkan Peninsula, and regarded the Ottoman Empire with eyes as hungry as those that Austria and Prussia turned on the German Reich. If her greedy plans were to be accomplished she must eventually come into collision with Prussia, Austria, and Great Britain. In the Netherlands a dynastic and a popular party were engaged in a struggle that was really a contest between Great Britain and France. Agents of the King of Prussia went about Hungary and Bohemia stirring up national feeling against the Hapsburg dynasty.

Comte de Mirabeau predicted that a crisis of unprecedented violence would occur almost before Frederick the Great had been laid in his grave, and in 1784 Lord Malmesbury had already ventured the same prophecy: "The situation of Europe appears never to have been so critical at any epoch since the breaking out of the Thirty Years' War as it is at the present moment."

Least afraid of any were the kings. They were resolved on action and leadership and it was believed on all sides, and they themselves were certain, that they would not only bring about the anticipated great transformation but would reap all its benefits. Although their own majesty was palpably an offspring of the Middle Ages, they went rather far in their aversion to the sacrosanctity of the past. They denied themselves coronation ceremonies as outmoded nonsense, plundered the monasteries, sometimes attempted to rule without any censorship (which ultimately cost them dear), converted the universities into vocational and civil service schools, and defined the state as the greatest good to the greatest number. The sole stipulation was that the subject's idea of good must coincide with that of his sovereign, which seems to have opened the door to considerable misunderstanding.

It was expected that the new King of Prussia, Frederick William II, would do many of the things that would have to be done in one way or another, and Mirabeau called upon him to inaugurate a veritable revolution. Of course his subjects saw in their ruler, despite crown and purple, only such another as themselves, but, continued the French visitor, the royal might was proper and necessary if the desired changes were to be brought about. "Make free citizens of your peasant serfs," he demanded. "Replace military servitude with a citizen militia. Grant freedom to emigrate, freedom to acquire the estates of the nobility, freedom to industry, freedom of the press. Appoint great merchants to your ministries; they understand how to rule today. Proclaim the right to work, establish national workshops for the unemployed, suspend all excises and monopolies, make the interests of townsman and peasant your own. The concern of even the most absolute monarch lies wholly in the common good." Let the King retain his unlimited authority, to be sure, but what matters are law and economics, not political power. Let him use his authority for one last time only to renounce it, by emancipating his subjects and so making himself superfluous.

What would be left of the reformer after these reforms had been carried out, no one ever troubled to ask.

THE kindly, meticulous old gentleman, the austere and profound philosopher, Immanuel Kant, took Gentz into the intimate circle of his disciples, let him read the proofs of his writings as they came from the press, and invited the young man to his luncheons, where were incredible amounts of dried fish and for every guest a quarter of a bottle of Bordeaux. The conversation turned on the political events of the day: the designs entertained by Catherine the Great of Russia for aggrandizement and the all-too-radical reforms of the Hapsburg Emperor; not to mention such things, say, as the geography of far lands, marvelous tales of travel, and monsters of the animal world for whose sensational descriptions the old gentleman often relied on writers whom he would have done better not to trust.

Behind the lecturer's desk Kant was more grave and ceremonious, and still another person in his books. Through long, inspiring evenings Gentz lost himself in definitions of what we know, and what we never can know, and what we may believe, and what we ought to do. He read, also, the essays, in which the master attempted to introduce his dualistic principle into human history, and the *Ideas for a History of Man from a Cosmopolitan Standpoint* came out while our student was still in Königsberg.

Kant's philosophic demands on the individual and the state grew out of a profound pessimism. This devout scholar fixed on the nature of man a morose and penetrating gaze and held in low esteem the governments of his time, which were concerned only with war; preparing for the next one, and paying for the one just past. Pondering the advances that the art of war had already made, and was sure to make in the future, he asked whether a barbarous destruction of civilization by civilization itself would not be the inevitable end. But the rigid exponent of naturalism thought it illogical to assume that nature is purposeful in each of its parts, yet purposeless as a whole, and was unwilling to believe that the entire, immeasurable structure, culminating so obviously in man, was destined to no better fate than final destruction by man himself. On the other hand, he was realistically acute enough not to rely on any virtues of mankind in promising deliverance. Might not the obscure purpose of nature actually avail itself of the malice, selfishness, and belligerence of man that seemed so antagonistic to it, making possible in the end what was of necessity wholly impossible in a military state: the unrestricted development of all man's dormant gifts, the final completion of his task? Had not this purpose already, and in precisely this way, brought into being the state, which had curbed individual, uncivilized man just as the state, in its turn, would some day be curbed by a confederation of states or a superstate? Although fomenters of intrigue among the nations did not know it, the whole purpose of war was its eventual abolition; perpetual peace and the millennium that would arise under its beneficent sway. This might take a long while. But there was no need for haste; given time enough the race must reach its goal, or at least approach it in eternity. Individualism was a dream. . . .

Kant was a revolutionary. That is to say, he despised the primitive state of man, and regarded the civilization of his time as nothing more than the primal state refined by science, and mankind as but a pack of ravening animals that unfortunately had learned to use gunpowder. Up to then the state had been the outcome of mere chance, but in the future it would be the product of clear reason, deriving its every law from principles whose truth the scholar believed himself able to demonstrate a priori. The actions of the American colonists gave hope that all this might come rather soon; but perhaps it would be delayed; or never come; or perhaps the solution of the problem lay far in eternity. The old man gave his students no definite answer; it was enough that they should have something to think about for the rest of their lives.

To absorb such profound thoughts in all the plasticity of youth, while they are still new, or hardly yet formulated, and even to have the privilege of discussion with the great man who gave them life —that is an impression never to be effaced. To this extent it might be said that Gentz remained a Kantian all his days. Not, of course, in the sense that he swallowed the philosophy whole and was satisfied with it, for this he never did, even while his association was so close. He understood Kant as Kant wished to be understood; he learned how to think and how to question. Later he expressly condemned the sectarianism and intellectual epidemic into which, he said, the system had degenerated. "But that was entirely the fault of those who, in their clumsiness and stupidity, perverted this negative philosophy to a positive one, or, still better said, destroyed its original fluidity. In its more important and authentic features the Kantian philosophy will remain a living stream as long as there are minds."

To discover why Kant's philosophy never ceased to live in Gentz's own mind would be an intricate task indeed, for the study of philosophy in youth stimulates in many, many different ways. Whatever the reason, Kant's rigid ethics, his categorical imperative, and his idea of a league of nations can still be traced in the manifestoes with which Gentz summoned the world twenty years later to concerted effort against Napoleon. His thoughts revolved incessantly about the relation between morals and government, ideas and experience, right and might, and the impulse thereto came from Kant, since he followed Kant's lead in part yet in part, also, as an empiricist and a conservative, found himself in opposition. For even when Kant had become to him the very prototype of the rationalistic doctrinaire, who in reality can produce nothing but ruin, his denial still pursued a course determined by Kant. Only one who knows what "reason" and "ideas" are could be an "empiricist" like Gentz.

GENTZ returned to Berlin from Königsberg after an absence of two years. Here he came under the influence of those magazine editors, academicians, and theorizing democrats who later were to be included under the term "Berlin Enlightenment." At the "Wednesday Club" there gathered every week ecclesiastical bigwigs whose religious faith was nebulous and sophisticated, scholars who recommended abolition of the universities, ministers of state who found no fault with the demands of the Third Estate in France, and men of law who strove to give the Prussian legal code then in preparation a foundation that was reminiscent of Rousseau's republicanism. These representatives of a middle class bent on reform met in the Gentz home, and as the mint director's eldest son spoke with fire and intelligence they gladly welcomed him into their circle. Easily foremost among them was a certain Christian Garve, to whom the youth addressed long, profound letters, which have been preserved.

Garve, like Kant, wrote on the relation between ethics and government, though in a less radical tone. Kant, so he assured young Gentz, had but little to offer after all. His writings were unintelligible to the great majority, he saw the world in too tragic a light, and lost himself in desperate and futile dilemmas: nature, reality, sin, might, on the one hand; ideas, the right, duty impossible of fulfillment, on the other. How much better, said Garve, to occupy oneself with history and natural science than to explore the nature of everything, and tragically contrast what is with what should be, but never can be. Friendship, loyalty, and obedience to law were virtues of the individual citizen, but statesmen and kings, unfortunately, often felt it necessary to break through the rules of private morals and to put might before right.

The problems that we face are problems of evaluation, not of actual right, and Gentz ought not to perplex himself with abstract propositions but try, rather, to be a man of spirit and balance. What was gained when Kant taught his students that treaties must be lived up to under all circumstances? History could furnish instances enough where this just could not be done; and besides, if treaties were never broken there would never be any political changes at all. Or of what use was the assertion that all nations, the smallest as well as the greatest, are of equal dignity in the eyes of international law? Twenty-five million persons exercised both a physical and a moral ascendancy over a few thousand, and it was not merely true that pygmy nations yield to great powers but probably right that they should. If only a ruler fully realized his own interests and had the highest good of his people in view, combining it as best he could with that of all mankind, the ideal had not yet been attained, certainly, but it had been approached as nearly as may be in this world.

"Oh, would to God," wrote Garve, "that war might nevermore be waged or conquest attempted unless he who starts the one or seeks the other can show with at least some degree of probability that either would benefit his country, or even him! How tranquil would Europe be for years to come, and how peacefully could every man sit down under his own vine and fig tree!" Unfortunately, the race was still a bit far from this happy condition; and yet, what progress had taken place in the past few decades! Because of the interchange of knowledge, the similarity of customs, and the interweavings of commerce, war would become constantly less and less frequent; probably less savage, too. Men were no angels, but neither were they devils, and good will, education, and the dissemination of practical information could do much. In international politics a sort of blind instinct was at work, which functioned inaccurately enough, it was true, yet insured the reciprocal esteem of great powers nevertheless, and also kept weaker nations from being instantly gobbled up. Still, if a small, backward, decadent state were to fall victim occasionally to a great, rising power, where was it written that one must protest the violation, and cry aloud to high Heaven?

Young Gentz joined passionately in such discussions, yet the radicalism of Kant seemed to him nearer the truth than the cheerful empiricism of Garve. The mere good will of a ruler, he wrote, would be a highly uncertain guarantee indeed, and without law and the faithful observance of covenants no human society would be possible. "Might makes right" was impudent defiance, pure and simple. Of what value is a so-called realistic view of things that is based on momentary advantage only? Today a treaty is broken merely because it appears expedient to do so; tomorrow the transgressor himself is ruined by the default of another. It is easy enough to see the results of such opportunism: war and misery without end. No! Here theoretical solutions or personal good will are of no avail. Either one acts in accordance with certain principles, or one does not; one abides by covenants, or one does not. "So live always that thy principles can be made universal rules of conduct." This is the magic word upon which domestic and foreign policies should be based. So far it has not been done, but is it the business of philosophy to call everything that exists good, merely because it exists? . . . Arguments that Kant, for forty years an attentive observer of European politics, would have read with a melancholy smile.

Königsberg and Berlin, Kant and the Berlin enlighteners: such was Gentz's own more specific intellectual background. But to the wider influence of Rousseau and Schiller, shared by his generation everywhere, he added by study the less familiar teachings of Montesquieu, Adam Smith, and Gibbon.

MEANWHILE he was experiencing various other phases of life: the day's work, the evening's pleasure, love, friendship, and the gaining of a livelihood. He began as secretary to the *Generaldirektorium*, or Ministry of the Interior, then under the joint and wretched management of several ministers of Frederick William II, where there was much talk of reform and a fresh breeze, but little accomplishment. Only seldom could he discover any connection at all between his intellectual interests and his official duties, and complained that he was nothing but a scribbling slave. When he found friends who were not condemned to such drudgery, but all day could do things for which he had only his evenings free, he would fly into a rage, for he had been subject from early youth to a torment that never afterward left him entirely: the bitterness of envy.

In those days Berlin was for a short time what later it was to be again for a short time: a cosmopolitan, voluptuous, intellectually stimulating town. It had become so under the dreary militaristic rule of Frederick the Great. The diplomatic corps was prominent, and besides its members there were independent agents of all sorts, transient scientists, and globe-trotters, all of whom had hurried there to study the atmosphere and organization of the great Prussian power that had sprung into being overnight out of nothing. Then there were rich Jews, still living under degrading and restrictive laws though willing to free themselves from their own customs, gladly visited because of their pretty daughters and bountiful tables, and contributing still further toward a dissolution of the conventions of old Prussia, which even without them would have been too narrow to encompass this new social order. A great capital without tradition, an intense intellectual life with no past, or at best a shabby, mean past. *There* was a motley garden! Even during the lifetime of the old King the middle classes of Berlin had been thought uncommonly extravagant and immoral. Desiccated little government officials blossomed out as nighthawks and alcoholic phantoms, and did not hesitate at throwing away in a bordello a whole month's salary in one single night.

Young Gentz followed the example of his colleagues, and gambling debts, whisky, and so-called actresses came to occupy a large place in his life. His inordinate love of amusement was unconquerable, for he suffered from his inferior social position and wanted to show the world how meanly and deceitfully it was treating him; and, too, he really enjoyed his qualms of conscience, the feeling that he was better and purer than his deeds. At least these were the motives offered in letters to his friend, Elizabeth, in Königsberg. He complained of the futureless slavery of his calling, the morass of his twenty-three years of life, but boasted of something within him that could not be defiled, no matter what his excesses. Indeed, he offered his hand again more or less definitely to the unhappily married girl. The young wife's answer has not been preserved, for though Gentz's friends almost invariably kept the letters that he wrote them, and thousands of these are still in existence, he nearly always threw away immediately those addressed to him, for he could not bear such reminders of the past.

In any case he had the good fortune, not enjoyed by many, though it seems to have been more common then than it is now, to find congenial associates of his own generation against whom to measure himself: chiefly Huguenots, cousins and nephews of his mother. These descendants of Protestants who had been driven from France a hundred years earlier kept to themselves in their colony, where they enjoyed the privilege of their own schools, churches, and courts of law. Originally inclined to austerity and thrift, even they had begun to show of late a certain laxity in their habits, a more pretentious and graceless behavior that was especially noticeable because their young people spoke only French among themselves and scornfully held aloof from their fellow citizens of German descent. Nevertheless, or perhaps even because of this, many succeeded in reaching high government posts. A cousin of Gentz, Friedrich Ancillon, master of the oily word, later became Prussian Foreign Minister, and a second was none other than the notorious Cabinet Councilor Lombard, of whom we shall hear further particulars in the course of our story. As Gentz associated so intimately with these people he lived from the very first outside his fatherland, as it were, and no one who professes to interpret a person in terms of his environment can ever neglect the Huguenot, rhetorical, supernational element in his early training.

Wholly congenial with the Ancillons and the Lombards was a young Swede, Gustaf von Brinkmann, touring Germany in order to make the acquaintance of her great writers. Possessed of uncommon social gifts, a poetaster of charm in four or five languages, amiable, a little windy, he returned later to Berlin as Swedish Ambassador. A thorough cosmopolite also was Wilhelm von Humboldt, a junior barrister in the court of appeals, and the most intimate among all the friends of Gentz's youth.

Humboldt, Fortune's own child, twenty-three years of age when they first became friends and thus three years younger than Gentz, came from a more prominent social set, and was entirely familiar with the south German and French scene. In August of the preceding summer, 1789, he had listened to the debates of the French National Assembly and had visited Rousseau's grave. He had made the acquaintance of Georg Forster, most enthusiastic and most unfortunate of the German revolutionists; of young politicians of the English school educating themselves in Hanover; of Johannes von Müller, the herald of Swiss freedom; and, just recently, of Friedrich Schiller, with whom he got on famously. High officials in Berlin were not above listening respectfully to the unbiased opinions of this boy, or making him formal offer of a post in the civil service. But all to no avail; the young baron lived only for his own improvement. He felt himself on the heights that had been attained by German intellectualism at such dizzy speed, and to his friends seemed phenomenal, a prodigy. He was rich, and if not handsome at least presented the smart appearance that wealth can bestow. In the first raptures of his betrothal, reveling in the intellectual as well as the material, a dilettante, he was a little arrogant, a little crafty, a little cold. What the more unruly, emotional, and passionate Gentz realized from early youth, that life is no serene delight, this man seemed destined not to learn until he was old.

It is highly interesting to review their correspondence, Humboldt's with his fiancée and Gentz's with the older Garve, to compare their ideas of one another, and to see how this friendship began.

It commenced like so many others. At first Humboldt could not endure Gentz, whom he thought presumptuous and unreliable and met with hearty disdain, though well aware of Gentz's interest in him. "Gentz could not get a word out of me in spite of all his efforts, and thinks me insufferably arrogant." Of their first conversation he wrote: "He told me that this evening had affected him deeply; he had been much annoyed, but, considering me highly superior, had received a very favorable impression of me. I went to call on him soon afterward, and from then on we saw one another oftener. I discovered more and more evidence of a keen intellect, and little by little turned our conversation to those ideas that are least susceptible of proof and yet seem to me so real. He showed such deep interest, and discussed them so profoundly, that we were drawn closer and closer together until we were seeing each other every day and he had developed an enthusiastic love and esteem for me. How deep it is you really have not the faintest conception. . . ." And a little before this: "I spent most of last night with a man that I am beginning to like very much. His name is Gentz, and he, also, is at work here. He has a truly penetrating mind and a highly ardent nature, but little grace, little esthetic sense on the whole, and in his character not enough flexibility; and yet, though he is a few years older than I he is still so youthful that it makes one happy just to be with him."

Two months later he seems to be describing Gentz again for the first time. "I spend most of my time now with a far more interesting man. His name is Gentz, and he is a few years older than I am." Then follows this synopsis: "He is not adaptable enough to cope with obstacles in his path, but whoever sees him from all sides must love him. For I have not often found in a man such warmth of character, such devotion to whatever attracts him, or such great modesty despite a manner that often seems determined, together with such high intellectual gifts. In many respects he means much to me, though I feel that he cannot be to me what I am to him, and often this hurts."

The self-confidence of the desperately struggling, envious, faithful, warmhearted Gentz, as quick to praise as to blame, was undermined by his association with Humboldt, and since there is no better protection than love against the overwhelming superiority of an intimate friend he threw himself bodily into love's arms. "No sooner had his image come alive in me," he wrote to Garve, "than I began to fear every moment that I should lose all sense of proportion, and that everything else would be magnified by it until the unusual seemed fabulous, the large gigantic, and everything improbable in consequence. . . . It flatters me infinitely to think that Humboldt should regard me so highly, and my vanity in this, together with a longing for endless discussions, drew me still nearer to him. Toward the end of January an indisposition that gave me an excuse to be with him almost constantly resulted in a deep attachment, and finally in a love such as I have rarely before felt for any person, though it is held in check somewhat by an almost embarrassing admiration. And now there blossomed before my eyes a character whose steadfast consistency, whose imperturbable singleness of purpose, and whose predominant strength could be understood and admired only by one who had studied him as I had. . . ." The amazing sagacity of Humboldt, his overpowering arguments, his comprehensive talents, and his kindness, so ends the letter, encourage the writer to idolize all mankind in his new friend.

A club was organized that met every Tuesday at the home of one of the most cultured women in bourgeois society. In spite of punch, and a singing teakettle, the conversation was earnest and scholarly, for the young members were no merely literary group but students of the applied sciences who were determined to get on in the world;

and three of the five did, in fact, become ministers of state in after years.

On Friday evenings Humboldt and Gentz met alone, then several times a week, then every day, and every night from ten o'clock until morning. Gentz led their talk as long as it turned on politics, for this was his passion and his profession; but when it came to the fine arts, antiquity, or contemporary literature the nobleman was teacher and guide. It was the era of conversation, and they discussed one abstruse subject after another: "Ideas, sensations, man, all tend toward the general." But today it is hard to imagine how such a night of words could ever begin, whether or not by deliberate plan, and how it could continue. Among countless other subjects they talked about the Revolution in France.

The French Revolution; an appalling social catastrophe to some, the funeral of despotism to others. Gentz favored, Humboldt opposed it. Gentz upheld it as a Kantian and a young bourgeois because it was "the first practical triumph of philosophy" and meant liberty, and deliverance from all the old evils. Humboldt was against it as a member of the ruling class and an intellectual aristocrat, as well as on the basis of a not unoriginal argument. In a "Letter to a Friend," which Gentz had thought directed at him, published in the *Berliner Monatsschrift*, Humboldt had asserted that no nation could be ripe for a political constitution drawn up in accordance with the principles of pure reason. It would be dangerous to stifle the individual, in all its might, with the theoretical; only through struggle between the human mind and more powerful chance could anything viable emerge. But the more penetrating Gentz was not disturbed by this argument. Even Humboldt's rejection of the abstract had taken the form of idle speculation; the supposed historical thinker had not furnished the rationalist with a historical example. Furthermore, was not the suggestion that "things" must be allowed to work themselves out alone superfluous, to say the least? Was not man himself, no matter what he did, a thing that worked in just this way? And even though he be thought of as mastering things in the role of a directing intelligence, did not his results come always and only from a struggle between more powerful chance and an opposing mind?

Gentz was as little shaken in his civism by such argumentation as by certain grave news that now began to filter in from France, and was perforce laid to the iniquity of the German press, the folly of emigrants, and the ill will of those enemies of liberty who still managed to remain in Paris. So far he had studied history as something past and over, something almost apocryphal, and had continued to live in an unconcerned and peaceful present. But now the past was growing dim, and the present itself was being transformed into history; into wholly gratifying, yes, unprecedented, history.

II

THE FRENCH REVOLUTION

WHO can say how the world would have looked if the French Revolution had succeeded, and come to an end peaceably and joyously with the festival of confederation on the Champ de Mars? In the summer of 1790, indeed, it was thought to be over, and brave hopes intoxicated the intellectuals, and even the masses, in Germany, in north Italy, and in Great Britain. Important changes had long been anticipated, and now at last they had come. Not exactly as had been expected, perhaps, but then, had they ever been really pictured in all their details? The American colonists, far away and much less numerous, had made a beginning; great, rich France had followed, and what she did the other European nations would soon have to do. The fellowship of all free men, a brotherhood of justice and perpetual peace, though still only a Utopian dream, had come appreciably nearer. Despots made war on one another, but not republics, for how could a self-governing people have any interest in war? Now, at last, the folly of the Middle Ages was over and a league of nations would shortly appear in the Old World, young and new as the United States of America, unburdened by the imbecilities of a benighted past, and entirely free at any time to do what was right.

Professor Kant's cheeks glowed when he seized the French newspapers as they appeared on the streets. Young Gentz, his pupil, thought and spoke with the rest. "Call it fanaticism," he wrote, "or exaggeration, or what you will. . . . The spirit of the day quickens within me, active and strong. It is high time that humanity awoke from its long sleep." In order that a few at the top might enjoy all the good things in life, the people had been suppressed; now they would emerge from night into day. But woe betide them, woe to all mankind, if the great attempt to establish a government on the principles of reason should miscarry! A second would not soon be made.

When a shrewd and crabbed citizen, Justus Moeser, of Osnabrück, openly scoffed at "the rights of man," and compared the state with a joint-stock company in which only stockholders had the right to vote, Gentz countered with his maiden literary effort: *Attempt to Establish the Chief Principles of Right.* The essay demanded a system of laws derived from conceptions of man rather than from pure theory, and it would have been quaint and rare had it not been but a transcript of what must be acknowledged quaint and rare in Kant himself.

But we carry forever with us a part of what we have learned, thought, and believed in youth, and whosoever at twenty-five had faith in the rights of man, in perpetual peace, in revolution, in progress, and in the sudden or gradual transition from evil to good in history will never lose this faith entirely. He may ridicule it, he may even betray it, but will never be as he would have been without it. No matter what happens, or what he himself does, it will be assayed over and over again, whether consciously or unconsciously, in the light of these early beliefs. On the other hand, it must be confessed that our minds are partly molded by what goes on about us, and that subsequent experience also affects our views.

In the spring of 1791 Gentz ran across a book that had rapidly become a best seller in Great Britain and France: Edmund Burke's *Reflections on the French Revolution.* He read it in a hostile spirit, for he knew that Burke violently hated this upheaval, yet he thought it beautifully written and replete with wisdom in its details, though wrong as a whole. Once again he read it, comparing its main theme with what had happened in France since its publication, and found it worthy of mature consideration. Three months later he decided that Burke was right, and began to translate the *Reflections* into German, clothing it in the ornate and flowing style of Schiller's *Thirty Years' War.*

Up to now conservatism had been practiced, to be sure; but, chiefly as a consequence of the revolutionary political "philosophy," there had suddenly appeared a conservative philosophy, which was not so much a doctrine of opposition as a negation of all political doctrine. Burke proclaimed the power of tradition, of belief, of prejudice, and maintained that man is unable to divest himself of these. Even the French revolutionists could not, and their prejudices were more barefaced, more offensive, more insane than those that held the British Empire together. These were dignified, old, the accumulated wisdom of the fathers; those, the spawn of a few impudent minds of the present day.

There were said to be eternal truths, but if Burke was to be believed truth is not eternal, not abstract, not some universally valid thing far up in the clouds; it exists, rather, in the actual conditions that obtain in a nation, and in its history.

". . . I cannot stand forward, and give praise or blame to anything which relates to human actions, and human concerns, on a simple view of the object, as it stands stripped of every relation, in all the nakedness and solitude of metaphysical abstraction. Circumstances (which with some gentlemen pass for nothing) give in reality to every political principle its distinguishing colour and discriminating effect. The circumstances are what render every civil and political scheme beneficial or noxious to mankind. . . ."

Freedom, for example, is the most treasured possession of man, and Burke prized it highly, but ". . . abstract liberty, like other abstractions, is not to be found. Liberty inheres in some sensible object, and every nation has formed to itself some favourite point which by way of eminence becomes the criterion of happiness. . . ." The freedom of the British would be nothing without their religion, and Burke doubted that freedom can exist anywhere without religion.

"You see, Sir," he explained with a certain brusqueness, "that in this enlightened age I am bold enough to confess, that we are generally men of untaught feelings; that instead of casting away all our old prejudices, we cherish them to a very considerable degree, and, to take more shame to ourselves, we cherish them because they are prejudices; and the longer they have lasted, and the more generally they have prevailed, the more we cherish them. We are afraid to put men to live and trade each on his own private stock of reason; because we suspect that this stock in each man is small, and that the individuals would do better to avail themselves of the general bank and capital of nations and of ages. . . .

"We know, and what is better, we feel inwardly, that religion is the basis of civil society, and the source of all good and of all comfort. In England we are so convinced of this, that there is no rust of superstition, with which the accumulated absurdity of the human mind might have crusted it over in the course of ages, that ninety-nine in a hundred of the people of England would not prefer to impiety. We shall never be such fools as to call in an enemy to the substance of any system to remove its corruptions, to supply its defects, or to perfect its construction. . . .

"We know, and it is our pride to know, that man is by his constitution a religious animal; that atheism is against, not only our reason, but our instincts; and that it cannot prevail long. But if, in the moment of riot, and in a drunken delirium from the hot spirit drawn out of the alembic of Hell, which in France is now so furiously boiling, we should uncover our nakedness, by throwing off that Christian religion which has hitherto been our boast and comfort, and one great source of civilization amongst us, and amongst many other nations, we are apprehensive (being well aware that the mind will not endure a void) that some uncouth, pernicious, and degrading superstition might take place of it. . . .

"Your literary men, and your politicians, and so do the whole clan of the enlightened among us, essentially defer in these points. They have no respect for the wisdom of others; but they pay it off by a very full measure of confidence in their own. With them it is a sufficient motive to destroy an old scheme of things, because it is an old one. . . .

"The science of constructing a commonwealth, or renovating it, or reforming it, is, like every other experimental science, not to be taught *a priori* . . . very plausible schemes, with very pleasing commencements, have often shameful and lamentable conclusions. In states there are often some obscure and almost latent causes, things which appear at first view of little moment, on which a very great part of its prosperity or adversity may most essentially depend. The science of government being therefore so practical in itself, and intended for such practical purposes, a matter which requires experience, and even more experience than any person can gain in his whole life, however sagacious and observing he may be, it is with infinite caution that any man ought to venture upon pulling down an edifice, which has answered in any tolerable degree for ages the common purposes of society, or on building it up again, without having models and patterns of approved utility before his eyes."

Such an admonition as this, a treasury of accumulated and glorious political wisdom suddenly revealed, was the more impressive because Burke consistently avoided or retracted the extreme, and made all those concessions that temperate critics could have demanded of him.

"I do not, my dear Sir, conceive you to be of that sophistical, captious spirit, or of that uncandid dulness, as to require, for every general observation or sentiment, an explicit detail of the correctives and exceptions, which reason will presume to be included in all the general propositions which come from reasonable men. . . ."

It may be that Burke had forerunners in Great Britain; on the Continent he had none, and for the young men who had looked up to Rousseau and to Kant as the preceptors of society his book must have opened an entirely new world: the historical and actual one. Gentz had learned from Kant that the Middle Ages represented an "inconceivable aberration of the human mind"; now he was reproducing Burke's lament over the passing of their chivalry in language whose stateliness surpassed even the original. The question that might have embarrassed Burke, whether the old order in France still met the needs of society to a "tolerable degree," and whether the very attempt at peaceful remedies would not shatter the whole structure, was not to be answered save by the most accurate historical research. But that which needed no such painstaking investigation, the current illusion, proved Burke to be right, and with every passing day more right. France had not found the goal that she was seeking, yet meanwhile summoned the world in menacing tones to imitate her tumultuous and bloody experiment.

It was in respect to this demoralization of the French effort at reform that Gentz exclaimed, in the preface to his translation: "The despotic synod in Paris, supported internally by their inquisitorial tribunals and externally by thousands of volunteer zealots, interprets with an intolerance unprecedented since the infallibility of the popes crumbled every deviation from their principles as heresy and abomination. . . . A gang of numbskulls who have abandoned all moderation now offer, not to the rabble alone but to an astonished Europe, a standard of human judgment, a theory of statesmanship, and principles of civic alliance; and with such brazen effrontery as no monarch has ever yet been guilty of wish to be recognized as universal lawgivers. All that mankind held precious they regard as trifling; all that gave happiness to millions is rooted out as vagary and perversion. From now on there must be one state, one people, one faith, one language. . . . And this more than tyrannical theory, whose results would mock all human calculation: Is it to gain the ascendancy without a misstep and without a struggle? Shall not those still untouched by the whirlwind exert themselves to the full to maintain at least a semblance of opposition? . . ."

THE events that drove the young author to such an outburst of alarm are already known to the reader.

In April, 1792, the imprisoned King of France had been forced by the Legislative Assembly to declare war on his brother-in-law, the King of Hungary and Bohemia, though as matters stood there was hardly need any longer for a "declaration." French representatives and writers had been outdoing one another for a year in frantic defiance of the whole Continent of Europe. In vain did the clear-sighted publicist, Mallet du Pan, warn his countrymen: "The conspirators to be feared are those who by threatening Europe may actually arouse her: they are the preachers of insurrection, the scribblers who insult every sovereign, the clubs who teach the art of anarchy in the name of philosophy, scattering their agents through every empire to stir up trouble, murder, and civil war. . . ."

Then, turning to the monarchs: "No epoch of history, ancient and modern, presents a crisis of greater severity. The sovereigns will perhaps presume too much if they think they can unravel it by the simple force of arms. If they neglect to appeal to public opinion, to point out that the interests of their subjects lie in the preservation of lawful government, the excesses of the French Revolution may well subvert Europe from one end to the other. . . ."

Too long had the masters of the old statecraft failed to grasp the situation. A war of ideas, a war in which public opinion was transformed into centralized power, a common interest in defense among all the European nations? Their vocation had not prepared the partitioners of Poland for anything like this, and when at last they did yield to the inevitable they proved to be incredibly maladroit. Throughout a few weeks that were heavy with destiny they gave ear to aristocratic émigrés, whom actually they despised, and let themselves be persuaded that war against revolutionary France would be the easiest thing in the world. After having avoided legitimate and prudent intervention for three years they now listened to talk of a bold interference for which they were morally and militarily unprepared; morally, because they did not really understand conditions in France and were half in sympathy with those against whom they now proposed to take the field; militarily, for reasons that will be shown.

The outcome of their action, at once inadequate and shameless, and paralyzed by concealed discord, was deplorable. "The foreign war, so much wished for," Mallet du Pan, now a fugitive in Switzerland, sadly wrote, "has completed the Revolution which it was intended to annihilate. Six months earlier, a defense line of sixty thousand men would have sufficed to keep it within some bounds of moderation and to facilitate its amendment. This opportunity lost, the armies of the two greatest military powers of Germany served merely to witness the triumphs of the Jacobins. . . . Generals, authorities, administrations, ministries, revenues, laws, hangmen, newspapers, instruments of public opinion—all these became their prey in an instant."

For years the revolutionary war party had done everything humanly possible to imperil France; now they declared her in danger, as, indeed, she was, and usurped authority. The King entered upon the thorny path of pity and ridicule that began with his formal deposition and ended with his death. The bungling invasion of neighboring countries inflamed the patriotism of the masses and effected a revolutionary concord. Because they attacked France the Germans were regarded as the aggressors, which this time they really were not. An army composed of former royal soldiery and revolutionary volunteers struck, and threw them back, whereupon the French assumed the offensive and within a few months became masters of the Rhineland and Belgium. Declarations of war against Great Britain, Spain, and Holland followed, and at the same time the National Convention addressed a proclamation to all the peoples of the earth, urging them to rise against their rulers and promising aid if they did so. Victories exceeding all anticipation emboldened the revolutionary leaders to new annexations.

Defeats, which were not lacking, precipitated events at home. The Republican party, having above all others provoked the war, fell because of it in the summer of 1793. Philosophers of the Enlightenment; friends of Voltaire who still survived; leaders in the practical sciences; writers; poetic glorifiers of the civic virtues of the ancients; champions of the people and of government by reason, if any there were, lost their heads on the Place de la Révolution, or fell by their own hands, or perished in flight of injuries and starvation. As Burke had prophesied, foreign and internal strife were intermingled; French peasants allied themselves with the King of England, and at the command of the Parisian despots French towns and cities were laid level with the ground. Yet at the same time the bleeding and burning country exerted itself to the utmost against attack from without, and under the dictatorship of a so-called Committee of Public Safety, and led by generals with curious names, held a united Europe in check.

Four years previously lasting peace had seemed in sight. Not entirely without cause, for the last great war lay several decades in the past, and much had happened since then to reflect the widespread instinct for peace. Had not the enlightened monarchs already abolished capital punishment? But now pacifism was a tantalizing or a monstrous dream, and Utopia was nourished only on its flagrant contrast with reality. The condition of the world resembled that during the last years of Louis XIV, if not during the Thirty Years' War. The old struggle between France and Austria, Bourbon and Hapsburg, and the newer maritime strife between France and Great Britain were blended with unfamiliar conflicting forces into a peril of which no one could see the end. Even where the war did not penetrate life promptly became wrapped in gloom, and far across the sea the young United States itself was driven to adopt a misanthropic foreign policy.

An international civil war? A new religious war? Burke had drawn this parallel in his *Reflections:* "It is a revolution of doctrine and theoretic dogma. It has much greater resemblance to those changes which have been made upon religious grounds." He had extended the warning that just as in the Thirty Years' War the Protestants had had their partisans and helpers in Catholic countries, so the French would have to wage war within and without at the same time, and had concluded that defense would not be enough and that only resolute and timely attack could save the monarchies. "If they were to guard against an invasion from France, the merits of a merely defensive resistance might be supported by plausible topics; but as the attack does not operate against these countries externally but by an internal corruption (a sort of dry rot), those who pursue a merely defensive plan cannot escape the danger." The same comparison was used in an opposite sense, especially by Prussian pacifists, who contended that war against France must be avoided at all costs, or quickly ended if it should break out, for the very reason that it threatened to degenerate into a religious war; and according to experience, wars between ideas were longer and more terrible than those launched by the mere volition of cabinets.

Why had the ideals of the Revolution been shattered? There were those who thought the human race not yet ready for such a fundamental transformation; others, on the contrary, believed that it was too old and corrupt, and that what would work in America would not work, unfortunately, in Europe; others, again, that the realization of a political ideal, if wholeheartedly pursued, is always horrible, or, conversely, if there must be a revolution its cost must be paid without too much lament; and still others, finally, that a state could have been established upon a rational basis if only the French reformers had been left to their work in peace; the venomous opposition of reactionaries at home and abroad had been the real cause of the catastrophe. This last argument was not wholly without foundation. Gentz, for example, conceded that advocates of the old order, and the émigrés in particular, had been as guilty as anyone in their position could be.

And yet, did political changes anywhere occur in a vacuum? Was it not necessary in this instance, as always, to consider the wishes of others, of strangers and opponents? The rational pursuit of a sound design is always frustrated by the irrational, by the projects and desires of established powers, and if these are not taken into account the rational course itself will finally become the most irrational of all.

But the transformation of rational into irrational, of high priests of reason into headsmen, was not fortuitous and imposed from without; on the contrary, it lay in the revolutionists themselves. They needed opposition in order to accomplish their design; by the most insane defiance they had provoked a widespread war that the world did not want, and would have liked to enforce concord in their own country, and then throughout the world, forsooth, on one universal principle. It failed to work, not only because they were surrounded by peoples whose wishes did not coincide with theirs, but also because their innermost desire, already detected by Burke in their master, Rousseau, was more the disruption of an old order than the creation of a new.

Despite the biting criticism that the state of the world now showered on his theory, Professor Kant still clung to it manfully. In an article entitled "On the Proverb: What Is Right in Theory May Not Work in Practice" the imperturbable philosopher explained that a sound theory, correctly understood, will certainly work in practice. If a republic is in theory the only good type of state, it cannot fail to be so in fact as well. Recent experience? "There can be nothing more pernicious, nothing more unworthy of a philosopher," he had written previously, "than the vulgar recourse to experience, for there would be no unfortunate experiences at all if mankind had acted from the first according to dependable theories, and if notions that were crude just because they were drawn from experience had not thwarted everything." What interested him about the Revolution, he now insisted, was not the acts of its leaders, of the corrupt politicians, but the idealism of the masses. It has been proved in our own day, he continued, that even though man is not good he carries within him the seeds of virtue nevertheless.

What other explanation could there be for the fact that hundreds of thousands of young Frenchmen had fallen, inspired in strife and in death by that highest of all ideals, the liberty and equality of man? Weighed against this, Marat's evil character was as nothing. Under other forms of government, too, there had been base men, but never the unyielding patriotism that the French had shown in their revolutionary wars.

At the other extreme a Savoyard aristocrat, Count Joseph de Maistre, now a fugitive in Switzerland, saw in events then current a proof not of the virtue of mankind, but of the inexorability and omnipotence of God. No human soul had planned all this. The men of the Terror were themselves only marionettes on invisible threads, and when God's will had been accomplished through them they would vanish into the abyss whence they came. " 'I can imagine nothing further' is heard on every side. It is a good expression if it leads us back to the supreme cause that is now teaching mankind such a terrible lesson, but a stupid one if it indicates only anger and doubt. Everywhere are heard the questions: How is it possible that the most criminal of all men can triumph over the whole world? That regicide can bring all the advantages so eagerly anticipated by its infamous perpetrators? That wicked men succeed in everything? That the most atrocious plans are carried out with ease, whereas advocates of the right remain unsuccessful and ridiculous in all that they undertake? That the most famous statesmen err continually and the best generals suffer one defeat after another?

"But these are the prime requisites of a revolution that has been willed by God. Nothing can stop it, and those who oppose it fail consistently. Never has the Divine Will been made more clearly manifest. . . ." The retribution of God had been visited on the whole French nation, yes, on all European civilization, which had become an accessory to the crime, for a common peace is wholly impossible in the absence of religion, of morals. And the slaughtered French nobility, so the stern de Maistre insisted, had had no more of either than their executioners. Now, however, necessity would compel new ways of thinking.

Friedrich Georg Forster, son of the German world traveler, and himself a cosmopolite, sought to oppose this religious view on a historical, a beyond-good-and-evil basis. "Who can say now," he wrote, "how deeply the French Revolution has affected the fate of the whole human race, and how it will continue to do so until the very end of time? Let him who is present at the deliberations of the gods decide whether there is an actual morality of deeds and events, or whether any occurrence, with or without regard to all its possible consequences, can be called either good or bad. Even our logicians will never be able to prove a thing reprehensible because evil men promote it, or because it can be used for wicked purposes." But his rejection of the moral in history brought Forster nothing; despondent and alone he died shortly thereafter in Paris, whither he had hurried with such fond hopes.

Besides the unimpeachable but fruitless opinions of the philosophers there were those of the masses, who understood nothing; of the politicians, who were just managing to scrape along from one day to the next; and of the émigrés, who placed all the blame on chance and a few wicked men. Gouverneur Morris, the American Ambassador in Paris, called the last "refugee talk," and recalled that victims of the American Revolution had taken just such a short-sighted view.

Only a few combined the philosophical with the practical, and earnestly sought means by which the conflagration could be extinguished, or at least kept within bounds. For such purposes a belief in Divine punishment was of as little value as refugee talk; the psychological, the military, the economic mysteries of the Revolution must be penetrated; its methods heeded and its innovations adapted for use. The most successful at this formidable task were Mallet du Pan, who dispatched wise, but mostly futile, advice from London: and Gentz.

THE arrows of the Revolution struck everywhere while Gentz was establishing himself as a political writer. The too radical fell, the too moderate fell; Robespierre's dictatorship rose and set; Belgium was conquered, lost, conquered again, and Holland followed after. Stripped of their all, ecclesiastical and secular dignitaries from western Germany drifted toward the center of the Reich. The British, who had arrived late on the battlefield, were the most steadfast in their opposition. Prussia was growing war weary, and seeking helplessly for a way out.

Gentz sent his essays to various periodicals and finally, in 1795, ventured to take over one for himself, the *Neue deutsche Monatsschrift*. In 1799 he founded the monthly *Historisches Journal*, of which he alone supplied the entire contents; and in addition to all this he translated the writings of the most prominent émigrés: Mallet du Pan, Mounier, and that great authority on French economics, d'Ivernois.

The superiority of France, Gentz explained to his readers, rested upon the fact that she was no longer like the other nations. True, she was still a despotic state, but her despotism was not of the old, familiar variety, where the subjects idled and slept away their energies. It was an enthusiastic despotism of the people over themselves that enforced the participation of every citizen, and turned the whole strength of the country on its foreign enemies. It depended upon one party alone: the Jacobins; able men, but wicked and bloodthirsty, who, as Gentz said, "were not in jest where power was concerned." In numbers they constituted but a small minority, and a mystery still to be solved was how they managed, notwithstanding this, to impose their will on the whole country. "The riddle is explained when one remembers that the Jacobin clubs and the Convention together form the roots of a great tree that has spread its branches over all France; over the smallest villages no less than over the largest cities. . . . Thus were the other inhabitants of a region to constitute a majority never so strong they would still be unable to offer even the slightest opposition to this organization because it would seize them singly, one after another, and strangle at birth any alliance that might be under consideration." A party despotism like this, that had emerged from the people themselves, touched the life of the individual citizen far more closely than the old kings, for all their police and their armies, had ever been able to affect it.

The French dictators naturally denied that their system was tyrannical. "Does our rule resemble despotism?" asked Robespierre. "Yes, but only as a sword in the hand of a champion of liberty resembles the sword that the tyrant turns against him." "Good," replied Gentz; "we all see the similarity. Now, then, show us the difference! Show us the transition from your tyranny to freedom! Show us even the possibility of such a transition. . . . Despotism is despotism, let its ultimate goal be what it may."

The ultimate goal! So much had been heard of it since 1789, yet mankind seemed to be traveling farther and farther away from it. There had been a time when it meant a community of free men, but now the state rigidly controlled the life of every one of its citizens. According to the soundest theory, what is the state? An epitome of its citizens, replied Gentz, and it is perfect when the rights of every last one are secure. But upon "the good of all" as an abstract basis any sort of tyranny could be established. "This wretched maxim, that the good of the people is the highest law, has been from time immemorial the death of all political morality and an excuse for the evilest deeds!" Against these the highly praised "virtue" of the revolutionary despots was no guarantee, the less so because the administration changed every month.

That was another subject for derision. He who today was the savior of the motherland, the archpriest of the revolutionary temple, became tomorrow an "antirevolutionist," an "agent of Pitt," a "Cromwellist," a monster that richly deserved death. Not a year went by, nay, sometimes not even a month, without these radical changes at revolutionary headquarters, without some sensation, some coup d'état, some so-called red-letter day. Often it was hard to say against which side the blow had been delivered, whether the reactionary or the ultraradical. Authority, vested only in itself, blindly pursuing a course whose congruence posterity might perhaps be able to recognize or explain, constantly vacillating between the extremes of ostensible moderation and ostensible radicalism, striking at one or the other side at short intervals if not simultaneously, now audaciously proclaimed the union of the two. What! Royalists and arch-Jacobins allied against the Republic?

The paradox was greeted with laughter by the other nations. Yet after all it was not so absurd, for there *was* a common foe, and even though their ideas were contradictory the leaders did not take them very seriously, for they identified themselves with the ideas until finally the ideas vanished completely and only the leaders themselves remained. Everything went according to the laws of social mechanics. That is to say, those who began the Revolution, or led it from time to time, were pushed aside until displaced members of two diametrically opposite camps found themselves for the moment in coöperation, while the victorious group attacked them both by exaggerating the extent of their alliance and substituting for proof, which they did not have, the most hair-raising fabrications. Posterity, thought Gentz, should study the evidence offered at the trial of Hébert's followers in order to realize the moral degeneration that marked the closing years of the eighteenth century. When the most successful of all republican generals, Pichegru, was arrested a second time for high treason together with some sixty leading politicians, Gentz wrote in a private letter: "I know well enough what to think of the recent happenings in Paris, but it is much too subtle, and the leaders are much too stupid to be honored by my telling them. So I shall do no more than try to confound, with the following dilemma, those who are still supporters of the unhappy Republic. Either it is true that the highest in office were traitors, or it is not true. If it is true, what shall we say of a Republic in which such rogues could become leaders? If it is not true, what shall we say of a nation that dares to treat its most faithful officials in such a way?"

Public opinion in Europe worried but little over this dilemma. What power the rulers had, to effect thus easily such a bold coup d'état as ruin of the most popular generals—this alone caused wonder.

What was the use of ridicule? What was the use of showing the revolutionists the contradictions in which they were involved? The danger of a complete triumph of the revolutionary principle, or, more accurately put, of the French Armies, was imminent. What could be done about it?

The allied powers had proceeded on the conviction that a revolution like that in France must weaken a nation morally, militarily, and economically. Even such an expert on the economics of the Revolution as François d'Ivernois saw substantial hope for the allied powers in the financial ruin of the Republic, and only too willingly did William Pitt, the British Prime Minister, give credence to this comfortable opinion. Meanwhile it turned out quite otherwise, for the nations that were not actually touched by the Revolution proved inferior by far in a moral, a military, and an economic respect, as Gentz was one of the first to see. Occasionally at first, then by degrees more consistently, he tried to make the monarchies understand what had been responsible for their defeat.

In examining the problem from the angle of morale and morality the highest discrimination was required. The French people fought enthusiastically and furiously, and all the military talent hitherto latent among twenty-five million people found a place; against them the rest of Europe sent conscripted or hired professional soldiers. But, curiously enough, the strength of the French Army lay partly in this, too: it looked down with scorn on the bloody morass of Paris, and at bottom was entirely out of sympathy with the Jacobins. Amidst the general lawlessness it became an independent organization with so proud and exultant a tradition that Mallet du Pan advised the drawing up of a peace program agreeable to the army, even though not to the Jacobins, with the object of driving a wedge between the two.

The unprecedented size of this people's army necessitated a theater of operations much larger than those of the past, and what had formerly been like a skillful game of chess in which only a few pieces are engaged now became a torrent that submerged whole countries. Rivers and mountains acquired the significance of fortresses, conquered provinces served as repositories for military stores, and the amorality that had distinguished internal revolutionary politics became the chief means in strategy. "The anxious and scrupulous neutrality that the Swiss cantons imposed upon themselves," wrote Gentz in respect to the invasion of Switzerland, "left the perpetrators of this crime not the slightest pretext for their interference; but it was all in vain. Switzerland was the most important strategic position in all Europe; nothing more was required to vindicate the outrage."

The most serious error was the universal belief that war could not be carried on without money. This may have been true for Prussia, where they had not even yet ventured to print paper money and the costs of war were paid in gold. Or for Great Britain, which was vulnerable in a different way; she was powerful and rich, but her economy was based on a complicated, world-wide system of credit. What could possibly endanger a revolutionary state that thumbed its nose at the friendship and credit of the whole world?

In correspondence with d'Ivernois the young writer in Berlin rejected any hope that France would collapse because of her financial burden. On the contrary, necessity would only drive these modern statesmen to fresh attacks and conquests. The internal economy of France was like that of an isolated farm, or, better, a robbers' cave. What did she own, after all? What could she dispense with? Or get from her neighbors? "The Revolution," Gentz recapitulated later, "provided France with means and resources of which no use could be made except under revolutionary conditions, and of which in normal times no one had the slightest conception. . . . It taught us that under certain conditions war can be waged with no money at all, and sometimes most successfully even in the total absence of all customary resources; that a truly revolutionary condition uncovers to a nation, once it has become involved in the upheaval, new and wholly incalculable means; that such a system can prevail over the soundest theories of political economy; and, finally, that cessation of trade, paralysis of industries, loss of ready money, deficits in revenue, total disorganization of the tax system, and all the evils commonly associated with the downfall of states are in a certain sense only relative, and that a great nation is never entirely exhausted so long as energy remains, even though it be the energy of crime. . . . When, by some extraordinary concatenation of circumstances all the forces of a great nation are concentrated on one single object, the probability of some remarkable success is always present, and if this single object happens to be military power there can be no difficulty in understanding how a state that pursues this to the exclusion of all else can quickly rise from the lowest depths of misery to the heights of a commanding splendor."

GENTZ, now thirty years of age, sat in his little home in Breitenstrasse, Berlin, poring over English and French journals though by then they were months old, abstracting and writing. When first his genius drove him to attack the Revolution with his pen, in the years between 1793 and 1795, and to fathom the nature of this interminable war, he had drawn no unequivocal, practical deductions. That came later. In fact, he still thought it possible, and sometimes, indeed, even desirable, to make peace with France and leave her to her own internal convulsions. "Either carry on this war with arms, as modern times demand, or abandon it entirely." Thus discreetly did he address the monarchies. It may be that he suggested the second alternative only that he might dare to express the first. Or it may be that, all young and still insecure as he was, he yielded a little to public opinion, for in Berlin the inclination to make peace was growing stronger and stronger and men whom he regarded highly, and with whose views on domestic politics he was fully in accord, were in favor of such a course.

Perhaps, after all, the Revolution was something to be imitated, for how was it possible to struggle against power whose overwhelming success rested upon the fact that it was so thoroughly in league with the spirit of the times, nay, even with the spirit of the future?

Gentz analyzed this argument minutely. If it proved valid the struggle would have to be given up. But no! It was not valid, at least in the sense in which it was employed by the advocates of capitulation. To refer everything to deep conspiracy, to avoidable treason and knavish trickery, as the émigrés did, was, of course, wholly unreasonable. But even more unreasonable and dangerous was the current belief in a historical predestination that accounted for everything, even the most distressing evil and bloodshed. "Mankind," so the adherents of this theory maintained, according to Gentz, "was ripe for just such an event. It was only a development, after all, of something that had been preparing in France for the past fifty or hundred years, and that must bear fruit through the irresistible power of an advancing intellectual civilization as surely as the grape-vine bears its grapes in the fall." If this theory were true then all that promoted the Revolution was noble, liberal, lofty, and humane; all that opposed it, base and servile, and any resistance entirely vain. The most dreadful suffering must be borne with unconcern if only it had been imposed by the great god, Revolution. It was, in a way, treating the present as though it were already past and irrevocable, or like sitting in idle contemplation over matters that could, and should, be settled by a little determination.

It is always unusual, momentous, and terrible occurrences that invite thinking men to appraise carefully once more their conceptions of the possible, the actual, and the inevitable. Gentz himself, a child of the eighteenth century, was well acquainted with the compelling trends of history. He was familiar with what later came to be called the "Bourgeois Revolution," which was, he explained in his journal, a result of both economic and intellectual causes.

Industry and trade should be freed of control by the state. The constantly increasing prosperity despite all wars; the discoveries of science; the development of world trade, especially in America; the dynamic power of money all pointed to a political upheaval. The great new group of capitalists had "one common end always in view: riches, as long as there were any more to be got; freedom, as long as they still felt restraint; and prestige and power, as soon as they had attained wealth and independence. No matter how successfully they might be repressed for a time they never lost their resilience, but unerringly seized the next opportunity. Once masters, they were not satisfied with the mere transfer of power to other hands, but knew no rest until this power itself had assumed a new character and new forms. Sooner or later this will take place in all those European countries where it has not already happened." Indeed, it had occurred in Great Britain, in Holland, and in America; and was it not really the background of the French Revolution? If it were admitted that the progress of the human mind and the casting off of old feudal chains by a middle class devoted to trade were both inevitable and advantageous, would not assent have to be given even to the French Revolution?

Never! According to Gentz, it is a mistake to judge individual cases and general theories by the same rules. True, the Revolution was associated with facts and ideas that were just and right, but the ideas had not required it for their realization. Those who were in their twenties before 1789 did not look back on that period as melancholy, as an aristocrats' lost paradise, but as optimistic, stirring, and modern. Never had there been a higher conception of man! The influence of the Enlightenment had spread so far that even governments as traditionally sluggish and hostile to thought as the Neapolitan and the Portuguese had to comply with the universal longing, and had hastened to share in the evolution that Prussia, France, and Austria had initiated. Thus in the good that it did produce the French Revolution was in no way foreign to prevailing convictions, but merely an example of a general tendency becoming concrete. Its misfortune was that it precipitated what would have come to pass far better without it; that it overthrew the good together with the bad; that it even converted good into bad and everything into its opposite, and thus sullied the very name of freedom.

"If only one had studied the true, historical, and social character of the Revolution, without favorable bias as to its origins, and had learned what actually were its immediate driving forces, what its implements, what its ends, and the methods of its instigators," one would never have sunk low enough to vindicate the massacre at Lyons on the score that it belonged to the current of the future.

The accomplished, the ensuing, and the strong were not identical with the inevitable, the rational, and the good. The present was not omnipotent. But it was not justifiable either to take refuge from today's horror in a denial of the world and a mysticism that looked askance at history. The duty of a responsible man was to guard himself against all the usual extremes and careless abstractions, and to think honestly, examine thoroughly, and discriminate fairly.

Our struggling young author fulfilled this duty by writing a history of the French Revolution in four thick volumes folio. He distinguished actual events from their general or ideological premises, and pointed out the underlying motives, the idiotic mistakes of the court and the émigrés, the presumption of individual revolutionary leaders, and the unconscious guilt of the masses. He showed that all might have turned out otherwise, and why things happened as they did. It was a faithful, laborious, and penetrating demonstration of cause and effect, yet in the end he did not publish it, because events were still in such rapid flux that no final conclusions could be drawn.

So PHILOSOPHICAL yet so practical, so emotional yet so temperate, were the writings of the thirty-year-old Gentz, and their effect was gratifying. In Berlin he was recognized before long as the most gifted political writer in the German language, and even in London his essays began to attract attention. But the financing of his journals still caused him the greatest anxiety.

Fame pleased him, and he never failed to choose for discussion such controversial subjects as would bring his works into the limelight, though in his own mind he was not nearly so certain of his ground as their tone might have suggested. Sometimes, when he abandoned himself to his thoughts, or saw the validity of an opposing argument, he would suddenly be plunged into the deepest melancholy. Why was everything that one wrote so inadequate, so powerless to penetrate the terrifying maze of reality? Whence the right to seek the moral in history, to measure what had happened by a few personal standards? Had not the world always been in the desperate condition in which it found itself today? Was the conquest of Belgium and Switzerland by the Jacobins any worse than the partition of Poland by the kings? Were not both sides equally wrong in this world war, and did not the simple truth lie in these words: *Iliacos intra muros peccatur et extra?* *

On such occasions as this, after he had sat helpless over his writing for a time, he would suddenly throw down his pen and seek distraction in highly questionable society. Befuddled with whisky, and seated beside some queer friend, or some so-called actress, the celebrated authority on international politics might have been seen thundering in a hired equipage through the night streets of the Prussian capital.

* Within and without the walls of Troy all goes wrong. Horace, *Epistulae*, 1, 2, 16.

III

PRUSSIAN POLITICS

IN MARCH of 1795 representatives of the King of Prussia signed a treaty of peace in Basel with the French Republic. The situation was a delicate one, for Baron von Hardenberg, leader of the Prussian delegation, did not find it easy to sit down at the same table with the murderers of Louis XVI. Yet he felt constrained to accommodate himself to their idiom and appeal with ironic pathos to liberty, the brotherhood of man, and the right of the masses to determine their own destiny. The Jacobin representative, on the other hand, François Barthélemy, proved thoroughly conversant with traditional European politics, and expressed the view that Prussia must certainly be indemnified for her war costs. This, he insinuated, could best be done by the annexation of certain small German states. Austria and England alone were to blame for this most unfortunate of all wars, and his stainless employers would be highly gratified at seeing progressive Prussia hold the balance of power in future over these two inimical meddlers with the peace.

Now here was a language that von Hardenberg understood. In the end France was awarded all German possessions lying on the left bank of the Rhine, and in the interests of the ardently desired universal peace Prussia was allowed to engulf those states that no longer fitted into the new scheme of things, either because of their small size or their obsolete forms of government. The negotiators drew an imaginary "line of demarcation" right across Germany, all to the north of which was to belong to a Prussian neutral zone, closed thereafter against the passage of armed forces.

War with the German Reich, with Austria, with Great Britain still continued, but France was now rid of her main adversary. A proud monarch, enamored of the past and definitely hostile to the Revolution, had recognized her as a legitimate power.

The secret motive for this separate peace, this breach of allegiance, was partly power politics, partly ideology. As for the first, the Prussian ministers were afraid that if France were annihilated the aspirations of Russia and Austria toward domination of the Continent could no longer be successfully opposed. It appeared to them more advantageous, therefore, to let the war pursue its endless course and in the meantime to share the remainder of Poland with Russia. As for the second, the King had advisers who believed that for one reason or another the Revolution was an inevitable misfortune of the times, and others, again, who thought that the war was the real revolution and that accordingly it must be brought to an end as soon as possible. "We cannot defeat France," they argued, "without adopting her own methods; that is to say, without descending to sans-culottism in both our army and our economy. Thus the very thing that we wish to preserve by the war, our way of life, we should actually lose by the war, whereas with a program of mutual tolerance we might hope to save it and even to exert some degree of influence over the Jacobins themselves. Furthermore, the Revolution is gradually dying out as it is. . . ."

But the French had something more than mere reciprocal toleration in mind. The intellectuals of various shades who now were attempting to guide French policy had believed for half a century that Prussia was the safest and most natural ally for France. For that reason she must be strengthened. In the interest of humanity, for the dissemination of sound philosophy, and to maintain the balance of power in Europe and bring low the House of Austria the German states must be organized around Berlin; the map of Germany, whose incongruities were a scandal to all enlightened thinkers, must be simplified and the Prussian Reich, thus regenerated, closely allied with the French Republic.

The first French Ambassador in Berlin, Caillard, had a military alliance in view, and all sorts of independent agents and cynical or doctrinaire charlatans of both nationalities pledged themselves to bring it about. The Prussian Foreign Minister, Count von Haugwitz, said neither yes nor no to their offers, but for the moment proffered cordial friendship, and favorable trade relations in particular.

To the rest of Europe the Peace of Basel was an unwelcome surprise. Indignation mounted as it came to light that the enemy was being furnished from Berlin with munitions of war, and that through the good offices of the banker, Itzig, the French cavalry had been reinforced with 10,000 horses from north Germany. Von Haugwitz swore that he wished this separate peace to be the forerunner of a general peace, and offered his impartial services toward this end. But no one listened to him, and the withdrawal of Prussia changed the course of the war hardly at all. In French domestic policy war had become the guiding principle, the key to and the support of power. The hope of change, of expansion, of plunder glowed ever more fervently in the breasts of Austrian nobles and French demagogues. The rulers of England would never admit that Belgium and Holland were now under the dominion of France.

In their extremity the allies began to sue once more for Prussian aid. Von Haugwitz did not wholly deprive them of hope, and continued in this way to lead all the belligerents on for ten years.

Amidst the welter of problems that confront us we are long in choosing a policy that will determine our future actions, but finally one is selected, perhaps because it seems an answer to the dominant question of our day, perhaps only because its realization lies most easily within our grasp. Until then thoughts and deeds have been inconsistent; we have changed our point of view, espousing now one, now another cause as our main interest, and letting ourselves be driven into positions that soon became untenable.

So it was with Gentz, who was hostile to the French Revolution, yet certainly not opposed to the separate Peace of Basel. It appeared to him that the war had long since lost its ideological character, to become only another great war between cabinets, an obsolete and bloody game in which north Germany would do better to remain an outsider. He saw that the allies could never win with the methods they were employing, and knew that the coalition was suffering from irreconcilable internal strife; he believed that Prussia was in need of thoroughgoing liberal reforms, yet realized that the war was fatal to them. For inside the state it was leading to untoward conditions, to reaction and censorship under which a sincere and conscientious journalist could no longer remain at ease. To oppose this reactionary situation, to be a reformer and at the same time an advocate of the war against the Revolution, required far more realism than could be expected of a young theorist. Two years after the conclusion of the Treaty of Basel Gentz was still advising that the Prussian separate peace be maintained.

This he did expressly in a pamphlet on the best form of government, an open letter that he transmitted in 1797 to the new King of Prussia. The act was unusual to the point of impudence, but the position of monarchs was now so insecure that they had to listen with polite interest to the advice of their subjects. Gentz imparted some useful truths to the young man, and boldly assured him that there remained only one way of doing honor to a king: to tell him the truth, that is, to recount the needs, the ideas, the facts of his time.

The private citizen, so wrote the young antirevolutionary, required confidence, law and order, peace and security. Foreign policy no longer deserved to take first place. To avoid war should be the highest ambition of statesmanship; unnatural alliances endangered peace. As for domestic affairs, the last trace of privilege before the law should vanish. "All that undermines respect for the law, all that condones arbitrary legal proceedings and in the sinister form of peremptory decisions seeks to drive the startled citizen from the last bastions of his security, is a desecration of the monarch's high office. . . ." Taxes should be few and the tax system more simple. "Everyone should be free to pursue his own interests in any legitimate way that he thinks will lead most quickly to his goal; to employ his capabilities to the best advantage." No government monopoly, no interference with private enterprise, should restrict him with superfluous regulations. . . . As a climax Gentz added to all these recommendations on economics some further advice on government, and demanded freedom of the press. Everyone must be responsible for his own deeds, but against erroneous beliefs only the truth should appear. Nothing on earth is less fitted to be enchained than the mind. . . .

The little article caused a sensation. Loud criticism was heard from the conservatives, and from Weimar Goethe declared himself outraged by such officious expressions of liberalism. But before long the bitterest enemy of the production was the author himself, who buried his face in his hands and turned aside whenever the subject came up. The opportunism of youth, he would cry; only the most audacious indiscretion and ambition could have suggested it.

Perhaps he was somewhat to blame, but certainly he had no idea of being appointed a king's minister, as was whispered about at the time, on the strength of his open letter. Indeed, when later he was offered a position in the Privy Council he declined, pleading that he was only a writer and shuddered at the very prospect of exercising authority.

He may have shuddered at authority, but he had no fear of popularity and fame; and besides, he had only to recall his background in order to speak as a liberal. The doctrines of Adam Smith were never betrayed by the disciple of Burke, and toward certain conditions in Prussia, where no one dared even travel the highways without special permission, where a valet's wages were set by the king, and heavy punishment was prescribed for importing mousetraps from Brunswick, a follower of Adam Smith could hardly accept conservatism under any circumstances.

The new King, an amiable but awkward and timid young man, read the letter, underscoring with approval the passage in which avoidance of war was said to be the highest goal of statesmanship. Frederick William III thought fundamental reforms inevitable, too, but feared those who would be at his disposal in achieving revolution from above. Because comparisons were in vogue, and it appeared only too probable that the experience of France would have to be repeated, it was the custom to compare him with Louis XVI. But he himself, instructed by a humanitarian diplomat trained in the law, was assailed by grave doubts of his own fitness and of the divine right of kings in general.

Those about him had soon come to the conclusion that the seething caldron of the French Revolution would have to cool off a little before anything suitable for use at home could be taken out of it. In the second year of his reign one of his ministers said to the Ambassador from the French Republic: "Here you have only the nobility against you. Our King and our people uniformly favor France. The highly profitable Revolution that you have brought about from below upward will come to pass slowly in Prussia from above downward. In his way the King is a democrat, and labors without cessation to restrict the privileges of the nobility, following in this respect the example of Joseph II of Austria, though he acts more cautiously. We shall leave the aristocrats their ribbons, which often take the place of pensions and so relieve our finances, but the necessity of living well will soon transfer them to more useful walks of life, to industry and trade. As the King has derived these ideas from the French Revolution our nobility detest your country, of course, above all else. . . ."

A commission was actually established to reform the administration, and because of his graceful literary style Gentz, now a clerk in the War Office, was made its recording secretary. But the aristocratic ministers thought it against the laws of nature to curtail the privileges of the nobility, and although the King had called for prompt action, "in the spirit of the times," lest otherwise the state itself be threatened with ruin, little or nothing was achieved.

Besides the ministers there was an unofficial center of power, the so-called Cabinet Council, private advisers of the King, who represented a sort of government opposition. Its members were of bourgeois, and often Huguenot, origin, and were more progressive than the ministers themselves. Gentz was closely allied to them by training, relationship, and interests and, indeed, might have joined them were it not that the more he learned about the affairs of the state the more he came to distrust these dilettantes of the innermost circle. They stood between the King and his ministers, who were rarely able to consult him, they intrigued, and they obstructed. The domestic reforms that had been planned weakened the foreign policy, but the same grave uncertainty that caused the government to lose all interest in foreign affairs and drove it toward reform now destroyed this, too, in its turn; and always there was present an increasing anxiety over the external situation.

Was this any time for peaceful innovations at home? The war that Austria and Great Britain continued to wage against France was becoming more and more bitter, and had spread to Switzerland, Italy, and even north Africa. The entrance of Russia brought the confusion to a climax, and it was apparent that it could end in but one of two ways. Either the allies must restore the balance of power, for which they would need Prussia's help, or France would win and then proceed to establish a revolutionary world federation that would be a constant menace: half empire, half chaos.

When Gentz founded his new periodical, the *Historisches Journal,* in January, 1799, foreign politics was his only interest, and in the light of this, which his philosophical training had once taught him to disdain so heartily, he now judged the attitude of all his political friends. Social reforms were to be desired, certainly, but were of little importance compared with the peril of Jacobin rule over Europe, and if they increased this danger they would be damnable. Damnable, also, were certain other plans which, even though they did concern foreign policy, kept Prussia out of the Second Coalition: designs against Austria, plans for easy gains at the expense of the belligerents, obsolete plans, brainless, heartless plans. It was time for everyone to coöperate and drive back into its place something that threatened to become stronger than all else together: this was now the keynote of his thoughts and his endeavors. As a youth he had imagined himself born into a pacific world of reasonable discussion, and for a few years had believed that one state at least, in the midst of a world drunk with war, could enjoy the blessings of a democratic peace. Now he could speak only of disturbances in the balance of power, and of war.

THE year 1797 brought an attempt at peace on the Continent. Even Austria became resigned at last to recognizing the French Republic, but the obliquitous arrangements upon which the peace rested, the division of north Italy between Austria and France—a sacrifice of the weak and neutral everywhere—did not result in the anticipated new balance of power. Although both parties to the agreement gained something, the victor came off with the lion's share and it soon became evident that they could not manage peaceably together in Italy. Much less could England suffer the English Channel and the shores of the Mediterranean to be controlled by the most aggressive of the great powers. The Old World had not yet reached the point where it could settle down quietly for a while.

Negotiations between the grotesque "German Reich" and its more modern conquerors dragged themselves out in a bizarre congress during 1798. In this year of peace Switzerland was lured into deceitful negotiations that affected her domestic affairs, then overpowered by arms and so heartlessly despoiled that the carriages of the French generals broke down under their burden of gold; the Papal States were made over into a republic and the Holy Father was dragged off to France a prisoner; the recently established Republic of Lombardy was so consistently annoyed by confiscation and coups d'état that even the dummy rulers appointed to administer this sister republic lost all pleasure in their autocracy; and the King of Sardinia was beleaguered in his capital, and allowed to remain there only because this infamous man was more docile where French interests were concerned than the Italian national revolutionists gave promise of being. General Bonaparte embarked on his attempt, in the new style,* to break Great Britain's hold on the Near East and block the land route to India. England answered him with the annihilation of a French fleet, the establishment of an income tax, and preparations for new alliances on the Continent. Here William Pitt pinned his hopes especially on great, powerful Russia. The steady approach of a Russian Army toward the west brought about a new coalition with Austria, Portugal, Bavaria, and Naples, and in 1799 war broke out again as though spontaneously, without a single power having "declared" it.

But to make it appear that all was as it should be, this one was promptly called the War of the Second Coalition and said to differ from that of the First Coalition in amplitude of plan, decision of

* The innovation consisted in lightning attack at a weak spot, penetrating the enemy's front, spreading out behind it, and cutting his supply lines.

attack, and loyal cohesion of the allies. Actually, however, the two together constituted one and the same war. A British expeditionary force landed in Holland, and toward the south there appeared an unprecedented sight: an army of Russians, of magnificently trained barbarians, pouring down the mountains toward the plain of the Po. In Germany, in Switzerland, and in Italy the French were routed and thrown back, their artificial republics shattered. The war began as a tempest that threatened to overturn everything.

For their part, the rulers of the French Republic resolved on a stratagem to save it and to win over the armed help of Prussia. To this end there appeared in Berlin a pale man in a black coat, the ostentatious and fanatical exponent of representative government, Emmanuel-Joseph Sieyès; but he was not welcomed with the honors that he expected. It was his conviction that the real activating motive between governments is fear, and he conducted his diplomacy accordingly. Radiating intelligence and rectitude although, to be sure, he had managed to put away several millions during the Revolution, the great man did his best, in a few dogmatically conducted conversations, to establish a conclusive French-Prussian alliance, but saw shortly that his attempt would fail. "As soon as one begins to reason the Germans think one is retreating," he wrote home. And, hitting the nail on the head: "I cannot repeat this to you often enough; the French err seriously in regarding Prussia as their natural ally for all time."

He made merry over the King's French and commended only that of old Prince Henry, the brother of Frederick the Great, with whom, he said, he felt entirely at home. "How different he is from all the others that I have seen here!" He called von Haugwitz the "Minister of Inaction," or the "Minister for the Obstruction of Foreign Affairs," and denied emphatically that he was a member of the faction sympathetic toward France, even though the English and Russians were unfriendly to him. Really, he did not belong to any party. He was a nobody.

After having stayed for a year Sieyès took his departure, firm in the conviction that it would be best to force Prussia toward the east, possibly unite her with Poland, and establish an alliance of small German states under the protectorate of France.

Whenever Sieyès made his ponderous exit from the Foreign Office Thomas Grenville and Count Panin appeared, Ambassadors Extraordinary of Great Britain and Russia respectively, to enlist the Prussian Army in the interests of their sovereigns. Could a great power like Prussia, they insinuated, possibly remain neutral amidst this unparalleled world conflagration? A sudden Prussian advance against Holland, and the specter of French control over Europe would unquestionably vanish as promptly as it had arisen. Von Haugwitz listened to them attentively, and there are documents to prove that this not unintelligent man, disheartened by the gradually increasing power of France, flatly advised the King to accept the English and Russian proposals; but Frederick William was wholly under the influence of his Francophile Cabinet Council, whose members still continued to believe in perpetual peace and so let their great opportunity slip by.

We owe to a clerk in the Prussian War Office, Friedrich Gentz, all our detailed knowledge of these intrigues and the connection between them. At this time he began to engage in activities that could hardly be reconciled with his official position. Enraged at what seemed to him the senseless conduct of his government, he began to denounce it secretly to the British and to throw out hints on how a change might eventually be brought about. The great gains of Austria and Russia had already been lost, and Bonaparte had returned from Africa to seize control in France by a coup d'état, when Gentz wrote his first secret memoir. He entrusted it not to the Ambassador but to a British agent named Stamford who was then traveling back and forth between London, Berlin, and Hanover.

Gentz did not think much of the motives that were said to be responsible for Prussian foreign policy: the traditional fear of the Hapsburg greed for territory, of Great Britain's maritime rule, and of the sinister Russian masses. Such arguments were employed simply for the reason that they lay ready at hand and seemed to justify an attitude indulged in because of a complete lack of vigor and honesty. Mediocrity, according to Gentz, was the key to the policy, or "absence of any policy," at the court in Berlin. "You, Sir, continue to believe that one need not despair of a favorable turn here; that what is not done today can be done tomorrow just as well; and that our trifling may perhaps be replaced some day by collaboration in the one cause that should interest the world just now . . ." "Because there is something so unnatural, so revolting, in the idea that this state should forget completely what it owes to itself and the rest of Europe, it is believed that the ignominious oblivion to which it appears condemned must of necessity be but a temporary phenomenon. From week to week, almost from hour to hour, the moment of our long-delayed awakening has been expected, and I greatly fear that even now this vain hope has not been relinquished." Politics, he continued, are the product of individual men, and from those in whose hands the King of Prussia now finds himself nothing decent or courageous is to be anticipated.

Gentz was not above reviewing their records seriatim. First, there was General Kökeritz, a man with neither brains nor education, common sense, nor the ability to conduct affairs, and possessed of no social gifts at all. A second, Herr Beyme, a Councilor charged with reporting on all domestic affairs, a lawyer, conceited, arrogant, and bigoted, was endowed at most with the poor attainments required to draw up a judicial opinion. A third, Herr Lombard, the real author of Prussian policy, was best known to Gentz, who was related by marriage to Lombard's wife and came from the same esthetic Huguenot set. Lombard had intelligence and wit, wrote tolerable German and admirable French, but otherwise he could not be too harshly appraised. "His only principle of action is to be of the same mind as those in power. . . . In some casual hour at night he leafs hastily through dispatches from the ambassadors to foreign courts, and while half asleep makes ready a report upon which the destinies of a nation may depend. . . . He treats the most important affairs of Europe as though they concerned some small town, prefers droll conceits to serious thought, and is pleased to sustain the aversion of the King to foreign transactions by consistently presenting them in a contemptuous light." Yes, more than once this adviser of the King had actually said to Gentz that it would be best if the Foreign Office were abolished. . . .

Under the dominion of these shortsighted, ignoble, and shallow men there sat a King who understood nothing of the world crisis amidst which he had ascended the throne. Whatever there was of wisdom or efficiency in Prussia they paralyzed, suppressed, and condemned to silence, and the mood of a public inimical to both war and politics gave them welcome support. How responsible statesmanship should handle this mood, disdain it, clarify it, educate it to truth, make it over, worried the Cabinet Councilors not at all. . . . "Who can fail to see and to understand today that, given the splendid opportunities of the past campaign, now, perhaps, lost forever, one single firm step by our side, just one decisive move against Holland, would have overturned the Directory and ended the Revolution before the Great Adventurer returned from the East to the misfortune of all mankind; would have restored the balance of power in Europe; and would have covered Prussia with lasting glory?" A little risk in 1799, and Napoleon's Empire might never have been. But three Cabinet Councilors wished it otherwise. . . .

Well, that was all past. As for the future, Gentz saw no need of reforming the internal administration, for though still burdened with many defects it was better than in most of the other nations; and even if changes were desirable, this was no time to discuss them. Arguments of that sort would divert attention from the one and only topic upon which it must now be concentrated." . . . "Before a house is decorated one must first be sure of retaining it."

What Great Britain should attempt to bring about first of all was abolition of the Cabinet Council and the formation of a representative ministry. The procedure of such a body in respect to the foreign crisis could not be determined in advance, though of course "it would not be governed by senile diplomats and maxims from out the past, but rather by new principles dictated by the complete overturn of Europe. . . . One of the first precepts might well be to regard methods exactly opposite to those that the present Council had followed as probably the best." A representative ministry could govern well even though no guarantee were given as to its personnel, whereas a Privy Council could not. If such a council were retained Prussia would sink in normal times to the level of a third-rate power; but under the present highly unusual conditions she was threatened with nothing less than final and well-deserved extinction. . . .

Thus the memoir. Its author must have been very angry as he prepared it, all unsuspecting that in the years to come he would have to write a hundred more like it.

It was at this time, in the spring of 1800, that Gentz received money from England for the first time: five hundred pounds from the funds of the Secretary of State for Foreign Affairs, Lord Grenville.

Public opinion on the Continent held that the situation was not favorable to England. Europe was tired of war, and as England had long been the champion of action against France, and for a time had held out entirely alone, a popular impression arose that she was chiefly to blame and must have started it all. How the war really had begun, eight years previously, and what its original object was, had long since been forgotten; the belief persisted, even though, as a matter of fact, the English fought neither willingly nor well, and upon landing in Holland shortly before had won no laurels. After having inveigled Russia and Austria into the second war England had helped them only with money. Then the bankers, who were the real rulers in London, had demanded this back with compound interest, if not actually used it to seize the industries of her partners, who had fought and bled for British interests.

How on earth did the British capitalists intend to finish this war with a victory? Or did they really want to end it, they and the lords, who determined British policy? "Restoring the established governments of Europe, not a thirst for conquest and plunder," was, according to a declaration of George III, the ambition of these plutocrats. But the nations for whose liberty they were fighting were treated exactly as enemies the minute they succumbed to French arms, and the most substantial help that the British ever gave them was to take away their colonies and ships. Even an Austrian diplomat did not deny himself the sarcastic remark: "Whatever the British do, it finally results in a strengthening of their fleet. . . ."

How long would Europe continue to procrastinate? No, not simply to procrastinate, but to belabor herself, to bleed, to burn, instead of leaving the rabid island to itself and taking steps to reduce the Continent to righteous order? This was the tone of French propaganda, reinforced by highly plausible though actually meaningless offers of peace. It spread and flourished in Scandinavia, in Vienna, in St. Petersburg, and Berlin was wholly dominated by it.

Gentz was now in financial as well as moral difficulties. When he founded his *Historisches Journal* he had enjoyed some support from Count von Haugwitz, but this was withdrawn as soon as the ministers realized that the young man had aims other than theirs. In his monthly articles Gentz demanded Prussian intervention as explicitly as he dared, and also praised British politics and the British way of life. His *Essay on the Financial Policy and National Wealth of Great Britain* in particular attracted attention in London. In it he gave the Continent an idea of Great Britain's invincible might, of the organization and development of a great modern economic structure, her system of amortization, the Bank of England, paper money, the income tax, and of the actual national income—the whole as complicated as French economy was primitive and brutal. The essay was translated into English, and Prime Minister Pitt himself read it with admiration.

The British Ambassador in Berlin, Lord Carysford, fully cognizant of the power of public opinion, invited the young man to call. A German so well versed in politics, in economics, in history, who was such a remarkable writer, and possessed of such brilliant social gifts withal, was really unique, and Gentz became a welcome guest of the Englishman. Through the mediation of Carysford he wrote Lord Grenville that the diabolically clever French propaganda must be opposed at all costs, that he could no longer support his journal, and that he needed money. Grenville received the suggestion favorably and thereafter money began to arrive irregularly from London: 100 pounds, 1,000 pounds, according to the whim of the donors. He who had begun ten years before to write as a philosophical young moralist on justice and liberty, had become a secret and highly paid international agent; a dangerous position, such as no one before him had ever held in Germany.

An "agent of Pitt," as the current French expression put it! Had the reputed strongbox of the Prime Minister corrupted even him? To answer this question in the affirmative would be a wholly unjustifiable simplification. Gentz had been expressing his opinions for ten years without ever being paid for them, and he changed them not one whit because now he had begun to receive money. Never, either then or later, did anyone pay him to hear a predetermined opinion, but only to have him express his own independent views; it was the personal integrity of an adviser that was bought. He took money, yes; as much of it as he could get, but only from those with whose opinions he was in accord, or who at least would permit him to speak without restraint. Those who were not wise enough to agree to this stipulation found negotiations broken off at once.

To be so passionately devoted to something, yet so greedy after the money that it brought in; to be so dependent yet so respected; so free, so proud; this was a side to his genius that he did not recognize at first, a side that he came to realize only by degrees, a phase that could not have been gauged by his contemporaries without the greatest difficulty, because it was unique.

On the evening when he visited the British Embassy for the first time he relinquished the career that appeared to have been marked out for him. That upon which he was now embarking had been as little foreseen, or deliberately planned, as anyone planned the French Revolution, or Napoleon's Empire, or any of the other important events that are begotten by time.

IV

GENTZ AND HIS FRIENDS

AT THE turn of the century Gentz was enjoying the friendship of a woman of Jewish extraction, no longer young, whose salon attracted diplomats, writers, and princes, foreign no less than native. Rahel Lewin, neither rich nor beautiful, was a pale, slender, elderly, unmarried woman with large eyes and a face that bore the stamp of suffering. Too fragile for love, she yet had something of the hearty and jovial in her manner. Uncommonly wise and good, incomparable as an inspiration, a mediatrix, and a confidante, she gave the north German capital a social and intellectual center that was half Western, half Germanic. Was it real, or apparent; or real, though only for one fleeting, happy moment? Who could say? In the shelter of Prussian neutrality, and for the time being, it was the best that Europe had to offer in the way of a cultural group.

Late at night there would gather in Rahel's attic room a circle of strange, disheveled, and often somewhat feminine figures; adventurers of the mind who, while General Bonaparte's armies traversed the Continent, pursued their bold inquiries, out of which were later to grow a new esthetics, Indology, psychoanalysis, and a new philosophy of history. Members of the group lived two or three together, exchanged sweethearts, entered into what they called "intellectual marriages" with one another, and talked the whole night through about the mysteries of the soul, dreams, love, death; about rediscovered mystics of the Middle Ages and fashions in art; but almost never about politics and the state.

There came the poet-philologist, Friedrich Schlegel, still but a youth, enormously gifted and just as cheeky; his friend, Ludwig Tieck, writer of entrancing fairy stories, who was shortly to join Schlegel's brother, August, in bringing out a translation of Shakespeare; the two Humboldts, Wilhelm, still a model of remarkable self-mastery, and his brother, Alexander, the explorer; Jean Paul Richter, whose tales, uncommonly charming, witty, and full of ideas, were abolishing the classical form of the novel and becoming the sensation of the book world; Majors von Schack and Gualtieri, military Bohemians, half Prussian and half French, intellectual libertines, buffoons; the historian, Johannes von Müller, political conspirator and author of a pompously archaic history of Switzerland, small, squeaky of voice, ugly as sin, expert in matters of love as he thought but in fact generally unlucky; and Prince Louis Ferdinand of Prussia, handsome and spoiled, half revolutionary, immersed in debt, permanently in opposition to his house and his station, talented but eccentric, and already drunk before noon.

Others joined the circle later. Clemens Brentano, for example, the poet, devoted to the Middle Ages and their folklore, discoverer of old songs and writer of new, transforming the eternal themes with his magic imagery; Friedrich Schleiermacher, highly cultivated pastor and philosopher, who understood how to make the Christian religion acceptable to freethinkers; and Georg Wilhelm Friedrich Hegel, whose powerful but extravagant philosophy of history captured the world.

Some would disappear; wander off or die, to be replaced by others, and so the circle continued until the middle of the century, though the quality of its membership underwent a gradual depreciation.

"The entrance of a man," writes a chronicler of such an evening, "whom the greeting, 'Good evening, Gentz,' caused me to recognize immediately as the celebrated publicist, created some excitement. I have seldom seen such a combination of shyness and assurance as this man presented. Timidly and irresolutely he appeared to examine every face and every chair, and seemed uneasy until he had investigated them all. I, as a stranger, was wholly without interest for him but he recognized the others as friends; only that Friedrich Schlegel caused a barely perceptible shudder, and he sat down as far away from him as he could. Safe and comfortable now, between Madame Unzelmann and Major von Schack, he entered into a conversation with them that soon became general. He said that he had lunched with Count von Haugwitz, the Minister for Foreign Affairs, met ambassadors and generals, and heard the latest from London and Paris. Madame Unzelmann, however, forbade all talk of politics and demanded only news in the discussion of which she, too, could take part. 'Quite right, my angel,' replied Gentz, 'but we talked least of all about politics; rather about different sorts of enjoyment and the various depravities that are turning up in Paris again; about love affairs, the theaters, and the restaurants. Fine subjects for conversation, aren't they?' Von Schack, recently back from France, asked a few questions of Gentz, who answered but briefly and seemed upset by Schlegel, who kept glowering more and more

JOHANNES VON MÜLLER (1752–1809)

fiercely at him. The muttered words: 'Mercenary scribbler, good-for-nothing enemy of freedom,' and other such amenities characteristic of the then revolutionary and republican Schlegel, did not reach Gentz's ear, to be sure, but his intuition seemed to sense every malevolent whisper from afar.

"Demoiselle Lewin rescued him from his embarrassment by asking after a woman in whom he must have been deeply interested, for he began to speak with the greatest ardor of an irresistible fascination and a beautiful character that had enraptured him and plunged him into the depths of despair. He accused himself of the most culpable weakness, 'but,' he continued, 'what can I do about it? Love is blind, and has bandaged my eyes, too.' 'No, no,' cried Demoiselle Lewin, 'there I would change mythology. Love is not blind, and her eyes are not bound. On the contrary, she looses every bandage and sees sharp and clear; and that she should continue to love in spite of all she sees, that is her most precious insigne!'

"At first Gentz was inclined to deny this, but gradually gave in and ended by proclaiming it the most wonderful of all beliefs, which from that very moment he would undertake to advocate and spread abroad. 'The theme is surely unexhausted and inexhaustible,' he said, 'and you, O searcher of hearts, shall have the credit of uttering a truth before which the errors of ages, yes, of mythology itself, shall crumble away in ruins.' He went on in this vein, speaking of the happiness and unhappiness of love, of its beginnings and its limitations, its consequences and its death, at first only in short sentences addressed in a conversational way, diffidently, to those near him. But gradually he forsook this dissembling tone, spoke with more warmth, ventured upon more explicit and audacious assertions, and when he felt entirely sure of his listeners seemed to open all the floodgates of his eloquence, whose mighty stream now flowed irresistibly and filled us all with amazement and delight. He spoke with fire and passion, with discernment and exuberance, with such a succession of happy expressions and constructions, and such smooth transitions, that never since that night have I been so persuaded and captivated by anyone. He held everybody's attention and gained everybody's applause. Only our hostess, her serious eyes riveted upon him, cried out from time to time: 'Right, Gentz!' 'Magnificent!' or 'Bravo!' with 'Certainly not!' or 'Oh, no!' interspersed. The rest listened in complete silence. . . ."

Because he stimulated everyone and made everyone productive his friends, as we have seen, called him the Nile. A British traveler who met him at Lord Carysford's remarked that he had the divine gift of transmitting to others whatever was in him; himself electric, he electrified his listeners. One alone among the companions of his intellectual adventures and his debauches outshone him, by virtue of his name, his looks, his music: Prince Louis Ferdinand. Gentz was no virtuoso; he was so preoccupied with the written word that he gave no heed to either music or the graphic arts, whereas Prince Louis, slow of speech and a stutterer even when he took to the pen, was ravishing at the piano. Stirring and rare his fantasies, singing out through the open window in all the stillness of a winter night. When he had finished, Rahel's guests would steal away to their homes, to sleep or, like Gentz, to spend the rest of the night at their writing.

Then the next day was depressing. Again our eyewitness is at Rahel's. Conversation was interrupted by a surprise, he says, that bordered on the ludicrous. "Unexpectedly Gentz burst, literally burst, into the room. Without taking the slightest notice of us two strangers he threw himself down on the sofa, crying out as if beside himself: 'I *can't stand* any more! What weariness! What torture! Writing, worrying, all last night! From five o'clock on, the damned creditors! I meet them wherever I go! They hound me to death! No peace, no rest anywhere! Do let me sleep here for half an hour in safety!' The fascinating conversationalist of yesterday, the influential writer and authority on statesmanship, had seemed to be in a pitiable condition, yet already he was lying there, his arms folded, his eyes closed, apparently able to secure the peace that he craved provided only he were not disturbed by anything outside himself. Demoiselle Lewin, whose deep sympathy could not conceal a smile, left the poor fellow in undisturbed possession of the space that he had preëmpted. . . ."

SINCE 1793 Gentz had been married to a young woman whose maiden name was Gilly and who was, like his mother, a member of the French "colony" and of irreproachable ancestry. The poor girl thought that she had married an upright Huguenot-Prussian official like her father and her brothers, but soon found that she had been transplanted into a circle of highly gifted debtors and men about town, among whom her husband was easily the most notorious. Good to others, and only too good to himself, our young hedonist, laughing and lamenting by turns, was now involved in the most wretched irregularities. Debts, love affairs, the vexations of his calling, and gossip gave him no peace. On one occasion he even went into bankruptcy, but without worrying overmuch. "He is," wrote Humboldt, "entirely unaffected by it. The bankruptcy has had no effect whatsoever, and I very much fear that he has made a new promise to pay off the balance of his obligations." Gentz loved the passing moment too much, he loved himself too much, to be capable of improving his position.

He needed people and longed for their company, but acquired a reputation for viciousness because of his curious discrimination between the spiritual and the physical. There were women whose images filled his eyes with the tears of innocent admiration, yet who forever remained to him only images; there were persons of both sexes, wise and fine, with whom he would pass whole nights in conversation; and there were affairs for which he paid, and ended the matter there.

Among the first was Demoiselle von Imhoff, sensitive and poetic maid of honor to the Duchess of Weimar, whose acquaintanceship he hoped would be the great purifying experience of his life. At least she filled his hours in Weimar with the highest rapture; enriched his return in the post chaise with dreams and tears; and caused him, who had something of narcissism in his nature, to luxuriate in his own virtue and purity while thinking of hers. This harmless indulgence gratified him all the more because of the strange contrast with his own disordered life.

Rahel Lewin loved him more deeply than he loved her and gave him the flattery that he liked so well, and he repaid her with suffering and pain. He made her the confidante of all his emotions but never, as she secretly wished, their object. The sincerity that marked so many attachments in those days characterized this romantic and nebulous relationship, too. Their correspondence, sometimes active, sometimes sporadic, went on until the end, and she who had watched so solicitously over the love affairs of the youth was still troubled over those of the graying man. Like all her contemporaries she kept a diary, and to it she confided her troubles: "My whole life is a misfortune. God alone hears my heart's cry. . . . Gentz and all my surroundings hurt me." To him she wrote later: "You will be mine as long as one world holds us both. . . . Who has always been in my mind; for whom have I trembled? You, everlasting, ever-beloved friend. What was it that distressed me most about all the disorders of our times? That they separated me still farther from you. You may have changed as much as you like; you are still the same! Ever the same to me, dearly beloved friend; dear old fat Gentz! . . . Oh, I shall still see you. How long, how *deeply*, have I grieved over our separation! Of course, such a friendship as ours is rare, for not many friends understand one another so well. And still, I know that *you* have forgotten me; that I am never in your thoughts at all. . . ."

He to whom the letter came answered with almost brutal frankness: "It was really an immense mistake—shall I say of ours, or of nature?—that we never fell violently in love with one another. It would have been an affair such as the world has rarely seen. Instead of that we have both wasted our best on mere 'people,' as you so appropriately call our whole group, and each in his way has been impoverished thereby. But the fault is mostly yours. You stood higher, saw farther and more clearly than I, and for the sake of my soul, still innocent though wrapped about in soiled raiment, you should have set aside all conventional shyness and made me inordinately happy, even though it had to be done by force. . . ."

Ordinarily, however, one searches his letters to Rahel in vain for any more personal candor than might have appeared in the most important of his papers on statesmanship: "Just as soon as I dared put aside my pen I busied myself with nothing more than the arranging of my room. I am constantly trying to find some way to get more *money* for furniture, perfumes, and all those little refinements that are called luxuries."

For his lights-o'-love money was badly needed, as his bought and degrading pleasures continued. In September, 1804, he wrote, concerning his adjustments of nature's urge in middle life: "I began an affair with a girl of low station and very little charm, whom chance had led to my household. . . . During the following winter I supported this person more or less, and paid dearly for the pleasure that I had had of her. Fortunately, however, she was possessed of more good qualities than bad, and as she had become the mother of a son I have continued to treat her with consideration to this day. . . ."

The last of his Berlin period was passed under the sway of Christine Eigensatz, an actress to whom Rahel had introduced him, and the situation led to a divorce from his wife and brought the entanglements of his private life to a climax. There exist excerpts from diaries, abstracts or astonished commentaries, that were written down twenty-five years later before he consigned their French originals to the flames; a summing up of life and all its impulses in a man that the aging Gentz could hardly believe he once had been; a man whose hastily noted confessions he understood only in part, or often not at all, and weighed, and condemned or ridiculed. Even this brief record conveys a dismal picture of his last days in Berlin.

"October 24. Departure of Lord Carysford from Berlin. Confession that I had somewhat neglected him because of my recent continuous dissipation. On this same evening lost 74 louis d'or in gambling.

"November 2. Made an arrangement with a lawyer (pawned a manuscript, which I did not redeem until twenty years later) by which I got 70 louis d'or. Lost them that night in gambling.

"March 13. Declared my passion for Christel in unmistakable terms, and she allowed me to spend the next night with her. But right afterward, partly through my own wretched behavior and partly through the arrival of her established lover (Zinnow), there was the devil to pay.

"April 15. Is it possible? The most real, the most urgent, of my misfortunes has been the impossibility of making a gift to Christel, who had her benefit performance today. And on this very day fate sends the unworthy writer of these lines a remittance of 1,000 pounds sterling from England!

"On February 21, when I got home at two in the morning, I found a letter from my wife that decided my life for me. On the following day our resolve was made. Presumably we shall be divorced, but this did not prevent me from going to a ball that night, etc.

"March. A three or four days' visit to the Humboldts at Tegel. When I returned to Berlin things were in a terribly bad way with me. As I entered my house its loneliness, together with all that I knew, all that I felt, and all that I dreaded threw me into a perfect horror of despair. . . ."

At first blush the writer of this diary might be taken for a licentious young bachelor of pronounced masculine type, yet in one of his franker letters to Rahel he calls himself a receptive creature who produced nothing, "the foremost among women," and twenty years later Prince Metternich said jokingly that Gentz really should have been a woman as his delicate skin, his coquetry, and his sensitive nerves all suggested. But where psychological matters are concerned, extremes meet more often than anywhere else. Gentz's intellect was entirely masculine, and lucidity was its most characteristic feature, though as his mind was analytical rather than constructive he owed his success principally to his talent for exposition. He could not do things, merely hint at them in secret memoranda so that others might do them. He was a brave man, courageous enough to defy convention, challenge public opinion, and even a despot who was apt to have such adversaries shot if he could catch them.

On the other hand, he could be ridiculously nervous. As a youth he had an unconquerable aversion to soldiers in uniform, later could not bear the sight of a full beard, and thunder and lightning made him jump out of bed at night to call for help; hence, with scientific exactitude, he sought out places to live where thunderstorms were few. All his life he avoided funerals, for whenever he was struck by the realization that he, too, must die he became half crazy with anxiety and bewildered dismay. He would shed bitter tears over the death of a dog and, indeed, wept at the slightest provocation. His passions were sensual and dissolute, yet his genius for friendship and conversation was remarkable. He was attracted by the hyperfeminine, lush type of woman, and by frail sisters of the night, too, but was equally fond of clever, handsome young men, and was attractive to them in turn.

So say young people who were living in Berlin at the time, and afterward made a name for themselves. Thus a Baltic count, Nesselrode, who forty years later became a Russian Imperial Chancellor, wrote: "Of the friendly relationships that I entered into at that time, none turned out more to my advantage than that with the celebrated Gentz." And a Lieutenant von Nostiz, afterward chronicler of the Vienna Congress, said: Gentz and Gualtieri ". . . noticed me among the host of young men in uniform because of my high spirits. In grateful appreciation of their kindness I sought the company of these brilliant men, and saw them almost daily. . . ."

But the friendship with Adam Müller, a student at the University of Göttingen, was the most enduring and is worthy of note because of its intellectual setting.

Adam Müller, twenty-two when Gentz first made his acquaintance, was one of those alert but unreliable young intellectuals that the awakened spirit of the time hatched out in such great numbers. He could write beautifully, knew something of literature, and was not without philosophical insight and intuitive understanding. His head was full of ideas, some good, some absurd. But through all his metaphysical bombast there shone forth a subtle judgment of men, of facts, and of situations. His manner of speaking fascinated both men

ADAM MÜLLER (1779–1829)

and women, though there were some who thought it a little forced and pert. Müller was a charming but affected and perfidious young man. This base disciple of Burke was not ashamed to address letters to his old father from various European capitals while living comfortably as a private tutor on a Polish estate. One foggy night he left —with the wife of the owner.

As a social philosopher he objected to cotton wool on the ground that it was a highly artificial product; therefore he went clothed in sheepskin summer and winter. Both he and Gentz practically lived on the money of the rich and influential, but whereas Gentz would make no concessions in return, letting each situation develop by itself, as it were, Müller toadied all his life long to money and princes. He aped Gentz's career, but without his genius. "I live and move in the political world," Gentz once wrote to him, "and have found in Lord Carysford a first-rate authority." Müller replied: "You will already have learned that for the past four weeks I have lived and moved in politics, and that I have made connections with the English Ambassador to this country," and so on. But Gentz's position in the world, and especially in England, remained without a parallel and Müller, seeing this, actually resolved to join the British Army, at the time when French invasion threatened; however, he ultimately dropped his noble idea.

Gentz was fascinated by this extraordinary specimen, and preserved the friendship as he did almost no other. He entertained him, gave him money, later shared all his own prospects with him, and provided both employment and a title, so that Müller's entire existence came to depend virtually on Gentz, who was wholly captivated by the shameless boy prodigy. Pathetically the elder and more famous praised him: "This have I reared, and of this I am proud, even though the pupil has outgrown the master. It is my most valuable bequest to the world." To Müller himself he wrote: "It gives me the greatest satisfaction to think that I discovered the extent and profundity of your mind so long before anyone else. There is no denying that in the days to come you will tower high above me." Müller received such compliments as a matter of course.

This shrewd judge of human nature once expressed the opinion that Gentz was a mixture of the "North and the Orient," meaning thereby that he was a combination of austere, lucid intellect and an impressionable disposition inclined toward fantasy. It appears that the irresistible and acquisitive Müller could arouse the "Oriental" in him as no one else. The two friends enjoyed veritable orgies of talk together, and spoke of them afterward, "our night in Dresden," for example, as one might refer to a night of love.

Müller was for Gentz the epitome of all that he himself did not possess, and did not even want: the romantic, the speculative, and the poetic. Other and better exponents of all these had never been far off, but fate had thrown him Adam Müller, and he took real pains to educate this picturesque young friend and train his all-too-ductile mind. "I shall never forget," he once wrote him, "that I was almost thirty before I had achieved a clear understanding of myself and of the world, and that I reached this happy position at last not by my own efforts, but through the help of others. What happened to me may, and must, and will happen to you, too. So you must expect me always to be a strict censor, and whenever you hear me say 'I do not understand you' you are to seek the reason, though occasionally the fault may be mine, in the immaturity of your thought. Do not, my friend, I entreat you, let yourself be deprived of the divine clarity of the mind, the pinnacle of all intellectual heights, by the mysticism of a generation that oversteps itself! . . . Live and think in yourself!"

But only a few years later Müller was given clearly to understand that he was unteachable, and that nothing of value would ever come out of their conversations together. "What is called a quiet discussion was possible between us only when I listened to you passively. There can be no music unless instruments are in tune together, but either you have no conception of how to tune yourself, or I cannot be tuned. Be that as it may, this much I know: That contrary to the spirit of real analysis our talks always began with a clear, or at least a fairly clear, thought; that this gradually became more and more confused; and that our conversation finally ended in what I call, and shall always have to call, mere twaddle."

Of Müller's "organic" theory of money, Gentz said that one single chapter of Adam Smith would do more to advance knowledge than a hundred volumes filled with this sort of "fantastic and mystic apothegms."

In 1804, impelled by genuine religious doubts and fears, by his social and political speculations, and by a snobbish admiration of its hierarchy, Müller betook himself to Roman Catholicism, and from similar motives others of his type followed. They were afraid of their own thoughts, which had been upset by the intellectual revolution of the time, and of the masses, who had been equally stirred by the social revolution. They were enchanted, too, by the discipline and tradition of the Roman Church, this bit of a gorgeous past set down in the present, no less than by the arrogant and supercilious Austrian-Spanish aristocracy, whom none but Catholics could approach.

Gentz was all approval, but despite tempting and admonitory pleas by the newly cleansed Müller refused to join him. Catholic he would never be. When asked why not, he would reply that he could not, and offer no further explanation. He was too conscientious to take the step without some sort of conviction, whereas Müller had no convictions of any sort. Gentz admired the Catholic Church from afar as a historian, an esthete, even as a statesman, and understood fully its power to unite not only individuals but the masses, yes, whole nations; but as for himself, he was unable to become a part of it.

Not that he lacked all sense of the eternal questions. He knew well the fear of death and infinity, the consciousness of duty and of sin, yet belonged among those perplexed souls who are not devoid of profound religious feeling but are too judicial, too independent, too critical of self to embrace one religion in preference to any other. These can exist neither with nor without belief. They believe, but do not themselves know what they believe.

When Adam Müller once asserted that the judgment of the individual must bow before laws by God made manifest, Gentz returned this precise and earnest response:

"If it is to have any validity, all that is appreciable to the reason must be brought before the bar of reason for judgment; and by everyone for himself: Who has the sole right to be lawgiver? But universal laws, you will say, are revelations from God, against which there can be no appeal. Then I would ask: Has God communicated them directly to you? If your answer should be Yes, I would reply, without arrogating to myself the right to question your statement, so much the better for you! I have not been vouchsafed such a favor, although I may not be numbered among the least deserving of all mankind. Therefore you and I belong for the present in two entirely separate categories. If your answer should be No, then your conviction as to these revelations must be based wholly upon a faith in what has been revealed to others. Now I, myself, have no such faith, though I have striven long and earnestly to accept from others the revelations that have been denied to me; you are a witness to that. I have failed. The disposition to believe is not in me. . . . So long as you are unable to resolve this fundamental difference between us you must forgive me for regarding many of your most emphatic assertions as wholly dogmatic."

Writers interested in Gentz included him for many years among the "statesmen of romanticism." Later it was decided that he had always been a rationalist at heart and belonged not in the nineteenth but in the eighteenth century. What is to be gained by attempting such distinctions? No active mind can be subordinated to any "ism"; and Gentz's views were more independent than those expressed by most of his contemporaries. There are certain lasting political tendencies, shared by him, that might be called romantic, among them a clear sense of the identity of all Christian civilization. But even this may have a tinge of rationalism; churches and traditions unite, and so does reason. Again, some intellectual trends could be called romantic; for example, delight in the subtlety of thought for the mere sake of thought, or in the magic of wit and word. To such proclivities Gentz was no stranger, and he could pass whole nights in talk.

Gentz's chief contribution was not romantic, and just as little rationalistic, if rationalism is construed as the pedantic habit of thought that preceded romanticism. His method was of no school, but that of a bold, vigorous intellect. He hated all that was subjective, biased, arbitrary, or irresponsible, and was contemptuous of literary cliques and their intrigues. This gifted and inquiring man was delighted by the intellectual and the new, but the idly experimental, an obscure and diffuse style, and the stupidity of all despotism repelled him.

He was too well acquainted with French and English literature of the eighteenth century to be wholly satisfied with the new literature of his own country, saying that the German romanticists lived in a "region of caprice, egoism, anarchy, and gloom." "I feel toward this book as I do toward almost all the productions of this annoying school. I am always ashamed at first of having understood so little of them; then I am ashamed of having been ashamed. . . . What these people call *writing*, I should hardly call drivel. How is it possible for us who are familiar with the best writing in all languages to speak of *style* in these formless compositions, where the greatest confusion of ideas competes with the most wanton negligence of expression!" The profoundest literary experience of his youth, Edmund Burke, still remained his model, in writing as in thinking. Again and again he marveled as he read him. "Can the halting prose of our own leading authors be even compared with his? What fullness, what rotundity, what rhythm! So would I write, if only heaven will vouchsafe it! . . ."

GENTZ appreciated the romantic school without belonging to it, and the classicists as well, those old gods of German literature who dwelt in Weimar, three days' journey from Berlin, enjoying an old-fashioned and perfect life. On one occasion he found them all gathered about Goethe's table; Goethe himself, Herder, Wieland, Schiller; yet the evening seemed to him "indifferent and almost dull." On the other hand, he could hardly tear himself away from Schiller after five hours of talk, and what these two had to say to each other about the inner meaning of everything, about history, the rights of the upper and lower classes, about freedom and restraint, not to mention Bonaparte and Europe, must have been of the highest that the cultured interchange of ideas could produce anywhere in the world. In the evening he was taken to the ducal theater by Schiller, whose masterpiece, *The Death of Wallenstein*, was then being played. There, in his private box, might have been seen the majestic poet and the elegant, nervous publicist, bending toward the footlights, reaching out for an opera glass, or whispering to one another.

Gentz did not fare so well with Goethe. The mind of the political writer was too eager, too importunate by its very intensity, for the author of *Faust*, who would contribute but little to a social conversation, whereas Gentz gave freely of all that he had. "You hate dissection and analysis," he wrote to Rahel after another visit to the master, "and not wholly without justification. But I really must insist that there are two men in Goethe: a sort of Mephistopheles, and not an agreeably provocative one; and the overpowering poetical genius. At first, just as a man, he was repugnant to me. This summer I have learned to tolerate him, though only because I began to realize that I had paid him too high a compliment in disliking him; there is nothing whatever to be gained from personal acquaintance with him. I hate to speak so freely, and God forbid that you should let it go any farther. . . ."

This trip to Weimar, in November, 1801, proved to Gentz in the most agreeable manner possible how far one could go as a publicist in his day. The little capital, recently become famous, though still somewhat isolated for all that, was hungry for fresh intellectual fare, and snatched eagerly at the new guest. Karl August, the Duke of Weimar, founder of this august literary center, invited him to the castle and seated him at table next to the reigning duchess. With visiting, music, and amateur theatricals he was royally entertained, but found Mozart's *Requiem* only "mildly diverting."

Here it was, in the soft eyes of a maid of honor, Demoiselle von Imhoff, that he found inspiration for a new and nobler life.

To be on a friendly footing, about 1800, with the gods of poetry in Weimar; with the romanticist authors, the philosophers, the speculative naturalists, the gifted Jews in Berlin; and shortly afterward with the famous musicians of Vienna, to say nothing of ministers and diplomats of the great powers—that was something of an achievement, a bewildering social and intellectual opulence. Perhaps in no other country, at no other period, has there collected such a galaxy of genius; and during the time that Europe was politically dominated by France it was conquered intellectually by the literature, the philosophy, and the music of the hitherto unknown and half-barbaric Germany.

Between these two conquests there was a certain connection. France, having dissipated her powers in revolution and war, was unproductive in the sphere of the intellect and the arts as never before, and her delirious pretensions had prompted the contemplative Germans to meditation, to comparison, and to a philosophical interpretation of history. Secondly, it was precisely the miscarriage of the Revolution, that grand illusion, that permitted a return to the old political complacency of the German intellectuals, who with clear conscience left politics to the politicians and devoted themselves to the play of abstract thought. Schiller, in particular, subscribed to this principle. But in the third place, it soon became manifest that history would repay a purely contemplative attitude toward it with humiliations of all sorts; with poverty, hunger, and thirst. Whereupon a rigid self-discipline set in, during the course of which literature, and even philosophy itself, became national, and not to their advantage.

But had this sudden flowering of German literature been wholly natural and sound? Gentz, the political agent, who had his native country always much in mind, doubted it. All had come about too quickly. A German classicism appeared, thanks to a princeling and two or three geniuses who leaned heavily on Greek or on English; one hardly knew how. Then a few dozen writers arose, gifted, but without tradition, without metropolitan background, emerging suddenly from some obscure province under the patronage of aristocrats, and understood only by Jews; inclined toward intellectual or social aristocratism, they either moved in cliques or were stifled in loneliness.

"The human mind," wrote Humboldt in a letter to Gentz, which the latter annotated, "requires time in which to progress, but in Germany doctrines of all sorts have accumulated too quickly, only to be displaced. What seems to me the most ominous symptom is that it has now become so common to employ in both prose and verse a style to which a certain degree of adequacy cannot be denied, but which opens up vistas so profound and sublime that I doubt whether it is susceptible of further development. Only when the road to sound experimentation has been lost does such dangerous facility appear, to invert the long-familiar until it begins to take on the aspect of the new. The reason may be that our literature has never been popular, even in the slightest degree. (Bravo, Humboldt, bravo! Yes, there's the rub!) All our good authors and their readers resemble a Masonic lodge. . . ."

It should not remain without mention that Gentz sometimes attributed the rapid blossoming of German literature, and its lack of any contact with the people, to the emancipation of the Jews. In a bon mot he called a certain sort of critic "indirect Jews." "Next to real Jews, there is nothing more terrible than these indirect Jews, the tyrants of literature." Now Gentz was not ardently antisemitic. As a journalist and a government official he did what he could for the Jews, and they paid him for it; and he was entirely at home in the salons of the rich Jews in Berlin: the Mayers, the Fränkels, the Ephraims. It appears, too, that there was a tender episode with the daughter of Mayer, the banker, afterward the Princess Reuss. In a word, like most brilliant Germans he could not live without the Jews, yet he often ridiculed them, and was impatient of their intellectual pose.

They had rapidly become partners in the literary life of Germany; in fact, had even helped to make it, for at the beginning of the century that was now so rapidly drawing to a close there had been none. And though they had brought forth no great genius of their own they had at least proved themselves capable of recognizing one; Jean Paul Richter, for example, owed them his fame. They had an instinct, too, for the fashionable, the startling, and the diverting and were, indeed, the real driving force of the whole literary movement. Mesmer's hypnotism and clairvoyance, Gall's sensational phrenology, and the theories of Sieyès on constitutional government were exactly to their taste. So it seemed to Gentz that the metropolitanized Jews of Berlin were at once the creators and the product of the "so-called eighteenth century"; thus he spoke of it when it had but just passed: "The half wisdom, the shallow wisdom, of the so-called eighteenth century, that brought forth nothing but ungodliness and the French Revolution."

The deadly sin of the Jews, he continued, was intellect. "The curse laid upon them, which was to follow them even unto the ten thousandth generation, is really that to their own and the world's annoyance they cannot escape being intelligent and intellectual, but must continue to be so until their black souls are on the way to Hell. Wherever there is intellectuality, purblind, wanton intellectuality, these monsters usurp the leadership, for it is their own proper field; they are born exponents of atheism, Jacobinism, the fashion of enlightenment, and so on."

Intellect was all very well. Gentz himself was not devoid of it, but alone it was inadequate for this life. Not less requisite were solidity of character, earnestness, and faith. And because they lacked faith the intellectual Jews of the new metropolis, though able to understand all that came up, were overpowered by these very happenings and unduly impressed by any and all accomplishments. They were defeatists par excellence. Their enthusiasm for the French Revolution could be excused; others had been similarly enraptured. Now, however, they were making themselves into unpaid propagandists for General Bonaparte and, furthermore, were disseminating the inadequate though fashionable pacifism that determined the Prussian policy of neutrality, and had so long been challenged by Gentz.

"I am now fully convinced that the ordinary war is less of a hideous evil by far than those babblers about humanity and those cheats of all sorts who would hoax the world with pretty stories." War could be prevented, he maintained, only by good statesmanship, not by abstract peace cults and the unreasoning pacificism that had been an accessory in bringing about an endless chain of wars. He related the Francophile Jews more or less to this catastrophe and once went so far, indeed, as to say in jest that it was the Jews alone who had made Bonaparte an Emperor. Such remarks as this were never made wholly without a laugh, for all matters that concerned the Jews moved him to mirth.

Gentz ultimately became estranged from his literary friends in so far as he mingled in government circles; to be sure, the connection between the realm of wit and the realm of power was closer than once it had been, though not yet so close after all, and the nearer a man came to one the farther he receded from the other. Such a writer as Gentz had never before been accepted by the aristocratic rulers of Prussia. The Ambassadors of the allies, Carysford (Great Britain), Stadion (Austria), and Alopeus (Russia), were pleased by his antirevolutionary writings and his brilliant personality. The Prussian ministers treated him with apprehensive respect because public opinion had begun to play a role in politics; they no longer dared give him money for his journals, yet endeavored to remain on friendly personal terms with him.

A list of his acquaintances in the Berlin period begins with "Observations," wherein the following passage occurs: "In 1800 I really began to live in the great world. Since then I have known men of all classes, for society has been my main interest, and I have learned how to adapt them to my own ends."

The roll is enormous. Princes of the royal house; all sorts of dukes and counts; and the whole corps of domestic, foreign, and visiting diplomats appear on it. But had he been really a snob, these pampered gentlemen would not have accepted him so freely; he was born for society, and through it he worked. Sometimes this preoccupation went as far as disdain for all that was not human, or of the city. "I did not promise myself much," he wrote of a trip on the Rhine, "because for some time now I have been rather bored by all inanimate things, including even beautiful scenery, and interested only in man and his doings."

Human activities! Yearly thereafter he would send forth thousands of letters into the world, to statesmen, to scholars, to younger friends; always eager to stimulate, always looking for help, for contacts, for the select few. The many, he used to say, behave like fools.

The winter of 1801–2, the winter of European peace, was the most brilliant that Berlin society had yet enjoyed. Masquerades, theatrical performances, and sleighing parties followed one another in unbroken succession though English visitors, it must be confessed, thought that the arrangements were a little too economical and that everyone drank too much cheap punch. Morals were free and easy, men showed themselves in fantastically colored uniforms and, contrary to the prevailing fashion in the antirevolutionary capitals, Vienna and London, everyone aped the Paris of the Directory.

Late at night Gentz would appear, still without decorations, though at least he did have a snuffbox beset with diamonds with which the Austrian Emperor had honored him shortly before. He would draw the Austrian Ambassador into a window niche and begin to explain at length why the French First Consul was not, nor ever could be, the man of peace that he represented himself.

V

FLIGHT INTO AUSTRIA

WHEN Bonaparte took over the government of France on November 9, 1799 (18th Brumaire), he was widely admired and accounted a hero and a philosopher. He was young, spirited, virtuous, a man of bold deeds yet conciliatory withal. The European intellectuals of the Left idolized him, and even in conservative circles it was believed that affairs would now go more smoothly than under any of his predecessors since 1789.

As to the historical import of the 18th Brumaire opinions differed considerably. Those who had brought about the coup d'état strove to retain the revolutionary centralized power and to cleanse the Revolution from its dross of the all-too-human, a resolve that was applauded by most democrats throughout the world. Others, who since the publication of Burke's *Reflections on the French Revolution* had been awaiting the appearance of "some victorious general," thought Bonaparte a "Cromwellist," a dictator, and an assassin of liberty. Still others, finally, were not satisfied to swallow whole either abstractions or superficial historical analogies, preferring to stick more closely to solid fact.

In the December number of his *Historisches Journal* Gentz ventured upon a bold assertion: Bonaparte's republican system of government was nothing less than monarchy, and in all its essentials nothing less than the old form of monarchy. Not, of course, that there would be a return of kingship, but that Napoleon would take the place of a king, and was about to erect the new structure with the stones of the old. This paradox, which historical research has succeeded in unearthing after years of work, did not escape the sharp eye of the journalist at the very moment of its birth. Bonaparte's "Prefects," he wrote, had a sinister resemblance to the "Intendants" of former kings, and his two fellow consuls were unnecessary creatures of the First Consul. The parliamentary bodies, the Senate and the Tribunate, were artificial creations; lifeless, and powerless against the First Consul except, perhaps, that given the opportunity they might overthrow him. So, continued Gentz, after ten years of agony and convulsion we have monarchy back again, only under a new name and in another garb: an event of enormous interest and surpassing irony.

He who had opposed the Revolution for eight years certainly had no occasion to resent such a cycle of occurrences. Those who hitherto had favored the "good cause," and continued to defend it enthusiastically even now, when in all essentials it had developed into its very opposite, might see how they could escape the ridicule of posterity. "The overwhelmingly great majority of the friends of the French Revolution appear to have made it an invariable practice to call good everything that it brought forth. Guided by this maxim they had passed happily and safely from the Constitution of 1791 to the National Convention, from this to the revolutionary government and Robespierre's Reign of Terror, then again to the Constitution of 1795 and through all its consequences, and now they seemed to rejoice as heartily over the undoing of this Constitution as they had over its existence."

But the logic of history is not the logic of geometry, and the cycle of revolutionary events was not so simple as the circumference of a circle, with its return to a starting point. Bonaparte, retracing the thousand-year-old course of monarchy, was at once the heir and the captive of the Revolution, particularly in respect to that which interested Gentz above all else: the sphere of foreign relations.

In discussing this situation the greatest caution was necessary. The war-weary world looked to Bonaparte for peace, and whoever undertook to demonstrate the essentially military character of his imperial adventure might easily achieve the reputation of being himself desirous of more bloodletting. As a matter of fact, Bonaparte had offered peace, particularly to the King of England, in an admirable and philosophical letter that said much about the griefs of their own senselessly bleeding nations but nothing at all about Holland, Belgium, or Italy.

The letter remained unanswered. The peace offensive had miscarried.

Matters began to assume a wholly different aspect when the First Consul thereupon made a dramatic passage across the Alps, struck at the Austrian Army in Italy, and forced its commander to sue for an armistice. The monotonously repetitive character of this event led to the conclusion that resistance was of no avail after all and that now, in 1800, Europe would have to resign herself to what she could have had even in 1797—Napoleon as conqueror.

But the attack showed, too, that no peace guaranteed by an undefeated France was permanent. How was it possible to escape from this circle? Only by continuing the war more vigorously, Gentz assured his readers. If the Prussians had helped the British troops in Holland, if the Russians had not withdrawn inopportunely from the coalition, if Bonaparte had not been allowed to slip away out of Egypt and return to France, the allies would be in Paris by now. Instead of that, alas, everything would have to be begun all over again, and no illusion could alter this fact.

"By extending its theater so widely the French Revolution had made war much easier, contradictory though this might seem, because it had taught at least one nation the secret of regarding war no longer as the road to exhaustion, but rather as a means of increasing its power. Sooner or later all the other nations would have to heed this teaching or else renounce their autonomy and independence. This fact alone explains in advance the events of the years to come."

These Gentz actually foresaw, and never have prophecies been made more truly or in bolder outline. "In foreign relations it has become almost ludicrous to count upon anything that cannot be acquired or defended by force of arms. The uncertainty of all possessions and rights has gradually led the one to such ruinous depression, the other to such arrogant presumption, that nothing but power now commands respect. . . . That not only peace, but even the possibility of peace, is far remote today, that war is everywhere the watchword and will continue to be so for many years to come if some extraordinary change does not succeed in averting our unhappy fate—this depressing truth is only too evident. . . ."

Thus did he close his *Journal*, in December, 1800. In February, 1801, Austria abandoned the struggle, and by the Treaty of Lunéville accepted again the provisions of the Peace of Campo Formio. This time no mere truce was intended, but a final cessation of hostilities.

Great Britain remained alone.

In order to isolate her still more, Bonaparte hastened to confer on this new order of things the appearance of something voluntarily accepted by the nations and moral forces of the Continent. If he succeeded, Great Britain's persistence in the war would become a sort of macabre folly. With imagination, and unencumbered by any theoretical bias, he went to work. Flattery of the half-insane Russian Czar with gifts and pretty talk was a means that he did not disdain to use; in return for real though stringently limited concessions the Pope was persuaded to recognize the French Revolution, with no mention of the fate that his predecessor had suffered through it; the internal affairs of Switzerland were arranged by Bonaparte's arbitration; and the Lombards had to elect him their president, in consideration of which their Republic was given the highly auspicious name of Italian.

In the antechamber of the Consul were to be seen, beside blood-flecked Jacobins, descendants of those who for centuries had served the kings.

For what on earth could Great Britain still be fighting?

THIS derisive question was posed by a nobleman of great name in the service of Bonaparte, Count de Hauterive, in a skillful piece of propaganda that he called *The Situation of France at the End of the Eighth Year*. It was a presentation of the causes and effects of the great war as those in Paris wished the world to see them. De Hauterive asserted that in 1789 Europe had been in a state of political and moral anarchy; that not France, but Prussian militarism, the appearance of Russia in Western politics, and, above all, Great Britain's infamous greed for trade, had been to blame for the condition of affairs; that the war against the French Revolution was not in any sense an ideological war but a war of plunder, whose purpose it had been to prepare France for the fate of Poland; that its outcome was a sign of eternal justice; and that Spaniards, Italians, Dutch, Swiss, and Germans might congratulate themselves on having found once more, in French power, their traditional protector. If, however—de Hauterive suddenly broke out in threatening tones—they should refuse to recognize their true interests one would know perfectly well how to deal with them over the heads of their rulers. It was high time that Europe became united, united against Great Britain, who alone did not wish to see such a coalition; and France, by reason of her power without and her new blood within, was ordained to preside over it.

The book did not fail to make an impression on the war-weary people of France and Germany. It rationalized the inherited hate for the coldhearted selfishness of the mercantile nation. It employed arguments that are always valid: for example, that the horrors of the day were not so unprecedented after all, and that before they descended on the world all had not been so well with it as one would like to believe.

Gentz was especially interested in the work because the polemics of this mouthpiece of Bonaparte were directed explicitly against him, who was called the warmest and most accomplished advocate of Great Britain, "instructed, and probably paid." Now of course the whole world knew that he received money from London, but he could not remain silent under the charge that he was an unprincipled and corrupt partisan, and accordingly determined to refute de Hauterive.

The result was: *On the Political Situation in Europe before and after the Revolution,* for years the last of his longer political writings. Once more he gathered all his forces in order to convince the world of the justice of Great Britain's cause. He admitted that the years before 1789 had witnessed no paradise of perpetual peace, but could that ever be expected in this world? Under existing conditions there had been, however, such a thing as international law, which had automatically come into being through the balance of power and the force of public opinion, and never had it been stronger than before the Revolution. This balance of power, above all the concern of Great Britain, had formerly protected Prussia against France and Austria, and Austria against France and Prussia, and it would have aided France, too, had her expulsion from the European game been the object of the coalition instead of the limitation of her aggressive predominance. Great Britain acted in her own interest; what state did not? But what truth was there in the biased representation of "British politics as an endless labyrinth of intrigues and cabals, of deliberate vacillation, and of systematic perfidy? Where are the wars that Great Britain instigated, the alliances that she entered merely to break them up, the deceitful combinations that she established? The history of the eighteenth century says nothing of all these transgressions. . ."

If war was to cease, the enmities on which it was nourished must cease. Even a relatively favorable situation such as that existing before 1789 was impossible in Europe as long as the atrocious predominance of France continued. No single power in the world could contend with her, and no alliance in which at least all four great powers did not participate could oppose her with any hope of success. Where then would be peace, and the balance of power? It was a world given to extremes, even if Bonaparte, of whose character the less said the better, had honestly wished to keep within bounds.

"Some political truths," continued Gentz, "are so depressing, and some relationships so critical, that they can be dealt with only in the most general way." This he did, summing up his evidence in vague terms. So wrongly, so wretchedly, had the situation been allowed to develop that there now remained for Europe only the distressing prospect of still another coalition if an artificial balance of power were to be maintained; another coalition, with its innumerable defects and dangers, but a coalition of all. For nations that did not participate but, like Prussia, feigned neutrality, would succumb only too easily to the temptation to attach themselves to Bonaparte, the overwhelming opponent.

Gentz published his book in fascicles, but when he had come so far he was warned by the Prussian censor to stop. To call for a third Coalition when the Second had just perished so miserably; when Europe had been at war for nine years, the number of slain ran into the millions, and all the comforts of life threatened to disappear; and when the new ruler of France, God be praised, was an enlightened and peace-loving man—this exceeded the patience of the Prussian Government, and even of the public. Gentz was cried down as a dangerous dreamer, a bloodthirsty Don Quixote who, besides, was in the pay of a foreign power, the only one that could have any interest in a renewed decimation of the youth of the Continent; and his notorious prodigality left no doubt as to why he had accepted such an office.

Gentz opened his eyes to find that he was as alone in his native land as Great Britain now was in the world, and he began to scorn the society in which he lived. Certainly there were arguments enough against him. It was only too probable that Austria and Russia nourished sinister designs; it was certain that the British Cabinet had only their country's naked interests in mind and that these were often vindicated in curious ways. Arguments were as plentiful as blackberries, and each nation could blame all the others with considerable justice. It was even true that the French had introduced valuable and permanent reforms in the lands that they conquered, that a new spirit breathed wherever they went, and that changes like those they were making would soon have to come in Germany.

Gentz denied none of this, least of all the last. Yet facts, after all, could be arranged in a scale of importance and at the top of this, irrespective of who was to blame, stood the menace that one nation, France, had been able to inflate herself almost without limit. The threat was palpable, the superstate already half accomplished. Under no circumstances must she be allowed to bring the process to completion, whether international politics were regarded as a game, a contest of peoples and governments, a regulator of internal social conditions, or the arena where freedom, the highest of all ideals, was won. Under no circumstances!

And now Great Britain, too, left the struggling publicist in the lurch. A difference of opinion with his King that was concerned with the rights of the Irish Catholics, and thus only in the most indirect way with the war, drove the proud and weary Pitt out of office in March, 1801. His successor, Henry Addington, could not resist the vision of peace with which Bonaparte's skillful propaganda had bewitched men everywhere. Negotiations with France were begun, continued for nearly a year during which all decisive questions were enveloped in an atmosphere of ambiguity and vacillation, and concluded with an agreement in which Great Britain, according to the French interpretation, renounced her position on the Continent, though without seriously intending to do so. A highly favorable trade treaty was to follow as a consolation, but never did. Assurances of mutual confidence and of hopes for an unclouded peace crowned the work, while each of the contracting parties exhorted the other to begin putting the treaty courageously into effect.

Sadly Gentz admitted himself outdistanced. He had no faith in the Treaty of Amiens and could not understand how the British could humiliate themselves so deeply and, as it seemed to him, so uselessly. Since he had no connection with Addington's administration he received no more money from London. His enemies thought he had reached the end, tormented by debts, without real occupation, disillusioned and embittered. With his whole heart he had counted on the war and on a defeat of the Revolution, and the negotiated peace that was now being ushered in marked the close of his career in hyperpacifistic Berlin. He who had been condemned to devote his whole life and soul to international affairs could not but turn cynic when he saw the moral and political demands that he had made on his period consistently neglected; equally so when he saw the state that he had served pursuing a catastrophic course despite all his warnings. It was an expedient that helped for a while, but it could not long satisfy a nature such as his. He fled, from himself and from the environment that had made him what he was.

THE German Empire, or the Holy Roman Empire, was, as the reader knows, a union of several hundred states. The great majority, bishoprics and sovereign abbacies, margraviates and free cities, were being done away with under pressure from France and incorporated with some of the larger states. The two most important, Austria and Prussia, belonged only through some of their possessions; the King of Prussia through his old Electorate of Brandenburg and the King of Hungary and Bohemia through a few holdings that were called "Austria," Tyrol, and so on. In its entirety this monarchy of the Hapsburgs did not even have a name. It was a mélange of a few countries where German was spoken with more where the Latin, Slavic, or Hungarian tongues prevailed. Nevertheless, the head of this remarkable Empire was accounted more German even than the King of Prussia, say. The Hapsburg domains had always seemed to the Germans to form an empire, as it were, because they united the most various autonomies and traditions, languages and races, into one multifarious whole. The individual, national states were mainly Protestant, the Empire as a whole was essentially Roman Catholic, and the traditional arch-Catholicism of the Hapsburgs contributed to their domain the dignity of a superstate; the dignity of an, or *the*, empire. Furthermore, a Hapsburg monarch still bore the title of Elected German Emperor; had he not, it would have been difficult to know just what to call him. Under the second predecessor of the then reigning monarch, Joseph II, an attempt had been made at centralization, Germanization, modernization, and, if one may say so, Protestantization of this old conglomerate, but it miscarried because internal conditions made it impossible, and because of the French Revolution. Under Franz II there was a return to the principle that the emperor must be not creator but administrator, chairman, and solemnly threatening overseer.

In all his life Gentz had never been farther south than Weimar, and he had no real conception of the great, checkered states lying to the south and east; of their thriving rustic villages and baroque churches, of their mountains, their soldiers, their bureaucrats, and their monks.

He knew that the French "philosophers" and revolutionists had always seen in Prussia a friend, in Austria an execrated enemy, and this was now for him a bond of sympathy. Then, too, Austria had shown an astonishing vitality during the past nine years of war, and if Great Britain had been the world's chief adversary of France, on the Continent her strongest foe had been Austria. Austrian diplomacy was regarded as instinctive by tradition, covetous, crafty, and unscrupulous. How far a devotion to the Church, or to the German Empire, or to the mighty dynasty of the Hapsburgs prompted this diplomacy to resist the world revolution so obstinately might be answered thus or so; in any case, next to Great Britain Austria was the power that one could depend on above all if one was set on preserving the old Europe.

The first opportunity presented to our publicist for serving Austria was a mournful one; the assassination of the French delegates to the peace congress at Rastatt in 1799. These unfortunate diplomats, self-important yet essentially good-hearted men, were stopped after they had left the abortive congress one night and just before they had reached the Rhine, dragged from their carriage and, though they showed their safe-conducts, shot and stabbed. Two died on the spot; the third, pretending to be dead, escaped, and it was through him that the identity of the murderers was discovered. They were Croatian hussars, Austrians beyond any shadow of doubt. The Francophile world was aroused to fury, though part of it may have rejoiced in secret; the neutrals were enraged; the exponents of counterrevolution were deeply embarrassed. What of the struggle between right and wrong, when the right itself acted so abominably?

Gentz thereupon entered into a widespread and passionate public discussion. It was unnecessary, he wrote, to place the blame for this monstrous occurrence higher than where it so obviously belonged; on a few brutalized soldiers of the lowest class. What possible advantage could the Austrian ministry anticipate from it? But what immeasurable harm! The argument was sound, and he advanced it in good faith. Not for decades did he learn that the crime had been instigated, if not by the ministers themselves, at least by those close to the Generalissimo, for it had been hoped that important papers compromising Prussian policies would be found on the delegates.

The Emperor Franz had Gentz's article distributed in the form of reprints, and rewarded the author with a gold snuffbox. The Austrian Ambassador in Berlin, Count Stadion, a liberal-minded man, sought him out.

Stadion, it appears, was the first to conceive the idea that the great publicist might be of use to Vienna, since he was no longer of value to Berlin; for though the important role played by public opinion in this world crisis was suspected even in old-fashioned Austria, the employment of a well-informed Protestant writer to direct it had never occurred to anyone before. But need teaches prayer, and even a conservative may do something at last for which there is no precedent.

Stadion could give Gentz nothing to help him on his way save letters of introduction and promises of friendship, but Gentz was so depressed, and a change so imperative, that he snatched eagerly at even these straws.

Together with Adam Müller he left Berlin in a post chaise at three in the morning on June 20, 1802, his pockets empty except for his permit to leave. Gloomy adieus to his family and one last "celestial night" with Christine, the actress, had preceded this departure, and he had promptly lost in play the money with which he could have begun life in Vienna. In Dresden he made the acquaintance of the young Austrian Ambassador, Count Clemens Metternich. At Teplitz, in Bohemia, the pomp of the Austrian nobility was first disclosed to his envious eyes, and he was received by the Lobkowitzes, the Wilczeks, and the Choteks as though he were one of them. On July 27 he arrived in Vienna, and thought it forlorn.

It was so big, so hot, so dusty, and seemed so unintellectual and slatternly that he lay crying in his hotel room. Sadly he lost himself in the past, and was overjoyed when some Jewish bankers called, bringing with them a little of the atmosphere of north Germany. Toward the end of August the situation had improved. Nobles and diplomats returned to town, highly placed government officials began to notice the unbidden guest, and Count Cobenzl, the Foreign Minister, an elegant, skeptical, and indolent man, asked him to call.

A court ceremonial from out the time of the Spanish Counterreformation introduced Gentz a few days later to the Emperor's audience chamber. Franz was young and mistrustful, lantern jawed, with cold, languid, ungracious eyes, and a stony expression.

"Are you the man who is an author?" This was his customary opening question to writers. Though the conversation was carried on in German the Italian-educated monarch was limited to the Viennese dialect, which made him appear more closely connected with the life and feelings of the people and thus more affable than he really was. Gentz's beautifully fluent Modern High German annoyed him, and he referred to it afterward as "bloated, flatulent gibberish," that secretly must have something or other to do with Jacobinism. The Emperor was no friend to intellectuals, and the audience was dull and entirely barren of result.

But although, or perhaps because, the Emperor would have nothing to do with the dissolute Prussian official, a group quickly formed that unconditionally demanded his collaboration. Two Austrian Ambassadors who were thoroughly familiar with foreign affairs, Count Stadion and Count Metternich, intervened with urgent letters and the Emperor's brother, the Archduke Karl, invited Gentz to call. Even von Colloredo, the highly influential Chief of the Imperial Cabinet, gave a favorable opinion of him, for the times unfortunately were such that it was unsafe to disregard entirely the temper of the public; and this man had the reputation of being an expert defender of authority. Furthermore, an acquaintance with the difficult problems of paper money was attributed to him; and besides all this, he could no doubt tell something about the secrets of Prussian politics if one were to catch him in the right mood.

So Gentz received an appointment as Imperial Counselor, with an annual salary of 4,000 gulden.

This required only that he take up his residence in Vienna, and prepare an occasional article of unbiased advice. It might be said that he became a sort of paid volunteer. He could now hope to do more than merely create illusions out of thin air; indeed, could look forward to developing some effective connections in those quarters where decisions were made. This prospect was especially agreeable because he would be able to gather more concrete material for his reports to Great Britain, a phase of his activities that naturally was well known to those in the Austrian capital. Nevertheless, some government secrets were revealed to him.

He came to know why there had been a falling out with Russia, and what were the real grounds for the hatred against Prussia. He received information on the strength of the army, the size of the national income and the national debt, as well as on what was readily available and what still lacking. No Protestant stranger to the capital of the Hapsburgs had been honored with such confidence since the world began, and his position there showed the times to be wholly without parallel.

So situated, he wrote a frank and dignified letter to the King of Prussia, asking permission to resign. He emphasized the disproportion between his official position and his literary talents; his political convictions; and even his domestic difficulties. Frederick William replied with a not ungracious Cabinet order, and von Haugwitz, the Foreign Minister, solaced himself with a jest: "Now, at last, we are quits with Austria. We took Silesia away from her; we return her Gentz."

To his friends the new Austrian wrote that he recognized fully how much he had left behind him in Berlin, but that between his deeds, his debts, and his tormentors on the one hand, and his new position on the other, there had been no choice. He added such lofty assurances as this: "It is no little thing to be able to tell you that I am now as familiar with the secret driving forces of the Austrian monarchy, and with all that passes for government here, as with the streets of Berlin. . . . I have not heard much to gratify or console me, but have learned an infinite amount. Now I understand how deep the wounds of Europe really go; but I know, too, where the healing herbs are to be found. If you realized how much good I have been responsible for in Vienna, how much advice I have given in these past two months, what measures I have devised, and how many minds I have electrified you would be amazed. . . . If a war should break out anywhere in Europe you may be sure that it was I who started it. There can and must be no peace as long as wanton mischief reigns unpunished. I would rather see the whole world go up in flames than sink under this deadly marasmus."

Of himself he wrote: "My hour has struck. My long, long youth has run its course. I renounce all the abundance of life and dedicate myself to the austere activities of my mind, which fortunately has not yet begun to age. Henceforth I shall live a more arid, more insipid life, but, I sincerely hope, a more regular and harmonious one. And on the ruins of all my old passions, and inclinations, and indulgences there shall arise an ambition for true fame and a certain hitherto submerged pride over something that lay wrapped about in alien folds far in the depths of my being."

Brave hopes! Good resolutions!

He wrote, also, of his regret for past sins: "Believe me, I shall never think without blinding tears of my wife, always dear to me for so many reasons; of my honorable old father; my kind and loyal sisters; my wonderful mother, now sinking into her grave; or of so many other dear ones, bound to me by the closest and most sacred ties: whom so often through the unfortunate disharmony between my wild and aspiring nature, with its thirst after achievement and indulgence, and their own more tranquil and ordered lives I have inevitably harassed and grieved. . . ."

Well, all that was over. A foreign emperor had made the poor journalist his independent adviser, and he had escaped forever from the restricted ambit of the middle class.

Unfortunately he was bade to return once more to the city of his past to make final and orderly disposition of certain official, financial, and court affairs. All went well until he reached Dresden, where he stopped over because he could not bear the thought of going on. The British Ambassador there, Hugh Elliot, advised that instead of returning to Berlin he make a trip to London with him. Good! But where to get the money?

Gentz borrowed 150 pounds sterling from Metternich, won from General Armfelt 200 taler in play and got another 100 pounds sterling from him as a loan, then felt in a position to accept Elliot's proposal. He hurried on ahead to Weimar, saw Demoiselle von Imhoff, borrowed 40 louis d'or from the Duke, and in Frankfort beguiled the time at the homes of well-to-do bankers until Elliot arrived.

Berlin never saw him again.

PART TWO

GENTZ IN EUROPE

VI

LONDON, 1802

HUGH ELLIOT, Gentz's traveling companion, was a true cavalier of the eighteenth century. In Berlin he had challenged Frederick the Great with his arrogant repartee; in Naples, seduced the Queen; in Copenhagen, declared war on the Danes on his own responsibility. His mission in Dresden, which bored him not a little, was a sort of punishment. When asked where he got news for his courier twice a week he would reply: "Nothing more simple. If I discover anything of interest to my government, I send it. If not, I invent a report, and contradict it by the following courier. In this way I never lack material." On his trip across the Continent this eccentric diplomat could not have wished for better company than Gentz, and their evenings passed agreeably with liquor, politics, and trifling. Only a trip on the Rhine, made in deference to the nature-loving Briton, was disastrous. Gentz soon consigned castles, cliffs, and forests to the Devil, retired to his cabin, suffered an attack of seasickness mixed with fear of an accident, and finally had to be carried ashore half dead.

Not without some trepidation the pair crossed the French border at Coblenz, or the border of what then was called France, for the Rhineland and the Netherlands, long since occupied, had been finally recognized by the Treaty of Lunéville as French possessions, though without much regard for the wishes of the inhabitants. Brussels, once so full of activity, Gentz found poor, subdued, and lifeless. Even Talma, the great actor, whom he had the good fortune to see, could tempt only the officers of the French garrison into the theater. By day, the inhabitants went about with mournful looks; by night, the streets were deserted.

"Before the 18th Brumaire," Gentz wrote to Adam Müller from his hotel, "the thought that the horrors under which people groaned must necessarily be transient offset, as it were, any excess of troubles. But now those laboring under the yoke feel only the monotony of a comfortless and apparently lasting, cold, hard, cruel, insulting despotism, especially during the past year since the reigning Sultan has felt sure of his throne. . . ."

Yet combined with hopelessness he found rage; and with rage, hope once more. "Hatred of the French has attained an appalling strength in every heart. All the way from Coblenz to Brussels, even with all the differences of speech, of customs, and of previous forms of government, in free cities, bishoprics, large and small provinces, in Bonn, in Cologne, in Jülich, in Aachen, in Liége, in Brabant we failed to find a single person who was not inspired by the same hate, the same wish, the same hope. It will not, it cannot last, was the perpetual refrain of all those with whom we talked. . . ."

Naturally Gentz did not send this letter off from Brussels, but for safety's sake carried it on his person to England.

THE reception accorded him there was unprecedented. An article in the *Morning Post* read: "Mr. Gentz has just left the Prussian service, and entered into that of Austria, and his reception in London has certainly been more universally favourable than that of perhaps any other private foreigner who ever visited this capital. But its universality is a sufficient proof that it depends on personal merit and just celebrity, without any mixture of secret political views. It has been confined to no party. Lord Grenville and Mr. Windham have vied with Mr. Addington and Lord Hawkesbury in their attention to this celebrated writer. There is no need of any mysterious cause to explain why Englishmen of all parties should show their gratitude to the ablest defender of England. . . ."

It is not necessary to discuss at length for the English-speaking reader the significance of the names just mentioned. Henry Addington was the Premier, and Robert Lord Hawkesbury the Foreign Minister, of the government that had concluded peace with Bonaparte in the preceding spring. Lord Grenville had been the Foreign Minister, and William Windham the Secretary for War, in the administration of William Pitt. They hated both the peace and those responsible for it, yet one might have seen Addington and Windham together at a dinner given by the Duke of Portland in honor of Gentz, where the natural courtesy shown by the two opponents to one another filled the stranger with admiration and envy.

What a company! What splendor from out the past; what familiarity with the present! What conversation, when after three or four hours the dinner came to an end, the gentlemen remained behind, and the port wine unloosed their tongues! In Berlin there were both brains and politics, but the two were separate from one another; the intellectual lost touch with reality and politicians were narrow and malicious. In Vienna, strictly speaking, there were neither intellect nor politics; only foolish sensuality. In London the politicians were intellectual, equipped with classical no less than modern knowledge; acquainted with Horace as well as with international trade.

Naturally there was much talk of Bonaparte and of the dubious peace, for this was the most recent development. After nine years of isolation it had at last become possible to study the situation in Paris on the spot, and a few of those in the highest circles had taken advantage of the opportunity. Among them was Charles Fox, Leader of the Opposition. The First Consul had eagerly seized the chance to predispose such an influential man in his own favor, and had said to him—and Gentz listened with a bitter smile: "Monsieur Fox, I am happy to meet in you a man that clearly realizes the folly of war. It is just this conviction that draws you and me together. Ah, Monsieur Fox, when shall I see all mankind united in one single alliance that could be symbolized by two clasped hands, a black one and a white one?"

To call such beautiful ideals lies one would have had to be courageous enough to draw the logical conclusions from bitter experience; for unquestionably they were beautiful ideals.

Yet Francis Jackson, the British Ambassador in Berlin, described Bonaparte's manner as sarcastic, vulgar, and impertinent, though his remarks showed subtlety and understanding; and Talleyrand as the most shameless liar he had ever met. Of the suspicions that were rife among the various subrulers on the Continent, their fears, their jealousies, their hates, no one in England, he continued, had the slightest conception. Members of the diplomatic corps were treated little better than prisoners, and one must expect to encounter Fouché's secret agents in every salon. Tyranny stifled all social life.

The most cordially hated man, said Lord Pembroke, was undoubtedly the Dictator himself, as he had noticed in Paris a hundred times or more, but this should not encourage the false hope that his overthrow was imminent. Pembroke knew no way of wresting power from a man like Bonaparte, once he had it thoroughly organized. Besides, though the French did hate the First Consul they hated or feared Great Britain still more, and the Tyrant understood well how to bring this feeling to a white heat in order to make his subjects more submissive to his rule. Here Gentz said to himself: And yet you made peace with this man and actually believed that it would be permanent!

Lord Hawkesbury remarked that news reaching his office fully justified the conclusion that Bonaparte was insane. "It is just as it was with the Czar Paul; the scenes in which he indulges clearly prove that he is crazy." But the skeptical Lord Malmesbury reminded the party of a letter of the year 1741, or thereabouts, in which a British diplomat had said the same thing about the King of Prussia; yet Frederick the Great had reigned for forty years after that without anything more having been heard of his insanity.

The German guest contributed his share to conversations of this sort. Bonaparte was better understood in the corrupt capitals of the Continent than in London, he suggested. On one occasion he spent four hours in talk with William Windham, the most severe antagonist of Addington's peace policy, and it is not unlikely that this interchange of ideas was reflected in the speech before the House of Commons in which Windham soon afterward resumed his opposition to the Treaty of Amiens.

It was the second session of Parliament since the union with Ireland, marked by universal doubt that Addington's administration could endure, and a complete lack of confidence in the permanence of world peace, though both should have stood firm. In court dress, his three-cornered hat under his arm, Gentz sat in the House of Lords while the old King read the Speech from the Throne. It was still George III, who forty years before had won Canada and twenty-five years before lost the American colonies; master of the older and the younger Pitt; an incarnation of the eighteenth century. Naturally everyone knew in advance the contents of his speech. He praised "the numerous blessings enjoyed under the protection of our happy constitution," referring with satisfaction to the prosperity of the nation and its citizens. He emphasized his love of peace, but added that his government would always have to watch the European situation attentively and would not be willing to depart from that wise course "by which the interests of other states are connected with our own." This passage, a hundred times weighed and filtered by royal offices and advisers, was as interesting to Gentz as to the French Ambassador, who also was present.

The debate attending the Resolution of Thanks for the speech brought violent attacks upon Addington. Lord Grenville called the Prime Minister's foreign policies "a series of ignorance and disgrace. If, however," he concluded, "there be any hope, it is to be found in measures of decision and firmness—in a bold and animated tone, held by a leader of courage and capacity—not by any of the men now in power, but by him to whom Europe looks up at this awful hour for the preservation of their dearest rights and liberties."

The situation was described even more clearly in the House of Commons, where the Speaker, Charles Abbot, had reserved a place of honor for Gentz. Windham maintained that the situation between Great Britain and France was actually war, and that words were powerless to change it. Great Britain was the bulwark between Bonaparte and world domination. Did anyone there present believe that the First Consul's thoughts and aspirations were fixed upon aught but her destruction? Already the conditions laid down in the Treaty of Amiens had been broken individually and collectively, which surprised him less than it did the ministers, for from the very first these conditions had been hypocritical and untenable. Not only did the First Consul now direct the world, Holland, Germany, Switzerland, Italy, as though it belonged to him; he actually dared to meddle with the innermost affairs of Great Britain; he threatened her freedom of speech and the press, shamelessly played her political parties one against the other, and no doubt would soon dictate who was to rule in the United Kingdom.

Yet against all these incursions, these annexations and usurpations, Mr. Addington had not once dared to raise his voice in protest. In the face of peril that was deadly beyond all precedent there was talk of reducing the army and the fleet, and of lowering taxes. Was such a course really approved by the nation? If the citizen thought more of his bank book than he did of his native land, then Great Britain was lost. Yes, and she deserved to be lost. The speaker could not hide from himself that all this was more or less merited, and that the modern Romans, pursuing their objective of world dominion with unparalleled energy and boldness, had not been so far off in their estimate of the situation. If the nation could not be fired with a spirit of self-sacrifice equal to that which animated the French, if Bonaparte's evil genius were not opposed by a tutelary spirit of the same courage and breadth, Great Britain had better make herself over immediately into a French province.

A corpulent young man with the Bourbon nose who sat near Gentz bowed to him and whispered in German, but with a foreign accent: "This means trouble," his expression plainly showing that he was pleased. He was, as Gentz already knew, an émigré from France, Louis Philippe, Duke of Chartres, or, as he was more correctly known since the sad death of his father, of Orleans; and none other than the son of Philippe Égalité. The checkered course of his life was well known. A military career in the service of the Republic; then flight to the camp of the allies in company with General Dumouriez; exile in Switzerland, where he became a teacher of mathematics in a boys' boarding school; next, in the United States; and finally in England, where he was reconciled with his family and began to receive money from them again. Louis Philippe sided wholeheartedly with Addington's opponents, as another war seemed to him inevitable, and desirable no less for the world than for him, who now had been living for ten years in exile.

"Is anything more required," he asked Gentz at the end of the debate, "for a vivid picture of the state of Europe than that six months after signing of the peace treaty a British Parliament can discuss nothing but the question whether there shall be war or peace with France?"

Addington thought it best to meet Windham's deluge of oratory with icy calm, answering it in a soft voice and with nothing but the bare facts and figures. He showed that the army and the fleet, though smaller than during the war, were still considerably larger than before it, in accordance with his principle of choosing the golden mean between a war footing and designs appropriate to assured peace, which, he confessed, was not enjoyed at the moment. The great advantages of peace were apparent in the development of foreign trade, which had increased since the Treaty of Amiens by not less than four million pounds. Of course, he acknowledged, the honor and safety of the kingdom took precedence over all else; but was the situation really so grave that the one must be regarded as lost and the other as seriously threatened? "There were some gentlemen who were in the habit of making exaggerated statements and using language tending to war; others, on the contrary, seemed ready to make any sacrifice for the maintenance of peace. Ministers would not follow the advice of either, but adopt a middle course, which should be at the same time firm and moderate."

Charles Fox, the elderly fop and *bon vivant*, the gambler, the most astute politician in the world, parried the attack on Addington's moderation, though with a certain showing of disdain. He deplored the situation in which they found themselves, blaming not Addington, however, who had occupied his responsible office for hardly two years, but his predecessor. The fault, if this talkative darling of the gods was to be believed, was William Pitt's, for he had conducted the world war, which could have been avoided, at once inflexibly and feebly, and therein lay the difficulty.

The deserted Addington plainly showed his gratitude and relief while Fox spoke, nodding his head in affirmation. This, so the young Duke of Orleans explained to his neighbor, betokened a political sensation. Fox was Pitt's greatest opponent and rival. Addington was regarded as Pitt's friend and successor, in whose selection Pitt himself had had a voice, and it was rumored that he had undertaken to advise and support Addington with all the authority of his name. He had persuaded his friends not to deny Addington their coöperation, and to spare the nation all the dangers of a fundamental change in government during war.

Now the fact of the matter was that Pitt had gradually become more and more convinced of Addington's incapacity. He acknowledged that Addington was not the man to contend with Bonaparte, and that the futility of his policies accelerated rather than delayed the war while making alliances impossible. Addington did not regard his role as it was originally conceived by his party. He took his mission, which seemed to Pitt's friends a sort of comic interlude, very gravely and solemnly, consistently showed a wooden obstinacy, and was driven by vain ambition to settle the policies of the nation entirely on his own responsibility. And as his decisions were highly unfortunate, and he asked Pitt's advice only as a matter of form, Pitt found himself identified with a policy over which he had no real influence, and which he actually condemned, while at the same time his delicate sense of honor forbade him openly to say so. Giving ill health as an excuse he therefore absented himself consistently from the sessions of Parliament and took the waters at Bath, but deceived nobody thereby. Furthermore, Fox was making advances to Addington, who at least did not refuse to accept his help. This was fortunate, for an ally of Fox could under no circumstances remain an ally of Pitt.

The young speaker who followed Fox did not fail to make use of this opportunity. He attacked Addington, praising Pitt and contrasting the capabilities of that great leader with the fruitless muddling of his successor. His name was George Canning, he was thirty-two years old, the leader of a group of young men who were sworn to restore Pitt to office, and his special pupil and adherent. His speech was not eminently classical and spiced with Latin quotations, as Windham's had been, but supercilious and aggressive. The pleasure that he appeared to find in baiting the Prime Minister with questions and mordant sallies was shared by his listeners, and Duke Louis Philippe leaned over to Gentz several times to murmur in his Swiss dialect: "This means trouble."

When at last the session was over it was midnight, and it had opened at noon. Gentz had sat through it all in his hot court costume, without food or drink, nailed to his seat, and wholly unconscious of the passage of time.

A FEW days later the King and Queen expressed a desire to see him, and accompanied by the Austrian chargé d'affaires he called at Buckingham Palace. Old George III, crafty, headstrong, charming, spiteful, crazy, had already forgotten who was being introduced and the Queen, a plain, simple woman of the Mecklenburgs, tried to save the situation.

The Queen (in German): "You were presented to the King yesterday?"

"Yes."

"I was sure it was you. The King was not quite certain, and did not dare address you as the great author, but I said immediately that you were he. I am glad to bid you welcome to English soil. You have done England a great service."

Gentz did not know wherein this service lay, and still less how news of it could have crossed the Channel.

"English and French translations of your excellent book have been published, but I didn't need either of them. I cannot be too grateful to my son, Adolf, for sending me a copy of the German edition a year ago. But what did you think of the translation?"

"I think the English one is admirable, and regret that I cannot say the same of the French."

"After all, that doesn't surprise me very much. How could you expect the French to make anything but a garbled translation?"

"But what Your Majesty appears to take for granted is not so. That translation was made in Berlin."

"In Berlin? Well, that's not much better than France, either. But tell me: you're no longer in the service of Prussia . . . ?"

Here the account breaks off. What else the Queen said about Prussia could not be entrusted to the mail.

It was particularly this reception at Buckingham Palace that crowned Gentz's reputation among both friends and enemies. The Prussian Foreign Minister, von Haugwitz, remarked to Bignon, the

French Ambassador, that the way in which Gentz had been taken up in London held out little promise of European peace.

"Gentz earns his money," wrote Bignon in a report, "and it is clear that he must have a great deal to do, for his pay is generous. He is now getting 800 pounds annually from England, and 4,000 gulden from the court at Vienna. If there is one man who can be called the champion of the counterrevolution, it is he. . . . In Berlin he was constantly tormented by debt, always seeking some way to keep body and soul together, and finally confirmed his theory of loans by fleeing from his creditors. In London and Vienna, on the other hand, he is received in princely fashion, honored, and showered with money. This one example, though it concerns but a single person, to be sure, clearly shows the differences in custom among the three courts. . . ."

As to the size of Gentz's income at least, the offended diplomat had not been poorly advised. The Austrian salary actually was 4,000 gulden, and the year's stipend that he took home as a result of his visit to London may safely be set at 1,000 pounds; at any rate, he received a bill of exchange for that amount in 1805. This seems a great deal of money when it is recalled that the celebrated Doctor Johnson was very happy on 300 pounds a year, and still more when it is reckoned by Continental standards. On the other hand, it was not really so much when the demands and passions of our publicist are taken into account.

In return he was expected to influence Austrian policy in Great Britain's favor and periodically to write reports, advice, and propaganda such as he had formerly produced when an independent writer. That it should have been the pacifistic government of Addington and Hawkesbury that rewarded him seems curious enough, for it was said of the former that he feared above all things any association with Continental nations, any so-called entangling alliances; and naturally he knew only too well that as far as the Treaty of Amiens was concerned Gentz was ranged on the side of his most implacable foes. But perhaps he thought a resumption of hostilities with France probable after all; or perhaps he merely wanted to procure the support of a foreign authority whom all parties were equally desirous of consulting.

Among the host of political friends that Gentz made in London there remain to be mentioned in particular the Duke of Portland, Lord President of the Council and subsequently Prime Minister; Nicholas Vansittart, Secretary of the Treasury; and George Hammond, Undersecretary for Foreign Affairs, all of whom were later to be of use to him. Whether he made the personal acquaintance of Pitt is not so clear; he would have had to seek him out at Bath, where the former Prime Minister was living in retirement. A letter of introduction from Canning, or Lord Malmesbury, or Lord Grenville would have gained him entry, and it is highly probable that Pitt would have been glad of an opportunity to meet the writer whose *Essay on the Administration of British Finance* he had once read with such great admiration. In any case, it is known that Gentz later wrote to him directly.

Another noteworthy friendship was that with James Mackintosh. Edmund Burke had always connected the two, for Mackintosh's first literary success had been gained ten years previously with a defense of the French Revolution, an attack on Burke; and Gentz had added to his translation of Burke's *Reflections on the French Revolution* the *Attempt at a Refutation of the Defense by Mr. Mackintosh*. These events, combined with Burke's influence, had turned Mackintosh, too, into a conservative, and to any who would listen he was fond of relating how Burke, in a single conversation, had established for him the magic power of tradition and shown him the way to a coördinated political system. Thus Mackintosh's development corresponded rather closely with that of Gentz. With his fascinating personality he was regarded as one of the foremost men in London, though actually he had no great achievements to his credit.

No longer were there many French émigrés in London. The great majority had taken advantage of the First Consul's amnesty and hurried back to France, where they lived the life of second-class citizens under humiliating police supervision, if indeed they did not die immediately as did the unfortunate Calonne after a twelve-year exile. The sad happiness of a return to their native land was denied only to the Bourbons and their immediate circle, and in their unassuming homes on the outskirts of London two or three little groups held ghostly court, awaiting meanwhile with haughty patience the downfall of Bonaparte and the triumph of eternal justice. Louis Philippe of Orleans had a country place at Twickenham, and there Gentz passed his final English week end, as the guest of a man for whom the future seemed to hold great things in store.

For as Gentz wrote to Adam Müller: "By his unusual mind and his extraordinary character this one single Bourbon atones for the unhappy weaknesses of three whole generations of his line. You will be astonished to hear that this young nobleman, among all the men that I know, is most in harmony with my present political ideas, the one whose conversation is most instructive to me and from whom I have learned most, even about England. . . ." Historical comparison, he continued, is still the best means of forecasting the future. The English revolution of the seventeenth century had ended by elevating to the throne a so-called younger line, and Louis Philippe seemed at least as well adapted to reconciling past and future, to combining tradition and progress, as William and Mary.

Only the pity of it is that historical parallels, as a rule, do not come off.

GENTZ was in high spirits when he left London during the Christmas holidays after a two months' stay, his trunks, which he sent by sea to Hamburg, full of the secret documents and parliamentary reports that had been entrusted to him. "England now belongs to me," he boasted. "I know all the sources of direct information, and have a hundred connections whence I can obtain the most dependable news in any given case. . . ." At last he understood fully, and for the first time, why Bonaparte counted Great Britain his chief enemy and why she alone, despite the Treaty of Amiens, continued a war that the entire Continent had given up. Only the British, he thought, were a real nation, a thoroughly organized society. "And note that this is the one thing to be considered in any attempt to attain a reasoned opinion on this great nation: Nothing in Great Britain is isolated. Everything hangs together; everything affects everything else; all is united, combined, blended. I have no words adequate to express to you this accord, this amazing ensemble, though of course there may be other countries that outshine her in certain respects: Germany in profundity, for example. . . ."

"Why should I not be happy in England? In this paradise of Europe, this garden of the gods, this last stronghold of true middle-class welfare, of morality and harmonious civilization, of sound ideas and real humanity? How necessary, how absolutely necessary it was that I should have seen this country! I came to London better prepared, better equipped, than any other foreigner; on this everyone agrees, even here. But how vivid everything became that until then had been only a silhouette! Such a complete whole; a society so perfect from whatever aspect; the only nation at present that possesses a definite character; a civilization not fragmentary, like the others, but comprehensively and systematically organized, and a temperament that embraces, penetrates, and is interwoven with it all. Such a captivating show of practical wisdom, of quiet and unassuming greatness, of widespread and deep-rooted bliss I am fully convinced the world has never yet seen. . . ."

But the admiring envy of the stranger blinded him to the shadows that lay over the land. Men like Mackintosh could have told him that even here the French Revolution had frustrated many of the bravest hopes of the eighteenth century. The Tories were counting on a long, rigidly conservative reign. None mentioned any longer a reform of the House of Commons. The union of Great Britain and Ireland had taken place the year before under dismal auspices, after the quelling of a revolt incited by the French. Again and again the liberties of the citizens had been curtailed, their immemorial rights temporarily suspended. Still, all this was child's play compared with what had taken place in France, and certainly it showed poor judgment on the part of the Opposition to inveigh against "Pitt's Terror" while putting up with the Jacobin Terror. Those accustomed to the illiberal, bureaucratic states of the Continent must have thought the British lack of restrictions gracious and free and the Commons a stately forum, despite the medieval way in which its members were elected.

The Whigs and the Tories both were as little interested as Gentz in the benefit of the common people. In this respect he belonged to the generation of Pitt and his friends. Like them, he thought in terms of politics and political economy, not of human welfare. When he spoke of the "whole" he meant the public schools, the universities, the banks, the East India Company, the press, the navy, the clubs, Parliament, and the court; all these, and the relationships between them, but not the workers in Blake's "dark, satanic mills." He would have been far ahead of his times indeed had he made their weal and woe the chief concern of political science.

As GENTZ made his way back to Vienna across the wintry landscape of the Continent, prosperous and in high spirits, Great Britain and France were rapidly nearing a break, and in March, 1803, the two nations were again at war with one another. But a whole year was to pass before Addington realized that his position had become untenable and Pitt resumed the premiership.

VII

STOP BONAPARTE!

TO ANYONE coming from London, Vienna must have seemed narrowly restricted. Its political activities were shabby, its public life was nonexistent, and history was being made there by bureaucrats whose names the people hardly knew. Sheltered behind the barriers of an antiquated Spanish court ritual the Emperor lived in complete seclusion, watching over the affairs of the state with jealous nicety but too timid and proud to speak even with his ministers or his brothers. The most influential man in the country was Count von Colloredo, Chief of the Cabinet. Without aim in life the nobility frittered away their time in social activities, and all that was expected of them was to act as patrons of the arts, and particularly of the great musicians. Among the people two parties were recognized, the "Archpatriots" and the "Malcontents," of which the latter was said to be increasing in alarming numbers. The nation was impoverished, bled white by the long war, its currency was declining, and attempts were under way to prevent the threatened overindustrialization and unemployment by prohibiting the establishment of new factories. But the most urgent problem of all was to preserve peace as long as might be feasible.

Why not try to influence the First Consul toward peace, since it would be so clearly in his own interest as well? Young Count Metternich, leaving for Berlin to take up his post as Ambassador, was told: "All will depend upon whether Napoleon really is obsessed by the insatiable lust for power of which England and her partisans accuse him; or whether this shrewd leader can be persuaded to substitute for the reckless policy hitherto forced upon him by the pressure of his extraordinary situation and the unexpected submission of European sovereigns, a more moderate course that nevertheless would assure continuation of his power and remove any of his grounds for distrust." "Unusual complaisance," "actions that do not seem consistent with the personal dignity or honor of the First Consul," were by no means to be demanded of him. For the rest, the possibility of a new alliance with Russia must always be kept open, though without endangering peace with France, an event, so ended the instructions, that would find us between the hammer and the anvil.

Amid such surroundings there was no place for the logical, mettlesome Gentz, with his insistence on decisions, any more than there had been in Berlin, and he soon came to hate his chief, Cobenzl, the Foreign Minister, as cordially as ever he had hated the members of the Prussian Cabinet. Evidently the same fetid air lay over all the Continental capitals, and the sickness that he had formerly thought distinctive of Prussia he now recognized as European; as a disease that could not be escaped by the simple expedient of emigration.

Doctor honoris causa Louis Count Cobenzl had all the advantages that were to be expected in a chief of the Austrian diplomatic service. He was well groomed, imperturbable, with a fair knowledge of law and of public affairs, and had distinguished acquaintances everywhere in Christendom. He could say, "My old friend, the Russian Foreign Minister." Indeed, he could say, "My old friend, General Bonaparte," for in 1797 he had negotiated with him at Campo Formio, and in the interests of peace had even brushed the haggard cheek of the Revolutionist with his lips. But of what actually was going on about him, or of what underlay the great crisis, Count Cobenzl had no official knowledge, and regarded those who could have enlightened him as mere underbred Utopians.

So it was, for example, with his new volunteer assistant, Gentz. He wrote: "I regard you as a reserve corps, of which much is to be expected," but at the same time had him spied upon and intercepted his correspondence; thus he was not long in discovering that in London Gentz was working against his ministry. The influential man of letters had proved to be an unwelcome acquisition.

But, as Cobenzl explained to his companion, von Colloredo, it was impossible to get rid of him, because he knew so many secrets now that it was better to keep him under the eye of the Austrian police than to dismiss him. "It is not wise to let writers meddle too much with politics," confided one of these aristocratic friends to the other; it was necessary to make use of them, but they should never be allowed to become too independent. Finally it came to an open rupture between the chief and his assistant, who nevertheless remained an assistant and unblushingly continued to fulfill the duty for which he was paid; that is, to say what he thought.

Here he relied upon his English connections, and also upon a political group in Vienna itself that opposed the policies of Cobenzl and was called the "War party," or the "Anglomaniacs." It was an international circle of émigrés and exiles; clever, adventurous, and intractable men who met at the home of Count Panin, one of those responsible for the assassination of Paul I of Russia. Among them was the Corsican, Pozzo di Borgo, who wanted to convey his native island to Great Britain, and possessed the advantage of having been acquainted with Bonaparte from early youth. The Dictator did not shrink from furnishing personally to the police a description of this hated comrade of his boyhood days: "Charles André Pozzo di Borgo, of Corsica; five feet, five to six inches tall; rather thin; hair and eyes brown; complexion dark; face plump; nose long; mouth average, teeth excellent; generally dresses in black; speaks English and French well, German poorly; crafty, spiteful, and intelligent; talks fluently, and raises his voice in a discussion; has graceful hands and likes to show them."

Another prominent member of the group was the Swedish General Armfelt. Wild adventures in peace and in war; a sentence of death for treason; exile; then sudden restoration to favor, and advancement, had made this emotional man still more intolerant and angry, and it was related that he had once publicly called Cobenzl a blockhead, and threatened him with a beating.

The British Ambassador, Sir Arthur Paget, was as closely associated with the War party as his delicate position would allow. He was young and inexperienced, and sometimes his reports contained nothing but what Gentz had dictated or insinuated to him.

The objective of the War party was a general European conflict or, as Gentz understood it, a coalition that perhaps might still be able to prevent it. Its members were intimate with certain representatives of the General Staff, and particularly with General Mack, a then modern military theorist whom, unfortunately, they regarded as a genius. Among them Gentz stood out as the one who thought, spoke, and wrote to better effect than any of the others; who understood most thoroughly the situation in Berlin and in London; and who could boast the largest number of intimate personal connections. Within a few months he had become the most important member of the circle and it was in Panin's salon, between eleven at night and two in the morning, that he first introduced ideas which, worked up later into letters and memoirs, caused Cobenzl so many anxious hours and incited his opponents to active measures.

His notion was one of indivisible peace and indivisible war. It was his firm belief that the former was impossible with Bonaparte, the illegitimate ruler, and that a coalition of all Europe must force him either to relinquish his conquests, or into war; that if such an alliance were to be formed, and, even more, attain its ends, a change of responsible government officials must first be brought about. Lombard and von Haugwitz in Berlin, Cobenzl and von Colloredo in Vienna, were of as little use as Addington, in London. The type of man who had wrecked the First and Second Coalitions would do nothing. In a manuscript that he intended to call *A History of the Balance of Power in Europe* Gentz recapitulated the conduct of the European rulers as follows: "The sum of all statesmanship seems to be to escape the common danger in any way possible or, if participation cannot be avoided, to limit it to the most inadequate and ineffectual measures and to leave the scene at all costs the moment that a means of escape appears; and fortunate it is if the hope of seizing some temporary spoils before their own huts go up in the general conflagration does not transform these egotists into secret enemies of one another."

Those who indulged in such methods were certainly not the ones to build for the future, or to put into effect what was so urgently needed in the present. "Expressions like 'The fate of this or that part of Europe does not concern us' or 'We limit ourselves to the maintenance of order in such and such an area' and so on should never again pass the lips of a ruler or a statesman." "No isolation, no absolute neutrality, no outright exclusion from any important negotiations! The fear that such a policy, the only dignified and proper one, will lead to endless quarrels and perpetual war is entirely groundless! . . . The more vigorously and courageously injustice and force are attacked at their first appearance, the less often will it be necessary to take the field against them in battle. . . . The more sensitive is every part to injury of the whole, the less frequent will wars become."

Golden words, understood by nobody!

A war between Great Britain and France was, after all, but a war between Great Britain and France. It would serve to weaken both powers, and to divert the revolutionary war machine from Central Europe toward the English Channel. This was a drama that Count Cobenzl could view with not wholly unpleasant emotions.

An invasion of Great Britain threatened during the fall of 1803, and 400,000 volunteers gathered to defend her shores. Pitt, still without office, exhausted himself as Lord Warden of the Five Ports in drilling his regiments. Across the Channel, near Boulogne, Bonaparte assembled his army and the small, flat boats that were to carry it over. "I tremble for England's fate," wrote Gentz to a friend, "and I should tremble for the rest of Europe, too, if it were possible to take any lively interest in what one despises beyond all measure. . . . My hatred for France, and for this perfidious, vain, bigoted usurper, forced first by the infamy of contemporaries into greatness and then into the excesses of greatness; this wanton, blaspheming, villainous bandit, has become an obsession with me; my only one at present, and it gnaws at my vitals. If anyone today could predict with certainty that I should never contribute toward the downfall of this Monster, my whole life from now on would become a burden and a loathing. . . ."

But to overthrow the "Monster" mere defense was not enough, no matter how greatly one admired the resolution of the British in their isolation. It was essential to seize the initiative and try to land on the Continent; in Holland, Belgium, Portugal; perhaps even in France, to rekindle the civil war there. Thus did Gentz advise the British Government in a memorandum, to which Nicholas Vansittart replied in October: "We begin to await the invasion rather with curiosity than anxiety. With a triumphant navy and 500,000 men in arms, it will exceed the greatest wonders in history if any impression is made on our coasts. The delay of attempt is advantageous to us by affording time to organize the new levies more completely. But whatever confidence we may feel in our security against any attack, I am convinced that it is only from a vigorous system of offensive operations conducted on the principles you have laid down that we can expect a result honourable to this country and advantageous to Europe in general. . . ."

Assuming, of course, that there was a "Europe," and that she would recognize her own interests and coöperate effectively. But that was out of the question.

There were moments when Gentz hated the men of his own faction more than he hated the enemy, and wished that they, and he himself, and the whole world might be annihilated. "Everything is dead and decayed," he wrote. "No, no! We shall be destroyed, and it is wholly right that we should be destroyed. Anyone of real moral sense must passionately long for the political downfall of Europe. . . . A general deluge, whether physical or civil and political, must sooner or later overwhelm the world in order that an entirely new harvest may arise from the corruption as from a plowed and fertilized field. I should prefer the former, and would gladly go down in the flood myself if I could but see the millions of human beasts being drowned too, and only the animals saved. Under present conditions, the belief that anything good can thrive in its customary way is the purest folly."

But what if the defeat of the "Good Cause" did not necessarily mean the "downfall of Europe"? What if the enemy were to triumph without committing too many atrocities and his ideas, no matter how insolently and odiously expressed, turned out to be right? What if the world adapted itself to his views and, contrary to all expectation, did not fare too badly under his rule?

Such a possibility was the most abominable that could be imagined, and as tormenting as an imp. " 'The most terrible thing of all would be to have such canaille proved right.' These words you did not merely copy from my heart; you tore them from my heart. I, too, no matter how I am cast down by the thought that such a disaster is actually possible; I, too, when I search my heart, cannot conceal from myself that the most awful of all awful things, truly much worse than the destruction of the world, more unspeakably dreadful even than a collapse of the whole solar system itself, would always remain for me the triumph of such canaille. All other evils can be cured, or they lose themselves in a general downfall, but the idea that the rabble may be right has in it something imperishable. . . . In this notion is to be found the real source of all my antirevolutionary tendency."

A rule of moral conduct: here indeed was a guiding principle hard to maintain in politics. Bonaparte would not prove right in the end if he merely succeeded in perpetuating evil conditions by violence and trickery; he would prove right only if he created something timely, inspired and enhanced life, and increased the happiness of the people. But was there any higher goal for statesmanship than this? Could one remain his enemy if, by whatever means, he succeeded in doing so? Would not one have to recant then, for very shame, and forbear? But instead Gentz saw the success of Bonaparte's venture only as a terrible misfortune; not to his own vanity, but with respect to the world and to God.

By stifling his doubts, to be sure, he could easily prove that whatever good or useful came out of evil was only relatively so, and always colored by evil. But good or useful for whom? Hardly for nations other than France. Foreign domination was bad under all circumstances and Bonaparte's, despite certain institutions that were valuable in themselves, was burdensome and rapacious. This he had seen with his own eyes a year previously, in Belgium and the Rhineland. Here the happiness of the many had not been increased, to say nothing of the few, the intellectuals. Never had the struggle led by Gentz been so truly a national one as during this period, from 1803 to 1807: the freedom and dignity of Europe lay in the freedom and dignity of her several nations.

The winter passed without invasion. In the spring of 1804 attention was diverted from the coast to Paris, where there were sinister happenings. A plot against the life of the Dictator, undeniably instigated by the Royalists, if not by the British, came to an end with the execution or flight of some in high places. The young Duc d'Enghien, a nephew of Philippe Égalité, who was living in Germany as an émigré near the French border, was arrested in his neutral retreat at the command of Bonaparte, taken to Paris, accused of some vague crime, and shot. The most innocent member of a family that was not wholly guiltless toward the regime, he had, in the words of Napoleon, "been sleeping too near the edge of the precipice."

Soon afterward the First Consul proclaimed to the clansmen of the victim, the kings of Europe, that he was now one of their number by assuming the title of Emperor. Once more three and a half million French had assented to an already accomplished fact, and it seemed implicit in this wonderful new arrangement, the plebiscite, that it never could return a negative answer.

Count Cobenzl announced to the French Ambassador that although as a man he deeply regretted the death of the young Duke, as a responsible statesman he did not wish the event to become a source of trouble between France and Austria. As for Napoleon's assumption of the title of Emperor, no objection was made in Vienna. His opportunistic and vigorous rule pursued its vacillating course between revolution and counterrevolution, disconcerting thereby all those who believed that a government must be either frankly revolutionary or conservative. Ambassador La Rochefoucauld pointed out that the new Empire meant "the death blow to the Revolutionary Hydra." These words, so pleasing to Cobenzl, threw some of the German republicans into a frenzy of grief, but at the same time the Empire was represented as the apotheosis of democracy, the crown and safeguard of the Revolution, and this interpretation, too, was applauded.

Gentz entreated Count Cobenzl in a memorandum to deny recognition to Bonaparte's Empire. Many deeds of violence, many injustices, had later been commended as right, but only in themselves; they never had been validated by such far-reaching results as the elevation of a revolutionary officer of tarnished ancestry to a rank equivalent to that of a Roman Emperor and all that this implied. Once this had occurred the situation was irremediable, and the dignity of imperial authority, like so much else, would be gone forever.

But suppose the objection were made that refusal to recognize the new Emperor would mean war? "I," wrote Gentz to his chief, "an unknown, insignificant man, a deeply interested but passive observer of this sad spectacle of error and folly; I, who watch and condemn every single step of your pernicious course and disapprove of your whole political system"—would choose war. Through their "gross delusions, their tardy and paltry measures, their unremitting absorption in their own ignoble interests," all sovereigns were to blame for the dilemma that they now faced, and they would have to pay. But lacking the courage to enter into coalitions or engage in war they should at least protract their negotiations and let the impudent upstart swallow his impudence; so, at any rate, they could try to exploit their shameful capitulation on behalf of the balance of power in Europe—not, of course, on behalf of their own interests.

In such words as these did the idealistic commoner remind the cynical aristocrat of his duty.

He could hardly have known that certain rulers, the King of Prussia, for example, had actually urged the First Consul to assume the crown, and that nothing was more comforting to them than the prospect that the Revolutionist might be tamed by clothing him in all the regalia of sovereignty. "Come, be one of us; share our private interests, and be happy!"

Count Cobenzl was familiar with all the requirements of politics, and thought to steer the ship of state through the stormy seas of this vexatious period without regard to scruples that would influence the private citizen. That he acknowledged the ennoblement of regicides caused him not the slightest qualm. He read the memorandum of his subordinate and later, before the eyes of the French Ambassador, ostentatiously burned a protest against Napoleon's ascent to the throne that the poor Bourbon pretender had addressed to what he thought were friendly courts.

Gentz's "Memorandum on the Necessity of Not Recognizing the Imperial Title of Bonaparte" was a declaration of war on the Foreign Minister, who thenceforth refused to see him. Agents of Napoleon soon got possession of this inept document and Otto, the French Ambassador to Bavaria, sent it to Paris accompanied by a malicious biography of the author. Gentz, he wrote, "had recently been in London, where the ministers had been very friendly with him and had represented him to the King as a man who was in a position to rekindle the war should such a course become necessary. His ardent, tireless passion for Great Britain, or at least for the money that he received from London, could find no better opportunity for expression than over the question of the imperial title. . . ."

The malice of his enemies might have been agreeable to Gentz if only he had been more certain of his friends. But as things were his political and financial existence hung by too thin a thread, for he had been useful to the British not so much by reason of his disinterested advice as for his knowledge of Austria and his influence there. If he were shut off from the secrets of Austrian politics because of a too-vehement Anglomania his repute in London would suffer. Furthermore, he was at odds with the irritable Paget, probably over an unfortunate question of money. The homeless wanderer was playing a dangerous game. He could not resort to publicity in opposing the rulers, because in Austria there was no such thing as publicity; because he had ruined his chances with the public of north Germany; and because it would have been unseemly in an advocate of "conservative principles" to appeal to the reading public against governmental authority. To retire to England was not the solution, for his very function was to work for Great Britain from the Continent. But how, and through whom?

He redoubled his surreptitious efforts to explain, to incite, to convene. He entered into correspondence with Francis Jackson, the British Ambassador in Berlin; he urged his friend, Johannes von Müller, the historian, then living in Berlin, to place his influential pen at the disposal of the Prussian opposition; he congratulated the King of Sweden, the only European monarch who had dared to snub Napoleon, in a proud and pessimistic message. Only a few, he wrote, understood the immediate great crisis as His Majesty and he himself understood it. "The catastrophes that we now witness are but secondary phenomena, only signs and portents of more serious troubles to come. . . . We live in one of those ominous periods when the whole established social structure breaks down, to give place to a new. We are too weak to arrest the general decay." But was that any reason for acquiescence? For not making some effort at resistance? "To defend valiantly and keep inviolate the social order to which we were born, its laws, and the religious, political, and civil institutions upon which it rests; that is the line of conduct marked out for us. And whereas the Supreme Arbiter of our destinies makes use of evil doers to effect great upheavals, it is His will, nevertheless, that the good resist them; and though they perish in the glorious attempt, meet death with their weapons in their hands. . . ."

Defeatism lay concealed in this letter, with its mixture of dramatic chivalry and sociology. But King Gustav knew very little about sociology. He rewarded Gentz with the Order of the North Star and elevated him to the nobility. Thenceforth he was called Chevalier de Gentz, or at least he called himself so.

Another romanticist of royal blood was the Archduke Johann of Austria, younger brother of the Emperor, and influential in military circles. Him Gentz besieged with arguments to the effect that Napoleon could never be induced to make an honorable peace, and that a great war was inevitable. "What seems to us the most dreadful of all misfortunes is an unavoidable evil against which neither the highest political skill nor the most cringing subservience can protect us indefinitely. In accordance with the eternal nature of things, an elemental force that has been torn from its beaten track and has broken down all barriers and all opposition to sweep forward without purpose or limitation cannot possibly bring itself to a standstill."

But Count Cobenzl, he continued, is a man who never inquired into the eternal laws. "We live only in the present, see only the immediate danger, and shut our eyes to the future, which we think of as lying only just beyond the current year or at most the year following. . . . And precisely this is responsible for the depth of our degradation. . . ." The Emperor paid a Foreign Minister, who had many assistants, ambassadors, and consuls; he paid a great army in order to give Austrian foreign policy the necessary weight. Yet Austria had no foreign policy. "Let us close our eyes and our ears to all that goes on beyond our borders! Away with all our visions of influence on foreign affairs and a balance of power; of measures to be taken against a predominance that never can be overcome once it has been established! Let Europe help herself as best she may! What obligations have we to Europe? Our duty is to protect ourselves, and no one will threaten us directly if only we can keep out of foreign quarrels."

This, according to Gentz, was the political creed of Count Cobenzl. Its final corollary was that even complete capitulation, even the decay of the state itself, would in reality be no great misfortune.

This admission Gentz had actually drawn from certain close associates of the Foreign Minister!

Was it worth the trouble of refuting? Perhaps it might be, for once this distorted opinion gained ground there would be no stopping it, and strange notions, incited by French preponderance, were already circulating through the land. It was being said that national honor was not real; that the state, the nation, was not real; and that whereas life without money, or with part of the body shot away, was no life at all, life without national honor was still life, and very well worth while.

Were they right, those who thought so? Never, Gentz insisted. "A life without honor is a life without happiness and without value." What the self-centered private citizen might put up with if he had to, the state should never condone. "Only shortsighted idiots; or apathetic, crude, and hardened egotists; or willingly dazzled statesmen purposely fostering foreign delusions could be satisfied with our present situation. . . ."

What was the way out of the difficulty? Obviously, an alliance of all the other nations against France. Monotonous advice, to be sure, but monotonous only because the mistakes of the European statesmen were so pitiably monotonous. An alliance of Austria with Prussia, Great Britain, Russia meant salvation; above all, with Russia because, Gentz warned, she was the only power that could tolerate a monarchy comprising the whole of Europe, and come to terms with Bonaparte. An isolated Russia would be driven into the arms of the Tyrant, who was only waiting for just such an opportunity. "Instead of drawing closer and closer to Russia the Austrian ministers exhaust their whole store of fawning and skulking political maneuvers in order to reconcile Russia and France, and congratulate themselves on having been able to delay the departure of the Russian chargé d'affaires from Paris by a few weeks! Such an extreme of delusion and weakness actually transcends all imagination. Posterity will refuse to believe it, and even we, who are condemned to be living witnesses, often ask ourselves whether it really can be true or whether we are not being fooled by dreams."

Further submission and isolation, concluded Gentz, only invited Bonaparte to fresh deeds of violence and meant war eventually under the most dangerous of all conditions, with ruin in the end. An earnest and energetic collaboration of the great powers, on the other hand, meant war under the most favorable conditions, and perhaps even peace; for it was not yet quite certain but that Bonaparte might give in if he suddenly found himself confronted by a united opposition, to which so far he was wholly unaccustomed. "These are neither the visions of a dreamer chasing rainbows, nor the vaporings of an overheated brain that would see the world drown in blood, but valid and practical conclusions demanded by irrefutable evidence!"

"Other men and other measures!" With this demand Gentz ended his emotional outburst.

The developments of the next few months proved him right. They necessitated other measures indeed, but brought no other men to the rescue.

THE weakness and vacillation of Europe tempted Bonaparte to deeds that he did not think would endanger peace. Already he had transgressed often enough the terms of the Lunéville Treaty and no one had cared. He had evacuated neither Holland nor the Kingdom of Naples; bent Switzerland to his will; annexed Piedmont; and occupied Hanover, which, though it belonged to Great Britain, was at the same time an integral part of the German Empire. As he had now gone so far, it was necessary to go farther, from fear that his potential foes would attack him as soon as he came to a halt no less than because of the arrogance induced by his feeling of superiority.

Accordingly he let it be known that the war with Great Britain had forced him to consolidate his position on the Continent: but this war, in its turn, was only a result of the impossible stipulations of earlier peace treaties.

He said that he did as he liked only with regions in which neither the Czar nor the Austrian Emperor had any interest: but Austria was interested above all in north Italy, and south Italy pointed toward Egypt and the Near East.

He insisted that the Mediterranean must become a French lake: but the Mediterranean Sea lay at the very heart of the Old World.

He promised that his imperial rank would in no case be higher than that of the Hapsburgs, the German, or recently the Austrian, Emperor: but according to tradition there could be only one Emperor, only one successor to the Romans and to Charlemagne, and of this he seemed well aware when he received the homage of the German princes at Aachen, the ancient capital of Charlemagne. Indeed, the City Council offered the Empress Josephine a bone from the skeleton of the founder of the imperial title, who lay buried there.

By such acts as these Napoleon finally succeeded in arousing an alliance against him that no one on the Continent except Gentz had either desired or planned. It began with an agreement for defense between Austria and Russia, which was but a poor scrap of paper after all for everyone knew that Napoleon would be careful not to attack either of these great powers. The second step was the dispatch to London by the Czar of a confidential agent, Count Novossiltsov, whose instructions were novel enough; they suggested that the wind should be taken out of French sails in the matter of freedom, and that all peoples should be given the right to decide their own destinies. Pitt, skeptical from long experience, thought that world peace, or a coalition at least, would be more safely assured if Belgium were given to Prussia and north Italy to Austria. Gentz was of essentially the same opinion when he wrote to George Hammond in November, 1805: "The sacrifice is heavy, and only with sad hearts will those who dreamed of a workable European federation pronounce the death sentence on the last of the small states to survive our century's terrible crisis. But necessity knows no law, and it still is a thousand times better to divide Europe into a few great powers than to deliver her over to the tyranny of one. . . ."

In March, 1805, Napoleon notified the world that he had found it necessary to convert the Republic of Lombardy into the Kingdom of Italy, and to accept the crown that had been offered him. The name "Italy" suggested claims embracing the whole peninsula, and perhaps even more. There followed a triumphal progress through the new kingdom, coronation ceremonies in which the insignia of Charlemagne and the iron crown of the Lombards appeared, and arrogant and threatening speeches.

In April Great Britain and Russia signed a compact of alliance at St. Petersburg. But the patience of the Continental powers was even then not exhausted. Alexander of Russia preferred the role of peacemaker to that of instigator of a world war, and hoped, also, that perhaps with the aid of Napoleon he might realize certain plans concerning the eastern Mediterranean and the island of Malta to which Pitt would not have acceded. His final offer of compromise, sent to Paris in May through Count Novossiltsov, was sufficiently acceptable. Great Britain was to relinquish all her colonial conquests, and if not Napoleon himself, then at least one of his brothers, was to be King of Lombardy. But Novossiltsov had gone only as far as Berlin when he learned that the Ligurian Republic, formerly Genoa, had been incorporated into the French Empire by one stroke of the pen, and was ordered to return to St. Petersburg.

At the same time, Cobenzl came to his senses. "Recent events in Italy fully prove that the Emperor Napoleon is obsessed by an insatiable lust for aggrandizement. . . ." The Austrian monarchy, he continued, was in "lethal danger," and nothing remained but to accept the proposal of Russia. Mack, the "modern" general, the "genius," received supreme command of the army that was about to be mobilized.

The War party, the "Anglomaniacs," and Friedrich Gentz, their leader, had triumphed.

If matters were skillfully handled the Napoleonic era could now be brought to an end almost before it had begun. But Gentz was in deadly fear that they would not be so managed. How, he asked, could they conduct a war successfully who had bungled and lost the peace? The handful of men constituting the government of a nation have a mysterious power, for upon them depends the enthusiasm or the cynical indifference of millions of soldiers and civilians. Under the leadership of Cobenzl Austria could never win a war. Secondly, and above all, the aid of Prussia was indispensable, since Prussia and Austria combined meant Germany, meant non-French Europe. But if Prussia remained neutral the direction of the coalition would fall to Russia. The Russians were far away, hindered in their communication with central Europe by this very Prussian neutrality and, on the whole, for reasons more easily felt than explained, incapable of deciding the important affairs of Europe. Prussia must therefore be won over, and before hostilities began, for once they had broken out her ministers would trim their sails in accordance with the fortunes of war.

Now in St. Petersburg and London there was a plan, to be sure, to force Prussia into coöperation by a military demonstration on her eastern border, but Gentz understood his touchy friends in Berlin far too well not to know that such a gesture would have exactly the opposite effect, and drive them straight into the arms of Napoleon. The "advocate of war," as he was called, the European warmonger, if one there really were, would have preferred no war at all to a war without Prussian help. In vain did he redouble his prophesies of evil to Jackson, the British Ambassador in Berlin, and to Hammond, Undersecretary of State in the British Foreign Office. In September, when the decision had been practically made, he addressed himself personally once more to Pitt: "You allow the war to begin without having effected any change in the Austrian Government, and without having won over the King of Prussia. Within a short time you will bitterly rue both these mistakes. This war cannot succeed; its planning is fundamentally wrong; Almighty God himself cannot save us!"

But Gentz, the intellectual, had no power over those whom he advised and, moreover, he had set his heart on something that was entirely beyond his control. William Pitt, himself a strong character, did not realize the inferiority of the men who ruled the Continent, nor were the Austrian ministers any longer masters of the situation; resolved too late upon war, they could not choose the moment when it should begin.

Napoleon chose it for them.

Even Gentz thought for a moment that the Dictator was merely bluffing, and that he would make some concessions when he suddenly found determined opposition arrayed against him. "Bonaparte, as we now see, blusters in word and deed only as long as he knows he can do so with safety. He does not want war. His plan is to conquer the world without it, to make a show of arms while others sit with their hands in their laps."

Even Gentz, for an instant, could not escape an intoxicating joy when Napoleon abruptly accepted war. "The star of the Tyrant pales! Such a moment the theatrical monarch has never yet experienced, and all the gentlemen-in-waiting and masters-of-ceremonies that he has ordered to Strassburg cannot help him!"

An impressive reconciliation took place between Cobenzl and his troublesome adviser and, it having been arranged that Gentz should complete and publish his *History of the Balance of Power in Europe* as a sort of war manifesto, he settled down to the task in welcome tranquillity in his villa at Hietzing.

He wrote with the freedom that the war at last permitted him, directing his accusations at France, at Europe, at the whole world, and showing that the victims of the great crisis were almost as much to blame for it as those who exploited their weakness and greed. An order that did not tolerate the existence of small states was only chaos and jungle. The antagonism between France and the rest of Europe had revolved principally about the continued life of small nations, but instead of coöperating to save them the natural enemies of France had shared the plunder with her, without being clever enough to see that he who can and does seize the lion's share of the booty will later turn upon his accomplice and rob him, too; first of his spoils, and then of his lawful possessions. If there were no longer to be any small states there would soon be no large ones either, because the one that is most powerful would swallow them all. The crimes committed against Savoy, Geneva, Venice, Switzerland, and Holland, peaceable, civilized communities, were the beginning of all the injustice and suffering of the times. No one could deny that they had hindered rather than advanced the common cause by their scrupulous neutrality, their egoism, and their ill-advised conservatism, and made it difficult for the great powers to help them. Yet there had been means of saving them, even against their will, and those ways would still be effective. If a federation were not arranged through which the great nations could protect their own rights and those of the smaller ones, a single great police state would surely arise from the chaos. There was no third possibility now; only a choice between these two.

For what did he hope as he sat writing there? Alas, the new war was already as good as lost while he remained at his desk, bewitched by the clarity and integrity of his thoughts.

Napoleon had not been bluffing. He did not expect that Austria and Russia would take the annexation of Genoa in bad part, yet was well prepared for such an eventuality. He had not consciously desired the war, but only as a man must desire opportunities to practice a trade in which he knows that he can excel all his competitors. "I must have battles and triumphs," he had told Fouché not long previously. "I shall strike before the coalition is ready. The old fogies do not understand our times and the kings have neither energy nor capacity. I am not afraid of the old Europe."

The only power that he did fear was Great Britain, and now the war on the Continent gave him an excuse to abandon an invasion that from the first had been more or less chimerical, and to win laurels where they were more easily to be had. His plans had been laid long since, and he had determined that he would respect the neutrality of neither Switzerland nor south Germany; indeed, he was certain of active help from the latter.

General Mack, the "genius," deciding on an offensive war, took up his march through Bavaria toward the Rhine, but suddenly realized that he was surrounded while he believed the French to be still in the interior of France. In the fortress of Ulm, on October 20, 1805, the Austrian commander ignominiously surrendered his not inconsiderable army.

An appalling, an almost incredible beginning! For a long time nobody in London would believe it. But at last, so great in theory was the preponderance of a united Europe, there arose the hope that his victory at Ulm might mean ultimate disaster for Napoleon if he allowed himself to be decoyed farther into Central Europe while Prussians, British, and Russians attacked him from the rear. Now, more than ever, all depended upon the entry of Prussia.

Naturally, Bonaparte's most charming intermediary, General Duroc, had reached Berlin far in advance of the allies' special commission, where he appeared early in September, with a highly tempting offer of coalition. His game was actually half won when the news came that Napoleon had sent an army corps through Prussian territory. Deeply offended by this breach of neutrality, King Frederick William turned to the allies, so it happened that the Czar Alexander, traveling to Berlin incognito as the Comte du Nord, arrived in the very nick of time. A treaty was signed, according to which Prussia bound herself to enter the war after December 15, provided that Napoleon did not accept before then the equitable conditions for world peace that Frederick William was to transmit to him.

But political morals had sunk so low that in order to give even a semblance of weight to this treaty the King and the Czar thought it necessary to descend into the family vaults of the Hohenzollerns and there, over the casket of Frederick the Great, swear eternal friendship.

What good did it do? "Even during this scene," Lombard, the Cabinet Councilor, told the French Ambassador soon afterward, "the King was thinking only of how he could best escape the Russian pressure."

Hardly had the Comte du Nord left Berlin to rejoin his army, then operating in Bohemia, when Lord Harrowby, a member of the British Cabinet and an intimate friend of Pitt, arrived. "The whole fortune of the war," said Pitt, in explaining the nature of his mission to the distinguished but frail statesman, "and the destiny of Europe may turn upon our having a person on the spot at Berlin in whom unlimited confidence can be placed and who may turn the favourable disposition at Berlin to the best advantage. . . ." "The encouragement you are enabled to hold out, and the knowledge of our naval victories will, I trust, add all that is wanting to bring forth the full exertions of the Continent. In that case, the past misfortunes, and even any that may happen in the interval of the next three weeks, will be soon repaired: and we shall still see Bonaparte's army either cut off or driven back to France, and Holland recovered before Christmas. . . ."

All this, no doubt, was far from impossible. But Lord Harrowby was delayed by fog over the English Channel, and what he was forced to hear when at last he reached Berlin was of such nature that he suffered several immediate and violent hemorrhages, and begged Pitt to send a ship to Hamburg with his coffin.

"It grieves me to the soul to think that your sanguine expectations of the immediate junction of Prussia are so likely to be disappointed. . . ." The first disappointment was that Prussia wanted to wait until December 15, when perhaps all would have been lost in Bohemia. The second, that in return for her help Prussia was to receive Hanover, which Napoleon had already promised her in any case; and how could a representative of the Elector of Hanover, who was also the King of England, acquiesce in such a monstrous extortion?

All that Lord Harrowby and the Czar could achieve was the information that von Haugwitz, the Foreign Minister, had really set off to meet the irresistibly advancing Napoleon somewhere toward the southeast, and submit to him the Prussian offer of mediation. But von Haugwitz traveled slowly, for in Prague he was attacked by diarrhea, from which, he wrote to Berlin, he must first entirely recover.

Bending over his maps in London, Pitt wore himself out in waiting and hoping. "Nothing from Harrowby?"

In Vienna, Gentz reviewed his prophesies. Good God! What sort of statesmen were these? When there had still been a chance of winning Prussia over they had neglected her, and now they were fawning upon her with humiliating entreaties. "No, no!" he wrote to Hammond, who also had hurried to Berlin. "Prussia must intervene as an auxiliary power, not as a protector. . . . If our forces are well organized we *must*, together with Russia, be strong enough to defend south Germany and Austria. All that Prussia can and should do is to carry out a great and conclusive diversion, an attack on Holland and Belgium. . . ." Still more emphatically did he oppose the idea that Prussian intervention might lead to a restoration of the conditions that prevailed before the war. "This war was not undertaken to preserve the status quo; it was undertaken to change the status quo, and woe betide us if ever this should be forgotten.

It was undertaken to drive the French out of Italy. It was undertaken to restore their independence to Holland, to Switzerland, and to the German Empire. . . . And if it does not lead us to that goal there will be good proof that no other will ever be able to do so. If this war should be lost there will be nothing left but to resign ourselves to the general destruction. It *must* not be lost. . . ."

It distressed Gentz to close such a letter with a request for money, but the French had marched down the Danube without encountering any resistance, and unless some miracle happened they would soon be in Vienna. Then where should he go, and where could he get the necessary funds? For Gentz never had any money ahead.

"Unfortunately the enemy may appear any day now before the gates of the city. I know that my name stands very near the top of the black list drawn up by these criminals. . . . Therefore I must disappear in good time. . . ."

The advocate of coalition was physically no great hero; self-seeking, highly intellectual men seldom are. The collapse of his dearest hopes; the realization of his worst presentiments; the approach of the triumphant enemy; the incapacity and carelessness of the men about him; his loneliness amidst a group whom he served but who did not understand him, and mistrusted him as an alien —all this was thoroughly depressing. He was shaken by sobs as he left Vienna, on November 8, in the carriage of a military friend, with little money and many unfinished manuscripts in his pockets. Alas, "not to succeed at the moment when everything of value in life depended on success; not to succeed, but instead to read the triumphant reports in the damned newspapers of this hellish band and the exultation of their adherents in Germany; it fills my mind entirely, and leaves no room for other sorrows. The rabble here, and this time I mean the higher nobility and the army, are able to see at present only the immediate future, which is a matter of complete indifference to me. May the Devil take us if we do not deserve to live!"

Johannes von Müller consoled him with historical analogies.

In long lines the carriages of the court, the ministers, and the nobility rumbled along the highway toward Bohemia. Brünn, the capital city of Moravia, selected as a temporary capital, seemed halfway safe, for strict orders had been given to blow up the bridges over the Danube as soon as the French were in Vienna. They marched in without a struggle and the Municipal Council announced itself at their disposal, anxious to help in preserving order even under the heel of the conqueror. The bridges were not destroyed, and on November 20 Napoleon set up his headquarters in Brünn.

But by then Gentz was some hundred miles farther on, in Olmütz, where the Austrian Emperor and the Czar held miserable council together. The monarchs embraced, and their officers glared at one another while recriminations over the war and the defeat flew back and forth among them. Negotiations with the enemy went on almost uninterruptedly, imperial messages were exchanged, and couriers sent hither and thither. The ostensible purpose of all these schemes was to delay Napoleon's military activities and divert his attention until December 15, the day upon which the Prussian decision fell due.

It was only too apparent, however, that Cobenzl had wholly different possibilities in mind. He was, indeed, toying with the idea that through a separate peace he might be able to buy off himself and his like from further difficulties and anxieties. It was definitely stipulated in their covenant, to be sure, that Russia and Austria would under no conditions make peace separately. But was there any treaty against the breaking of treaties? Was there even an Austrian Empire any longer? The civil administrations in its main centers were in the hands of the enemy, and functioning perfectly; in the farthest corner of the land cowered the legitimate government, protected by Russian troops, impotent, and ignorant of the fate of the last Austrian Army, now moving about somewhere in Hungary. Was not the surrender of a few provinces better than this intolerable situation, if one could only continue to govern the rest in peace, and draw taxes from them? On the other hand, Cobenzl weighed the possibility of retreating over the border into Prussian Silesia.

If only Prussia would make up her mind!

On November 28 von Haugwitz, the Prussian Foreign Minister, actually approached Napoleon at Brünn, but met an icy welcome. The Emperor sent for a coach and horses and ordered the exhausted diplomat taken to Vienna, where he arrived in a state of complete physical and mental collapse. There he was to discuss provisionally with Talleyrand his proposals for mediation.

He who for years has piled error upon error seldom lacks opportunities to forsake the downward path and save himself before it is too late, but it is highly improbable that he will take advantage of them; else he would have done so long before reaching his final unhappy situation. Even toward the end of November, 1805, the allies could still have destroyed the absurd Napoleonic Empire before it had reached its zenith. It was only a matter of avoiding battle and luring the Intruder after them until the northern powers could attack him from the rear. Gentz, though a dilettante in military affairs, saw this, and explained it at headquarters to anyone that would listen. In Olmütz, a little town overtaxed by the presence of two emperors and an enormous, idle political machine, the incurable adventurer sat and cried out that they should wait now for Prussian help. Secretly, he had almost lost hope. "What depresses and torments and unmans me, often brings me close to despair, and makes me want to abandon the whole thing is the everlasting pettiness of the men and the means by which this Austrian state expects to be saved!"

Napoleon succeeded in making the Czar believe that he feared above all things a decisive test of strength, and that his enemies would therefore have good cause to put one in motion. Young Alexander accordingly resolved to do so, and the town of Austerlitz, where the stage was set, has given its name to one of the world's great battles.

From Olmütz Gentz had turned farther to the northeast, toward Troppau, probably because he feared for his safety. In this beautiful city, with its baroque architecture, he stayed over for a few days as the protector, or the protégé, of two highly placed ladies who were generously supplied with money and equipages and here, during the night of December 3–4, he received the bad news. Napoleon, disregarding as always the established rules of warfare, breaking through with concentrated power at one point as was his custom, and then spreading out behind the center of his opponent to cut off his retreat, had won the battle. It had been a bitter and a bloody day, and looking about him toward evening Alexander found no means with which he could continue to resist; nothing at the moment; nothing, that is, that these gentlemen were capable of conceiving. That battle lost, the war was lost.

Lying in his hotel bedroom at Troppau, sleepless and with furiously pounding heart, Gentz envisaged all the inevitable misery of the future. The mob of professional politicians, the ministers, and the generals probably did not understand their predicament. He, the writer, driven into politics by his passionate inclination, understood it for them. The coalition had come to an end. The war had come to an end. Freedom in Europe had come to an end. Languid hopes, springing up in the very face of these facts, were considered for a moment and then brushed away: Prussia is still there, and under obligations after December 15—but one need only know von Haugwitz and Lombard. At a rather liberal estimate the Russians alone still have more troops than the "Demoniac." The Archduke Karl must be somewhere in Hungary with an undefeated Austrian Army—but he admires Napoleon and has always opposed the war, and certainly will do nothing now to prolong it. Cobenzl will no doubt be forced out of office, though not because of his actual misdeeds. His successor? Where is there even one competent successor? Even if there were one he certainly would not be appointed, for the very reason that he is competent. No, Great Britain will not capitulate, at least while Pitt continues in office. But suppose he were to fall, in consequence of the deplorable miscarriage of his policies? Suppose that Fox, god of the pacifists and friend of Napoleon, were to succeed him? In such a case another Amiens does not seem so impossible. Are not the British always in a position to remain independent, to blockade the Continent and leave it to its own shame? Does the Continent really deserve any better? Is this not exactly what a true friend of Great Britain would now have to advise?

But in that case what would become of him, of Friedrich Gentz? He was not at all deeply impressed by Napoleon's triumphs, for he understood far too well his own period and the nature of those whose cause he had espoused and who should have defended this cause, his and theirs, yet did not. He was not impressed. Not he! But the masses, after their nature, would now regard the Conqueror as a god.

"I have long foreseen what is happening," he said to himself, "but now that it is actually here I cannot help being overcome by rage and pain, and hardly know how I shall be able to go on living." Naturally, the catastrophe had not seemed to him unavoidable. He had hoped for the best, and had imagined, dreaded, and anticipated the worst only as a possibility. But when an evil that we have feared really comes to pass we easily convince ourselves that we had always recognized it as inevitable, so that we may be right in one thing at least. In the present instance there had been ample cause for pessimism. The selfish indifference, the overweening ignorance, the contempt for everything unfamiliar, the indolent bureaucracy of the leaders; yes, alas, and the unholy Peace of 1797 and the disgraceful sharing of Italy with Bonaparte: nemesis, nemesis! The

Conqueror could hardly be expected to relinquish lands that he now occupied; there would be new, high-sounding names and another so-called final arrangement of the Continent.

Well, nothing was final. The war had been conducted just as politics had been conducted during the years before it broke out: blindly, from day to day. And now peace would be concluded in the same manner. Already there were new illusions, hopes for chivalrous coöperation with the Victor. Chivalrous coöperation with Bonaparte! A group of spineless characters could never prevail against a single strong one; by virtue of mere numbers they should be able to, but the necessary resolution was lacking.

The next morning Gentz began writing letters, and gathering up the broken threads of his political connections as best he could. If Austria made a separate peace, all was lost for him. Had he not been the leader of the War party? He was Warmonger Number One. That he had persisted in his admonitions against making war as long as Cobenzl and his group were in power, persisted until his blood had boiled and he had nearly gone mad, this would hardly be taken into account now. He would be regarded as an alien, an immigrant who had abused the hospitality of Austria in order to satisfy his hatred. Had not his Viennese friends already begun to treat him with marked coolness?

To Johannes von Müller he wrote: "To these sordid minds nothing else is of consequence if only 'He' would give up Vienna. If they were to go down with it, what joy the fall of the Empire would bring!"

He said in a letter to Francis Jackson that the only hope for the defeated nations was to make a common peace, disregarding the loss of a few provinces, for a new peace could not well be more impossible than the old one; and if Great Britain, Austria, and Russia only remained in close agreement the war could be resumed after a few years.

Soon, however, both Russia and Austria were on better terms with France than with each other, and Napoleon was far from lying when he said that he could easily make a covenant at any time with either one of these partners against the other; the rage of the Russians toward their allies, according to Gentz, "amounted to frenzy."

Austria deserted the coalition two days after the battle of Austerlitz. Thus her Emperor, as Gentz reconstructed the scene, "resolved magnanimously to betake himself to the headquarters of the shameless Usurper, who awaited only this one last triumph to regard the Continent as his own private property. The Imperial Charlatan, surrounded by all his generals, gentlemen-in-waiting, and masters-of-ceremonies, was gracious and mild. He actually guaranteed peace, and declared that he would be found moderate and reasonable. . . ." Cobenzl, the "putrescent corpse," had preferred to remain away from the meeting. The first condition of the armistice was that the Russians must evacuate all Austrian territory, and this they did, ostensibly under compulsion but in fact not unwillingly.

Gentz, who wanted above all things to keep out of the hands of the French, fled before them in company with his two aristocratic ladies. In Breslau, the capital of Silesia, there lived an old friend and former chief, the Provincial Governor, Count Hoym, and here Gentz hoped to receive temporary asylum. Hoym received the fugitive kindly, but no one can escape anxieties by mere change of scene. Breslau was swarming with Russian officers, making their way through Silesia back to Poland, and their open contempt for Austrians, and particularly for Germans, was to Gentz intolerable.

"I know well that we can hardly uphold our honor as Germans any longer; our rulers have seen to that . . ." he wrote to Johannes von Müller.

For his part, Napoleon made use of this estrangement to play Germany against Russia, and to rally Europe by rhetoric against Muscovite barbarism. "Plundering, burning, and murdering are the favorite sports of the Russians," read one of his bulletins. "They kill even priests before the altar! Woe betide the ruler who summons such help into his land! The battle of Austerlitz was a victory for *Europe*, since it destroyed the spurious renown of these barbarians."

Europe against Russia, Europe against Great Britain. Peaceful Europe, united at last!

When Gentz looked away from the Russians to his own compatriots he saw that they heedlessly swallowed this fabricated nonsense as though it were eternal truth itself. To Jackson he wrote: "Bonapartist, philanthropic, pacifistic reptiles swarm here like earthworms after rain."

Meanwhile, he knew exactly how von Haugwitz, the Prussian Minister, would fulfill his mission of intervention in Vienna, though actually he had received no information of any sort. "After the battle von Haugwitz will not have dared to submit his proposals to the Man, and even if he had he would have been laughed to scorn. . . . The French will ignore him in his role of negotiator for the coalition, treating him as a representative of Prussia who is empowered to adjust the little differences that may exist between Prussia and His Napoleonic Majesty, and instead of listening to his conditions will lay before him those of the Emperor of the World. . . . Von Haugwitz will have the interests of England, of Austria, of Russia, the honor of Europe, and the balance of power as little in mind as he has the moon and stars. But he will not forget to mention certain Prussian desires for expansion. . . ."

Precisely this was taking place in the castle at Schönbrunn while Gentz, in impotent rage, was depicting the scene in Breslau, and the final result was an alliance between France and Prussia. For the British diplomats, who had had a melancholy rendezvous in Berlin, there was nothing more but to leave the Continent immediately, their hearts filled with bitter contempt.

"Heavens!" wrote General Paget to his brother, the Ambassador, "What has Prussia to answer for! For nothing less, in my mind, than every calamity which has befallen Europe for more than ten years."

For almost ten years Gentz had recognized the significance and the delinquency of Prussia in this great crisis, and the furious contest that he had waged since 1799 against Lombard, a petty Cabinet Councilor unknown to the world, had been in reality a well-intentioned struggle for the future of Europe.

Nevertheless, he was now inclined, as he wrote to Johannes von Müller, to lay the blame for the collapse of the Third Coalition principally on the British Government; ". . . almost always competent in domestic affairs, sadly ignorant, pertinacious, and incorrigible in foreign affairs. The chief fault was London's. Four or five statesmen there simply would not listen when qualified observers shouted themselves hoarse, and gave themselves writer's cramp, in an effort to explain that unless the Austrian ministry were overthrown every attempt to cast off the shackles of Europe would be wholly in vain; that to let Russia occupy the foreground and play the chief role, instead of keeping her in the rear merely as a bulwark, was a perverse and ruinous line of conduct; and finally, that without Prussia's full and timely coöperation against France it would be utterly impossible to accomplish anything."

It was said, to be sure, that Pitt could not alter the base characters of the Continental statesmen; but one was in duty bound to understand the men with whom one worked, and to take all their faults and weaknesses into account. Here the reproaches of Gentz coincided with those of the British Opposition. Was delaying the danger of invasion for five months the sole result of such desperate exertions and chances? Why had no effective diversion, no landing on the Continent, been undertaken to relieve Austria and Russia? What negligence, had a landing been possible! If impossible, what an outlook for the future!

It may be that William Pitt had been overwhelmed in the Lower House by such importunate questions as these. In any case, he replied to them no longer, and four weeks after the Austrian separate peace he died, brokenhearted. The last book that he had ordered from a circulating library in Bath was Schiller's *Thirty Years' War*.

Gentz learned of the death of his great patron, in Dresden whither he had gone from Breslau. After Prussia had openly allied herself with the new order it was impossible that he should remain there any longer, but Saxony was neutral and for the moment forgotten, and here the last, scattered members of the disbanded War party assembled.

VIII

WHY PRUSSIA FELL

WAS the war over? For Austria, yes, and her defeat had been so prompt and so overwhelming that Napoleon might well hope to bring the nations still involved to full realization of the true state of affairs. Theoretically the Russians were still engaged, though without a proper front. The British, too, continued in the war and had recently become undisputed masters of their own theater, the sea, but they could not operate directly on the Continent. Feeble efforts at an agreement between Great Britain and France, and between Russia and France, had been inspired by the apprehension that this war could never be ended by hostilities; yet for the hundredth time they led to the conclusion that it could never be ended by peaceful means either.

Meanwhile Napoleon reaped the fruits of the Austrian collapse, tearing down and building up on the Continent as though sure that his creations would last forever. How easy then to make and unmake! Monarchistic systems were preserved and even enhanced, but vacant thrones were given over to the ludicrous family of the Dictator, which, whether he liked it or not, was the surest way of making monarchism ridiculous.

The new governments combined the spirit of absolutism with that of the Revolution; privileges disappeared, boundaries were wiped out, and new political units arose as the times demanded. But was it so easy to contend against all this? Would not an opposition in its turn have to employ essentially the same measures? And where, after all, was the opposition whose triumph ought to be so ardently desired? Was not everyone, or almost everyone, affected by the victorious spirit of the times; committed to it and identified with it?

The south German rulers, in so far as their domains had not vanished, seceded from the Holy Roman Empire and formed the Confederation of the Rhine, with Napoleon at its head. Nothing remained for Franz II, Holy Roman Emperor, but to surrender the ancient crown of Charlemagne, which his family had worn for so many centuries, and content himself with a new title created beforehand as a precaution: Franz I, Hereditary Emperor of Austria.

Gentz's comment on all this was: "Everything is surely over now, for the little that remains can be so easily supplied in imagination that even the pleasure of surprise no longer remains to us." Who could have foreseen these things ten years previously? But now that matters had gone so far the incurable moralist could not help seeking moral grounds for such an incredibly rapid transformation, and found it in the fact that what the Germans themselves had done to the Poles Napoleon was now doing to them in return.

Gentz remained in Dresden, for it had become clear that he would no longer be of use to Vienna unless he exercised more restraint in the future over his writing and talking. But this he would never do. "The times are too serious for life to be wasted!" Dresden, capital of a small neutral state lying between Prussia, Austria, and Russia, was a suitable place in which to stay, for it boasted the presence of a diplomatic corps, and many travelers passed through it. It appeared doubtful in the extreme, however, that this vestige of a happy freedom could be preserved much longer. "Saxony is like an island in the midst of a raging ocean," he wrote to his friend Mackintosh, in Bombay. "It is impossible that it should long continue to enjoy this fortunate privilege. . . . I have followed from here in torment the drama of the great dissolution, consoled only by the presence of so many curious émigrés from all parts of Europe."

Thanks to his old patron, Lord Grenville, who now presided over the "cabinet of all the talents," Gentz continued to receive money from London and could afford to live in the best hotel in the city, the Golden Angel, which soon became the center of his political intrigues. Here he was visited by Count d'Antraigues, the veteran agent-in-chief of the French emigration, he who once left his portfolio in an Italian hired carriage and thus became responsible for the discovery of so many conspiracies. Here might have been seen, also, Count Clemens Metternich, the newly appointed Austrian Ambassador in Paris; and the influential spokesman of the Prussian opposition, Baron vom und zum Stein, stopped over at the Golden Angel and aroused in Gentz the highest enthusiasm. "Minister vom Stein, who stayed here for a few days, is the foremost statesman in Germany. If I lived in Berlin I should certainly make use of him. With his deep insight and fine character it would be only a question of guaranteeing him support, for he is fully resolved to act. But even he cannot act entirely alone. . . ."

Vom Stein wanted to replace Lombard in the Cabinet and force Prussia's entry into the war, and this was Gentz's wish also.

So much was clear: That only Prussian intervention would

cause the war to flare up again and pass from sinister smoldering into an active phase. But it might be asked whether a new front offered by Prussia would not be more helpful to Napoleon than to the allies; for was there any reason to hope that Prussia would fare any better than Austria? Was it not plain obstinacy for Gentz to pin his hopes on Prussia once more? Now? After all that had happened? Like an unskillful chess player, moving one piece after another in the hope that a fourth will succeed where a first, and a second, and a third failed?

Johannes von Müller, friend of Gentz, famous historical writer, who still drafted the proclamations of the Prussian War party, did not want to be longer associated with such gamblers and was inclined to abandon them. Immediately after the debacle at Ulm he proposed to Gentz that they go to India, "the British Empire on the Ganges," whither, he thought, many Europeans would now flee. For this reason he preferred to seek introductions there rather than in America, where, he said, there were only tradesmen with no sense for literature. After the Austrian separate peace he had made up his mind to follow the example of King David: ". . . While the child was yet alive, I fasted and wept. . . . But now he is dead, wherefore should I fast?" Accordingly he went to work again on his history of Switzerland, but became more and more restless. Could it be possible that he, the *Geheimrat,* had made a mistake? At least from a practical standpoint, and in the final analysis from a historical standpoint as well? To give up politics and dwell in the seclusion of a Swiss mountain valley would be pleasant indeed. But what to live on? "I cannot live without any salary," he wrote to Gentz, "especially if all my literary earnings stop." "The passion for the common good that might otherwise inspire me has cooled down not a little, for the common good is disappearing; but it is impossible to enjoy a salary without doing some work in return. . . ." In the summer of 1806 he began to talk of a Tusculum,* of peace, of purely literary activities. "I do not want to be involved in any more useless controversies. . . ."

Gentz, who knew his friend well, tried in vain to stop this trend toward civic and moral cowardice. "It is true that the times are appalling and every day become more appalling. But were we not prepared for all that is now taking place?" "Under their present governments Russia, Austria, and Prussia are wholly incapable of

* A country resort just outside Rome where Cicero wrote his *Tusculan Disputations* and other philosophical works.

any good, and to about the same degree. That is my firm conviction. What, then, is to be done? Must we despair of everything, surrender everything? By no means! We, that is, you, I, and the few who are with us, must act constantly as though the great powers would come to their senses at any moment. For us to be misled by their wickedness, their moral bankruptcy, would be dangerous in the extreme; to share it would be base. The problem that we must solve is to combine a clear insight into the endless difficulties of our position with the unrelenting courage and active resolution that are the first proviso of salvation. . . ." "Does the world stand still at some unhappy point? Does not its perpetual rotation bring new combinations and new hopes every day? Do not desert the cause, I implore you. . . ."

On one occasion von Müller even visited Dresden, and the disgusting old man was so entranced by Gentz's personality as to send him the most nauseating love letters. But his morale was not conspicuously strengthened.

In the awkward situation wherein Gentz found himself the young Count Metternich became his best intermediary with Vienna. Gentz admired in him the consummate air of "the so-called eighteenth century"; he admired his *savoir faire*, his tempered narcissism, his smiling calm, his comeliness, his youth; all of which was combined with the friendliness and intellect to be expected in one of his class and calling. Here was a man of a type wholly different from the wretched Cobenzl; a man whose bearing could impress even the new barbarians and who still realized what principles meant. As early as 1805 Gentz had recognized in this thirty-two-year-old diplomat the future political chief of Austria.

"I have piled memoir upon memoir, contrived one artifice after another, to induce the Emperor to put you in charge of affairs. . . . For all in all you are the one man in the monarchy who has all the qualifications for management and the fewest defects." Thus it was with deep regret that Gentz now saw Metternich accept the ambassadorship to the Court of St. Cloud, a post where the wretchedness of the European situation was more profoundly felt than anywhere else and which, so he feared, might sully the principles of this young knight.

But Metternich thought otherwise. He believed that a man must adapt himself to his surroundings, and that even at Napoleon's military and *opéra bouffe* court it would be possible to live the life of a polished cavalier. He had sufficient aplomb and enthusiasm for the purpose. He allowed Gentz, his mentor, to see only his most thoughtful side, and wrote to him at length about the complete overturn that his own generation was condemned to experience. "Europe is going up in flames. Those who will not conquer will be conquered. Of this eternal truth *the only man in Europe who wills and acts* has given us dreadful verification."

But was his actual subjugation necessary? In their conferences at the Golden Angel Gentz explained to the young diplomat that it was not a question of overthrowing the Conqueror but of opposing him with new moral weapons as well as with military measures. The capitulation at Ulm, the lack of Prussian help, the catastrophe at Austerlitz, and the Russian retreat were not mere chance events. On the contrary, they were the expression of one single and repeatedly demonstrated fact: the weakness of the allies.

Where were these new moral weapons to be had? Gentz could think only of an alliance of *all* the remaining powers, the appointment of strong ministers, and the renunciation of every selfish motive. Yet even then one could hope only to counterbalance Napoleon, "to protect the tottering old building against the oncoming flood." Little enough to ask, surely.

The opinion spread furtively about that Napoleon's "new federative system" was inevitable, circulated by those who knew what they wanted and accepted by those who wanted no more than a merely tolerable life but who, even at the opening of the war, had hoped that the allies would win. Now they were coolly saying, as a foregone conclusion and not without malice toward those of opposite opinion, that the future belonged to the French. And why not? The Emperor Napoleon was a great man, whereas his adversaries apparently amounted to nothing. Gentz read it in the newspapers and pamphlets of the day, he heard it in the salons of the aristocrats and the shops of the people. Once more truth seemed to be on the side of the liar. That there was little to admire in Napoleon's enemies, who could deny? Gentz held his peace.

He roamed about the beautiful city of Dresden and saw everybody enjoying the spring, the young people beginning to bathe in the Elbe as usual, and realized that not one of them all had the slightest interest in international politics. Could it be otherwise? But should it be so, when there was one man, Bonaparte, so desperately in earnest about politics? Was not that nation already lost without knowing it whose citizens, whose youth, pursued their daily life in accordance with the maxim: "*Edite, bibite, post mortem nulla voluptas*"? * Was not this selfishness of the masses the real basis for the "new federative system"?

He had to set it down: All that he knew about the latest happenings; all his disillusions and his hopes; the past, the present, and the future; as well, as exactly, as impressively as he could.

"When a people," he wrote, "are so immersed in their own affairs and have such a mean and limited outlook that all public interests are alien to them, when the value of independence is balanced against the smallest and shabbiest benefits, and the loss of all freedom and dignity becomes a matter of indifference, then the time for appeal to the nobler sentiments has already passed by. Subjection is complete even before the tyrant appears; the state has dissolved even before its visible collapse; and at the first test by catastrophe those who no longer had the energy to maintain a place in the sun will surrender to the powers of darkness." Then the people, impatient of public affairs, must surely learn what they refused to hear while there was yet time: that honor, freedom, and power are no illusory notions, and that their loss means also paralysis of industry and trade, unemployment, poverty, hunger, and thirst. A world tyranny like that of Bonaparte had no respect for the dignity of a conquered people, for their culture, their industries, or their personal security and freedom. It could not respect them, Gentz prophesied with grim satisfaction. The indifferent; the cynical; the practical; and youth, in all its greed for pleasure, would realize too late upon what their most intimate joys, love, marriage, and gaining a livelihood had really depended.

All were to blame. He himself had often said that the governments were at fault; and so they were, as far as any government could be. But though virtually exempt from popular control they had acted at bottom, nevertheless, in accordance with the temper of their subjects.

"Rulers, it is said, educate their subjects, and in a certain sense this is true. But in a higher and more general sense it will be found that subjects educate their rulers and that these, regarded as parts of the whole, are continuously and necessarily the product of their total environment. Even the most exhaustive account of all the blunders and faults of the rulers will not fully explain the dreadful turmoil that Europe has gone through in the past decade. The history of this disorder will remain for posterity an incomprehensible chaos,

* Eat, drink. There is no pleasure after death.

an empty outline, unless it includes a clear and vivid description of the condition of the various nations; their share in the general debacle, their progress toward good or evil, their aspirations, their endeavors, their mistakes, their moral and political decay. All biased criticism of their rulers, all accusations directed at these alone, are due either to prejudice or a lack of understanding. The fairest and the hardest, the best and the worst that can be said of them, is this: they faithfully represented their own times."

It was the duty of the leading men to rationalize and express in official terms what the kings and their subjects alike wanted to hear. "From these men we have experienced the uttermost. Year after year the seducers of a gullible age have left nothing undone to ridicule and cast suspicion upon those who were bold enough to draw aside the curtain that concealed the horrors of the future, and have recommended precisely those measures that would exclude any chance of improvement. It was only necessary, they said, to remain discreetly silent, calm, peaceable, and, above all, inactive; of itself the overflowing stream would soon return to its proper bed. Dominion of the world, they said, was an obvious impossibility. The possession by France of a few provinces or strongholds more or less would have no permanent effect on Europe; all the larger nations still stood fast. French domination had reached its natural limits, and her new ruler would be too wise to stray beyond them. For the present there was nothing further to be feared, they said, and time would take care of the rest.

"This soporific and perfidious doctrine was applauded by the people and all the various courts. Among the causes of our present ruin it has been the most effective, for out of it have come nearly all the inconsistent suggestions, the inadequate measures, and the political and military mistakes to which we owe the disaster of the recent campaign. When this catastrophe had reached gigantic proportions, first through the natural growth of an irresistible lust for power, and then through inept and feeble attempts at salvation, precarious in nature and patched up with crumbling and reluctant material, those who had nourished and assisted it by their treacherous reasons for complacency took refuge in a new sophistry to reconcile their dupes to what could no longer be concealed. It cannot now be denied that the predictions so often ridiculed have been amply justified and abundantly fulfilled; and that one single lawless will has 'redistributed the nations, stolen and dispersed their resources, and overthrown their peoples'; that there are hardly three independent rulers left between the Tagus and the Volga; and that the time between the actual completion and the formal declaration and ceremonious recognition of world domination is now to be measured not in years but in months and days. All this is so appallingly clear that no one would be daring enough to conceal it from the blindest of eyes.

"But even yet the store of deception is not exhausted. What can no longer be scorned as vagary, or rejected as fiction, is now called an endurable evil or even an advantage, and the frivolity of the times keeps pace also with this willful misconstruction. He who still has the heart to observe attentively the state of mind that prevails today, the political talk, the temper of society, and the progress and direction of public opinion will soon be convinced that, except for the infinitely few who with genuine patriotism and real international consciousness (which in their higher sense are identical) deplore the humiliating decline of Europe, the masses in all countries can be divided in a general way into two groups. One, and by far the larger, regards the events of this destructive period with indifference; the other, with satisfaction. . . ."

With satisfaction! "It is not merely grounds for consolation that we are offered, wherewith to soften an unavoidable fate, but unmistakable congratulations; exhortations to courage and joy. One assures us with philosophical profundity that what appears so dreadful may very well be, when seen in its true light, the easiest and surest road to perpetual peace; war, the unparalleled evil, would soon vanish from the earth if all acknowledged one ruler. Another believes, and not entirely without reason if only the conclusion followed from the premise, that the old political structure has become so weary and lifeless; the ties between individual members everywhere so loosely knit; and the spirit that ought to hold them together so exhausted, so weak, and so petty, that its extinction must not be inordinately mourned but rather desired and encouraged as a token of better things to come; the vigorous and productive rule of an absolute sovereign would rejuvenate and revivify everything. A third relies on the personal greatness of the man selected by Providence for a guarantee that the world will be governed according to His design; when all strife is over and all hampering enmities are removed, his mighty genius will repair everything, and transform a happily reunited Europe into a scene of well-being and abundance, of brilliance and renown.

"The people listen, not with perfect confidence, perhaps, but at least without antagonism, and in the minds of most there is something that predisposes them favorably. They long for peace. They firmly believe that the present tormenting, deranged, and turbulent situation indicates some definite outcome: either order will be restored, or the disorganization will finally be complete and everything will have to begin anew. But as the road to the former seems much longer and harder than the road to the latter they gradually accustom themselves to regard this last extreme of evil as a sort of haven, and little as they may originally have contemplated becoming accessories yield at last to the most guilty of all wishes."

If this was the psychological situation, if both the leaders and the led were thinking along these lines, where in all the world was help to be found? Gentz had tried to revolutionize governments, and had failed. That the masses everywhere were to rise against France—this had never occurred to him and his mind was so constructed that it never could have occurred to him. He lived in the belief of a community of states that transcended nationalism and was founded on a Christian civilization, which was everywhere the same. But this community, in so far as there still was one at all, was a company of the elite, of the aristocrats and the educated; the masses had no share in it. To win them over, more vigorous, selfish, and irrational motives would have to be invoked; motives opposed as much to cosmopolitan partnership as to Bonaparte's universal domination; motives such as democracy and nationalism. For this reason Gentz had never appealed to the masses.

He realized that Napoleon's triumph rested largely on the cynical indifference of the vanquished, but his reaction was contempt, not a wish to reform. It would have had to be a democratic reform, hence its language could not be other than demagogic, and here the great expert on political methods reached the limit of his powers. Casting about for a savior between leaders who did not lead, and the led, who could be drawn hither and thither, he came upon those who neither governed nor would be governed, who lived in the clouds, and among whom he himself belonged; the detached, the intellectuals. Them he addressed as "the strong, the pure, and the good." "You, who in the shipwreck of our times are beset by death and ruin yet continue to preserve those first and most precious of all blessings: a free and comprehensive mind; a brave and faithful heart; a reverence for what is sacred to all mankind; the courage to sacrifice everything for it; and faith in the future; you, staunch heroes of the century; tried by fire; undismayed by the general despair;

always triumphant in mind and in deed; misjudged by the multitude; and, fortunately, perhaps, despised and hated by those flatulent demagogues who would take the world by storm and whom the rabble revere as gods: do not tire and do not lose hope! . . ."

It was an escape into the realm of personality and into the reaches of the mind that the author-statesman so suddenly effected here. Where he and his compeers dwelt there was everlasting freedom, and all Napoleon's meddling with history vanished like a bad dream.

With this appeal he concluded the Preface to his *History of the Balance of Power in Europe*, which he had begun in the preceding fall with such brave hopes. It was published as a fragment, ostensibly in St. Petersburg but actually in Riga, by Hartknoch. It was a bold step, for if he had fallen into the hands of the French there is no doubt that he would have been shot, as was the Nuremberg bookseller who dared to sell a brochure directed against the Emperor.

But what did life matter? Anything that remained unsaid now could soon not be said at all. A few months hence not a printer on the Continent would touch such an article. That was in the nature of things, from which there is no escape, and least of all when misfortune threatens.

Hardly had he finished his swan song, however, when hope, irrationally enough, began to flicker in him once more.

Prussia entered the war. Why just at this time, in September, 1806, no one in Dresden knew, though why she should have entered at all was as clear to Gentz as the simplest of diagrams.

During the six months preceding, Prussia's base rulers had learned what Napoleon's friendship was worth. He had cynically betrayed them, now that they were isolated; offered Great Britain the very Hanover that he had spurred them on to annex, and thus involved them in war with her; kept none of his promises; dealt with Germany as though her rulers did not exist; and met their anxious protests with assurances that he was a lover of peace, with plans for the benefit of mankind, and with crude witticisms. The Cabinet of Prussia, he wrote to his Foreign Minister, "is so contemptible . . . that this power cannot be counted on. They will continue to act as they always have acted. They will mobilize, demobilize, mobilize again, absent themselves during the crisis, and then come to terms with the victor." Napoleon had good reason to despise such adversaries. Whether he reduced them to impotence and endless resignation, or finally drove them to a desperate outbreak, was all one to him. In either case he was sure of his next step, for the Prussian War was already in his mind while he was still engaged in hostilities with Austria.

Meanwhile the Cabinet Councilors in Berlin were becoming more and more anxious. No longer could they hide from themselves the unwelcome knowledge that inevitably the moment was drawing near when they would have to choose between a war that would make ruin probable, and a peace that would make it certain. As they were not traitors to the fatherland, but only weak men governed by the exigencies of the moment, they began to steel themselves to the idea of war and to set the most favorable time for beginning it.

Naturally, they made the worst possible choice.

The situation was not really urgent, for in August of 1806 Napoleon was no more of a threat to Prussia than he had been in the months and years preceding. To wait until Austria had recovered herself a little seemed the obvious course, but it was written that every one of the old states should be weighed in the balance and found wanting. Austria's trials over, Prussia's began. Having long betrayed all principles of decency, long been dishonored, discredited, and universally disliked, she now threw herself into a struggle that could have no possible end but disaster.

Nor did anyone try to profit by the experiences of the past year, and the blunders that had ruined the Austrians were repeated with painstaking precision. Once again the attack was made by those who had long endured the most unjust aggression for the sake of peace, so that Napoleon was in a position to entreat the King of Prussia not to have recourse to the madness of war. And once again those who had made the first move believed that, according to precedent, the whole initiative lay with them and must be retained. Instead of delaying matters by negotiations, therefore, instead of beginning the war with a retreat, and relying on Russia for help, they sent their army, far inferior even in numbers, toward Thuringia to meet this experienced master of war.

Experienced? To them he did not appear to be so, as long as they had not tested him for themselves.

The tactics of Frederick the Great were now more than forty years old, and while Prussia was still said to be the traditional military power that she had been in his day there was ample room for doubt. Nevertheless, this was the consensus, for nothing was known to the contrary. Most of the higher officers were actually of that legendary period, but beside them, or under them, there were younger, more mettlesome, more thoughtful officers, writers by avocation, of whom a group headed by Prince Louis Ferdinand swore on the eve of battle "to stake our lives without question and not to survive this war, where fame and high honor await us, or political freedom and liberal ideas will be stifled and overthrown if it should turn out disastrously." An extraordinary reversal of values, though these men were unquestionably sincere to the highest degree. They were defending liberty against the Revolution or counter-revolution of the equalitarian Tyrant who was no longer an equalitarian—but let us abandon all such generalization and hairsplitting. Revolutionary or not, Napoleon represented bondage, and it required no subtle discrimination to recognize this instantly. Those who lived under him felt it instinctively.

A high summer of despair gave place to an early and distracted fall. Prussian troops entered Dresden and Louis Ferdinand called on Gentz. There was time for discussions, for love affairs, and for suppers under the trees that shaded the mansions of the rich across the mountains. While couriers rode, and armies marched, fate came slowly on.

On September 30 Gentz was invited by von Haugwitz to visit Prussian headquarters at Naumburg, where important matters awaited his decision. He left on October 2. What was desired of him was vaguely expressed, yet clear enough. The half-Austrian, half-European agent and political sage was asked to mediate between Prussia and Austria, and perhaps Great Britain; clear up "misunderstandings"; court good will; and, in short, to help. Those who had scoffed at his warnings five years before and scornfully let him emigrate now awaited his assistance and greeted him with anxious friendliness. So eagerly did they receive him, and hang on his words, sighing in unison a relieved, "Thank God, you are here," that he, who by nature was not insusceptible to flattery and emotional gratification, was painfully embarrassed, disquieted, and before long desperate.

Gentz kept an account of his visit to the Prussian Army in a special diary, which was first published after his death in an English translation, and may be numbered among the most successful of political memoirs. "That is truth, that is history," cried Leopold Ranke, the historian, upon reading it; and if what goes on in salons and at headquarters is "history" it must be acknowledged that the days preceding the defeat of Frederick's Prussia could not have been described more authentically.

The mood of these notes is that of a dream whose calamitous end the dreamer mysteriously knows in advance, though they were written down day by day and Gentz could not have foreseen the outcome. But it was to be read in the expression of those with whom he consulted. These unhappy men had humiliated themselves year in and year out, yielding ground both politically and morally, and merely because they were "at war" could not now suddenly become strong, independent, and fired with a spirit of aggression. The less so because the very war itself showed that their former policy of appeasement had been fundamentally wrong, and they were tormented by the consciousness that if it was right to take the course to which they were now committed it should have been taken long since.

None of them had deserted. All were present at headquarters: the friendly enemies of Berlin days, Kabinettsrat Lombard; Kabinettsrat Beyme; Marquis Lucchesini, the Prussian Ambassador in Paris; and Foreign Minister von Haugwitz. There, too, were the ranking military officers, ludicrous old men, maliciously whispering against one another and against the whole system: a ponderous, creaking machine that had not been tested for many years.

A preliminary five-hour talk with General Kalkreuth introduced Gentz to the military situation, and particularly to the conduct of the campaign. It was Kalkreuth's conviction that the mediocrity, the weakness, and the jealousy of the Duke of Brunswick, the Generalissimo, were enough to ruin even a more auspicious undertaking. "Now, remember," said the General at the end of a talk spiced with bitter sarcasm, "if there is not a complete change in our organization within the next eight days this campaign will end in the same way as that of 1792, if not in a catastrophe that will overshadow the battle of Austerlitz."

Unfavorably impressed by the arguments of this shrewd officer, Gentz continued his journey. He spent the night at Weimar, where in bygone days he had passed such delightful evenings with Amalie von Imhoff, but where now all was confusion, and reached Erfurt on the following day. Here he met von Haugwitz, who entertained him at dinner and afterward led him to a private room where the fullest disclosures could be made respecting the purpose of the invitation. "It was more than good of you to come," said the Count with excited amiability. "What we want is only to hear your impression of our undertaking. You must be our friend, and surely you will be if you will just listen to me for a while."

Then von Haugwitz explained how everything had come about; how Prussia had achieved her reputation for duplicity, though in fact her conduct had always been irreproachable. "For a long time we have been convinced that Napoleon and peace are incompatible, but all we could do was to adopt a peaceful disguise, and the dissimulation thus forced upon us could not be abandoned for several reasons. First, because the King, too strongly prejudiced against even the thought of war, deceived himself from year to year with the notion that Napoleon's Empire would collapse through some chance event as suddenly as it arose, and thus we should be saved from a grave crisis to which he could not be induced to expose us save under the most extreme necessity. Secondly, would it not be desirable amidst such threatening conditions that at least one state in Europe should remain intact and prepared for a serious emergency?

"Nevertheless, we were ready to intervene last year. Then, unfortunately, came the battle of Austerlitz and I, entirely alone in Vienna, had to conclude with the Victor that pact of friendship for which I have been so severely criticized. But I swear to you, and have witnesses to prove it, that I myself was opposed to this covenant, and that upon my return to Berlin I implored the King not to ratify it, but to dismiss me instead. My request was not granted. Then I was sent to Paris, where I realized for the first time how the French felt toward us; how they could not stomach our existence with a large, undefeated army; how Napoleon had already selected the moment when he would fall upon us with all his forces and how Talleyrand alone had hitherto delayed the attack. I concealed none of this from the King, and since then we have arranged accordingly to keep Paris in suspense and meanwhile have sought agreements with Russia and the German princes. What else could we do? Do you not admit that our policy was wise, and meant for the best, and that we have nothing to retract? Pray speak with the greatest freedom."

Gentz: "You know what I think of Prussia's policy since the unhappy Peace of Basel. All deference to the King's love of peace; it explains much to me. But I cannot forgive your actually having concluded an alliance with the common enemy and shared his illicit spoils; I cannot possibly reconcile myself to such a violation of principle. War is not always the worst of all evils, and there may be alternatives to which it is preferable."

Von Haugwitz: "Oh, of course! There may be various opinions on such difficult questions. But to be practical, what can we do to clarify our position and come before the world with clean hands, since we really did have the general good always in view?"

Gentz: "I shall give you only this one piece of advice: Let bygones be bygones. The present is bad enough. Let your conduct be unequivocal and firm now; the world will side with you and soon cease to refer to the old mistakes and offences."

This pleased von Haugwitz greatly, and now he asked whether his guest would be willing to support him with his pen; to go to Vienna and there present the Prussian attitude in its just light. Gentz replied that he was at Prussian headquarters without Austrian permission and without any definite connection with the new Austrian Government. Besides, he added, the responsible men of Prussia would never in the world have undertaken such a dangerous enterprise as war against France without first having come to an understanding with Vienna. Von Haugwitz was deeply embarrassed by this remark. No, curiously enough, nothing of the sort had been done. . . .

Hoping that out of the mouths of two liars, who were laboring in the same cause yet were anything but bosom friends, truth might come, Gentz called on Marquis Lucchesini after he had left von Haugwitz. Lucchesini made no essential alterations in the picture, but thought von Haugwitz most to blame. He himself, as Prussian Ambassador in Paris, had long been convinced that the relations between France and Prussia could not continue as they were; but, he assured Gentz, "the great misfortune was that Count von Haugwitz had deluded himself so far as to fancy that he had this man Napoleon in his pocket."

In Vienna Napoleon had flattered the Minister with pretty talk and easy promises. Then, continued his colleague with malicious pleasure, on his subsequent trip to Paris the Minister's eyes opened in horror.

But that Lucchesini himself was not entirely free of blame Gentz learned from a third source. Madame Lucchesini, so it was said, would have been very reluctant to give up her Paris salon, and this was the reason why the reports of the Ambassador had always been couched in such a cheerful and optimistic tone.

The mood at headquarters was so excited and expectant that everyone willingly passed on any secrets that he might possess, even to those whom he did not know.

Gentz found his old enemy, Lombard, in pitiable condition. The man who had twice prevented Prussia's entry into a coalition was now so crippled in hands and feet that it caused him agony to be moved only from one chair to another, and to the tortures of gout was added the exhaustion of an attack of fever. "Oh," he wailed, "if you only knew what miseries I have suffered in the past few years! I have been treated as though I were a criminal, and branded throughout Europe as a traitor, bought by Napoleon. Yet I am as poor as a church mouse, and all I ever wanted was just an armchair and a pipe of tobacco. And von Haugwitz is in the same fix. He hardly knows which way to turn to feed his large family, and is besieged by his creditors every day. No, truly, we have always acted as well as we could according to our lights. I have known for years that the war was unavoidable, and we have been able to escape it so far only through all sorts of subterfuges. . . ."

Gentz: "If you were so sure that it was impossible to avoid war, why did you neglect all the opportunities for the King to enter it under the most favorable auspices?"

Lombard: "Oh, ask Lucchesini, ask von Haugwitz! They will both have to admit how I have felt about it for years. It is true that I let myself be duped for a moment by the Monster who is now devastating the world. When I met him in Brussels in 1803 he knew very well how to take me in; not so much by flattery as by feigning pacifism and generosity. But the illusion did not last long. I soon realized that this devil would not be stopped in his terrible course until he had annihilated everything, and though his charlatanism still continued to impress certain honorable men I was in a state of perpetual despair, for I could do nothing. . . . Do you know the King? My justification lies in this question. . . ."

It was the same King to whom a young man named Gentz had written ten years previously that the avoidance of war should be the highest, indeed the only, goal of statesmanship, and who had underlined this passage with approval. Gentz had abandoned the philosophy of peace that he had espoused in happier times when he realized that it did not correspond with reality, but the poor King, with his less adaptable mind, had remained true to it.

Lombard swore that his master was still a pacifist at heart. "Finally, as the confusion increased and the nation loudly demanded a change, he had been forced to yield; but there is no question that he would much rather withdraw. No one would wish that. But could anyone wish for what will come if we do not withdraw?"

Lombard himself expressed the most anxious misgivings, and cried in his feverish excitement that there was nothing for him to look forward to but the grave.

On such evil days had this archappeaser fallen, and Gentz was overcome by compassion. He treated Lombard with the greatest consideration, and even helped him to improve and translate into German a vapid war manifesto that the Kabinettsrat had written in French. Napoleon later ascribed this declaration of Prussia to the world to "a miserable scribe named Gentz, one of those dishonorable men who sell themselves for money." But in its clumsiness and gloom it bore, rather, the stamp of Lombard, or at least of a joint product weighted down with his inept schemes. Lombard had taken special pains to enumerate all the monstrous crimes of Napoleon, and all that Prussia had done for him in spite of them:

"French policy for the past fifteen years has been to scourge all mankind, and sad to say it remains the same under her new ruler. . . . It would be superfluous to enumerate all that Napoleon owes to Prussia. She was the first power to recognize him. Neither promises nor threats could shake her neutrality, and whatever allegiance could be demanded of a good neighbor she generously accorded for six years. Nay, more; Prussia held in high regard the brave nation that had learned to respect her in peace and in war, and recognized the genius of the French Emperor. . . . Thus for several years a curious struggle had been going on between a restraint that overlooked everything, combined with a sincerity that stood by its promises to the end, on the one hand; and on the other an abuse of force, an overconfidence in alluring luck, and a habit of relying on this alone. . . .

"Any contest between a policy that goes as far as it dares, and an honesty that still believes in duty and especially in promises, is bound to be unequal. The King approached the moment when he was to learn this by experience: the saddest moment of his life. . . . Finally Napoleon notified His Majesty that he had been pleased to dissolve the Holy Roman Empire and establish a Confederation of the Rhine, and called upon him to institute a similar confederation in north Germany. It was the customary and long successful procedure at the birth of a new scheme to offer some sort of bait to any court that might put obstacles in its way. . . .

"There was no longer any doubt that Napoleon wished either to overwhelm Prussia by war or to make her forever incapable of war by reducing her to a political degradation and impotence in which she must bow to the will of her menacing neighbor. . . ."

And so on.

This was not Gentz's style, and could not have been even though he had written the manifesto alone. For he did not write well, he was not himself, when it came to vindicating a cause of which he did not approve; still less when the cause, like that of Prussia, had long been repugnant to him.

The most depressing of all his discouraging conversations was that with the Generalissimo, the Duke of Brunswick, the once universally admired philosopher-prince and friend of Mirabeau whom certain of the French had once demanded as their King; now an old man, whose unfitness for command was revealed in his bewildered eyes.

"In his whole attitude," wrote Gentz, "in his appearance, his glance, his speech, there was something uncertain, something furtive, something weak; a sort of courtesy that seemed to ask forgiveness in advance for any reverses that he might suffer. . . . He spent a long time over flattering remarks that seemed to me highly inopportune at such a moment, and made me furiously impatient. . . . I was greatly embarrassed during this conversation, and although I sought from time to time to give it a concrete turn I failed consistently. He merely kept repeating, time after time, in a tone that drove me nearly frantic: 'Provided that one does not make some grave mistake. . . .' When at last I took the liberty of saying: 'But, Sir, surely it is to be hoped that under your leadership none will be made,' he replied, 'Alas, I can hardly answer for myself, and now I am required to be responsible for others. . . .' "

Gentz left the Duke with the feeling that all hope must now be abandoned, that only the extent of the disaster still remained in doubt, and that even before he had reached Vienna this, too, would long since have been decided.

With endless difficulty he made his way back to Weimar along roads choked with artillery. Here he learned that French troops had attacked the Prussians from the rear at Jena, just as at Ulm, cut their lines of communication, and destroyed their stores; that the Prussian vanguard had been annihilated, and that their commanding officer, Prince Louis Ferdinand, had fallen. Louis, the idol of Rahel's Bohemia, the companion of his intellectual Berlin nights!

It was too much for one who was unaccustomed to personal terror and pain, and confusion in defeat. Here there was no further use for his manifestoes and advice. Blind with horror the herald of the coalition war stumbled to his carriage, rolled away, and arrived in Dresden after an adventurous trip of five days during which he was in constant danger of falling into the hands of the French. There he heard of what he already knew: the end; the destruction of the main Prussian Army at Jena, and all the rest.

Off again in haste together with others who dared not await the arrival of the Conqueror, this time to Bohemia. Now north Germany was in the war and Bohemia neutral, and so it went, back and forth. "When I left Vienna," thus ends the diary, "the door of hope seemed to me closed forever, to Germany and to Europe."

Gone the hopes and adventures of his first emigration. A harsh, tedious exile began and once again he was in Prague, living there as one is forced to live who has no money, and in complete uncertainty regarding the future. Gentz was now little better off than any prisoner, for he could go neither to Germany, to Vienna, nor to Russia. From time to time he asked his patrons in Great Britain for permission to seek refuge there, but it is hard to see how he could have made the trip; though Madame de Staël, to be sure, went by way of St. Petersburg.

THE sequel to the battle of Jena was short and bizarre. For ten years the question whether Prussia would enter the war or not had kept the world on edge. In ten weeks her attempt at intervention was crushed. This famous military power now appeared as a nation in which there were citizens and gendarmes, but no will to a national existence, no capacity to withstand, and no honor. Wherewith there came to light at last, also, the basic reason for Lombard's appeasement policy of so many years' standing. Armies had let themselves be surrounded and disarmed, and strongholds that were believed impregnable had capitulated as though overcome by some magic power. Money, it was said, had played a role in all this.

Two weeks after the battle Napoleon was in Berlin, whence he decreed the exclusion of British trade from the Continent. The royal family, humbled under the biting contempt of the Victor, fled to the Russian border. The help of Russia was their last hope, though now no longer to be relied on.

There were five European nations that were accounted great powers: Great Britain, Russia, France, Austria, and, up to this moment, at least, Prussia. Among them all there was enmity, and actual or latent war: a negative relationship that dominated the political scene. For that very reason its abrogation and transformation into the opposite was to some extent a relevant idea; a secret hope, or fear, that never ceased to smolder in the minds of diplomats.

The enmity between France and Great Britain overshadowed all the others, though vague feelers were constantly being put out because of the notion that if they could unite there would be lasting peace and the whole world would belong to them. There was antagonism between France and Austria, a classical bitterness running back to the Renaissance in spite of their having tried twice during the past century to end it and rule the Continent together; in the Seven Years' War and in 1797. There was ill will between Prussia and Austria, a German and European resentment, yet German patriots were haunted by the idea that an alliance between these two powers, that is to say a federation of all Germans, would be stronger than the rest of Europe combined. There was hostility between France and Prussia, too, at least from time to time, but the alliance of these two progressive states was a favorite project of the French revolutionists. And finally, there was hatred between France and Russia, though it was generally believed that if these two powers were to unite they could dominate not only Europe alone but Africa and Asia as well, and destroy British world power.

This idea was not so bizarre as the others, though the various coalitions in which Russia and France found themselves side by side during the eighteenth century were not preliminaries to such a compact. The idea was revolutionary and despotic, and wholly modern, and had not escaped Bonaparte's restless, exploring mind. Once, indeed, six years previously, he and the Czar Paul had made some considerable progress with it, but the assassination of this madman by aristocratic and Anglophile conspirators in St. Petersburg had raised to the throne a young man who lived in a dream of Christian chivalry. Alexander I fancied himself a dragon-killer and deliverer of the oppressed, though he liked to play other roles as well. Gentz, who had an opportunity to study him in 1805, did not trust him, and called him a "ridiculous puppet emperor."

Gentz knew that among all the concealed possibilities for a sudden underhand union and overpowering diplomatic surprise an alliance between Russia and France was the only one that could produce the results expected of it, at least for a time. He had always warned against it, most earnestly in the book that he had directed at de Hauterive, and the following passage in particular had created a sensation in London five years previously:

"I am speaking now of the best interests of Europe, and consider the policies of the individual states from this standpoint alone. Speaking thus, I assert with the deepest conviction that an alliance between France and Russia such as was feared a few months ago, and surely not without reason, would be of all political combinations the most formidable and the most ruinous; that if European politics still retained even a shred of concern for its honor, its aims, and its duty it would oppose this final and most terrible of all evils with its last breath; and that if ever such an alliance should be realized the hour when it was consummated would certainly be the last hour of independence, security, and peace in Europe, save for the peace of the grave."

Russia was not really a European nation. Compared with Great Britain and the Continent she was a third power that merely trifled with Europe. She played at war on her borders, yes, and of late far beyond these; even as far as Switzerland and Italy. But Europe's sphere was not her sphere, Europe's ways were not her ways, and so in the end she was perfectly capable of dividing the world with the Despot who represented a Europe united through despotism. But even this would not be the end of the story by any means. No treaty of alliance could prevent a clash between opposing ambitions to rule, and it would become clear in the long run that Europe was no ordinary world power among others, and that her compulsory fusion into one would not be tolerated by any of the competing world powers.

For the moment, however, the hostility between France and Russia was such that its removal would have the most gratifying results for the Despot of the East and the Despot of the West, and the worst possible consequences for all those who were caught between them. No time would seem to be more favorable for a dramatic stroke like this than the hour when all the intervening nations lay exhausted. It was on this account that Gentz implored his Prussian friends not to depend on Russia, but to make peace before the Czar, who held all the trumps, could steal a march on them.

Of course his advice was not followed. A cruel winter and spring campaign on the plains of Poland brought matters to the point desired by Napoleon. The Czar sent word to the British Government that they had shown more interest in Egypt and Buenos Aires than in the Russian front, and that he was tired of all European chivalry. A meeting took place between the two warring monarchs, and within a few hours Napoleon had captured Alexander's imagination, with all its thirst for friendship and great deeds. The alliance between the two became an alliance between Europe and Asia.

"Having just proclaimed themselves the leaders of Europe against France, the Russians now praised Bonaparte's system with the same enthusiasm that they had formerly devoted to its abuse," wrote Gentz, still amazed in retrospect over such juggling.

The King of Prussia was allowed to retain half his territory, "in deference to the Emperor of Russia," and his nation was reduced to the position of a poor, vassal state. The rest was made into a kingdom for the youngest Bonaparte, so that now all the dutiful brothers of Charlemagne paraded under crowns.

Great Britain was to be given one last chance to join the two mightiest powers as a third and somewhat smaller ally, but in the probable event of her refusal was to be forced into capitulation by a commercial blockade.

Many incredible events had marked the preceding fifteen years, but the Treaty of Tilsit was the most unbelievable of all and, in addition, as it appeared, the concluding one.

At the head of the occupied, impoverished, and paralyzed remnant of Prussia moved Baron vom Stein, friend of Gentz. Curiously enough it was Napoleon himself who had advised the unfortunate King to appoint this great and progressive man. Lombard had been dismissed and imprisoned, but no one knew exactly whether because he had made war against France or because he had so long refrained from doing so.

Bitterly and understandingly Gentz followed from Prague all these events that he had long since foreseen. "It is perfectly obvious," he wrote to one of his remaining friends, "that this union of robbers, this unnatural, outrageous duumvirate, will eventually come to the same end as others of their sort. Octavian shares the world with Mark Antony only to rule it alone after another battle of Actium, which may not be so far distant. The Emperor of Russia will be punished! But we ourselves, in the meantime . . . ! This barbarous struggle over the question whether the world is to belong to one tyrant or two brings to a close the eighteen-year-old drama whose theme was universal freedom!"

When the next battle of Actium was to take place neither he nor anyone else knew. For the present Great Britain was alone once again, and more seriously threatened than at any time since the drama opened.

IX

NEW FACTS, NEW IDEAS

THE forty-three-year-old man who now watched from Prague with considerably tempered emotions the establishment of the "new federative system" found himself in a curious position. Incomparably shrewd, he was accounted among the best minds of Europe, and he himself shared the view: "I wish to say it, and I can say it without arrogance, as one of those representing the common mind of the present century. . . ."

Yet something essential seemed to be wrong with the ideas of this intellectual spokesman for his own time. Ever since he had begun to think politically he had gone from one defeat to another. How could that be? He had fallen into a world revolution, the nature of which he soon recognized but whose tremendous repercussions he had nevertheless underestimated. He had believed the political system that had survived the last preceding revolution, that of the Thirty Years' War, could be preserved through the present one, strengthened and renewed. He had inherited from thinkers of the seventeenth century and from their later commentators the political terms in which he thought: balance of power, peace, progress. Never war between peoples, and only seldom between states. If it did break out it was a misunderstanding, a stringently regulated and superfluous venture that could not, and ought not, advance matters. Progress should come through the discoveries of the sciences, of geography; through world trade and appropriate systems of government, with a union of the German states as spiritual head of a league of all the peoples of Europe; with Germany, aware at the same time of her national and cosmopolitan role and her European responsibilities, peacefully and, as it were, passively, leading the other nations; by concerted action against the Disturber of the Peace who threatened this system; with deeds attuned to principles, the principles of political logic, tactics, and morals; even by means of war and often necessarily by war.

Fundamentally an advocate of peace from early youth, Gentz had thrown all his pacifistic ballast overboard as soon as a real enemy appeared. But nothing was done according to principles, no one acted according to principles, and what seemed the reasonable course was nowhere pursued. Individual men were sensible, but governments were as stupid and lacking in discernment as dumb animals, and men appeared to become so, too, as soon as they were chosen to represent the state. One could know nothing beforehand, demand nothing; only will. But as volition in its origin had nothing in common with knowledge or with morals, the only ones whose commands were crowned with success were the immoral and the ignorant; the tools and the playthings of God.

What should occur peacefully by evolution occurred by war and revolution, and even then was by no means what had been desired and confidently expected, though resembling this, to be sure, in many of its features. Here decisions were no longer made in deference to moral principles, no matter how highly these were regarded. One floated around in a whirlpool where neither compass nor rules of navigation mattered any longer, but only strength.

Perhaps against his will Gentz had been instrumental from the first in presenting this, the truest and darkest side, to the reading public. But he had not been able to act accordingly. Defend valiantly the order to which we were born: this was the watchword. Yet again and again, for ten years, if affairs were not better managed about him in Prussia, in Austria, he had explained it by the evil characters of those in charge. His political letters were dominated by a consistency, indeed a monotony, of which no doubt he was unconscious, and during the crisis of 1805 four main arguments appear repeatedly:

1. Public opinion on the true nature of Napoleon must be clarified. This was his special concern, and he liked to quote a sentence of Burke's: "The public must never be regarded as incurable."

2. The four great powers must unite, and Prussia must be among them; not through compulsion and with a promise of military aid wrung from her, but voluntarily.

3. Russia is not to be trusted. She should be held in reserve, not be given the chief role.

4. The Austrian Cabinet must be overthrown. This thesis, which had to do with the ineptitude of the individual men, lay nearest his heart and was reiterated with the most patient impatience; the change of mind, the reformation of the individual man interested him above all else. So deeply, that when a rumor spread of Napoleon's death in Paris by slow poison Gentz immediately explained that he expected nothing, even though the hope were realized; Napoleon might die, of course, but another of the same kind would

soon take his place as long as his opponents remained what they were.

They remained so.

Cobenzl was dismissed after Austerlitz, and at first Gentz anticipated little more from the new administration of Count Stadion than from the old. Prussia had not been won over to the Coalition of 1805, and a year later she fought alone. The guidance of Europe had been left to Russia, and the men about the Czar Alexander took advantage of the situation in which they thus found themselves to change their course abruptly, go halves with Napoleon, and establish a dual French-Russian hegemony over two continents.

Such a system seemed strong, even final, and as final it had to be calmly accepted. "It could not be otherwise. The present catastrophe is the most terrible of all because in a certain sense it is the last; yet never have I been less shaken. For the past three months I have been living with the idea that it was inevitable."

He told friends of his resolve to publish no more for the present.

Had his politics been at fault, then? Philosophers are at odds over the question whether right or wrong is equivalent to successful or unsuccessful. No doubt Gentz was fond of philosophizing, but he was too unconstrained, too mobile, too weak to entertain a consistent philosophy; nor was his mind always capable of running counter to the universal undercurrent of German thought, which held the already accomplished to be the true and the right. He never doubted for a moment that his advice had been sound, certain specified values assumed, and that it would have had the desired result had it been followed in time; but only if these values were assumed.

Yet how could anyone take the validity of the old order and its values for granted when its official representatives had failed so notoriously? The strength, the claim of Napoleon lay not in the man himself, but in the proved nullity of his opponents. In respect to a pamphlet attacking the nobility, and published by one Buchholz, Gentz wrote to Adam Müller: "It pains me to think what will become of the members of our nobility who still subsist. The accusations of such a rash demagogue are really hard to answer, and the more intimately one has been acquainted with the nobility the more difficult is it to defend them with a clear conscience. And so it is with several other cardinal values. Who would have the face to approve still the old political system of Europe after the rapid succession of mistakes and insane acts that have brought it down at last to total ruin? Generally speaking it is true that a lost cause can be led only by great men. All others, slaves to success and for the most part even when this is but ephemeral, secretly find something offensive in the idea of anyone continuing to maintain his point once the issue has been decided against him."

Success! It was a matter of course that now, more than ever, voices should be raised in exaltation of the great monarchy; that the tempting theories so eloquently denounced by Gentz a year previously should be advanced even more cheerfully than ever; and that those who fifteen years before had pointed out the inevitability of the French Revolution, or their followers at least, should represent the collapse of the old states as something that must necessarily have occurred just at this time, even without Napoleon.

In their writings there was no lack of gibes directed at poor Gentz; sometimes he was called, with malicious flattery, "the only brains in the coalition." "On October 14 [the battle of Jena], to the music of the spheres, God weighed the old and the new order," wrote a former adherent of Gentz to Johannes von Müller; "the scalepan of the North went up! Now we must accept His decision." And he told with relish how, at a banquet in Dresden, he had proposed a toast to "the peace and him who brought it"; to "this destroyer of old, worm-eaten, decayed methods, this chosen instrument of God, baptized in genius and in fire"; and went on to complain impatiently that some people refused to hear the stroke of the hour.

Now with the recipient of this letter, the great Johannes von Müller, matters stood thus. Whether from lack of resolution, or worry over his financial situation, or perhaps because of some secret expectation, he did not leave Berlin when the French Armies drew near, and this eminent spokesman for the Prussian War party, this friend of Gentz and the slain Louis Ferdinand, was summoned by the Emperor Napoleon to an audience at the very palace where once he had chatted with Frederick the Great. Von Müller was by way of being a collector of great men, and never could resist them. Trembling with curiosity and unwonted happiness, the old historian drove up to the entrance, climbed the familiar steps, and was escorted to the inner rooms by a company of officers glowing with youth and talent. What took place there between him and the god during the next hour and a half was so sacred that he never could bring himself to share the details with anyone. This much only did he commit to writing: he had found the Emperor vigorous, profound, and unfathomable, but considerate also. In keen glance and breadth of vision Frederick the Great could not begin to compare with him.

What would become of Prussia would henceforth be a matter of indifference to Johannes.

The herald of Swiss freedom soon began to praise the Confederation of the Rhine in articles that appeared in the *Jenaische Literaturzeitung.*

It was Adam Müller who gave Gentz all the latest details of this aftermath of Napoleon's power and charm; not entirely, it may be suspected, without malicious joy. "Have you had enough of the incredible?" he wrote, in concluding his report. "Such are the men who study history for the sake of its great specimens!"

The final apostasy of his ally, after a long process of weakening, was hardly a severe blow to Gentz, but he recalled to mind and set down all his thoughts during these difficult months on the cogency of success and the accomplished fact; on exultation over victory, from which even the vanquished did not wish to remain excluded; and on the pusillanimity of man. The most significant passages in the farewell letter that he addressed to Johannes on February 27, 1807, read as follows:

"I realized that you have long since lost the courage and inclination to fight for a dangerously threatened cause. I knew that even last spring you would have deserted it wholly but for the continued exhortations of your friends; your respect for some, your fear of others. . . . Thus I was only mildly surprised that you should remain in Berlin. . . . Once this had occurred I was fully prepared to see you, with ambiguous confessions and explanations, disavow and abandon your principles, or at least those that have up to now passed as yours, in cowardly submission to the Victor and in clandestine negotiations with him; and sacrifice your reputation, your friends, the cause of Europe, and everything great and good that you have preached and fought for these many years. But that you should betray all that you ought to hold dear, and that you should be capable of renouncing it openly—such heights of presumptuous treachery I had not thought to find in you. . . . The veil fell from my eyes as I read: 'The energy that has been fruitlessly squandered on the decaying old must now be dedicated to the new; we must change our way of thinking.' And so on.

"It is unnecessary to say that nothing more is needed to effect the breaking of every bond, the dissolution of all relationship between us. . . . Has your clear and penetrating intellect become all at once so sadly overclouded that today you think good and honorable what barely six months ago you would have seen in all its abomination?

Or has some base interest, some servile fear, seduced you into writing against your better judgment? In forming their opinion your contemporaries will snatch at one or the other of these explanations. As for me, I accept neither. I flatter myself that I have understood you better. . . . You are, and always will remain, the plaything of every passing impression. Ever ready to recognize and accept as valid, to embrace, to espouse whatever happens to attract your attention, you are incapable of either thoroughgoing hate or complete loyalty. Your life is an endless equivocation. If the Devil himself were to appear upon earth, I could show him how to make friends with you in twenty-four hours.

"This time you have gone astray merely because, separated from all decent people and surrounded by scatterbrains or rogues, you have heard and seen nothing but the bad. If you could have made up your mind to leave Berlin, you probably would have been saved. Your real culpability lies in your having remained there; everything else has been an inevitable consequence of this. . . .

"Do not imagine that I have written you such a harsh letter without the deepest pain. Whether I have been capable of esteeming you let the past, let your heart, tell you. So I am capable of feeling, also, what it means to lose you. As champion in a holy cause I pronounce an inexorable sentence of condemnation on your outrageous apostasy; as a man, as a former friend, I feel only compassion for you. To hate you is beyond my power. If God fulfills our wishes, and rewards my efforts and others similarly directed, only one verdict awaits yours. But this is of fearful consequence. . . ."

Müller's answer was sorrowful, but full of dignity. As always, he sought vindication and solace in Roman history. Had not Livy acted in the best interest of mankind when he reconciled himself to Octavian's usurpation, thus winning freedom to finish his scholarly work instead of leading the fruitless life of an emigrant?

After the Treaty of Tilsit Müller visited Napoleon at Fontainebleau and soon afterward, instead of migrating to the "British Empire on the Ganges," entered the service of Jerome Bonaparte, the new King of Westphalia, as his Secretary of State. Here, in Cassel, its capital city, he died only two years later, in 1809, suspected by his new master; an errant and deeply melancholy man. Gentz often returned subsequently to his writings, and soon began to judge him more leniently.

For he gradually came to realize that it was easier to shout down enthusiasts for the Conqueror than not to capitulate in the long run, holding out to the end with the unholy agents of misfortune, the allies. Indeed, he did not actually hold out, for he believed that he himself and all his manifestoes had been wrong. "On the whole, I appraised the rulers far too highly, the masses much too ideally, and was more of a poet than I knew. Had I correctly estimated my contemporaries in good time I should have tried to direct them by other means, and thus perhaps might have averted much evil. . . .

"The attempts of the past four years to preserve freedom in Europe have all been, in my opinion, feeble, ill-timed, or wholly preposterous. The measures taken by the British Government were wrong almost without exception. The planning of the Austro-Russian War of 1805 was misconceived to the point of absurdity, the Prussian War pure madness. Russia I do not wish even to discuss, because any criticism of these past political events would have to hinge principally on the fact that Europe was so deluded as ever to expect salvation from Russia. . . ."

Nevertheless, the mood of this long summing up is not that of despair. "I, too, believe that a new and better order of things will arise from the present chaos, for to our joy and solace the instrument of a chastising justice has been vouchsafed power to destroy yet absolutely none to rebuild. *But the new order will not come about through agencies that are well known to us, and, sad though this may be, possibly not in forms with which we are familiar. . . .*"

This was not capitulation. Resignation, rather, connected with, or based upon, a realization of the necessarily transitory nature of all historical phenomena.

The view, which had taken shape during the Prussian War, and to which he gave ever clearer expression in the ensuing and relatively peaceful years, was as follows: Napoleon had triumphed at Tilsit as decisively as anyone could. So much the worse for him, since an empire like his begins to disintegrate at the moment when it stands completed. But not so much the better for us, perhaps, because for us to be considered right his alliance with Russia, the parceling out of Europe, the crowning of the brothers, and all the imperial hocus-pocus should never have happened at all. And yet, so much the better for the cause. Europe is not adapted for welding successfully into a single monarchy. We thought to prevent it, we fought against it in vain. It is here. But surely, and before very long, the end will come. How, we cannot say. We have learned by experience that all historical prophecy is presumption.

A second view, which concerned Napoleon's character, had now begun to dawn upon Gentz; namely, that it had been a mistake to regard him as a mixture of god and devil, a planning colossus, and to deal with him in such an exaggerated way, as though he were destiny itself; for this only incited him the more to assume the role of destiny. It was better to meet him with irony, with merriment; as a buffoon, a juggler, an impostor. This idea first came to Gentz when Napoleon threw himself into the arms of the Czar at Tilsit, and established the artificial Westphalian Kingdom. His thought was the result of three defeats.

A third view was the most astringent. Even as early as his Prussian period Gentz had come to the conclusion that the spread of the revolutionary spirit throughout Europe must in the end react inimically upon its source; that France would be struck down with her own weapons, and that this logical repercussion, if not the salvation of the epoch, would in any case be its lot. It would not restore the past, but the new would be tinged by the old and a tremendous confusion of ideas and facts would result. Out of the paroxysm there would finally emerge a third phase, whose nature no one could foresee but which Gentz at least ventured to believe might be based once more on the balance of power, on liberty, and on peace. This is what he meant by agencies still unknown, and, however sad they might be for him, unfamiliar forms.

There are no unmixed and unequivocal tendencies in our world or in our thinking. Even if there were, they would never be able to prevail as such but would be frustrated by others, which, if not already in existence, would in any case be engendered by them. No age follows one simple trend. No nation, no people, no idea monopolizes world history for more than a passing moment.

For two years Gentz remained in Prague and at the Bohemian spas, Teplitz and Carlsbad. The time passed, he knew not how. He called himself a "privileged idler," "an exiled crank who can produce no more." Europe's half ruined aristocracy apparently thought it their duty to accommodate with money the singular man who needed it so badly and whom they had once accepted as their own. According to a statement of Hammond, the Undersecretary of State, he obtained 4,500 pounds from London between 1806 and 1809; more than was received by an Undersecretary of State. What he did in return is not quite clear. The British felt so isolated from a Continent forced into enmity against them that the mere good will of a gossip who consorted every summer with the upper ten thousand of Germany and Russia may have appeared to them worth the outlay. Furthermore, he still continued to send memoirs to London, employing for the purpose two of his servants, the brothers Krauss, whom he had trained as confidential messengers. They risked the trip either by way of Prussia and Hamburg, through a net of French customs inspectors and censors, or by the Mediterranean route. George Canning, Foreign Secretary from 1807 to 1809, declared himself "rather a believer in Gentz," even though he was said to be an "enthusiast" and a "terrible spendthrift." When money arrived from London Gentz had his equipages and his chef, and spent his nights at the gaming table, but soon was as poor as a beggar again.

He strolled about with summer guests who had succeeded in reconciling themselves to the Napoleonic world; Goethe, for example, and the Duke of Weimar; with politicians out of office; with emigrants who passed their days in protest against the new order; with young German writers, who suffered agonies under the prevailing conditions because nothing was produced in the theaters save translations from the French, and nothing printed but glorifications of the Grand Empire. When these guests departed Gentz looked after them in bewilderment; he could not follow. Austria, though poor and restricted, was still an independent power and as such protected him, but at the same time supervised his movements.

Even neighboring Saxony now belonged to Napoleon's Confederation of the Rhine, and woe betide the "miserable scribe named Gentz" if ever he were caught there! Friends living in Dresden had to cross the border in order to see him; these were Adam Müller and a young and highly gifted but hapless dramatist named Kleist. There they published together a periodical called *Phoebus*, which annoyed Gentz, at least in so far as concerned Müller's contributions. Müller was not a hero born, and the days when he had wanted to join the British militia were long since past. He managed to think up the most distorted little ideas with which to lull himself into political indifference; under existing circumstances surely agreeable to Dresden, now that it was in the Confederation. Everything was right, Müller argued, if only it were done in the right way. Napoleon's amalgamation of Europe was the necessary even though radical answer to its earlier inordinate multiformity. One extreme leads to another, and so on.

Gentz, who scorned all such quibbling, wrote his two friends that he wanted to hear nothing further of their theories, and felt himself still more alone in the world.

Madame de Staël, a singularly clever woman, tells how she was attacked by a sort of anxiety and shortness of breath upon hearing of Napoleon's coup d'état, on the evening of the 18th Brumaire, and added, in 1810: "Since then it has never left me, and I fear it has become the illness of a whole Continent."

The people of Germany groaned under Napoleon's closure of the Continent to British trade; groaned, paid, obeyed, and waited. They were hungry; only tallow candles were available for light; and people went afoot, even to the court. How long one would continue to receive his salary was uncertain; a neighbor's had just been stopped. But everyone kept on working and making plans for this year and the next, realizing meanwhile, to be sure, that the fate of each depended upon circumstances over which he had no control. Worst off of all were the intellectuals; the group of professional writers and thinkers, whose inner and outward life, even in normal times, depended on such intangible supports. The majority followed Johannes von Müller's example, but those who were more conscientious did not know what to do and were driven about from pillar to post. No one had the slightest conception of what the future might bring. Napoleon, wrote Baron vom Stein, might die, and his Empire disintegrate; but on the other hand he might overcome the last obstacles in his path. "Then wars between nations will no longer break out; the world will be racked instead by civil wars and political uprisings; national unities will be crippled or destroyed, and the management of all important human affairs will be entrusted to a bureaucracy under the control of a remote and unknown director. Such a condition of affairs may last for a long time, as the history of the Roman Empire proves."

But then, again, in a letter to Gentz: "I, too, believe that Bonaparte's system will not be of long duration. It rests on foundations that are too rotten; on force, and the most despicable artifices of government; there is not a sign of humanity, of breadth, of nobility in the whole structure. It will be a great misfortune if all power, all influence should long remain in the hands of this man. Of course resentment is growing stronger and more general every day. He feels this, and the prospect will make him even more obstinately

JOSEPH GOERRES (1776–1848)

determined to continue the annihilation of everything that could be depended upon for resistance. . . ."

In the words of Joseph Goerres, a publicist and scholar of the Rhineland: "The old French horticultural custom that trimmed trees in the shape of men now prunes men into trees and hedges. Indians, Persians, Turks, New Zealanders, everyone, will be furnished with prefects and subprefects, with the Code and the censorship. . . . They have taken the smallest measure of man as a standard, and all that makes anyone greater will be cut down. . . ." But: "The delight in reading and study is not interfered with, for the government is afraid of no opposition but the material. Literature has been regarded for so long as the plaything of the nation that no one would try to snatch it away. To suppress national movements is not the Emperor's way. . . . The very fact that he has been unable to find any real national feeling among the Germans has been a puzzle to him." Well, they would show him that they did possess a nationality. Offended even by the way in which he offered his benefits—though his innovations were sensible in part; only ungracious and cold—they would prove to him that they were different from the other peoples whom he dominated; indeed, that they were unique, and had been from time immemorial. Their nationalism became exclusive, and sought its roots in the past.

In chaotic and creative times ideas are fluid, and pass easily one into the other. So, also, do men agree who it is thought must become enemics at first sight; and others are in conflict who later seem to be comrades. Ideas are still in a state of fermentation, not yet labeled or classified; men feel their way, still unconstrained by definite party lines.

Thus it might be thought that Gentz, the salon politician who had scarcely any contact with the people, the agent of Great Britain, the cosmopolite, must necessarily have been hostile from the first to the evolution through which German thought was now passing. But he was not. On the contrary, he was well content with it. "Europe," he had written in his *Preface*, "fell because of Germany. Now through Germany she must rise again." For this it was essential above all things that there be an awareness of German national unity. The secret of Europe's vitality was the diversity of her nations, and Germany should not be an exception among them. Gentz had pondered this difficult question often enough in the past. "We should have been a nation." Not a centralized national state like France; Germany was too large for that, too dangerous to her neighbors, and in too perilous a situation; too near the center of Europe. She should have been a federal union, unwilling to attack yet prepared for defense; a patriotic and cosmopolitan league. For a long time Gentz had been mulling over the difficulties of such a unique combination, and when certain writers, under the burden of the universal monarchy, sought to instill a national consciousness into the Germans, it was not in his heart at the moment to oppose the idea.

Other peoples reacted differently under Napoleon's exactions, and not merely in the heads of their cloistered writers. Soon after the Treaty of Tilsit—the final conclusion of peace—the will-o'-the-wisp of an entire Continent united against Great Britain drew the French Armies into Spain, which had long been submissive to the new order though not wholly servile. Charles IV, his coarse and blatant queen, and his son Ferdinand, an infamous and dishonored lot, were forced to abdicate and Bonaparte presented the Spanish people in exchange with Joseph, another of his ever-ready brothers. Though it meant chaos and death, the reply was the first uncompromising No! that any of the Continental peoples had dared to raise against Napoleon. Only gradually did the rest of Europe see, and grasp, what it meant.

THE ideas that simmered in the heads of German patriots had been aroused and influenced by the French Revolution, though without their realization, and directed against it. The reaction of the Spaniards was unconscious, too; the blind urge of hate, and a natural pride and conservatism. But at the same time there developed a conscious adaptation and imitation, under the influence of humanitarian ministers in Berlin and Vienna.

Both political leaders were old friends of Gentz; Baron vom und zum Stein, and Count Stadion, former Austrian Ambassador to Prussia, who first thought of bringing Gentz to Vienna. Stadion was busy with the task of converting the patrician army of Austria into a citizen's army, and Stein, the more radical of the two, was transmuting into a modern, postrevolutionary state the image of woe that still went by the name of Prussia.

Here was the "sans-culottization" that the appeasers had maintained, ten years before, would be the only means of conducting successfully a war against France, though of its very self it would rob such a war of all purpose. Now it was being introduced, yet without Prussia's becoming a Napoleonic state in consequence. For adaptation to external conditions does not mean sacrifice of the inner self, and he who is sheltered within his traditions need not embark upon the hateful course of the enemy merely because he has put certain of his practices into effect. Political customs are what we make them, and we make them what we ourselves are.

Stein was a modern and a liberal statesman, who had received more of his education in Great Britain than in France, yet at the same time had a feeling for tradition, looked to the past, and was filled with romantic yearning. He did not believe that the continuity of history would be broken if he adapted the part of Germany that had been entrusted to him to the demands of the present, and still less did he think that in so doing he would be conferring a favor upon France. On the contrary, he felt certain that his reforms, even those that he had copied from the French Revolution, could and should be directed against Napoleon. "We must pursue the good, the true, and the right with an energy and perseverance equal to that with which Napoleon carried out the French revolutionary system," wrote one of Stein's collaborators, "and to this end try to unite all that is fine and noble. Such a system, similar to that of the Jacobins, except in purpose and the employment of criminal means, and with Prussia at its head, might be effective in the highest degree."

Stein himself wrote: "I think it important to break the fetters with which bureaucracy has hampered the progress of human activities. We must destroy this spirit of greed, of base interest; the lifeless mechanism upon which this form of government depends. The nation must grow accustomed to managing its own affairs if it is to emerge from the immaturity in which an always anxious, always paternalistic government has kept its people." And certainly self government like this would prevail in the end against Napoleon's tyranny. The Prussian people would possess after all something that was worth the struggle, while for a long time yet the French were carrying on war merely for the sake of war.

Stein and his collaborators did not accomplish all that was in their minds, but they accomplished much. They emancipated the serfs; freed every sort of property, occupation, and profession; initiated autonomy of the municipalities; democratized the army; and humanized and vitalized education. And they did all this under difficulties that mock description; in a country that had been cut in two and hardly deserved the name of state any longer; a country whose public spirit was broken; a bankrupt country, whose citizens were ruined; under the very eyes of a French General Intendant who exacted the war levies, and whose demands Stein prudently and punctually fulfilled while seeking at the same time to placate him with favors; under an alarmed and stubborn King; and in the face of a reactionary nobility whose representatives did not hesitate to denounce the Minister to high French military officials as a dangerous revolutionary.

It was this remarkable combination of indigenous reactionaries and foreign ex-revolutionaries that eventually defeated Stein. He threatened the existence of the Junkers; was it not being said that the nobility were to be done away with entirely? Even the French nobility had been overthrown in 1789, and the French Commandant of Berlin had been among those who profited by their downfall. But these usufructuaries of the French Revolution had become conservative in the meantime, not to say reactionary, for Napoleon's hierarchy, loaded down with money and titles, wanted no further democratization; certainly not in France, and still less in conquered lands, where, as the Counterfeit Emperor fully realized, democracy would ineluctably assume an anti-French character.

The Junkers, in their turn, hated the democratic Stein more than they hated the foreign oppressor, and the alliance between the forces of French occupation and the domestic reaction finally proved too strong for him.

A letter was intercepted from which it appeared that Stein, despite his perfect adjustment to the situation at the moment, had wholly different plans for the future; plans that would result in a national uprising for the delivery of Europe. Napoleon was in Madrid at the time, but his decrees embraced the Continent; Stein was outlawed wherever the arm of the new order extended; his property was to be confiscated, and if he approached an area controlled by French or "allied" troops he was to be taken into custody. Now Berlin was only too obviously such an area, and Stein had to flee; to the heartfelt relief of the King and the derisive laughter of the Junkers, his soul filled with anger and contempt for the servility of his countrymen. What? Never a protest, after all he had done for them? The most complete indifference to his fate, to this flagrant injustice?

It was an audaciously independent act for Austria to let the outlaw pass her borders, though of course she did not neglect to keep close watch over all his omissions and commissions. He arrived in Prague on January 6, 1809.

HERE the European Agent still lived as a "privileged idler," though he was now free of the apathy that had held him in thrall since Jena and Tilsit. History does not stand still, and a man of forty-five must not give up. Two years before that everything had seemed frozen and dead; now it was as though the rustle and thaw of spring were in the air.

Under no circumstances would the Spaniards accede to what Napoleon had planned for them, and their opposition had slowly spread through underground channels to the regimented peoples of the Continent. Until now, cried Sheridan, leader of the British Opposition, "Bonaparte has contended with princes without dignity, numbers without ardour, or peoples without patriotism. He has yet to learn what it is to combat a people who are animated by one spirit against him!"

Under the inspiring leadership of George Canning Great Britain had taken advantage of this opportunity to gain the Continental foothold in Spain that she had never been able to secure in the Netherlands, and for which her self-seeking allies kept offering such miserably inadequate substitutes. At the same time, the first rumors of the recent meeting between the two partners in world domination, Napoleon and Alexander, began to leak out, in which it was maintained that they were no longer on such cordial good terms as Caesar would have the world believe. Outwardly, of course, all had been pomp and humility in 1808 at the congress of kings and princes in Erfurt, but underneath this much was certain: the Eastern youth with the melting eyes had defied his powerful friend with the utmost politeness. He found it reassuring that, besides Russia and the Grand Empire, the Empire of the Hapsburgs was still in existence, albeit somewhat reduced; and the net result of all the parleys between the two autocrats, all their manifestations of friendship, and all the fulsome and festive scenes put on for the benefit of the public, was that he completely frustrated the plan for a full disarmament of Austria under pressure from France and Russia. Furthermore, he had talked not only with Napoleon but several times in private with Talleyrand, his Minister, no one knew about what.

But Count Clemens Metternich, Austrian Ambassador in Paris, had an inkling. He was acquainted with those French politicians who were turning away from Napoleon with cool regret because they realized that his attempt to organize the whole Continent after his own plan had already failed, despite all his achieved and potential triumphs. Their only concern now was to preserve the advantages that had accrued to them through this autocracy, and they insinuated to Metternich, foreigner though he was, that the French no longer stood behind the Emperor; that all his conquests were to them a matter of indifference, yes, even of loathing. Metternich advised Vienna to this effect.

Gentz, in Prague, who knew of these reports, pieced them together with the conflagration in Spain and with the plans of George Canning, which obviously included the armed help of Austria. Could it be possible that despite everything, and with help from such an unexpected quarter as Spain, the end of the long adventure was so suddenly drawing nigh? "The experience of the ages has taught us," wrote Gentz philosophically, "that all human acts and endeavors, especially the unjust and the violent, prosper only up to a certain point. Napoleon appears to have reached his limit. Since the Treaty of Tilsit, and above all since his ill-advised attack on Spain, his progress not only has been stayed but his star, of such evil portent for the world, has unquestionably begun to set." And once again, for the third time in ten years, the veteran agent began to instill the idea of war into the ears of the Austrian statesmen.

It was under such circumstances that he met Baron vom Stein, and this time the sensitive, vivacious Gentz was wholly captivated by the brusque and turbulent reformer. In his shabby lodging, in cafés, in their strolls along the Moldau they discussed the future of Europe.

In England, where he was highly esteemed, this distinguished emigrant would have been only one among many but in Germany he was, like Gentz, phenomenal. He embodied that mixture of tradition and progress, of chivalry and industrialism that was the secret of the British upper classes alone. Stein was no Prussian. He came from a region of the German "Empire" that was richest in tradition; from Nassau, in the west, whence it was not far to Holland and to the British electorate of Hanover. He had been educated in law, then had entered the Prussian service, and had supervised commerce and mining for thirteen years; in this position, as he said, solitude, exercise, and the consciousness of doing some good were his pleasures.

He had been drawn into the political arena gradually, and against his will, or at any rate without any definite plan. Of the purely intellectual he had no very high opinion, and once reproached Gentz for not having taken his place among those "whose lives had been dedicated to research and discovery." The most insulting word in his vocabulary was "metaphysician," and he never let an opportunity pass to storm against "the undeserved honor in which the speculative sciences" were held. "The anomalous and the inscrutable attract the attention of the human mind, which surrenders itself to idle brooding instead of engaging in vigorous activity." He thought the German philosophers of his day little better than crazy.

Nevertheless, he read widely, especially the British historians and economists. His vehement nature was moderated by an aristocratic upbringing; he wrote to his mother only in French. His taste was faultless, and all ugliness hateful to him. In a word, he was the best leader for the Germans that could have come forward in that hour, and Gentz clearly recognized this. "For my part, I hereby declare that if today I could have Your Excellency made dictator, in the real old Roman sense of the word, over all that must be undertaken for the salvation of Germany I would depart this world tomorrow well content with my day's work, and assured of the result and of the future."

But truly good men are seldom raised by the world to dictatorship.

Stein and Gentz were agreed that the situation in Europe was unendurable, and that her peoples were gradually getting into a mood where they preferred a disastrous ending to an eternal state of somber despair. "Even though all love for the fatherland, all national pride, and every honorable impulse in Germany were extinguished," Gentz read to the Minister from a memoir that he had prepared for Count Stadion, "the immediate pressure of foreign domination, the hardships, the deprivation, the daily recurring perplexities and annoyances that hang over people and their rulers alike would engender the lively conviction that until we are freed of foreign interference no national prosperity and no peace worthy of the name can be even thought of.

"This persuasion actually is present in every heart, though fear in many, some ignoble private interest in a few, and in the majority a self-centered indolence hold it in subjection. . . . Everywhere the unhappy people are oppressed by an unwonted burden of taxation; an odious and unaccustomed system of conscription, imposed in alien form and for the benefit of alien designs; the scourge of incessant and immoderate quartering of passing troops; and the unnatural vexation of double rule. At the same time, a merciless hand robs them of the last means of producing the wherewithal to meet present demands, or even to satisfy their former obligations. Every branch of industry is withered, for the trade that is necessary to give them life has been shackled with savage violence. For the sake of an absurd and waning effort to force Great Britain to her knees . . . of this attempt, conceived in blind rage and revived in a thousand different forms of impotent envy and desperate vindictiveness, Germany is condemned to destruction. All harbors are sealed, all centers of commerce devastated, all markets closed, all highways guarded by spies, and even the most innocent correspondence is barely allowed, while the extravagant cost of all the necessities of life completes the general confusion.

"Credit has disappeared, poverty and distress increase at an alarming rate, and to all these intolerable evils there is now added, though only among nobler minds, the humiliating consciousness of moral and intellectual oppression; the hateful omnipresence of a suspicious tyranny that inexorably thwarts all reciprocal communication of ideas; closes all roads to truth; tolerates no writer who will not eulogize their daily outrages, no journalist who refuses to be a servile copyist of their loathsome, mendacious press; and regards every complaint over the ruin that they have brought about as rebellion and high treason. . . ."

This, according to Gentz, was the true character of the "new federative system" in a country that had submitted to it with eager subservience as no other had, and that for this reason should have enjoyed at least some privileges. Was it possible for anyone seriously to believe in the permanence of such a situation? Yet, on the other hand, how could it come to an end of itself alone?

His answer was, another war. Another war, quickly, while Napoleon's best troops were bleeding and dying in Spain. The Austrian Emperor, Gentz advised, should rise up and say: "Matters cannot remain as they are. Give back now to the peoples of Europe their liberty." And if Napoleon ignored this challenge, as there was every reason to believe he would, then the blow should be struck. No negotiations seeking to shift to his adversary the odium of attack. First demand, then act!

Stein pledged himself to bring north Germany into the war, which here ought to assume the character of a national uprising. "What can be done by citizens under arms in coöperation with a standing army, when both are inspired by a common impulse," the French had already shown and the Spaniards were showing now. "We must accustom ourselves to the thought of privations of every sort, and even of death, if we are to tread the path upon which we are now entering. With our souls thus prepared, let us strike, in God's name, if a favorable opportunity should arise, always remembering that with courage and fortitude great things may be accomplished through small means. But we must rid ourselves of all unresponsive men, blunted to the nobler feelings, who cripple and destroy everything and are concerned only with the undisturbed enjoyment of their own infamy."

Stein himself had given up his position, his future, even his home for the sake of the cause.

And suppose all were to go well? After victory, what? And after that? Would it not be necessary, before rending the iron clamp that bound Europe, and in order to burst it, to know exactly with what one wished to replace it? Well, with what? Gentz and Stein asked themselves.

Return to the past? To the Europe of 1789? That was not to be thought of; not in France, not in Germany, hardly even in Italy or Spain. Nowhere. The Man had not been able to build anything permanent, but had proved himself eminently successful in destruction; and whether all that he had undone was ripe for extinction, or still deserved to live—a difficult question—what was dead could not be brought back. The essential thing was to act against Napoleon as Napoleon himself had acted. The men and the aims must be different, but not the methods; at least for the moment. "If Bonaparte tyrannized over the world to crush it," asked Gentz, "why should not others tyrannize over the world to save it? But they must be benevolent despots! Liberty will soon awake of herself."

But the aims? The two exiled politicians soon saw that it would not do to insist on these, for their solutions were much too far apart. Stein's ideas were grandiose and vague. He wanted to complete the revolution that Napoleon had begun but finally betrayed, and mentioned the necessity for individual states of all Germans, all Poles, all Italians: national and republican states. The German rulers, the Thirty Tyrants, as he called them, must all vanish from the scene; they, who had fawned upon Napoleon like dogs, must not be allowed to profit by his fall. But Stein did not hold very rigidly to his views, and was capable of suggesting entirely different ones at a moment's notice. Great Britain was really the power to which Europe would owe her new-found freedom: then why not give her what she wanted, in order to prevent once and for all any repetition of the present chaos? Why not make the whole of north Germany subject to the British crown? The Germans would fare very well under the British constitution. . . .

Gentz listened to all this sort of thing with polite interest, but thought to himself that no one should venture to have any part in such schemes. One Revolution had been more than enough; nobody wanted a second. Nor would the prospect of another be apt to attract the men who were needed because they had the means to power at their fingers' ends: the rulers, the ministers, the generals. They demanded a program, and a program such as would provide at the very least for their own security.

Accordingly Gentz added to his plan for restoration a detailed sketch for a future organization of Germany and Europe; the first proposal for a "German Confederation." By all means Germany must be free and independent, as Stein wished, but she must be decentralized and federated, for otherwise she would be too much of a danger to Europe. The multiplicity of German states must therefore be preserved and, unfortunately, the situation created by Napoleon must be taken as a basis on which to build. "In all Europe," he wrote, "there is no country but Germany whose fate would be of such immediate and decisive importance to all the others. Germany is the true political and military center of gravity for the civilized world. . . . If a balance of power in any sense of the term is to be preserved in Europe, Germany must be the foundation for it. . . . The independence of Germany is the first political consideration, the chief common interest of Europe. If it can be guaranteed by an auspicious and vigorous organization such as we must endeavor to achieve, order, equilibrium, and peace will return once more. . . .

"Once Germany assumes the position that her dignity and her preservation, together with the preservation of all, make it her duty to adopt, even a Bonaparte will be unable to rob Spain and Portugal of their independence, trample Italy underfoot, or issue laws for Constantinople. Then even Switzerland and Holland themselves will arise from the dead. . . . When this idea is pursued further it is hard to imagine after all how any new and universal disruption, or even a long and serious war, could henceforth break out in Europe as long as Germany, under a good system of government, enjoys independence and the substantial power and legitimate influence connected with it. It is certain that if the perpetual peace that is so widely invoked should ever cease to be more than a poetic fancy it must descend on mankind in this way, and in this way alone. So intimately connected one with another are the great affairs of the world. . . ."

Perpetual Peace! The dream of Kant, the dream of his own youth! Alas, no! Who would dare imagine that he can build for eternity? A hundred years, even fifty years, was a long time in a period that had brought about such radical changes with such speed, and that still promised others no less dreadful. No plan, no wish, no design could expect to cope with stark reality.

"No edifice raised by human hands is complete," wrote Gentz at the end of his prospectus, "and none can count upon eternity. Even with the most felicitous organization of the future state and the fairest and wisest disposition of territories, the inflexible course of events may lead perhaps once more to critical situations that will bring repeated disturbances in their train. Still, if everything that we desire and expect today should come to pass, if the present misery should end, the abysmal disgrace of Germany be lifted, and the best system of which our insight is capable should then be established for the future, this period will have done its fair share."

Such the content of Gentz's discussions with Stein, and such the purport of a memorandum completed under their influence.

Gentz had been with Stein only a few days when he received an invitation from Count Stadion, the Austrian Prime Minister, to come to Vienna immediately. A manifest storm signal!

He left on February 1, 1809, excited as a child, his peace program in his portfolio: the program of the Vienna Congress.

X

HEYDAY OF THE EMPEROR

THERE are times in every story when the narrator must desert his hero, times when the fact can no longer be concealed that he himself knows more than the central figure. The hero, as he is presented, knows almost nothing but the present, whereas the author has knowledge of the future and thus can see the past in its true perspective. He is familiar with the whole story, from beginning to end, and can arrange it, divide it thus or so, do with it as he will, for he is in command. But try as he may to surrender himself to the gravity of a situation as it is felt by those implicated, his feigned ignorance must of necessity acquire a tinge of the ironical from time to time. How can he view the despair of his hero with entire seriousness when he knows perfectly well that within a few years it will have lost all semblance of reality and become only a matter for detached contemplation?

One need not be a genius today to understand upon what the Napoleonic Empire actually rested.

The French General had entered upon his historic adventure without a plan; how, he hardly knew; through opportunities seized without a second thought, through pressing necessity, or through the unexampled mediocrity of those whom he confronted and whom no one had prepared for such a test. The more he pushed forward, the more sorely was he tempted; if he retreated a step he would be followed and driven back, eventually to his starting point, where no further opportunity awaited him. From a historical standpoint, what was his great Empire in reality? Opportunity pursued to the uttermost; the necessity into which French politics had fallen since they had overleaped the boundaries of the old kingdom almost twenty years before, now driven to absurd lengths; the struggle between Europe and the French Revolution fixed at its culmination and exalted by additional dreams to seeming permanence; an outrageously enforced coalition of the Continent against Great Britain, decked out as an empire by the egotistic genius who had acquired his commanding position through impostures to which human misery docilely surrendered. The Great Man gradually became accustomed to regarding the Empire as a desirable consummation, as a goal in itself, and the war against Great Britain as merely a hateful interruption. But in truth the Empire was the fortuitous event, dependent upon the war with Great Britain, and the very principle to which it owed its origin and expansion was at the same time its destruction.

How simple, yet how dreadful, this mechanism! The desultory conquests along the Mediterranean and the English Channel, so casually undertaken by France, had precipitated her into a long war with Great Britain. France did not have a navy strong enough to subdue Great Britain directly. Great Britain had allies on the Continent, actual or potential, so these had to be overcome one after the other. By the time the second and third had been disposed of the first one had recovered, and now conditions had to be imposed that would prevent it from ever becoming dangerous again. Reconciliation and coöperation were subsequently offered, and the victim accepted them. What else was there to do? But the conditions were such that they could not be satisfied with honor, hence the least margin allowed for reconciliation and coöperation was devoted to preparations for renewed opposition. Then the cycle began anew.

Napoleon tried to turn the people against the dynasts and the ruling classes. But the people had to provide him with too many soldiers, and suffered too cruelly under the poverty that followed closure of the Continent to British trade. Thus the freedom of which he spoke to them was soon not freedom from their past, from their own rulers, but first, and above all, freedom from the foreign Emperor. The instinct for liberty to which he appealed was turned against him. He realized this, and now began to play the dynasties and the ruling classes against the people. They seemed willing. "The French kings, my predecessors . . ." said this Revolutionary when he annexed Rome, and no one said him nay. He asked in marriage a princess of old and august lineage; the request was granted. He offered his hand to his mother to kiss; that was thought only natural. He incorporated Holland in his Empire, and learned international jurists asked to whom, if not to France, such a manifest alluvium of French rivers should belong.

But subservient to his interests though they appeared the old powers were in fact no more easily conciliated than the people, because the antagonism between ranks is always less than that between a united nation and its foreign oppressor, and the rulers and the upper classes could not help sympathizing after all with the masses of their tormented compatriots. Furthermore, these powers had a presentiment that Napoleon would not and could not deal honorably with them. He had betrayed the Revolution effectually enough to alienate the people but not to win over their rulers. Unable to conjure up the patina of age for his own dynasty, he was as little able to turn the old dynasties to account as the democratic states, because he envied royalty and felt himself its inferior.

One of his generals warned a ruler born of a long-established line that Napoleon was resolved to exterminate all royal families. What he needed were manufactured dynasties, with artificial states set up in conformity with despotism and prepared to execute his orders; states without inner vitality and without permanence. For his own preservation he required the ephemeral and the impossible, and found himself enmeshed in the impossible.

Whatever still took shape under his hands turned out against him: in France, where ten years previously he had created a modern state that no longer needed an outmoded autocrat for its management; beyond her frontiers, in the "Empire," among the nations that he had swallowed up, the Italians, the Germans, the Poles, none of whom wanted to give themselves over to the sway of a single supertyrant.

This the Emperor could not understand. Anything that was contrary to his monstrous dream he called "anti-European," or sometimes even "Jacobinical." The British were "anti-European," all their friends, too, and not less so the consumers of British colonial wares. "Do you think I care anything about those Polish Jacobins?" he asked, under obligation by both logic and design to restore Poland, but prevented from redeeming his promise by his alliance with the Czar and even more by his own Empire, which would brook no free national state. He cheated the Italians in respect to their unification, having first suggested the idea to them. He imprisoned the Pope as an enemy of Europe, because the Holy Father had objected to the exclusion of British goods from his domains. The papal anathema that was issued in consequence "would certainly have been ridiculous," according to Fouché, "if the people had remained indifferent; but general indignation fanned into flame again a dying faith." Thus to the uprising of the Spaniards was added the patient enmity of the Church. The dynastic hocus-pocus, the golden cradle of the King of Rome, were meant to counterfeit the traditional, but remained only *opéra bouffe;* the new trend in romantic conservatism was not developing to Napoleon's advantage.

With remarkable insight one of the new conservatives, our friend Adam Müller, defined the fundamental contradiction in the position of the Emperor as early as 1808. He explained to his distinguished audience that in any political struggle there are always two parties: the young, who lean to innovation and accomplishment; and the old, who are inclined toward tradition. "A young statesman or general who declares himself wholeheartedly on the side of youth, and breaks through or overturns barriers erected by the past and safeguarded by the old; who employs the passing impulse, that heritage of youth, in his own interest; and who acts as though the world had only this one side, faces an awful and perilous moment when he crosses the inevitable divide into age, the other side of the world. Time and the natural law move on without interruption, compelling everyone, the entire social order, to traverse the hemisphere of youth as well as that of age, and the young leader is now upon the threshold of age. Other inclinations and other wishes spring up ineluctably. All the old institutions of the past that he reviled or overturned in his youth, all laws, all barriers, acquire an overpowering puissance and majesty for the hitherto rampant soul that must now adapt itself to wholly different conditions of existence. The higher he climbs toward the summit of life, the more clearly do the mountains of the past appear around him. The pressing requirements of his second period he himself has destroyed; he himself has given to the law of nature the power to crush him. The fame and the deeds of those days when he played at creating the world are necessarily effaced now that he has assumed the task of preserving the world, without benefit of the accumulated wisdom of the centuries that is so essential for preservation, because he himself has violated it. The earlier companions of this prophet of youth see him enter upon paths that are strangely incompatible with his former attitude, and are sensible of his inconsistency; in his own heart he, too, feels it, tries to preserve the bearing of youth, to blend hostile and eternally irreconcilable elements from both ages, and eventually succumbs to the jugglery in which he has been forced to take refuge. He imitates the habits of the age upon which he has entered, but its spirit will not be conjured up: prayer and cosmetics do not go together. . . ."

By employing such a profoundly philosophical style it was still possible for one to speak his mind even in Dresden, within the Confederation of the Rhine.

The so-called Napoleonic Wars may be classified in various ways. Those who lived through them day after day thought each one a new war, and called it so: "The War of the Third Coalition," "The Prussian War," "The War of 1809," and so on. But the truth is that when considered in the most general way they comprise, together with the wars against the Revolution, one single stupendous war that lasted from 1792 to 1815.

The British adopted this perspective intuitively, for they could see that although the sundry interventions and desertions of their allies shifted the world war from one theater to another, they did not interrupt its progress. As viewed from the Continent, however, the situation was entirely different. It might be said that from here three great wars could be distinguished: the war of the First and Second Coalitions, 1792 to 1801; the war of the Third Coalition, together with the tardy Prussian intervention, 1805 to 1807; and Napoleon's war against Russia, which developed into a general European war, 1812 to 1814; 1815 would be a negligible epilogue, 1809 a curious interlude.

Still another picture emerges when emphasis is placed upon the name and character of Napoleon. For although he fought in the war of the First Coalition, and, at the head of the Republic, terminated that of the Second, both had started independently of him. The first Napoleonic war was the War of 1805. The provocations of the new Emperor that led to it were the immediate causes of the Napoleonic Wars, and the Peace of Tilsit, which brought them to a close, was the real Napoleonic peace; it carried the "new federative system" to its zenith.

From 1805 to 1807 old Europe opposed the Emperor; during the years immediately preceding, 1801 to 1805, the appeasement period, she had tried to live peaceably with him; after 1807 she subordinated herself. But here again, in this classification, the War of 1809 against Austria is not easy to place. Certainly it was not, like its predecessors, conducted by a diplomatically arranged coalition. Austria struck because the situation in Europe promised success, and it seemed that action by one single power alone would be adequate to fan into flame the embers of opposition that glowed everywhere. But the fire did not burn fiercely enough.

There was civil war in the Tyrol, where, as in Spain, priests and peasants rose against their new oppressor, and there were rebellions of officers in north Germany. If to these are added the war that could no longer be suppressed in Spain, and a British attack on the island of Walcheren, in Holland, it must have seemed for a short time that the last hour of the "new federative system" had struck. But the preparations that Napoleon had been making while Europe slept proved too efficient. The insurrection in north Germany, scattered and planless, ended in mass executions; the attack on Holland failed; and the Russians, standing by the alliance between the two emperors, felt that they had done enough in not having taken any real action *against* Austria. South Germany and north Italy were secure bases whence Napoleon could launch his armies against Vienna, and though he had to overcome an opposition that was more dangerous than ever before, the new treaty extended his "Empire" down to the east coast of the Adriatic and the edge of the Balkans.

In reality an interlude, or a prologue, this War of 1809 seemed to many of those who were tossed about in the storm, ignorant of its true meaning, a final defeat that would seal the fate of the period. The Austrians had attempted resistance of a new type, with a modernized army and the whole nation in arms, but with no better success than in 1805. The reform Minister, Count Stadion, was dismissed. The program of his successor, Count Clemens Metternich, was one of complete adaptation to circumstances.

The remains of Austria concluded an alliance with France.
Napoleon married a Hapsburg princess.
What next?

GENTZ was among those who asked the question. We shall not relate what he went through during the war, or what he did, concerned lest we weary the reader with the monotony of this story that was all too real. Enough that when he returned to Prague after the frustrated offensive of 1809 he was an aging, prematurely gray, and disillusioned man. He was not so given to heroics as heretofore, but thoughtful, rational, and embittered. He doubted having managed his life to the best advantage. All his tormenting dreams he had seen come true, but none of his hopes. Behind him lay error and obstinacy; before him, the void. That he would eventually pass beyond its confines was as clear as day one moment, and so uncertain the next that he secretly feared its utter impossibility. Still another question was, how he could best order his life to traverse this waste; and a third, what would come then? Certainly not all that he had fought for, and fretted over, and insisted upon: re-establishment of the right and a revelation that the events of the past fifteen years had been mistaken and wrong.

He who came home after passing through three or four wars and wasting years of energy on a hundred memoirs, a thousand letters, ten thousand discussions, protests, warnings, recommendations—sound memoirs and good recommendations—left this question still unsettled. His mind was exhausted. He had so far recovered from the horrors of 1805, '06, and '07 that early in 1809 he had fallen prey once more to ardent hope. But temperamental excesses like this leave their mark in the end.

Toward the end of the year he wrote in his diary: "At first this year was bright with hope, then stormy, unhappy, and painful beyond all imagining; then peaceful again but somber, without interest, without prospect; my plans wrecked, the dreams of my life's most beautiful period shattered, nothing before me but a monotonous, fruitless existence. I have a feeling, too, that the whole thing will come to an end before very long." When he read these lines again, fifteen years later, he added: "I wrote that in 1810! *O vanas hominum mentes, o pectora coeca!*" Oh, the infirm souls of men; oh, their unseeing hearts!

In February, 1810, he appeared once more in Vienna, ostensibly as an expert in economics, to consult with the Minister of Finance, who stood helpless in the face of postwar inflation. He did, in fact, prepare "a few futile essays" on the subject of paper money, but his main purpose was to renew, and perhaps to profit by, his friendship with Metternich. "I even believe that in cultivating it I shall open up through him a new sphere of activity for myself." But the relations between these two men progressed with more difficulty than might be supposed.

Metternich's first important achievement was to bring about the marriage of Napoleon, in 1810, to the Austrian Archduchess, Marie Louise, daughter of Franz II. In this sensational union he saw a temporary expedient, and nothing more; surely a little moderation, a minimum of transient concessions, were to be expected from the son-in-law of the Hapsburg Emperor! In Metternich's eyes such benefits amply atoned for the sacrifice of the Emperor's silly young daughter. Every transaction with Napoleon was a recognition of his claims; the French aristocracy had served him long; princesses of the noblest families were closely associated with his brothers and his generals. If all these things lasted, it would be better to comply with them. If not, then all had been but trickery and disguise, the marriage only a mock marriage, and the child to be born of it would be a sham also. Thus whatever the future might hold, Metternich could raise his glass of champagne at the wedding banquet with a light heart to the eagerly expected King of Rome.

Gentz wrote no "Memoir on the Necessity of Refusing Napoleon the Hand of an Archduchess." What five years previously he would have taken at first for a macabre jest and then with raging thoughts and angry words tried to prevent, was now, to a mind disciplined and humbled by events, but sadly confirmatory news. He held his peace. He could not be present at the festivities, when Napoleon's marshal escorted in the imperial bride and all the men waved their hats in the air. Excluded from the celebration, he reaped the bitter reward for all his wasted years of struggle.

"The evening of the wedding ceremony," says his diary, "when all Vienna sparkled with lights, was one of the saddest of my life. I did not feel like going either to the church or to the court, and as I had nothing else to do I remained at home throughout the excitement. I was ill, and suffered terribly from rheumatic pains through the whole upper part of my body. I had no desire for anything. But in spite of all I went out for a little while about seven o'clock, saw the first of the illumination, heard the cannon announce the great event, and, prey to the saddest thoughts, cried like a child. After ward I went out twice more to see the illumination, but the crowds, together with my grief, drove me back again each time into the house. That night I could not sleep."

The years 1810, '11, and '12, the Emperor's heyday, were oppressive years, comfortless years. The worthless paper money would buy almost nothing. Life's little pleasures, tea and coffee especially, were not to be had, and there were no English newspapers; that customary diversion had been discontinued. There was dreary, monotonous news of the Spanish war, to which one gradually became accustomed. Even letters from friends were rare, and said but little when they did arrive, partly because of the censorship and partly because no one really had the heart for correspondence.

Gentz wrote to his old friend, Rahel Lewin, who was still trying to hold together her sadly attenuated salon: "I feel as though I were withered, sucked dry, finished. I cannot bear to dwell on the past, because I meet everywhere the ghosts of my own faults and my own mistakes. The present, naturally enough, is wholly without attraction, and of the future I know only this one humiliating fact: that in any case it must, and will, assume a form quite different from what I in my shortsighted philosophy had imagined. . . . Society, as it is called, has become so repugnant that it stifles and repels me by its monotony and its commonplace character. . . ."

In a letter to Brinkmann, his Swedish friend of twenty years before, now living a disenchanted life in his northern solitude, he said: "All we can do today is call out to one another from time to time that we still live." But when Brinkmann insisted, Gentz was ready enough to start a correspondence with him.

"As we both live in countries that revel in the felicity and serenity of Continental peace, and belong body and soul to the thrice blessed Continental system, no one can object if we communicate our simple desires to one another. And if we abstain from contraband colonial wares (which we never liked anyway, for as everyone knows we never drank anything but acorn coffee with beet sugar) and other anti-European fabrications (which we never wanted, even in our libraries) the most conscientious post-office official would never discover anything to find fault with in our correspondence."

But when he actually sat down to write, nothing cheerful occurred to him. "As all foreign policy has been reduced to the art of prolonging the miserable existence of impotent states by temporary palliatives, I have abandoned any real activity in this field since 1809." "For a year and a half I have suffered from an arthritic and gouty complaint; no real pain, but a condition that often affects the nerves and is associated with lassitude and general malaise. This, together with the discouraging outcome of so many fruitless endeavors and frustrated hopes after twenty years of effort, has dampened considerably my pleasure in life. . . ."

In October, 1811, he rented "a wretched little lodging" in Vienna's Seilergasse, which he gradually furnished in such manner that it was still suitable later, when prosperity came. There he led a self-centered and curious existence. For gambling, formerly one of his ruling passions, there was no money. He continued to meet occasionally the unpresentable Madame Swoboda, with whom he had lived at one time, and treated her with consideration for she had had a son by him. As far as can be ascertained, she had no successors. He took more pleasure in the home life of his servant, Leopold, whose flourishing family compensated for one of his own, especially at Christmas time. Before long there was added to his household a young secretary named Charles, actually a deserter from the Saxon Army, of whom the diary says: "I love that boy beyond all expression," and about whom there was some gossip, though probably it was unfounded. Gentz was always generous with his servants, and as much concerned over raising money for their New Year gifts as ever he had been about the birthdays of his "actresses."

His father, General Director of the Mint under Frederick the Great, had died in 1810, at the age of eighty-four. Since the flight from Prussia Gentz had never seen him again. His mother had long since died, and dead were poor Minna, the divorced wife, and his brother, Heinrich, a clever architect, who built the castle at Weimar. Two unmarried sisters lived in Berlin, to whom he wrote occasionally but whom he would not meet; in any case he had no desire to see again the city to which he had such an aversion.

Friends of his detested past sometimes turned up. In Teplitz he met Lombard, the former Cabinet Councilor, the ill-starred dove of peace, with whom he deliberately appeared arm in arm on the promenade: one does not avenge oneself on a fallen enemy. Humboldt, who had come to Vienna as Prussian Ambassador, he saw again for the first time after ten years filled with forgetfulness and pain. "I found him completely unchanged; as brilliant, as amusing, as irresistible as ever." Humboldt was better preserved than Gentz, having directed his life more wisely. He did not ask that the world be what it was not, and thought it only natural that everywhere and always treachery should be practiced, war carried on, and men harassed. Instead of fishing in troubled waters, where God alone knew what the catch would be, he lived for himself, his wife, his friends, and his own improvement. So he went along in Paris, in Spain, in Rome, as long as the course of events permitted, and he described Germany as a country in which he no longer had the slightest interest.

He was but little aroused over Napoleon, and spoke of him with unaffected respect as "the French Emperor"; and when the Dictator's brother-in-law, Prince Murat, showed his wife the courtesy of saying: "Humboldt, Madame, is an illustrious name," Caroline was genuinely touched by so much condescension. Later on, when Humboldt saw a way of helping the general situation and advancing his own interests at the same time, he turned toward the state and became Minister of Education under Stein. Then he changed over to foreign politics, as soon as there began to be a foreign policy once more, and with the rising hatred against Napoleon he, too, became a patriot and a Napoleon-hater, and so continued in pleasing harmony with himself and his environment.

Successful in managing his own affairs, Humboldt reviewed the evolution of his friend Gentz with grim interest. "This man has always lacked inner harmony," was his judgment. "His endeavors have always been directed outward; and not only that, but toward external activities over which he had scarcely any control. He never associated pleasure with something higher, and within himself, and so it was inevitable that he should succumb to satiety and exhaustion. . . . He has not found, nor ever can find, a dominant idea; the true, innermost man within himself and others has never been clearly revealed to him, yet his visions have been plain enough for him to make idealistic demands. Still, he has always been introspective, and despite all his inordinate desire for enjoyment has never entered upon unalloyed delight without a backward glance to evaluate the pleasure itself; thus he can see clearly the abyss into which he has fallen.

"Highly characteristic, too, is his insensitivity to all art, and his lack of any satisfaction in it. To him who has even a limited knowledge of art, nature shows an eternal opulence in all her phases and his imagination never tires. . . . Gentz has missed still another road to happiness; the shortest, the smoothest, and the most beautiful for him whose instinct leads him to take it: a taste for women. The feminine mind, though truly great in a few exceptional instances only, exerts a gracious power in many, and contains in a symbol that is easy to grasp all that would safeguard a man against such failures as his. This he has never realized, though still believing that he has, and he has often led the finest women to think that he understood them thoroughly because his imagination divined what his reason was unable to penetrate. Indeed, a certain kind of love affair has made him forever incapable of appreciating the best in women. . . ."

Humboldt, though too strongly influenced by the psychological patterns of his dead friend, Schiller, was a keen observer of human nature. Politics compel a man to take sides, and he who devotes himself to them heart and soul must become biased too. At least Gentz took politics "in grim earnest," as he said, whereas Humboldt turned out to be lukewarm and opportunistic.

Adam Müller, the aging divine youth, also appeared in Vienna, though Gentz tried to prevent the immigration of this once cherished friend. "I know from experience how hard it is here for a foreigner to carry out his intentions and to do a little good." Müller had been trying his luck recently in Berlin, where von Hardenberg, Stein's successor, had paid him for occasional advice and help with publicity. Müller accepted these opportunities gladly, but meanwhile tried to force the Minister into appointing him to a professorship in the University of Berlin by intriguing venomously against him, by playing a Germanic and cryptic economics against Hardenberg's liberal and Hanoverian-British system, and by placing his literary gifts at the disposal of the reactionary Junkers. Finally, Hardenberg could see no way to rid himself of the underhanded philosopher except to send him on a "secret mission" to Gentz. The errand was of little significance, and in order that Müller might have something to do Gentz had to arrange for him to give a course of lectures. In addition to delivering these, Müller transmitted reports to Hardenberg that were filled with insight and malice.

The Austrian people, he wrote, were demoralized, and despised their rulers. "The conduct of the Emperor and the princes of the Imperial House during and after the recent war: the obvious indifference to the suffering of the people and the personal avarice of the Emperor, to say nothing of the dangerous contrast between the proclamations of 1809 and the marriage in 1810, has discouraged all sense of nationalism."

His mention of proclamations was a thrust at Gentz, who had drawn them up. "Count Metternich, surfeited with great undertakings and indifferent to most of the nobler impulses by reason of his brilliant and precocious career, of course desires secretly to preserve a reputation for good intentions in respect to the freedom of Europe, yet will go no further than he conveniently can. . . . This spoiled child of Fortune has developed into a Minister of Neutrality. . . ."

In this opinion Müller was not wholly wrong. Just as he himself had a philosophy wherewith to explain and justify everything that happened, so Metternich possessed the secret of adjusting his policies to current predominations. He trimmed his sails according to the wind. And in the final analysis an opportunistic politician is much less contemptible than an opportunistic philosopher.

One day during the first year of his ministry Count Metternich was discussing with Gentz the question of what function Austria could continue to serve in a modern Europe. They agreed that her position must be a conservative one. During the past decades she had suffered more than enough changes and it was high time that peace should return as a stable condition. Austria was above all an Empire that needed peace and could bring peace; the intermediate state, the state of equipoise, *the* European state, if such there were: a bit of Germany, a bit of Italy, from a historical standpoint even a bit of Spain, together with lands to which no national name could be given and those where small but unruly nationalities adapted themselves to the civilizing influence of the Hapsburg rule. She was a state without social consciousness, without definite nationality, the state in which "domestic politics" themselves were actually a sort of diplomacy. She was the past in the present, and if the present grew too strong, too presumptuous, in comparison with the past, Austria could not survive. Metternich, the Rhinelander, and Gentz, the north German, recognized this danger more clearly than the native born, who accepted their milieu as a matter of course. As aliens these two men admired the magnificent scenery, and the curious political doctrine to which they had subscribed.

After this their conferences became more frequent, and as they proceeded Gentz profited more from Metternich than Metternich from him. We can never become more subtle than we are; and although Gentz had the richer and more profound intellect Metternich, whose mind was already quite adequate to his needs, had but little more to gain. Gentz, on the other hand, learned to moderate his demands and to adapt his level to circumstances; to separate philosophy from politics, and to view the latter as a mere trade. The vain Minister delighted in showing his mentor by means of the dispatches that arrived daily *quantilla prudentia mundus regatur*,* and how he exceeded most of his rivals in wisdom.

"Like all scholars, he is impractical," was his opinion of Gentz. "I know that he is apt to wander off if left to himself; for this reason he must not be allowed to remain unoccupied, but must be kept constantly busy." And later: "Herr von G. was always at one emotional extreme or the other, expecting certain victory or ineluctable defeat, and just as unstable in his trust or distrust of people. He was sure only of fundamentals, of general principles, but with these as a basis could orient himself after the widest divagations."

To this bundle of nerves, in his buoyant despair, the more limited and poised Metternich seemed increasingly the great healer, until

* With how little wisdom the world may be ruled.

the authority on the unscrupulous, wise in the ways of government, had become the mainstay and support of the skeptic.

And Napoleon? Gradually the disillusioned Demosthenes came to realize that Metternich did not take the Napoleonic episode too seriously. "The tyranny of Napoleon," he insisted, "is by its very nature a transitory phenomenon." This he may have learned from the Tyrant himself, who had blustered and shouted it out at him with angry laughter. Among all the foreigners there, Metternich, Ambassador in Paris from 1806 to 1809, best understood Napoleon. Gentz had struggled with an inflated phantom, a force devoid of human qualities, whereas Metternich had stood with courtly mien before the man himself as he raged back and forth in his audience chamber, and this irreproachable product of the eighteenth century had in no sense looked up to the god of the nineteenth. Metternich had good nerves—or no nerves, as another expression puts it.

Secure in the consciousness of all that he stood for, in his breeding, his appearance, his star-bespangled uniform, dignified and charming amongst the assembled court, he could let Bonaparte's vulgar and offensive outbursts of rage pass harmlessly over his head. The Emperor was always impressed by what he himself did not have. He treated the foreign Ambassador with less contempt than he did his own people, and it was not long before he began relating to him in detail and with overtaxed and unrestrained loquacity all the problems of his life and his position. Metternich put up with it, for from the standpoint of human nature as well as of his profession it was an interesting lesson. Although no genius, the young diplomat was shrewd enough for his office, in which a knowledge of human nature and the ability to put oneself in the place of others play such an important role.

The man whom the world knew simply as a Caesar seated awkwardly on his horse, as a god-devil, Metternich came to know intimately. He could see the commander, the man of imposing intellect, of the penetrating glance that laid everything bare; but he could see, too, the toils in which this egotistic nature had ensnared itself: snobbery, hysteria, theatricalism, improvisation, madness, and dangerous insecurity. It might be possible to get along with him for a time by wise and flexible management; in the long run he would no doubt be destroyed by his own folly.

How? When? Metternich pondered but little over these questions. He was patient and serene, with all the extrovert's complacency, which brings happiness and does not enervate; in love with life, and familiar with realms of pleasure that had no connection with politics. "But no dramatizing," he wrote under his portrait.

No dramatizing, but at critical moments the energy, the reticence, and the inclemency of a man whose progenitors had for centuries made government their special province. A ruling diplomat from youth, almost from childhood, indeed, he needed no painful disenchantments and inner strife to teach him what politics mean. Never an idealist, he did not become a cynic. Government to him was not so much action, fostered by brave hopes and plans, as it was mediation, balance, direction. He had been taught in youth that freedom and peace come from the mean, from equilibrium, from a balance of power among nations, among classes, and among ideologies. Ideologies were dogmatic, opposed to nature, and Metternich, a dilettante in the natural sciences, had no faith in them. Most of the men that he met he straightway pronounced crazy: rationalists and romanticists, revolutionists and counterrevolutionists were all idealists to him, fomenters of unrest and slaughter, thieves of human happiness, who in their capricious thinking perverted the true nature of things. It should be restored by a balance of political power, an artificial nature.

The Empire of Napoleon was such a monstrous absurdity, to be sure, so obviously a cause or a consequence of imbalance, that Metternich must certainly have wished for its dissolution. But why endeavor to attain this end by counterrevolutionary enterprises, by new bigotries and frenzies? Ridicule, evasion, and procrastination seemed to him more suitable measures; Napoleon should not be tempted as the terrified wayfarer tempts his murderer. Neither Russia nor Prussian Germany must be allowed to inherit the role of the Dictator in Europe. Merely to get rid of Napoleon there should never again be unleashed the Revolution that had brought him to the top and that he had subdued to his own ends.

The Revolution! "The appalling catastrophe of the French social revolution," as Metternich called it. He was living on the Rhine then, twenty years previously, and remembered with a shudder the macabre coronation ceremonies for the last German Emperor of the Holy Roman Empire, when his host, the Elector of Mainz, unveiled once more all the pomp of that antiquated structure, while the guests whispered to one another the most threatening news. "Your life may be very long," his old tutor had said to him, "but you will never live to see the end of this conflagration."

It was Napoleon who extinguished the flames, at least for the time being. He was revolutionary in his foreign policies, a conqueror who did not consolidate his gains, and through this he was to be destroyed. But Metternich esteemed him for having scorned, betrayed, and surmounted the social revolution. Both men thought alike in that they regarded government as the art of calming turbulent nature, sought reality in history, and did not believe in ideologies. Neither had any confidence in the rectitude or infallibility of "the people," and both were callous: Napoleon as a recognized monster, Metternich as a grand seignior of the preceding century; a logical, hard, and at the same time fastidious character in all his arrogance. But was it possible to get rid of the oppressor of the people without the help of the people themselves; of their fury, and all the mad ideologies that were now beginning to be connected with them?

For this reason the overthrow of Napoleon was not the exclusive goal of Count Metternich's efforts: a man of culture was not supposed, on the whole, to be limited to one single aim. If the Emperor does not mend his ways materially he must fall some day, from one cause or another. How, and when, let us leave to the future, and in the meantime make friendly attempts at adjustment.

Metternich even interceded with Napoleon for Baron vom Stein. That dangerous emigrant, he thought, would surely be pacified if only his confiscated property were restored to him. But by all means no dramatizing! This optimistic man even hoped to reconcile Great Britain herself to the new order, at least provisionally, though what would come later remained to be seen, and thus to crown peace on the Continent with a maritime peace. As he entered his coach for the trip to the imperial wedding in Paris he told interviewers that he earnestly hoped to bring such a peace back with him.

On the one hand, so he smilingly assured the British, his coöperation with the Victor was only apparent, and forced upon him by bitter necessity; he hoped no one would doubt that now, as always, his heart beat only for the cause of Europe's freedom. But on the other hand he invited them once more to join with him in his plan, and thus to make it possible of realization, for there could be no enduring peace on the Continent while these two great world empires continued at war with one another. Furthermore, the honor of Austria could best be restored by Britain's sacrifice of her own —by a uniform international lowering of standards, as it were. Metternich implored Gentz to use his influence in London toward an approach to this goal. It was the first command of the Minister to the adviser whom he had inherited from his predecessors, and there was nothing for the bankrupt idealist to do but fulfill it.

The "Memoir on Maritime Peace" was written against his better judgment, the first time in his life that he had ever done such a thing; but now he was a diplomat, ready to carry out all orders. In it he advocated a repetition of the attempt made ten years previously at Amiens, the infamy and despair of which he and a few others had penetrated and endured at the time. He arrayed the arguments with which he had been familiar for so long, and had so long hated: the elements of a balance of power in Europe were still extant, though formidably weakened; Great Britain would strengthen them by becoming once more a member of the general concert instead of continuing to wage a fruitless and alienating war; furthermore, she had become so rich and powerful during the long years of strife that she no longer had the slightest need for the classic balance of power, but in a certain sense was herself an equipoise for the united Continent; it was wrong to count on the suffering and hunger of oppressed peoples, for their miseries made them weak and incapable of resistance, whereas peace would make them stronger; the separation of the Spanish colonies from the motherland was ample compensation for the alliance of France and Spain; to disregard conquests that were already achieved was reasonable only when there was some expectation of recovering their fruits from the Victor; at present there was no such hope. In France herself the Napoleonic system had gradually become so firmly established that it must now be recognized as almost legitimate; instead of arguing about Napoleon's character, which would make peace forever impossible, it would be wiser to ask what was to his best interest; this was, to end the war, as it was Great Britain's interest also. Whoever insisted on the impossibility of a negotiated peace was insisting in vain, for it had now been proved that closure of the Continent had not subdued Great Britain, and that the banishment of French ships from the high seas had not overcome France; neither of these two powers had the means to end the war by force, and if there were no way of terminating it amicably it would last forever . . . and so on.

Gentz noted in his diary that he had tried to adopt a point of view opposed to his own, and that he was doubtful about the result. This was only to cause the saying in London that even Gentz himself had gone over to the capitulants. The Marquis of Wellesley, Foreign Secretary, acknowledged receipt of the letter in a frigidly polite negation. Napoleon would not give up his Continental system, and the requirements of the British Empire would not tolerate it. The Treaty of Amiens had not abrogated this basic fact, nor would Gentz's memoir succeed in doing so.

But the disfavor into which he had fallen in London was of short duration, for neither Metternich nor the British dared neglect each other for long. No one knew what would come of all this, and what some day they might like to have it believed they had planned and striven for from the very first. Great Britain now maintained official relations only with exiled monarchs, but there were still anomalous connections with the Continent. In a few capitals there were so-called Hanoverian ambassadors, representatives of a state that no longer existed, whose reports served the former Elector of Hanover albeit often in unbelievably roundabout ways. Disguised as harmless merchants, British agents traveled from Constantinople up the Danube to Vienna, whence they notified their principals that it would be hard to exert any influence over Austria without the assistance of Gentz. "As Gentz had the confidence of the last three British ambassadors and is one of the intimate friends of Count Metternich, it would be highly impolitic to drop him entirely. I have no reason to distrust his principles, but necessity is a poor adviser. If Gentz were to go over to the opposite side, neither Count von Hardenberg nor a single one of the British agents would have access to the Minister. Indeed, it is probable that we should all have to leave Vienna within twenty-four hours . . ." So through the agents Johnson and King he began to receive money again, three hundred pounds, six hundred pounds, from the pockets of British taxpayers.

Once more, for a few weeks, his household was generously supplied. And everyone kept all roads open.

XI

TRIUMPH AT LAST

WHEN Alexander, Czar of Russia, called in the summer of 1812 for the organization of a German legion, saying that he was about to draw the sword for the liberation of all peoples, Gentz emitted a derisive and bitter laugh. "It requires a singular degree of effrontery to summon one's neighbors to a common crusade after having cheated, betrayed, deserted, plundered, and sold them out individually and collectively for so many years. Above all it is wholly unparalleled to say of a war that was represented from the first as purely defensive, and that began with a retreat over the Dnieper, that its main purpose was the liberation of Germany!"

Since the opening of the war between France and Russia he had been obsessed by two thoughts. First: this is the long-expected and richly deserved punishment of the Czar. Second: but unfortunately he will be punished at our expense. Napoleon will emerge from this struggle mightier than ever, and whereas so far there have been at least two empires in Europe and Asia, from now on there will be only one. . . . He knew that there was a plan afoot to partition Russia and to set a French marshal as king over Finland, St. Petersburg, and the Baltic countries. Stockholm and Constantinople were to be incorporated in the French Empire, India would rise against British dominion, and the modicum of Austrian independence that Metternich had recently succeeded in conjuring up would inevitably disappear in the storm without anyone even bothering to ask after it.

In truth the attitude of the Czar and his advisers seemed hardly impressive from a moral standpoint. They had enjoyed to the full the ostentatious glitter of friendship with the Great Man as long as ever his magic held, meanwhile employing this alliance to broaden the scope of Russian domination and plunge Finns, Turks, and Persians into bloody involvements. At last they had learned, as all before them had learned, that with Napoleon there could be no question of coöperation between equals, and that he could not endure the proximity of a real, that is to say an independent, power; not, at least, while he continued at war with Great Britain. But the Russians, rulers of one sixth of the earth's surface, could not renounce their ambition to be a real power even with the best will in the world, which, of course, was lacking. Accordingly they began to withdraw from the Continental system and to follow their own course, which was bound to coincide sooner or later with that of the British since because of the antagonistic groupings in force at the time there was no third. During the long year 1811 the inevitability of the approaching clash was fully realized. It came as a result of the simple psychic and political mechanism that underlies the struggle for power, the mechanism by which world affairs are dominated and of which all apparent complications are but an expression.

But what were the sins of the past compared with the deeds and sacrifices that now were consummated? History is contemptuous of moral obstinacies, and states will forever continue to do what is enforced at the moment by their wish to survive.

Napoleon assembled the peoples of the Continent, French, Italians, Germans, Poles, against Russia, for it was his pride and his ruse to draw up Western civilization in battle array against the despotism of the East. Europe—France, Italy, Germany—did not say him nay but followed him in his mad undertaking, albeit with reluctance. It was Russia that said No; and the No of the crafty young man in his palace at St. Petersburg reflected accurately what his country desired; the wish of the peasants and even of the nobles, who with their own hands set fire to their castles so that an alien foe might not find refuge in them. The spirit of Russia had descended upon her ruler, who, furthermore, had been well advised; in part by an ambassador hurriedly dispatched from Great Britain as soon as it was clear that this time the situation was crucial; in part by the great emigrant, Baron vom Stein.

There came the customary news. The Emperor fought a great battle at Borodino as he had fought at Austerlitz and Jena, was victorious, and entered Moscow. This meant capitulation, or at least would have meant capitulation if the inhabitants had remained in their city, if the civil administration had placed itself at the disposal of the conqueror, and if the fleeing aristocrats had thought only of how soon they could return. Thus it had been in Milan and Rome, in Vienna and Berlin. As it was not so this time, for Napoleon entered a deserted and burning city, it availed him nothing that by the rules of the game as he knew them he had already won the war.

When finally he realized his position and turned back, it was too late.

The winter and the Cossacks did the rest.

That the defeated leader could even survive this grave retributive misfortune shows the weakness and decadence of his opponents, their inadequate preparation for this turn of events, the relative solidity of his system, and the force of his character. Muttering, and with clenched fists, Europe allowed his sledges to pass by. Paris let him collect a new army, govern, and make shamelessly brazen speeches. What would happen if he were no more?

Whereas so far the Russians had played the role of the attacked, for the sake of their country and aided by its very nature, they now came to a decision responsible for everything that followed. They concluded to pass beyond their own frontiers, ally themselves with the nations that Napoleon had intended to employ in breaking them, and thus convert the struggle into a general European war. It is perfectly well known who was behind this determination: Baron vom Stein, the famous expert in European affairs.

While Napoleon sought to catch his breath Germany burst into flame; too late for the honor of her people or, as Stein brusquely informed the Czarina, for the honor of her rulers. The blaze started from sheer necessity. Praiseworthy or not—that is a futile question in the face of stark compulsion. Most certainly it was not admirable that the popular wrath should break out only after it appeared highly probable that it could rage unpunished. By their long years of submission the Germans had led Napoleon to believe that they were a patient folk, with no interest in politics. Now of a sudden they were raving like furies, and a state system erected on a firm belief in their passivity broke down amidst all the brutalities and abuses without which such a collapse cannot occur.

British diplomacy, tireless and persistent, realizing at last that victory was almost certain, did its share to direct the unchained forces of opposition. Its representative in eastern Europe accomplished miracles of discreetly skillful negotiation. Encouraged by British-Russian promises the poor King of Prussia, in January, 1813, fled from his capital and turned toward Silesia. There his patriotic advisers extorted his signature to manifestoes that called first for the organization of volunteer corps, then for coöperation with the Russians, then for the mobilization of all young men, and finally for war against France.

Eight months previously the whole world had seemed united

against Russia. Now Great Britain was allied with Sweden, Sweden with Russia, and Russia with Prussia. If Austria declared herself at one with them there would be formed at last that world coalition for which Gentz had cried in vain fifteen years before, ten years before, even five years before. Had there been such a confederation then the world would have been spared untold anguish.

METTERNICH, and Gentz, his adviser, followed the development of this crisis with rapt attention. That Napoleon's spell was broken, or with the coöperation of Austria soon could be broken, was clear to them. Clear, too, was the goal: the restoration of equilibrium, military and political no less than social; the restoration of equilibrium, and nothing more. No new chimeras, no league of nations, no superstate; no German Empire, of which north German patriots had recently been dreaming; no Russian preponderance either, such as might so easily develop out of the valiant Russian contribution to this change in circumstances. A peace founded upon a group of states that were about equally strong, moderately governed, and not too hostile toward one another could be achieved only if Russia were kept within her own borders; if Prussian patriots did not transform themselves into pan-German revolutionists; if Austria regained the influence that she had exerted in the eighteenth century; and if France remained a great power.

Such was the equation worked out by Metternich and Gentz. To their coevals it seemed hardly enthusiastic enough for so momentous an era. But then, Gentz was no longer an enthusiast, and Metternich never had been one.

Both agreed in effect that Austria's role at first must be one of mediation. Still formally an ally of France, she must invite the warring powers to an interchange of views, and propose terms that would conform with Europe's legitimate aspirations. A victory by Napoleon over the united forces of Russia and Prussia would have wiped out his misfortune of the preceding year; a decisive victory by his opponents would imply the elimination of Austria. If Napoleon were defeated, Metternich's negotiations would ease the path for him. The Minister could intervene to arrange a tolerable peace for France that would assure the preservation of equilibrium.

But as his evil star would have it, Napoleon, still imbued by marvelous activity, won a few victories, or apparent victories, over his enemies and drove them back from Saxony toward Silesia.

Now Metternich had to interpose, in order that the allies might be saved; and not alone that they might be saved, but to bring to a head the situation resulting from the catastrophe of 1812. Napoleon, unconquered, would have to renounce his rule at least in Germany, in Poland, and along the Adriatic. The mediator could not ask less, because this, and more than this, could surely be obtained if Austria were to join the allies now; because the allies were determined to continue the war if these terms could not be obtained; because the spirit of the times peremptorily demanded it; and because he himself did not dare neglect any opportunity to turn the French world empire back into a concert of states.

"The question today," concluded Gentz, "is simply how, whether by war or by peace, Austria can best hope to expedite the overthrow of a dominance whose collapse is ineluctably ordained by its own shortcomings . . . Napoleon and all the world besides know that the Austrian Cabinet regards the present situation in Europe as impossible, and at odds with all conceptions of order, peace, and righteousness; hence abnormal and intolerable throughout. This is of greater import than six provinces snatched away from French rule."

In order to be nearer Saxony, the scene of strife and intrigue, Metternich and Gentz left in May for north Bohemia, and established their headquarters in a castle, Ratiborziz, that belonged to Metternich's mistress, the Duchess of Sagan. Early in June Napoleon arranged an armistice with Russia and Prussia, ostensibly to negotiate peace. In Marcolini Palace, at Dresden, the desperately struggling Dictator sat alone, still powerful, but threatened about by shadows; not far away, in a delightful chateau, his enemy, or exenemy, the confirmed adventurer, much sought after and courted by the men of the hour. The allied monarchs, the King of Prussia and the Czar, wandered about Silesia and Bohemia with their followers, and Ratiborziz was more than once the scene of their machinations.

GENTZ's letters to Metternich are the most interesting documentation of his thoughts and acts during this crisis, though allowance must be made for the artful cajoleries with which he managed the self-satisfied Minister. Highly informative, too, albeit written for a definite political purpose, is his correspondence with the Russian diplomat, Nesselrode, whom he advised periodically in return for an honorarium. Of late there had been still another who wished to be regularly informed on important European events: Prince Caradja, a Greek, the Turkish Viceroy in Bucharest. Gentz's dispatches to this potentate, living on the edge of civilization, begin in 1813 and are a brilliant journalistic achievement; the highly remunerative commission had been procured for him by Metternich. Then, in addition to all these, there are private letters in which he represented himself as he really was or, rather, as worse than he was, in compensation for his letters to the great leaders in which he had to make himself appear better than he was. The most unrestrained of all still went occasionally to the aging Rahel; the most serious to Metternich's secretary, Karl von Pilat, a young publicist who venerated him and whom he was endeavoring to train as formerly he had sought to train Adam Müller, Humboldt, Nesselrode, and the rest.

Nesselrode was now Russian Foreign Minister, though as such he played no great role, for the Czar wanted to be his own minister and, besides, was more inclined to listen to Baron vom Stein than to his Russian advisers. Humboldt was the Prussian Ambassador in Vienna, and the real leader in Prussian foreign politics; at the moment the capitals were of no significance, for Europe was concentrated about the traveling court cliques in north Bohemia, Saxony, and Silesia, and here Humboldt was to be found. The humanistic statesman was among the most rabid of the warmongers.

Not so Gentz. He who had desired this outcome and this war so ardently and so long now wanted peace; wanted Napoleon's amicable renunciation of all that did not rightfully belong to France, and gladly would have spared the world the agonies that otherwise it faced. In no case, however, must Austria oppose the other three great powers, and toward this end he worked. "Universal peace," he wrote to Nesselrode, "if this is in any way possible! If not, then universal war."

But as the Russians, the British, and the Prussians now feared nothing so much as Napoleon's compliance, and were secretly resolved among themselves to carry the war to the bitter end, he who brought Austria closer to the allied powers would be virtually promoting war. This he did. "Gentz," reported Humboldt, "is enormously useful to us." He could be, for he knew them all and could interpret them one to another. With Metternich he acted as an advocate for the Russians and the Prussians, and with these he interceded for Austria. He understood the nature of coalitions and knew how the most diverse class instincts, traditions, national or individual vanities, and ambitions to power are forcibly merged for the time being in the face of a greater common danger, while at the same time they are continually pulling apart. "The relations among the powers," he wrote, "intersect, interlace, intertwine, and conflict in such a singular way that even the most informed observer grows dizzy." All this must be accepted as it was, for it could not be otherwise. But as he, with jaded instinct and intelligence developed to the highest clarity, was passionately devoted to none of the partisans he could be friendly to all and show them how their differences could be adjusted. "All who deserve to be taken seriously have one common end in view: reciprocal abuse must be stopped. I shall never think him wise who can say at present of a radical and consistent advocate of war: 'He is a fool.' But he who reproaches a radical and consistent advocate of peace with being lost to all honor was never worthy of honor himself."

Talk continued from June until August, for those fine gentlemen who so long had been mere opportunists or lackeys now had the chance to make important decisions, and they tasted their power to the full. What were the minimal demands that could be made upon Napoleon? How could they be increased if he accepted them? If he did not accept, and the war continued, what was to be done with the liberated countries? What with France if—but only a small minority wanted to think so far ahead. Humboldt wrote that he hoped for everything through Napoleon's pertinacity; Gentz, that he hoped for everything through Napoleon's pliancy.

He conferred with Metternich before the Minister started in solemn mood for Dresden to hold one final discussion with Napoleon, and drove out to meet him on the highway when he returned, full of the dramatic scene with the Emperor in which he had been participating for eight hours. "The decision between peace and war lies in the hands of Your Majesty," Metternich had said. "There is an irreconcilable conflict between Europe and your aims up to now. Your conclusions of peace have always been mere armistices. The world needs peace, but in order to assure it you must limit your power until it is once more compatible with the general security; otherwise you will be defeated in the struggle. . . ." Excellent! If Metternich actually did say this he had expressed exactly Gentz's view.

But the lonely Tyrant could not agree. As willing as he was unable to make honorable concessions; prisoner of his past, his position, his nature; made still more obstinate by the presentiment that he was a lost man, and that for him there was no retreat; pierced by contempt for the kings whom he had so often seen as suppliants at his board, and who now acted as though they had never even heard of him; alienated from his own people, who cried, Peace! Peace! yet knew not what it meant; arguing over military problems like a professor of strategy, always striving to shift the blame for his Russian debacle; threatening: "We shall meet again in Vienna"; insulting: "Oh, Metternich, Metternich, how much did England pay you?" then, more like himself again, wheedling, almost imploring: "You would not declare war on me!" shamelessly exposing his predicament with exaggerated, hysterical laughter: "It may cost me my throne, but I will bury the world under its ruins!"

And yet, after the peace that Metternich had in mind he would still have been the most powerful sovereign in Europe.

The Dresden conference brought to light situations that no "negotiations" could bridge. Formally, it decided nothing. In the end Napoleon agreed to the calling of a peace congress, which was to be held in Prague, and thither everyone betook himself in June, Gentz among them as liaison officer and chief publicist. Sometimes, when he could stand no more talk, he sought solitude for a few days. "It is an inestimable boon in times like these to escape the turmoil for a few days and hear nothing that immediately concerns the present. On the whole the conviction grows in me that incessant talk about present or future events is the ruination of heart and mind."

Outside the conference rooms Gentz and his friends discussed not only the hopeless peace negotiations but God and man, the world and freedom. "Yesterday," Humboldt wrote to his wife, "I went to see Metternich at his request, and he seems anxious to have these meetings continue for he invited me again today, and we went for a walk until one o'clock; he, Gentz, and I. We discussed only things of the highest importance, and you would have found our conversation remarkable enough. Though one does not always agree with Metternich he invariably listens with attention nevertheless, familiarizes himself with the other side, and is never unreasonable."

This Gentz confirms in his memoirs: "I shall never forget certain walks with Count Metternich and Humboldt, over the bridge and through the streets of Prague, that often lasted far into the night." "As a rule Metternich and I took sides against Humboldt." For Humboldt believed in the people, and thought that this crisis must be resolved by them and not by aristocratic diplomats. "There are only two righteous and salutary forces in the world: God, and the people. What lies between does not count in the least, and we ourselves are of importance only in so far as we are close to the people." The friend of his youth was of another opinion; indeed, because of the spectacle that Germany was now offering, differed sharply from him. "How can the millions of ignorant babblers that make up a so-called public be capable in any way of deciding what should be done? One must have watched the ruling forces at close range, must have explored them, and thought oneself half to death over them if one is to understand how hard it is even then to arrive at a sound conclusion. After thirty years of effort I have at last reached a point where I can realize how a man must feel who is supposed to govern and to act."

Metternich, the man who was supposed to govern and to act, walked between the two others. The three had become acquainted as young men and now, influential ministers and councilors, they were strolling through the summer night, under the saints on the bridge at Prague, philosophizing and joking, their heads filled by the crises that marked the last years of Napoleon's reign.

As none of the delegates had any desire for peace or any faith in it, and Metternich himself may have had the desire but no longer had faith, the Prague congress degenerated into mere farce. The truce came to an end, and Austria entered the war against France. Metternich went to the headquarters of the allies, and Gentz stayed behind in Prague, the largest city near the front, where he opened a sort of press and publicity bureau. He wrote the Austrian war manifesto, as he had already done more times than he could count, edited the *Prager Zeitung*, and with the help of his young assistant, Karl von Pilat, arranged for the establishment of a daily in Vienna. He drew up pamphlets, which, in pursuit of an audacious idea, he distributed by the thousand; perhaps, for example, to attract the public of Saxony to the side of the allies. Thanks to Count Metternich, he was no longer a secret agent but the authorized director of public opinion, the increasing importance of which he had so early recognized. His lodging was the center upon which all the reports from the battle fronts converged, he had money to distribute with a free hand, and he should have been happy.

He was not.

THE war, in the final and complete actuality that it now assumed, was not a struggle between two clearly antithetical forces—"old Europe" on the one side, "revolutionary France" on the other. It was a chaos of opposing tendencies that one hardly knew how to allocate. The revolutionary Caesar had become a conservative and so could adjure the German rulers to support him, their protector against dangers from without as well as against dangers from within, by which he meant national democracy. In this sense the war against him was now a revolutionary war, a people's war. So the Russian peasants understood it, and so the German students understood it, too, and expressed themselves openly.

What had Gentz to do with a revolutionary war? Was it on these grounds that he now wished to save Napoleon? But Napoleon's world empire surely meant permanent revolution, and social peace was impossible without the existence of independent states, without equilibrium. Hence the forces of conservatism, the governments and the aristocrats, had valid reasons for making war on Napoleon. The conflict was waged by conservatives and revolutionaries together, though of course neither side clearly recognized the ephemeral nature of their alliance or its inconsistency. There were innumerable and subtle variations of opinion, from the extreme of those who would make over Napoleon's counterfeit into a genuine new Europe to the opposite extreme of those who wished to restore the old Europe. Many inclined toward both at once. What, for example, would have been the restitution of the German Empire, for which all Prussian patriots were now crying? The old? Or the new, with all its threat for the future? Who would be able to reduce the welter of affirmative and negative forces that always develops in such a crisis to a single, definite antithesis?

The aging Gentz, the man who ten years before had struggled for the victory of the old Europe over the new France, was distressed by the turmoil. Impulses that he felt would prove discordant in the long run were now momentarily united in a common effort; states, social tendencies, and states that were identified with certain social tendencies. It was clear that the Russians would assume an important position in the new Europe, thanks to their decisive achievements in 1812, and as a guarantee of equilibrium and of peace Russia would be welcome. But suppose the Czar Alexander nourished more ambitious plans? Suppose he hoped to become Napoleon's successor, as it were?

Prussia should regain what was hers before 1808; this, but certainly nothing more. Furthermore, she should take no part in that social tendency for which no one yet had a definite name, but that Gentz now began to call "Jacobinism," or "Teutomania." This it was, besides the danger of Russian hegemony, that worried him and claimed his attention above all else. It was a delirium of hatred, and crudity, and bad taste, and curious philosophy, and vague demands for supremacy such as had been expected from the Germans least of all. Perhaps it was necessary. Perhaps the Napoleonic plague could never have been lifted without the fury of the Prussian militia, the *Landwehr*, and the stimulus of the third-rate poets who enkindled it. In any case Gentz himself had certainly demanded, or at least predicted, such a revolutionary participation by the people ten years before; a new order of things that might be painful for him.

Now it had come, and it wounded his sensibilities. "Foreign trash"; "Treacherous Frenchmen"; "Freedom's blade drawn! Hurrah! Plunge the dagger into the throat!" Such expressions were offensive to the man of the eighteenth century. "Just take one look at all that is being printed today! Would it not make one spit with disgust and die? And at the sight of this filthy scribbling does not the thought sometimes come over you that despite all our show of success, fame, and splendor there must be something unhealthy about our whole condition?" In respect to his supervision of the Austrian newspapers he said: "The first period of my censorship is made very bitter for me. Every day there come pouring in the most abominable diatribes against Napoleon, which are meant sometimes to appear in the papers, sometimes to be printed separately, sometimes to be arranged for the theater, and sometimes to be set to music and sung in public. It seems to me wholly absurd that at the very moment when we are negotiating with Napoleon we should brand him unceasingly as the blackest criminal ever spewed forth by Hell." "All things considered, I feel that there is much greater need of reforming or controlling public opinion than of accepting its decrees. Things must not remain as they are, lest a prepotency much worse than the French follow in consequence."

When a principle like nationalism first arises, spreads, and grows there are still old-fashioned folk left, heavy with years, who, because they belong to another age, see through the intruder and oppose it as best they can. Then comes a spell of pronounced optimism; the tendency that was once so unfamiliar becomes predominant and widely accepted and the blockheads are scorned who, no doubt for pay, hold it their duty to fight against it. But in its turn this phase, too, passes and that which arose, spread, and grew is finally deposed and by its very nature goes down to destruction, though not without an agonized struggle. Self-confidence evaporates, and those who at first warned against the new departure are remembered with affection; thoughtful men they, and not untouched by a certain measure of tragedy, who showed us by their forebodings how everything had to happen as it did.

The new patriots, and even old friends who now swam happily with the current, began to hate and revile Metternich's "gray eminence." * "Nothing is more ruinous than a half-French diplomatist like Gentz," wrote Friedrich Schlegel to his brother August. "Surely you do not know him well. Hatred of the people is his ruling passion, to which all else is secondary. Because of a few proclamations, which were silly enough, to be sure, but insignificant after all, and not so blameworthy at least as an indifferent, stupid neutrality and inactivity, he has developed a downright antipathy toward everything German. He never speaks of Germany but with the most supercilious contempt. . . . I do not write you thus to upset you, and cause you to express your opinion of him perhaps in bitter words. On the contrary, I recommend the utmost prudence for he now has influence and at least can do much harm, though there is no hope of his wanting to do much that is useful. . . ."

Others, more favorably disposed, sought to arouse Gentz to some enthusiasm for the war of liberation. Was it possible that the Old Master had so far forgotten his own past, his burning desire of ten years before, now that it was finally stilled? Von Pilat reminded him of his finest production, the celebrated *Preface* of 1806. "My dear friend," Gentz replied, "who should teach me if not I myself? Have I lived for twenty years in vain? Am I deceived by a caprice, a delusion, a momentary figment? You are living in the year 1806, I in the year 1813. That is the real difference between us."

But was it not Pilat, rather, who lived in the present moment? And what did it matter to the young people who had been children in 1806 if the past seven years had affected the aging man thus and not otherwise? "No, I am living in 1813," Pilat might have answered him; "you are not, because you anticipated it, because you would not let the period mature." Thereupon Gentz: "A fine ripening indeed! Not only must the right things come; if they are to preserve their true nature they must come at the right time. . . ."

The dictates of reality, the noise of battle, and the jubilation of the public would have ended the discussion.

AUSTRIA declared war on August 12, 1813. Had it not been for the cautious leadership of the allies, all unaccustomed to victory as they

* The reference is to the Gray Cardinal, Père Joseph de Tremblay, private secretary to Cardinal Richelieu; hence, a confidential agent without official powers.

were, Napoleon would hardly have been able to remain in Germany for the two months that the "new federative system" had still to live. The armies of his marshals were driven back and annihilated in several bloody battles; before his own forces the allies recoiled until he had been encircled by an overwhelming preponderance of power. Then came a four-day slaughter, in which the number of troops engaged and the casualties were wholly unprecedented, and in which most of the nations and races of the Continent took part. Then a sudden and calamitous disintegration. The road across Germany toward the Rhine, over which the beaten Dictator preceded the remnants of his great army in flight, was marked out by the dead. His brothers, the kings, fled from their mock kingdoms and assembled in Paris. The foreign rulers, his vassals, crowded into the camp of the allies, where Metternich, regardless of their past infamies, received them amicably; for they had need of one another and in the end as much, or as little, cause for joint recrimination.

Dynasts whom the Emperor had exiled returned to their capitals, and even the princes of the House of Bourbon, the forgotten royal family, grew restless and began to remind the allied powers of their existence.

After the dazed and bewildered Emperor, in headlong flight toward Paris, pressed the allied forces; in their train the sovereigns, the ministers, the chief intriguers. Gentz, too, was ordered to the temporary headquarters at Freiburg. Hardly accustomed to such a triumphal progress, and exhilarated by the enormous tasks facing them, those at the top were in generous mood, and rewards were distributed with open hand. Metternich was created a prince, and Gentz received the highest Russian order together with a letter from the Czar, who publicly addressed him as "Chevalier of Europe." The order, a social asset, pleased him, for he had never enjoyed a rank commensurate with his position; *Hofrat*, an honorary title of dubious merit, was merely ridiculous. But he sniffed at the new title. Chevalier of Europe? That was no high honor when bestowed by the Man of Tilsit. He had watched events too closely for twenty years to have any heart now for the common triumph.

Hardly had Napoleon's "new federative system" been destroyed before the coalition began to totter. Hardly had France ceased to exist as the oppressive superstate before Austria, Great Britain, and Russia began to wonder what position she would occupy among the Continental states of the future, and how she could best be exploited for the special interests of one or the other. Everyone wanted the future government of France so qualified that it could be influenced by his own state in particular, and prepared for alliance with it. The Bonaparte family, defeated yet still continuing to reign, seemed particularly susceptible to the influence of Austria.

What was to be done with Holland, Belgium, west Germany, Italy, Poland? What were the intentions of an inflamed Prussia in respect to Germany?

The coalition, in so far as it had not originated in a genuinely catastrophic movement, a revolution, was a union of selfish state interests, and not all the spoils had been snatched from the beaten Conqueror before the victors fell into sinister quarrels about their redistribution. Only the war, and the fact that Napoleon did not wish to make peace, held the allies together. It was decided to break down his obstinacy by an invasion, but in the meantime to negotiate further with him.

Armies and headquarters, four-horse traveling carriages by the thousand, and a great deluge of intriguing government personnel spying on one another poured through Switzerland into France. Gentz gazed scornfully after them. In Freiburg he had to await the arrival of Lord Castlereagh, the British Foreign Minister, who came hurrying over to act as arbiter and curb the rapacious appetites of the Continental powers. He arrived during the night of January 17–18, one of the coldest in the memory of man, and went immediately into conference with Gentz for several hours; then, in the early morning, continued his journey toward the Swiss frontier. In honor of the war, whose theater he was approaching, and all unaccustomed to such scenes, he wore under his fur-lined cloak a fantastic uniform with scarlet breeches, while after his assistant there trailed actually a long Turkish saber. In respect to his mission, however, the young Minister turned out to be assiduous, deeply conscious of his responsibility, and able to think in terms of European public affairs.

Gentz had no really consistent opinions to impart to the British representative, and it would be an exaggeration to say that intellectually he mastered the situation completely.

Through all the chaos of the fallen new order there moved a few men who passionately strove for some definite goal. Baron vom Stein, for example: his aim was the shackling of France for a long period after the fall, or perhaps the death, of Napoleon, and the foundation of a German national state. Others less fanatical, but pliant, rather, and practical, held themselves ready to do whatever was opportune but to shun the dramatic wherever practicable. Still others saw all the possibilities and all the dangers, and hardly knew what remained to be desired amidst this welter of conflicting uncertainties.

Gentz was one of these. While he was penetrating the egoism of others with bitter gaze he, too, became an egoist and was thrown back partly on himself and partly on Austria, the country to which he had given his allegiance. The confirmed European often insisted now that he had become "a thorough Austrian," "even to hating the very words 'Europe,' 'world freedom,' and so on." Yet these were words that he had passionately disseminated ten years previously. Beyond question his wish was: Stop! Make peace immediately! But do not overshoot the mark, which is to end the domination of Europe by France, but not to replace the Empire with national revolutionary excesses.

If he had any influence whatsoever at this stage of affairs it showed itself in the peace conditions that the allies offered, first to Napoleon and then to the French people in defiance of Napoleon; a long and painful course of instruction that they finally took to heart. Even twenty years before it had been the constantly reiterated opinion of Gentz and his master, Mallet du Pan, that a coalition could never achieve peace with France unless she were first offered clear and moderate terms; that war should be waged only to restore order and not for the unjust advantage of one of the participants. To this principle Metternich now adhered, much to the rage of the Prussians, but he did not succeed in converting Napoleon to his view. However, through skillfully written leaflets he was able to make it appear to the French that the catastrophe of their Emperor was more personal than national. "The allied powers are not making war against France, but against the dominance that Napoleon, to the misfortune of Europe and of France herself, has so long exercised beyond the frontiers of his Empire. . . . The powers are ready to guarantee France an expansion such as she never knew under her kings. A great nation must not perish because she has finally been defeated in a bitter struggle through which she fought with all her accustomed bravery. For their part, the allied powers wish to live in freedom, happiness, and peace. . . ." This, even though Metternich wrote the declaration himself, was the spirit of Gentz speaking, the spirit in which the "Publicist of the Coalitions" had worked for twenty years and that now had actually achieved a belated victory.

Other influence he no longer had. After having done the honors of the Continent for Lord Castlereagh he returned to Vienna, and throughout the rest of the war remained merely an anxious spectator.

He harbored mixed feelings toward the Hero of the Century. Those of a more coarse and robust fiber, vom Stein, for example, can hate even in victory and push their conquests to the limit without mercy. But Gentz could not help thinking of the man who had defended himself to the last and was now wandering about through the wintry cold with his defeated thousands, and he was lost in contemplation and almost ashamed. He had never thought Napoleon a really great man, nor did he even now. His obstinate insistence on the human fallibility of this fortuitous demigod he described as a rash guess that had finally been confirmed. "God suggested to me that he was only human, and I should have died in this conviction even though he had conquered all Asia. . . ."

But because circumstances no longer favored Napoleon, because he faced alone the overwhelming power of a world arrayed against him, Gentz began to be more sympathetic. In particular he felt the absurdity, the infamy that lay in "overturning all Europe just to put one man in his place." And he had assayed Napoleon accurately: the desperate and almost magnificent activity in defeat; the invincible egotism; the impending downfall; the despondency; and all the bitter memories that he must now be treasuring up. He called him "a curious mean betwixt greatness and pettiness." "In their psychological and, I may well add, in their historical aspect no reading matter in years has interested me more deeply than the French *Bulletins* from February 1 to 19. Is it possible to imagine anything more remarkable in its characteristic aberration than the temper of a man who cannot cease from treating war as a subject for critical scientific examination, even in the moment of greatest danger? . . . Only a few in our time notice such traits, and those that do think at the most: 'That's all just trickery and affectation with which to deceive the world.' Even as mere affectation it should not be treated wholly with contempt, but I believe I am justified in thinking that it is true and real. Throughout his whole life long this man has done nothing but play a great military game with France, with Europe, with himself, and with his own fate. He remains the same whether on fortune's peak or the edge of the abyss. His voice is not that of a Nero, but neither is it that of a Caesar. The rare phenomenon that we call Bonaparte can be measured only with his own yardstick. . . .”

Though Gentz had never seen Napoleon he was now in close touch with him. He read his speeches and his *Bulletins* and listened to the tales of the diplomats whom Metternich was sending for the last time to the desolate leader. “When high ranking officers were delegated to confer with him on any sort of military affair,” thus reads one of Gentz’s dispatches to Bucharest, “he never took advantage of the opportunity, but true to his extraordinary character gave himself over to endless lecturing, to monologues lasting three or four hours, and instead of making concrete proposals continued to instruct the Austrian Emperor. . . .” He told the King of Saxony that he would never make peace, and that he was prepared to carry on the war for twenty years if necessary. To the Polish soldiers he said: “The whole world has deceived me. Germany has been attacked by a fever, but it will pass. I am as I have always been; I have not changed. Look at me. Have I grown any thinner?” When he heard that the Bavarians had turned on him he could not believe it for a long time, and at last said only: “Now you see what men are like. Now you see how far one can trust them.”

Who but one that hates implacably and is devoid of all imagination could withhold his pity upon hearing such things?

The pseudo-emperor and the pseudo-diplomat were both upstarts who believed in a special code of honor for the society into which each had gained entry, and for the kings, to whom Gentz had devoted himself as a servant, whom Napoleon, the revolutionary, had spared, and whom he had thought to be his allies. When Gentz now urged Metternich to prevent the deposition of Napoleon he adduced arguments on right, on decency, and on royal dignity, and as though to complete the irony of his own life appealed expressly to his old “Memorandum on the Necessity of Not Recognizing the Imperial Title of Bonaparte.” “In a memoir that I transmitted to the late Count Cobenzl in June, 1804, I availed myself of the following argument as the strongest: . . . ‘The decision to recognize Napoleon as Emperor would be valid for all time. No god would be able to reverse it.’ . . . On the basis of this recognition many covenants, peace treaties, alliances, and even family connections have been contracted with him. To endeavor to rescind it now would be an unjust and unworthy step. . . .”

Napoleon spoke in similar vein: “I never would have believed that the Austrian Emperor could treat his daughter as a stranger. . . . I really made a grave mistake in marrying an Austrian princess, though I cannot deny that the Empress is an incomparable woman. You do not appreciate to the full all her good qualities; perhaps on the whole I could have made no better choice. She will learn to govern as well as the famous Anne of Austria. . . ." Thus, blinded by the glitter of the crown, did he praise the silly girl, and realized as little as Gentz that those who had been infamous enough to send her to his bed could be infamous enough, too, to take her away from him.

In his anxiety over the post-Napoleonic chaos Gentz began to see the whole immediate past through the eyes of the Emperor, and to lay all his extravagant adventures to the clumsy opposition of Europe. It would have been possible to live peaceably with him, and it was still possible. "The source of all the grave mistakes and terrible sufferings of the era was the custom of regarding Napoleon wholly as a demigod, or a monster, or even both at once. At one time there were many, the Czar Alexander, for example, who thought that when such an extraordinary genius appeared on earth all must bow the head in respect; today the death of the monster is universally demanded. The question whether it might be possible to live politically with Napoleon on terms of independence and equality has never once been raised. . . . This is the place to ask it. If you [Prince Metternich] had only been minister of Europe before the War of 1805 we should all have been able to get along with Napoleon. Not in Arcadian concord and calm, for the era was stormy and its confusion could be resolved only by war. But how could it have occurred to Napoleon to subjugate Germany, Italy, Poland, and so on? He never would have reached such heights that a mighty opponent like the present coalition would be required to overthrow him. You could have prevented all these terrible calamities without much difficulty, merely because you understood his character and would have known how to set yours against it. All the rest of us took him much too seriously, and mismanaged him outright in consequence; then, after our first mishaps, no longer knew how to help ourselves, lost our heads, and abandoned ourselves to despair. Now that we are finished with him at last after superhuman exertions, and have only to enjoy the fruits of victory, we plunge into new dangers merely because it is still impossible for us to realize that such a 'monster of genius and infamy' actually has been conquered. . . ."

When all the world spoke of "the Emperor Napoleon" Gentz had called him "Bonaparte"; now he referred to him as "the Emperor." "That is his title, and the French would be fools to call him anything else." And when he was reproached with having become a champion of Napoleon at his time of life he said: "I wrote against him when it was more dangerous to do so than it is now." He wanted the beaten man treated with "tact and magnanimity"; but history, which had done so little to please him, failed him in this also.

It is remarkable how slow the allies were to realize that the war could not end otherwise than in Napoleon's downfall. To influence the domestic administration of an enemy state, to interfere in any way at all with the affairs of a foreign state, was unheard of or at least exceptional. Of course Napoleon's regime was not confined to internal French politics; it was world wide. But the idea frankly was to reduce it to a domestic French matter. That this would not succeed, that his system must either remain universal or be wholly destroyed Napoleon himself felt long before anyone else. Gradually the French people began to see it too, and only through them, through the conduct of Parisian politicians and Alsatian peasants, did it finally dawn on the leaders of the coalition.

More time passed before they realized that between the old royal family and Napoleon there was no third, serious possibility. There should have been a regency of emperors representing his son, and experienced politicians like Fouché and Metternich considered this plan: the Empire without an Emperor; all the advantages of the Napoleonic system without the disadvantage of his mad presence. But to ask that the tempest by which Napoleon had been overthrown should halt before his "dynasty," the most vainglorious of all his creations, was to demand too much of statecraft. All projects between the two extremes, emperor and king, were shadowy and unreal.

Another general? But why not Napoleon, then, the best that we have? asked Talleyrand. The Republic, the Directory, were so discredited that none among the rulers even thought of them. Napoleon's rule had lasted too long, gone too deep, leveled too thoroughly for the exhausted country to be able to furnish a new and dependable form of government now, in this her gravest crisis. And well did the Emperor know it. He despised the social revolution with which he had craftily threatened Europe, he disdained the liberal republicans, but he feared the Bourbons. Though no longer on the scene they had a thousand years' history behind them; a great force at the moment that was precisely assayed by this realist. The Bourbon party, sprung from almost nothing a few months before the final catastrophe, grew with extraordinary rapidity and when Talleyrand espoused their cause it seemed already three quarters won.

Well, restoration, then, "the worst revolution of all." Restoration, which twenty years before would have spelled for Gentz the highest rapture, but which he now summed up all the power of his logic to fight. Not alone because he always had to be "against," and shrank back before the realization of his wishes since he was better acquainted with ill than with good fortune; he fought it as a politician, as a historical and social philosopher. "Only give me back Europe as it was in 1789, and *then* the Bourbons, and I will be the first to sign Napoleon's passport. . . ."

The Europe of 1789! But this was the nineteenth century, modern to the last degree, with great countries and great armies, with a predominant middle class, with factories and newspapers. Napoleon's egotistic and fatal adventure had altered the condition and habits of millions of French people and brought forth new types, new callings, and a new attitude toward life. And now it was proposed that these people, changed as they were, should be ruled by fusty emigrants who had had no share in the glories or the sufferings of the past twenty years; who could not claim the slightest credit for the defeat of Napoleon save that they may have wished the allies well from the safety of their London salons.

One of two things: either the King would acknowledge the men and deeds of the Empire, in which case his office would be superfluous and an object of derision. Or he would not acknowledge them, and thus make the restoration in truth "the worst revolution of all"; then civil war, and world-wide misery once again. Probably he would do both. He would acknowledge, because such a five and twenty years cannot be rolled back; because except for a handful of emigrants there was no one who had not served Napoleon; and because then one could have reached manhood in France without ever having heard of the dynasty that had been eclipsed for so many years. Also he would not acknowledge, but make his own reservations, take revenge wherever this seemed possible, set spiteful and untrustworthy old men in the places so long occupied by Napoleon's efficient paladins, accumulate venom and rage, and unleash the old chaos again. The restoration would be deplorable if the King accepted things as he found them; frenzy if he did not. Kingship in the abstract was a beautiful dream, a noble remembrance, and a noble remembrance it should remain.

To these grave historical objections Gentz added others of a legal nature. The Empire would not be broken up even though Napoleon were forced to abdicate. He could be deposed—by his own Senate. The people themselves—ostensibly—could recall a king, so that the right to appoint and dismiss their rulers was implicitly conceded them. "But who really is the French nation, that must decide on this solemn undertaking? Where is its accredited mouthpiece? Where are its representatives? In a land where, for five and twenty years, first the all-leveling scythe of a people's wrath and then the policy of a military and despotic regime have obliterated every tracc of legal rights; where there are no longer any social distinctions, any organized trades, any privileges, any methods of orderly procedure save only those that the present government has created; nay, even any outstanding men save, again, those who hold office under the present government: in such a land it seems to me the most singular reversal of all reason to speak of a national will. . . ."

But perhaps he might have overlooked all these legal irrationalities, all this conflict with custom and principle, had he not seen the social danger that lay in replacing the Imperial Conqueror of the Revolution with royal incompetence.

Two French groups in particular wanted to take advantage of Napoleon's defeat by getting rid of him: the "ultraroyalist fools," as Gentz called them, and the incorrigible Jacobins. It was plain enough that the marriage of convenience between these two, which had been in effect occasionally even during the Revolution, would not long endure. "The revolutionary party are already sharpening their knives for their defrauded confederates. I have a deep suspicion that we shall have won, not for ourselves but for our worst enemies. A new war threatens, more grievous and bloody than the Napoleonic, and perhaps in the near future. And I fear that as far as this coming war is concerned we have destroyed our best ally." "Certainly I have no earthly reason to wish Napoleon well. As a man, as a moral witness of this world tragedy, it would be more fitting for me to welcome his fall. Many of those whose support and good opinion are not indifferent to me curse every thought of peace with him. The animosity, the demand for revenge, the enthusiasm for the Bourbons have reached such a pitch that it requires much more courage to write in Napoleon's favor today than it did to write against him three or four years ago. I know and feel all this. But I know, too, that other times are coming when other views will find acceptance, and that a balance between opinions is much more certain to be restored than a balance of power among the various states. If study and reflection do not at least put us in a position where to some degree we can advance to meet time or anticipate it, how is the thinking man any better in the end than the common herd?"

AT ALLIED headquarters Prince Metternich read this impetuous letter, and found himself to a certain extent in sympathy with the reflections of the writer. The misgivings that he expressed might well be fulfilled in the course of time; in decades, or during the current century.

But was this the moment to look so far into the future? For Gentz, perhaps, sitting alone in Vienna, deserted in his Seilergasse lodging and given over to his thoughts; certainly not for the Minister, on the scene of the most urgent decisions. As soon as Metternich realized that Napoleon would not let himself be saved, nothing remained but to coöperate in the restoration, so that the Russians and British might not be its sole beneficiaries. For the moment the old dynasty was a salutary convenience, but only for the moment, of course. Still, one lived only in the present. The immediate and burning question was how the French people could be put back on their feet again after such a series of unexampled adventures. This problem was solved with fair success, thanks to the extraordinary vitality and continuity of the nation, which, after all the storms that had passed over it, remained as it was before; but thanks, also, to the gouty old gentleman who in such dignified manner represented this continuity.

The outcome was as Gentz had foreseen from Vienna. If the allied monarchs come to Paris, he had prophesied, "nothing in the world will restrain the Czar of Russia, the Prussians, and the British from immediately attempting a counterrevolution in common with adherents of the Bourbons. Even though they pretend over and over again to fall in with our neutrality system, who can stop them from coaxing up by a thousand tricks, or organizing, or if necessary inventing, a so-called national demand and then saying that the citizens of the capital have spoken, and that their voice must be heard?"

After one last engagement under her walls the city of Paris surrendered. The Emperor, who had attempted a diversion toward the east but then hurried after the allies, arrived too late. And now, as he drained the cup of humiliation to its dregs in the palace at Fontainebleau, the anticipated and grotesque events were taking place in Paris. The allied monarchs entered the city in stately procession, were received with jubilation, and, having freed Europe from the French, so to speak, now were greeted by them as deliverers from their own Emperor; and all the plebiscites by which they had freely acknowledged Napoleon to be their ruler, and all that he had done through the people and never could have done without them, were forgotten. The victors, intoxicated by the atmosphere of this traditional wellspring of life and gaiety, by a community so exuberant, so rich in genius, and contrasting so seductively with the stodginess of their own capitals, succumbed to those who had long caused them such concern, flattered them, and promised them a just peace.

A just peace was to mean the boundaries of the ancient regime; this implied their King of bygone days. Paris was synonymous with the Empire, as ancient Rome had been, and since it appeared to have spoken in favor of the Bourbons, Napoleon was lost. The Senate, the very body that Gentz had prophesied ten years before could do nothing under the Emperor though it might endanger his sway, ordered him deposed. Regicides voted for the restoration of the late King's brother. The whole affair was engineered by intrigues, but by intrigues that would not have succeeded so well if they had not been aimed at what was logical and advantageous for the moment.

The Pretender, an infirm liberal, began his majestic progress across the Channel.

XII

VIENNA CONGRESS

GENTZ wrote to the aging Rahel: "I know *everything;* no one in the world is acquainted with so much contemporary history as I, for no one has enjoyed such deep intimacy with so many important factions and leading men *at the same time;* there *cannot* easily again be another such. It is a pity that all this should be lost to our contemporaries and to posterity, but I am too reserved, too diplomatic, too indolent, too surfeited, and too angry to talk about it; for writing I have neither time nor heart and, most important of all, youth is gone. . . ."

When a man of good will, named Luden, asked him to collaborate in a patriotic journal he replied that there must surely be writers who believed that somewhere in this struggling world there were justice and right. He himself had formerly been one, but was such no longer. "Through a concurrence of circumstances I have become familiar with the substance of great affairs; the secret ways of politics; the mind and character of almost all the leading men; the real import of nearly all political transactions; and the defects, delusions, and vanities in virtually everything that from a distance seems meritorious or imposing; so much so, indeed, that I am no longer susceptible to illusion. When one has reached this condition one can no longer exert a wholesome influence on the public. I hold it of the utmost importance that in politics especially there should be a group of writers whose fixed ideal is the highest political good, who assume that every important governmental measure is directed toward this end, and who treat the subject always as though in the final analysis real philanthropy, wisdom, and virtue *must* underlie all endeavor. But this demands above all that they come not too near the inner workings of the machine. . . . Once they have done so they may still be capable of useful memoirs (though only for posterity), but no longer can they be resolute, efficient, and inspired political writers. For such articles as you have in mind—in other words, precisely the sort to which I myself once aspired—I am now too stale and of no possible value. . . ."

Thus far had it gone with the man whom George Canning could

once deride as an all-too-rabid enthusiast. He was never more alone than in these days of his belated triumph.

When everything had favored Napoleon's venture, when in the pride of his youth he had trampled the old Europe under foot, Gentz had entered the lists against him, warning and accusing, and with no support other than his own courage. Now General Bonaparte's adventure was over, wrecked not by the diplomacy, the energy, the morale of his opponents, but rather by some inherent defect of his own. For ten years he had succeeded in doing the incredible, governing France and holding her in thrall and then, through her, a civilization ten times as great; now at last both rulers and their subjects had begun to oppose in earnest the foreign domination against which their fumbling efforts had been directed for so long, and the forces that had mobilized the Revolution in France were set in motion against Napoleon. His tactics were copied. The coalition of all, over whose necessity Gentz had sustained writer's cramp in 1804, was finally achieved in 1813, and after a few terrible weeks the "new federative system" lay prostrate in the dust.

As diplomatic agent between Austrians, Prussians, and Russians Gentz had not been wholly without a share in the debacle, but now he performed his tasks mechanically and without much inner satisfaction. His vehement longing could no longer be stilled because, after so much fruitless effort and passion, it was already dead. The Old World, he felt, had identified itself too thoroughly with Napoleon to be justified in ostentatiously separating from him now. The creations of his reign, which Gentz at first thought mere impudent jugglery, and historically negligible, had turned out to be lasting; so lasting, indeed, that even Gentz himself now wished to see no essential change made in them.

For this reason he opposed the restoration of the old French dynasty. "Only give me back Europe as it was in 1789, and *then* the Bourbons, and I will be the first to sign Napoleon's passport." Yes, he who once had lain sleepless with hatred toward the "blasphemous, villainous usurper" would now have liked to see him spared in his death struggle. This was in part obstinacy, weariness, reluctance to accept as such the belated and abundant fulfillment of his wishes, inability to share in the ecstasy of the masses; but in part, too, he disagreed with most of the allied powers on definitely political grounds. For although his cynicism was now often stronger than his good will he continued nevertheless to take a lively interest in the future of Western civilization, of Austria, and in his own future as well. As the glittering "afterward," the post-Napoleonic world, gradually became the present it assumed forms that in many ways were displeasing to him.

The downfall of Napoleon in 1814 differed in some measure from what it would have been in 1805; not merely because he had altered the world in the meantime, but more because the great nations of Europe had had to make themselves over radically in order to be stronger than he. In so doing they had developed previously unsuspected powers, military, social, and intellectual, that worked together against the common enemy yet at the same time struggled apart. The war that united governments had made their peoples egoistic, intoxicated with self, and hostile toward anything foreign. The great coalition of Russia, Austria, Prussia, and Great Britain, formed by the Treaty of Chaumont in March, 1814, was one outcome of the war of liberation; nationalism, the frenzied cult of national individuality, particularly in Germany, was another. Gentz feared this new German nationalism; he feared Russia; he feared Prussia; he feared a social revolution in France; he feared the whole great democratic effort without which Europe could never free herself of Napoleon, yet with which she would free herself so precipitately that one could not but ask what might happen, in the face of all this store of accumulated energy, after his disappearance from the scene. The present is never so beautiful as the future. Hardly are danger and suffering past before their very existence is well-nigh forgotten, and while we gaze after the disappearing thunderclouds new ones gather behind us.

That Gentz was only now at the apex of his foreign career was by no means a matter of chance. As long as he demanded of history what it did not give, as long as he angrily continued to reproach the rulers of Europe with the pitiful inadequacy of their endeavors, they looked down upon him in contempt and intimated that they understood their own business better than he did. But now that he kept his occupation separate from his inmost thoughts—routine here, secret mockery there—they accepted him as one of their own kind, and his face appeared in pretentious paintings among those of twenty leading ministers.

Napoleon's dream of empire had left behind it a multitude of realized facts; some of them structures that now could hardly be destroyed, others mere ruins by the wayside. An unprecedented task of clearing away and reorganizing remained to be done, and for this an enormous congress of European diplomats was assembled. The allies chose Vienna as its scene and, by acclamation, Gentz as its secretary, or chief of protocol.

WHETHER or not by chance, those who dominated the Congress of Vienna were old friends of Gentz almost to a man. Wilhelm von Humboldt, who with the title of Prussian Ambassador at the Court of Vienna determined the policies of Prussia, was the dearly beloved and envied friend of his youth. Count Nesselrode, the Russian Foreign Minister, he had discovered as a young man in Berlin, had attracted, and had instructed. Stein, adviser to the Czar, had been for a few winter months in Prague his partner in a political enterprise, but now they began to avoid one another because they entertained wholly different views in respect to Germany and Europe. He had met Lord Castlereagh in London in 1802, and had renewed the acquaintance in Freiburg a few months before the meeting of the Congress. Clemens Metternich could no longer do without Gentz as stimulus, companion, and admirer, and revealed to him his innermost thoughts on the tribulations of love no less than those that concerned Europe. The others did likewise; even the Czar of Russia, the fateful man of 1812, liked to promenade with him and show that although born to the purple he could still be both liberal and brilliant.

What it was that so commended the veteran agent to the confidence of these ceremonious and enigmatical leaders he himself hardly knew. Certainly it was not his discretion, for he might very well pass on to a second anything that he had learned from a first. His charm, his experience, his sense of what was fair, his inability to lie, his smiling candor even in corruption, but above everything else the superiority to all party politics and nationalism to which the events of the time had brought him explain his extraordinary position in a certain degree; unless one prefers to think that it was his unmistakable and inexplicable talent for inspiring confidence and making himself essential.

At Gentz's little lodging in the Seilergasse there appeared during that autumn of 1814 the flower of a victorious Europe. To the secretary of the Congress came all who needed his help; for as he had to arrange the agenda and had the ear of the Austrian, British, and French delegations everyone wanted something of him. Money flowed into his pockets, orders covered his dress coat, and imposing petitioners crowded his waiting room. "Could not receive the Crown Prince of Bavaria, the King of Denmark, etc." he noted under October 31. "At Castlereagh's, at Metternich's. Excitement, and transactions without number. Dined with some members of the Congress at Humboldt's. Important conferences at eight o'clock. Home about ten; worked until one."

And so every day. He had to prepare subjects for discussion; reconcile conflicting interests; draft declarations; outline speeches, and often both speech and reply; and, as its publicist, vindicate the Congress. In addition to all this there were those elaborate secret memoranda to be dispatched to the Viceroy in Bucharest. A position more suited to the display of his talents Gentz, the statesman without a country, could not possibly have imagined. He was the Secretary of Europe. He was spokesman for and adviser to a concert of states that had been in his thoughts for five and twenty years and that now, with their representatives all gathered in one place, seemed for the first time on the way to realization.

He slept in the morning, was busy with social matters and conferences until far into the night, and worked in privacy until dawn. Wilhelm von Humboldt was first to appear at his lodging for breakfast, and was continually amazed anew at the enormous appetite of his old friend. "He helped himself to everything before passing it to me. While I was modestly drinking two small cups of coffee he put down four and devoured two thirds of a *solila* as large as a plate, which, you must know, is a rich, flaky pastry swimming in grease and made into a sort of pie, that steams when it is opened; to say nothing of many *croissants* with half an inch of butter on each. . . ." Otherwise, Humboldt found Gentz unchanged. "I regard him always with interest and love, though at the same time I feel that others can and must have a different opinion. . . ."

Gentz's dinner parties were among the most select of those given in Vienna for the European rulers. Only an intimate circle was invited: the young Crown Prince of Württemberg, for whom he had a weakness and of whom the Empress Eugénie said a hundred years later to Wickham Steed that she and her consort had thought him the cleverest of the European kings, and had called him "the giant in the cellar"; Prince Metternich; Prince Talleyrand; Humboldt; Count Stadion; Count Wessenberg; not to mention such uncommonly brilliant women as Countess Fuchs and Princess Bagration. All praised his cuisine and his furnishings, but Friedrich Gentz, the writer, who had the audacity to oblige such guests to climb his steep stairway, was only half present at these gatherings. Sometimes, amidst the throng, he would suddenly withdraw into himself and ask: Good God, how did I ever get in with this crowd? Once he noted down: "I contributed almost nothing to the conversation. Metternich and Talleyrand went on in their usual way. Meanwhile I was overcome as never before by the futility of all human endeavor and the foibles of those who hold the world in their hands, as well as by my own superiority; but all this half unconsciously, and as though lost in a fog that descended on my mind from the empty twaddle of these gentlemen. . . ." As a historian and a philosopher he might have risen superior to all such human affairs at will, but so deeply had he become involved with the world that he could divorce himself from it only on occasion.

In age one achieves to the full the desires of youth: honors, money, and success. Lawrence, the portrait painter, who had hurried to Vienna to immortalize the great ones of the world in representations that were at once beautiful and true to life, was commissioned to paint him for the King of England: a dignified, important, and almost triumphant-looking man. Now when there was an illumination he did not lie weeping on his bed, as on the night when Marshal Berthier came to fetch away Napoleon's bride. Instead, it was the former Empress who sat stolidly in her apartment at Schönbrunn, and endured a recital of Zacharias Werner's tragedy, *Kunigunde*. Her little son, the King of Rome, "Napoleon's bastard," played at soldier in the garden of the palace; the unwelcome materialization of something that seemed never to have been, now that it was no more.

An extraordinary effort toward recalling the gloomy past was required if one were to have any satisfaction at all in the present; it was necessary to stupefy oneself with sensuous pleasures, as it was said that Gentz was now deliberately doing; as though he were Faust, dragged by the Devil through the wildest life, and enslaved through mean and shallow pleasures; so

> That to his hot, insatiable sense
> Meat and drink tempt greedy lips!
> In vain does he entreat refreshment . . .

Was there anything to justify this picture? Had he not faithlessly abandoned, in favor of politics and world frenzy, the dignity of the study and the struggle for truth to which he was predestined? Can political triumph satisfy the more subtle demands of the spirit? The writer administered the affairs of great men, but in his darker hours he despised them utterly. "When one observes the doings of the Congress," wrote its secretary, "one is no longer surprised that a man of iron like Bonaparte could overthrow all Europe, and would tremble for the future if the mediocrity of the one were not counterbalanced by the mediocrity of the other. . . ." Their talk was all of the noblest precepts, yet without exception they were concerned only with getting as much land and as much power as possible out of this their great opportunity. Gentz laughed bitterly over their "ideas"—his own ideas. "The magniloquent phrases about 'restitution of the social order,' 'the recovery of European politics,' 'enduring peace based upon a just apportionment of power,' and so on were trumped up only to quiet the masses and to confer on the Congress some semblance of import and dignity. But the real sense of the gathering was that the victors should share with one another the booty snatched from the vanquished."

Thus did he write in a résumé; he, who above all others was familiar with the proceedings of the Congress. Toward the end of 1814 he confided to his diary the following candid avowal of dismay: "The aspect of public affairs is depressing, not as formerly because of the frightfully threatening cloud that hung over our heads, but because of the miserable folly of all our public men. I have no cause to reproach myself, and so my intimate knowledge of all the wretched traffic and all the paltry men who rule the world troubles me no more; rather it exhilarates me, and I enjoy the whole spectacle as though it were given for my own private entertainment. The year 1815 begins for me under very favorable auspices. As for politics, I see clearly that it is idle to believe they can ever fulfill the hopes with which enthusiasts delude themselves, and which I have renounced forever." Such trial flights into cynicism were now becoming more frequent, but in the end he always found his way back.

During the months when new frontiers were being drawn, and riches divided, the secretary of the Vienna Congress might have had practically as much money as he desired. But he made no effort, and out of pure sloth would have little to do with the great bankers who circled about the feast. He accepted ready money, but only from leaders with whose politics he agreed, and only just enough to keep his devil-may-care household afloat. He set down such entries as: "Farewell call by the Grand Duke of Baden. He drinks tea with me and hands me a thousand ducats." Or merely: "Magnificent call by the Duke of Campociaro"; or: "A highly agreeable dispatch from Bucharest"; entries that will offer no difficult problem to the reader. Furthermore, he looked actively after the interests of the German Jews, and it appears that they returned his favors "in an interesting way." The largest sum of all, 24,000 gulden, came from Talleyrand; a generous amount, yet not so much when one recalls that it cost the King of Saxony six million francs to convince Talleyrand of the necessity for an independent Saxon state. Talleyrand's greed for gold was immense and he was ruled to some extent by this passion, whereas Gentz was only hedonistic and extravagant. He now ordered an equipage from London, in which he drove proudly about with Charles, the soldier; arranged masquerades for the personnel of his household; distributed gifts with lavish hand; and was never out of debt.

For love he had neither time nor inclination; at least, the secret police could tell no tales of such scandalous conduct as that of the Czar or Prince Metternich. In his diary are to be found only hasty, casual notes like "Saw for the first time a certain Toni," or "Passed an hour with Suzette, a very beautiful woman bequeathed me by Humboldt." There appears on the scene, too, a boy named August who insisted that he was Gentz's son and with whom, on the basis of this hypothesis, he spent "some delightful hours."

Gentz has come down in the imagination of a later era as one of the most frivolous principals at this frivolous world council, as a licentious old diplomat, a figure from an operetta; rouged, nibbling at bonbons, and slinking along behind court ballerinas, a *lorgnon* in his feeble hand. There is but little truth in this picture, however. Gentz was the most faithful worker of the Congress. He was there, as he himself said, "to lend style to the proceedings," to present them clearly in polished French or German. He was there to compose differences, so that at least a consistent account, an apparently happy result, might be possible. He was there, too, as a politician among others, to achieve or prevent certain things. For although he no longer expected any beneficent miracles from history he knew very well what he wanted of it for his own era, and even better what he did not want.

A POLITICAL assemblage like that at Vienna is a strange concourse of the most diverse forces. There meet ambitious men nourishing secret and contradictory designs. There meet states, partly to preserve themselves at any cost, partly to enlarge themselves at the expense of others. There periods and generations meet: the elder, who have power; the younger, who want it. Among all these conflicting wills a compromise has to be found, multiform and susceptible of modification, so that antagonisms, which always persist, may be held in abeyance at least for a time.

During its twenty-five stormy years Europe had become modernized. Everything that was to stir the nineteenth century was already there and discernible to the intuitive glance: captains of industry, proletarians, militarists and pacifists, nationalists and cosmopolites, atheists and neo-Catholics, yearning romanticists and revolutionary critics of society. There were young people, born into the midst of the great crisis, linked to the past by no close ties, their heads full of vague demands and dreams. But there were others, also, from the middle of the eighteenth century; these held in their hands the reins of power, and thought it their highest mission to prevent a repetition of the catastrophic occurrences that they had experienced.

Among the latter was Gentz. He longed for peace, and did not wish to see the French Revolution continued by new partisans in unknown and perhaps more dangerous forms. Hence he opposed Prussia and, for the same reason, the German Nationalists; the "Teutomaniacs," the "Germanomaniacs," the "Teutomagogues," or whatever else he chose scornfully to call them.

Here two main tendencies were clearly connected with one another.

The 1813 champions of independence were disgusted by the triumph of a fashionable diplomatic set that clung together indifferent to nationality. They felt that after the war things should never be again as they had been before. They wanted a more intense national life, a German empire, harsh punishment of France, impetuous leadership, enthusiasm, and an openly proclaimed national communality. "The recent war," wrote Caroline von Humboldt to her husband, the Ambassador, "told the masses only too clearly what they can do." "The people are good, but are not treated as they deserve." "Austria is such a heterogeneous mixture of diverse forces, and especially of nationalities, that I would wager any amount it will have ceased to be a German power before this century is out. German national sentiment is apparently increasing in strength, and Austria is not keeping pace with it. No power seems strong enough to halt the spirit of the times, and history furnishes plenty of information on what the future conceals. But evidently the gentlemen do not read history."

This clever woman sentenced Austria to death. Like all Germanomaniacs she wanted Prussia to acquire as much increase of power as might be, for the old Prussian greed for territorial expansion had appeared under a different guise during the past months. The patriotism of the German military had approached very closely a pan-German nationalism. They were credited with significant, even revolutionary, accomplishments in the war. The Germanomaniacs felt this, and noisily demanded at the Congress that Prussia receive the Rhineland, Saxony, and the largest possible slices of liberated Europe.

One must have pondered as deeply as Gentz over Germany and Europe to see how clearly all this was connected. He realized it more vividly than the Prussian diplomats themselves. They, Prince von Hardenberg and Baron von Humboldt, merely followed the immemorial custom of states when they tried to gain from the Vienna agreements as many subjects for the Hohenzollerns as they could, whereas Gentz saw that if Prussia overstepped certain limits the rest of Germany would fall to her sooner or later and that this, in turn, must eventually betoken a revolution compared with which even the Napoleonic itself would be mere child's play. No! No! Not for this had Europe undergone tortures to loosen Napoleon's hold; not to fall victim now to a domination by the Germans, which would be all the more oppressive and dangerous because it would depend upon overwhelming numbers rather than upon genius and momentary luck. A confederation of German states? Yes, by all means; but never a united Germany!

Consciously or unconsciously, it was precisely this upon which Prussia was now bent. "Prussia," so Gentz summed up the matter, "brought to the Congress only the one extravagant wish to extend her possessions at the expense of all, and without the slightest regard for justice or decency. . . . This system, followed since its establishment a century ago, has found new support in national enthusiasm, in the power of the army, and especially in a few distinguished military men to whom the government must now defer in every respect. . . . As they either cannot or will not enter into rivalry with Russia they concentrate all their efforts on Germany. The overcoming of Saxony, monstrous though it was, was to them but the first step in a series of operations through which they hoped sooner or later to acquire most of north Germany, put Austria out of action, and set themselves at the head of all Germany. Counting on the help of Russia to carry out this farseeing design, they wished at least to lay the cornerstone for their edifice during the Congress; and even though Austria did not succeed in thwarting their plans entirely it is no small gain that, thanks to our efforts, they did not achieve all that they had in mind."

But why no united Germany? What led the Prussian and German Gentz to oppose this aim as vehemently as once he had opposed Napoleon's superstate? The parallel is not out of place. An empire of all German-speaking peoples would signify equally, in one catastrophic way or another, nothing less than a European superstate. Gentz's realization of this was not so much a stroke of genius as mere traditional European statesmanship. He was acquainted with the masters of statecraft, whose principles and practices went back to the time of the great peace treaties, the Treaties of Westphalia, in 1648, and who had become increasingly perspicacious with the passing years. The international law that they had established was general, but also turned upon a particular truth that concerned both Europe and Germany. This was, that a great Germany would be too great for a small Europe unless certain shrewd and prudent conditions were met.

Gentz's execrated friend, the late Johannes von Müller, had expressed these many years before as follows: "Arms are Germany's profession. We bear them now to preserve order. But if a despot were to arise among us we should bear them against foreigners, for their money and their fair lands. . . . There are definite, insistent, eternal principles that some fortuitous circumstance or the rage of a minister might becloud, but that no number of alliances could abrogate. For Europe one of these is that Germany should maintain her political structure; that she should be strong of herself so that she need not depend upon the fortunes and designs of foreign powers. . . . For whom and in what cause her six hundred thousand warriors bear arms will determine all political balance, the freedom of Europe, and the good of the human race. . . ."

The Revolution and Napoleon had disregarded this maxim with crass ignorance. They had demolished Germany's old political structure, and in so doing had run counter to certain proclivities that were already present, since nothing develops out of thin air. Even before them there had existed the inclination and endeavor of the Prussian monarchy to extend its sway over as large a part of Germany as possible. In addition, and coeval with them, partly promoted by them and partly incited by their hostility, there was a German national tendency to restore the German Empire to its medieval form and grandeur. It was a romantic tendency, which looked backward toward the past but at the same time, since the past can never be regained, a tendency of wholly incalculable and wild revolutionary vigor. Germany with frontiers as they had been in the Middle Ages meant the fall of the smaller states, whose rape by Napoleon had been the real cause of the long war that only now had come to an end: of Holland, of Switzerland, of the Italian states. It meant the re-Germanization of regions that the more fortunate French nation had assimilated over centuries. It meant the dissolution of the Hapsburg monarchy. It meant the destruction of existing centers of order and civilization, a rousing of forces and harrowing of emotions such as even the great French Revolution itself had not achieved. It was a tendency whose end could not be foreseen; whose end no one had even tried accurately to foresee.

Should not the astute champions of the positivist school of constitutional law, Gentz and the others, have argued: "This nationalistic tendency is here, and will not rest until it has been realized. Let us take it from the hands of fools, therefore, and direct it toward ends that shall be just and tolerable for the world"? After all, a democratic national state was the aim of the French Revolution, and what Napoleon should have desired, but betrayed instead; was it not the duty of his victorious opponents to take over from him the great task? Who can say how much happier the nineteenth century might have been if Germans, Italians, and Slavs had constituted themselves national states while yet the idea was new and strong, and the national disposition still pliable; not through superior force, not through telegraph systems and railroads, but through common, voluntary resolve?

The answer is that Metternich and Gentz literally could not think along such lines. Too many old traditions, and aspirations to power, operated against it, no matter how much these might conflict among themselves. Indeed, their own principal, the head of the House of Hapsburg, would have discharged at a moment's notice any of his officials who even considered a thing so dangerous to his Empire. But even worse than that: they would have received no help, no guidance, from the new Nationalist party itself, for explicit advice could not be given by those whose own ideas were not clear.

Here, for example, was Baron vom Stein, the greatest and noblest of the Nationalists, with all his furious hatred of the German princes. He was in utter turmoil. He wanted a restitution of the Holy Roman Empire, with Austria bearing the imperial crown. At the same time he fought for an aggrandizement of Prussia, by means of which Germany's patchwork of states might be abolished. Although a fanatical believer in so-called Germanism he wished, notwithstanding, to treat the German problem as a general European problem that could not be solved without the Russians and the British. Most of his memoranda were addressed to the Czar, his patron, and critics insisted that he no longer knew what he was: European, or Russian, or a German nobleman. Without going as far as his friend General Gneisenau, who once flatly advised that Great Britain seize all north Germany and keep it—"The people thus united with Britain would be very happy under her liberal system of government"—he dreamed nevertheless of a union between Holland and Great Britain, a partition of Denmark, and other senseless projects whose blurring and disfiguring of the map of Europe were characteristic of a revolutionary era.

Stein, still an emigrant in the service of Russia, was profoundly embittered at the time, and thought himself betrayed by the entire world. He called Gentz a man with "worm-eaten brain and scorched heart." Nevertheless, Gentz was more useful to the Congress than Stein was, and if the latter had been entrusted with dictatorial powers to reconstitute Europe he would have produced nothing but confusion.

Wilhelm von Humboldt was another, though more moderate, leader of the Nationalists. Thanks to Napoleon, the humanism of this scholarly statesman had solidified into a belief in the people, whose voice he wished to heed. He involved himself in contradictions similar to those of Stein, speaking sometimes as though he were a Teutomaniac, and sometimes, again, as though he were not. He was far from contemplating dissolution of the old and tried Austrian state in favor of nationalistic states and warned against pan-German imperialism in memorable words that Gentz himself might well have uttered. "One must never forget," he wrote, "the true and actual purpose of the German Confederation, in so far as it relates to European politics. Its intent is to secure peace, and its whole existence is therefore based upon a preservation of balance through an inherent force of gravity; this would be entirely counteracted if there were introduced into the ranks of European states, besides the larger German states considered as single units, a new collective state prompted not by a disturbance in balance but, as it were, by deliberate act. . . . No one could then prevent Germany, as Germany, from becoming an aggressive state, which no good German can wish. For we know well what great superiority in literary and scientific accomplishments the German nation has achieved in the absence of external political aims; but no one knows how such aims might affect our future progress in this respect. . . ."

This was traditional eighteenth-century statecraft once more, founded on a sense of mechanical balance. But in spite of it Humboldt was tormented by the vague feeling that there was something essentially wrong with the European peace settlement. "To make a clean sweep of the evils that afflict our age, to suppress them completely and finally, the war should have been conducted and ended differently. Now a second war will be required, which inevitably will break out sooner or later, but in which the right, too, may succumb; for very few minds have come to a definite understanding of the situation. No matter how favorably events turn out nothing is and nothing will be clearly settled: not the war, not the Treaty of Paris, not the Congress. . . ."

But when has any political question ever been clearly settled? What new order does not carry within itself the seeds of fresh confusion? Right is often arrayed against right, greed against greed; mistakes cannot be avoided, and the final solution of the problem, harsh and detestable, easily gives rise later to the reproach: Why did you not solve it more skillfully at the right time? Those responsible, could they still speak, would reply: We could not. See what we had to deal with. No one in our place could have done better.

Gentz, however, was able to speak later, in respect to Germany as well as Italy. This he did, for example, in a short article that he called: "Could the Allies Have United Italy into One Single Kingdom in the Year 1814?" His answer was: No. Not because of principles urged at the Congress, to which there was by no means blind and rabid adherence when they conflicted with fact; not because of "Legitimism," not because of the Neapolitan Bourbons, not because of the Pope. But because the great majority of Italians were not prepared to accept a pan-Italian state; because there was nobody to organize one; because a great new state could not be founded by a few Lombardic intellectuals; because the arrangements that actually were made suited in all essentials the mood of most Italians. . . . Thus did Gentz defend himself when, in later life, he was reviled as a hater and destroyer of national movements; and historians of our own day agree that he was right.

For Prince Metternich there was no problem of national aspirations and conflicts; hence those to whom the question seemed urgent must have thought him frivolous and devoid of understanding. This Rhenish aristocrat, who spoke French better than he did German, still lived in a nationless antiquity. But Gentz, the writer from the middle class, was no cosmopolite. He had pondered deeply over the advantages for writers, say, or for politicians, of a political system based upon national unity: "We should have been a nation." During the struggle against Napoleon he had felt the lack sorely, and even now the universal function that he ascribed to the confederation of German states remained to his mind a lofty and responsible one. He had not frivolously ignored the problem of national unity, as he was reproached with having done, but had thought it through and abandoned it. Alarmed by the vague and threatening radicalism of the Teutomaniacs, he went to the opposite extreme, always conscious that political decisions must be one sided. This pupil of Immanuel Kant knew that positive, or established, law and abstract justice are two very different things, which never coincide entirely and whose coördination remains an eternal problem. He was no cynic, bowing to circumstances; no jurist, relying on dusty covenants. There was so much to consider, for one whose mind was open to the widest diversity of thought and fact. But the Teutomaniacs drove him to bias. In opposition to those who, for the sake of their nebulous idea of "nation," regarded as nothing all existing treaties, boundaries, and traditions, he became a positivist. In the interest of Austria, of German civilization rightly conceived, and of world peace the doings of the Prussians and the Nationalists must be stopped.

The first requisite was that the King of Saxony should come into his rights. This all-too-faithful henchman of Napoleon was a war prisoner of the allies. His country was occupied by Russian troops, and the Germanomaniacs burned to have it transferred to Prussia en bloc. In this they were supported by the Czar, because he planned to acquire in return the Prussian parts of Poland in conformity with the old *système copartageant*, or joint sharing of the spoils. To the others, the British and the Austrians, the question of Saxony appeared secondary for the time being, and for the sake of peace they were ready to accede. What the annexation of Saxony really meant only two at Vienna really understood, and they therefore began to confer privately together.

AMONG the innumerable members of the terrestrial hierarchy that gathered uninvited at Vienna—delegates and solicitants of all sorts, writers, bankers, ballerinas, portrait painters after fat commissions, physicians to cure the ills of the great by novel methods, father confessors and proselytizers, uplifters, somnambulists, and miracle-workers—there was to be found a certain Doctor Bollmann, who had just arrived from the United States of America; a man well versed in affairs and their reporting. Always ready to learn, Gentz did him the honor of inviting him to one of his gatherings. It was a typical European company: Prince Reuss XIX; von Humboldt; the Danish Ambassador, Count Bernstorff and his ladies; Prince Ferdinand of Coburg-Gotha; Count and Countess Fuchs; Carl von Varnhagen, the writer, with his wife, Rahel, nee Lewin; and others whom, in the words of von Varnhagen, "one was delighted to see and to hear." "Nevertheless," he continues in his memoirs, "the company soon fell silent just to listen to the marvels that Bollmann could tell of the United States of North America. This whole country had become remote from us because of the long maritime war, but still more remote was the idea of a republic whose development was a fabulous, nay, even an alarming example of how ordinary citizens can establish power and importance to a degree that we in Europe are still in the habit of associating only with the nobility and with royalty. Through the naïve questions of a diplomat who was present, and whose inordinate thirst for knowledge could never be satisfied, the talk gradually became a real lecture on republican principles and ideals, illustrated by striking examples, such as one would have thought hardly possible here at this congress of monarchs. Gentz was as though crushed by the weight of the thing, and as upset as though murder had been attempted in his presence. The good Bollmann, however, had not meant any harm. . . ."

Whence this uneasiness? They endeavored to "put Europe in order," and in so doing employed the words "European," "Christian," and "civilized" as though they were practically synonymous. Europe was the world. But no! It was the world no longer. Her traditional way of life was no more the only conceivable one; a monarchy not the only sound form of state. There was the great Republic across the sea. Gentz had long been acquainted with it and, indeed, had not lacked social contacts with the new country. Was not Alexander von Humboldt, Wilhelm's brother, an intimate friend of Thomas Jefferson? But mere acquaintance and the sudden sight of past, present, and future in one single image are two wholly different things.

Horror descended on the proud conservative as he listened to Doctor Bollmann's discourse. The picture of a rational, democratic society without a history, in which men could live comfortably, more abundantly and happily, in fact, than under the old kings—who listening to Bollmann could justly deny it? It was not the growing power of such a democracy that terrified him; fear he could cope with. It was rather the tormenting suspicion that the Americans were right; that he had chosen the wrong course and was an outmoded man standing in the way of progress.

Well, but had not the French tried to imitate America? And had not the result been Napoleon? Yes, to be sure, and so much the worse! So much the worse if the Americans were so superior in new developments that they could not even be imitated. While Europe was still exhausting herself in the Napoleonic Wars, which after all were but a sequel to this unhappy attempt at imitation, the Americans had been making their incredible progress. Bonaparte, like a fool, had sold Louisiana to the United States for a song, a region that alone could support more people than lived in all Europe. Yet no one could even begin to reproach him for it. Gentz himself had been heartily glad over the movement in the Spanish colonies for separation from their mother country, because thus they would be lost to Napoleonic Europe. Now Europe was Napoleonic no longer, but that she would regain South America was for those versed in history improbable to the point of impossibility.

The American democrats across the sea; the Prussians, the Nationalists, the Teutomaniacs in the heart of Germany; the incorrigible Jacobins and stubborn Royalists in Paris: No! Europe would never achieve the peace that was so ardently desired. Nor would she retain her place in the world. The Congress was undeniably magnificent; nothing like the golden Renaissance splendor of the great masked ball in the Hofburg would be seen in Washington for many a day. But it was a celebration by conquerors who in their darkest, that is their most enlightened, hours felt almost as though conquered themselves. Even the serene Metternich, who certainly understood nothing of what was going on across the sea, had attacks of this sort.

Well, God be praised, he, Gentz, surely would not live to see the worst of it. "After us the deluge," or those new things to which he did not want to oppose an unconditional No, yet to which, as the man he was, as an incarnation of the eighteenth century, he could not say Yes either.

TALLEYRAND was unpopular and lonely during the first days of his sojourn in Vienna. He appeared for the defeated, who so long had been insolent conquerors; that the allies had not fought the French at all, but only one evil man, was a pretty but rather artificial interpretation. His unsociability made it difficult for the Viennese secret police to watch him. "How hard it is to trail Prince Talleyrand," complained one of their agents, "will be clear to everyone who considers his character, and especially the arrangement of his dwelling house. It is like a closed fortress, in which he lives alone with his trusted circle." But in spite of all this the police finally succeeded in winning over an old serving man, and were glad to obtain a few scraps of paper from the wastebasket of the Prince.

At the receptions and masquerades Talleyrand stood about alone, waiting for someone to speak to him; powdered hair, livid countenance, supercilious stare, stupefied and seemingly lifeless eyes, and pendulous lips that betrayed both lechery and the blasé satiety of a surfeited man. His deformed foot was dragged behind him, rather than used as a support, and those watching him thought he looked like a legendary monster, half man, half serpent; or like a village schoolmaster, crippled, drunken, and old.

It was on such evenings that Gentz approached him and the two exchanged secrets of their political experiences. Once tempted into conversation, Talleyrand awoke, gathered himself together, and fascinated all listeners with his erudition and wit.

"France," said he, "after having set so many bad examples, must now furnish a good one; we must all be loyal Europeans. A fair distribution of power is all that we ask." Gentz thought this very true and accurate. Equilibrium, his philosophical life theme, had been the goal of prudent French politicians of the eighteenth century and Talleyrand, their pupil, turned back to them now. In this respect the interests of vanquished France coincided most auspiciously with those of the European community of states, or with justice itself. This was really the substance of the philosophy that Talleyrand brought with him to Vienna. After twenty years in the realm of raw, naked fact and constant war, amidst primitive conditions, there was to be a return to law and order. The "right of conquest," upon which the Prussians stubbornly insisted, was an unfortunate paradox. No sovereign could rightfully be deprived of his possessions unless he formally gave up all claim to them, and the European community of states recognized the transference of ownership. Thus Naples rightfully belonged to the Bourbon dynasty; thus, with very few exceptions, the political status of 1789 was still in existence and it rested only with Europe, assembled at Vienna, to sustain its validity. Voluntary and reasonable compromises naturally did not invalidate the general principle, provided, of course, that this was recognized as such. . . .

An eminently conservative and European doctrine, as Gentz acknowledged with the warmest interest. It presupposed a community of Christian states, united by and pledged to the observance of laws binding upon all. It was static, and it guaranteed peace; furthermore, it was exceptionally favorable to the French monarchy. For example, it would be more agreeable for the Bourbons in Paris to have Bourbons in Naples than "him who reigns in Naples." (Talleyrand could not bring himself to pronounce the name of Murat, the illegitimate King.) Again, Prussia would be more easily prevented from transforming Germany into a superstate.

In the long memorandum that he contributed to the report of the Congress Talleyrand did not conceal this more concrete side of his philosophy. "In addition to motives of justice," he wrote, "the more practical ones concerning French interests must be considered. The interests of the smaller states are the interest of France. All wish to preserve their existence, and we must help them to do so. . . . The pressure of Austria for expansion at the cost of Italy must be opposed. In Germany, Prussia is the great danger; her situation necessitates a greed for territory, and to her any pretext is justifiable. She knows no scruples; everything advantageous to her is right. . . . The terrible collapse brought about by her ambition has by no means cured her of it. At this very moment her agents and partisans are agitating in Germany, representing France as a power that is constantly planning new invasions and Prussia as the only one that can defend Germany, so that she must be delivered up to Prussia in order to be saved. Prussia would have liked to have Belgium; she wants everything that lies between France, the Moselle, and the Rhine; she wants Luxemburg; if she does not get Mainz all will be lost, she says; if she does not get Saxony she will enjoy no security. The allies are said to have agreed to keep her of the size that she was before 1807; that is, with ten million inhabitants. But if she has her own way there will soon be twenty million, and all Germany will be subject to her. Bounds must be set to this urge. . . ."

This was Gentz's view exactly, and His Highness reproduced it in every detail. For his own part, Gentz ventured to call the attention of France to a peril that was new, although related to the Prussian danger: the agitation for a united Germany by the so-called Germanomaniacs, who were carrying on their nefarious propaganda even in Vienna. . . . It did not take the experienced politician long to recognize the character of these mischief-makers. "German unity," wrote Talleyrand to King Louis, "is their cry, their doctrine, their religion, which they profess with true fanaticism. . . . Who can calculate the result if an agglomerate like the Germans, fused to a uniform whole, were to become aggressive? Who can say where such a movement would end?

Gentz succeeded in showing Prince Metternich the significance of the problem of Saxony in this connection. The reader knows the result: the common stand and secret alliance of the British, French, and Austrians that obliged Prussia to content herself temporarily with half of the desired kingdom.

The sensation of influencing a grave political resolve directly, instead of merely with his pen, went powerfully to the head of our intellectual: "This day is one of the most noteworthy of my life!" It was then that His Most Christian Majesty sent 24,000 gulden in gold. On the other hand, the hatred of the Prussians against their former compatriot rose to a white heat. "I hear," wrote Frau von Humboldt to her husband, "that Gentz is said to be one of our most zealous adversaries at Vienna, and that he takes all pains imaginable to restrain Prussia. I do not know whether I have told you that once, in the spring, when the armies were already in Paris, he said: When it comes to the negotiations I shall make every effort to cheat Prussia. And in February, when things were not going well with Blücher, he took a positively satanic delight in laying the blame on the 'conceited Prussian.' . . . The most sacred cause to inspire our era has never really touched him. . . . Do not trust him!"

Even his own brother, who had remained loyal to Prussia, said that he wanted nothing more to do with such an infamous man as Friedrich Gentz. Once more, as twenty-two years previously, when first he took up his pen against the French Revolution, his unjust opponents, blinded by their passions, could not understand that he was wholly sincere in word and deed, although he never accused them of sordid motives.

There is nothing remarkable in this for it is characteristic of nationalism, as of other fundamentally popular movements, that it impugns forthwith the morals of all who disagree with it. A conservative politician may have revolutionists prosecuted, but he never denies them all honor and ability. Gentz, in contrast, became for the Prussians a minion of Hell the moment they saw he was opposed to their religion; that is, did not want them allowed to annex the Kingdom of Saxony and dominate Germany and Europe.

To this it must be added that in the long view he was a poor Simple Simon, or else deluded; for Saxony, and much, much more than

Saxony, did fall to Prussia at last, and to this extent all his effort was in vain. A writer of our own day wishes to conclude from this that politics are wretchedly and wholly ineffectual. But what does this mean, after all? No man does more than he can. The vocation most intimately concerned with history, that of the politician, is at the same time the one most indissolubly linked with the present. "After us the deluge" is really the motto of every politician; or, if the inverse construction seem preferable: while we are here no deluge. Posterity must look out for itself.

As a result of Napoleon's return, diplomatic finesse lost in importance and Talleyrand's prestige suffered beyond repair. Only shortly before, his face wreathed in smiles, he had described the French Emperor as politically dead; now he sought to extricate himself from the affair as gracefully as possible through bitter complaints over the character of his compatriots. To Gentz alone was the new complication a challenge to deep thought. If even the slightest significance could be ascribed to the political doings of the masses, Napoleon's victorious progress was the greatest triumph that ever one man alone had achieved over the world and the people. It could not have happened in the absence of far-reaching social causes. Had he not said a year previously that the Bourbons would never again be able to govern France? On the other hand, this most insolent of all coups d'état could be regarded as a calamitous demobilization crisis, an event with neither meaning nor consequence; but this would imply holding the people, the soil from which all history springs, thoroughly in contempt. So Joseph Goerres, for example, did. He had counted on opposition by the Royalists, on civil war, and when this did not occur he sounded a shrill laugh of scorn in his *Mercur*.

"Once more it has happened that an era has strenuously endeavored to devote itself to the heroic, the dramatic, only to see everything turn to tragicomical delusion before its very eyes. There are things so fabulous and incredible to hear of that one might think they would shame the Devil himself, and with one of these the French have now provided us: the loss of an empire within twenty days, against the clearly expressed wish of twenty-four million men, and without a blow having been struck, to a bloodthirsty tyrant whom all execrated and cursed and who has returned from banishment with a bare thousand men. It is impossible to raise the virtuosity of wickedness to a higher point; and though we Germans, too, have given many wonderful performances of this sort in other fields all have now been excelled and eclipsed, and we are washed wholly clean of all stain. . . ." "France has humbled herself before him; he stands and waits to see how Europe will meet him. If we continue the course upon which we have embarked we shall contribute the second act to a French comedy and negotiate with him whom we have outlawed to gain a respite of two years, when his preparations for thorough eradication of the old order will be completed. As he brazenly preached freedom to the French, so will he tell the rulers of his moderation and how he intends to devote the rest of his days to the peaceful virtues. . . . He will give Europe what he promised as little as he will give the French their freedom."

Goerres' gloomy, threatening cry matched the general frame of mind. It was a genuine relaxation to turn back from the deplorable confusion of the Congress to the lofty flight of the common defensive struggle. Away, away with the mischief-maker, the devil, the spent actor, the monster, the fool! The new declaration of war that Gentz had to submit to drawing up was a declaration of outlawry. The allies were not declaring war on France, but all Europe, including France, was declaring war on this one man; a clever fiction that did not really square with the facts.

The armies, on their way home, turned back. Shrill cries resounded for a strong common leadership, for national unity, for the execution of the scoundrel, for the partitioning of his lands. Whoever was not indispensable at Vienna left for home. The diplomats were unmoved by any consciousness of the Great Man's tragedy as, after the rapturous delights of his return, he sat in the palace that had seen his former triumphs; half at home, half a foreign guest; surrounded by those whom he found completely changed and weakened in their convictions; whom he must pretend to trust and who distrusted him; left to reluctant creatures whom he had once despised; against him a merciless world. The letters that he addressed to his Empress, in Vienna, were opened in the conference of the great powers and heartily ridiculed, all the ministers coöperating in an effort to decipher the atrocious handwriting.

He had occupied the attention of his contemporaries too long and too exclusively, and everyone was thoroughly tired of him. All wanted to enter at last upon an era of peace into which this man did not fit, and the beseeching communications in which he protested his fervid wish to adapt himself to it were not even honored with an answer. What Metternich and the south Germans secretly desired no one knew exactly; they would not have dared to say. Gentz, who did say it—that now it would be best to leave France and the ruler whom she manifestly wanted in peace—was cried down as a hopelessly corrupt character.

Whether he was right rather than the indignant majority the author does not presume to decide. What Napoleon said to Benjamin Constant, the liberal, and repeated later as a captive with the patience of despair, seemed plausible. Wars such as he had been forced to wage were now obsolete. He could not accept the treaties of 1814, but as they had been accepted by the Bourbons he could put up with them as a condition for which he was not responsible. Now he would turn to internal affairs, and become a prince of peace, an emperor of the middle class, the workers, and the peasants. Why should he crave still further military fame? Oh, he would become a man that Europe could tolerate without difficulty. . . . Unfortunately he appeared gloomy and awkward during the festival of freedom on the Champ de Mars, and hardly convincing as a constitutional monarch. How could he and the freedom of the press that he promised be compatible? He, who disdained all orators, and all opposition? He understood the middle-class mind as well as any bourgeois, yet could not become bourgeois himself; he continued to say "My capital," "My subjects"; an outmoded hero who could not rid himself of his egotistic delusion. "He is the same madman as ever," said Fouché, and immediately set out to betray him.

How could he prove conclusively to the world that he had become another man? How could there be any confidence between him and the kings, after his escape and fresh usurpation? Gentz was asking too much of the art of diplomacy, as he had the year before. It was much simpler that the armies should turn back and bring the victory to an end; but this time to a definite end.

The glory of the revolutionary dynasty that bewitched the decades to come; the legend of Napoleon the liberal, the martyr to "modern ideas," rests essentially on the terrible episode that was about to begin. But it would hardly have flourished so vigorously had not the great mass of the mediocre thrown themselves pitilessly on the genius and borne him to earth before ever he could establish himself in his new role.

IN TOKEN of the new and militant determination the Congress functioned better than ever before. Early in June, while dreadful events were preparing in Belgium, everything was finished: a great mass of separate state treaties, definitions of boundaries, and alliances that had no connection with one another. It was Gentz who insisted, for good reasons, that all this should be given at least an external coherence; that the resolutions of the Vienna Congress should be incorporated in a single document. Together with Humboldt he completed the task in a few inspired nights, and the reapportionment of the Continent appeared in the shape of a fundamental European statute, at least on paper. More than this could not have been attained.

Perhaps this was the other, the positive, side of the course of instruction in politics that Gentz had undergone during the two years preceding: the conviction that in politics "more," the right, the absolute cannot be achieved. Though now he often appeared deliberately cynical and disillusioned in respect to the idealism of the study, he was proud on the other hand of his practical experience and held it to be the more useful, sound, and mature. "You live and move in a fixed political system," he would write in fatherly tone to one of his disciples. "You still cherish the youthful illusion that things must arrange themselves in deference to our wish, and that the world can be ruled in accordance with a few general principles. But experience and continuous meditation have led me to the conclusion—erroneous, perhaps, yet unalterable—that man and his world can dominate one another only in a reciprocal way; and that the physician learns the nature of disease far more often than he conquers it. For me there is no longer any system in practical politics. After all, it is only an art and the best artist is he who, at any given moment, is most completely master of his instrument."

According to the principle of Legitimism the Kingdom of Poland should have been restored, and Gentz himself would have ardently desired its restitution; the project failed because it ran counter to the wishes of mighty Russia. In deference to the new principle of national emancipation Italians, Czechs, and Serbs should have been made sovereign nations, which was impossible. The loose confederation of German states lagged far behind the original design; the concept of a great German empire. Even the Final Act of the Congress, an irrational collection of detached rules, reflected but dimly the idea of a legally instituted community of nations and perpetual peace. It is true that Gentz drew up a sketch for a general reciprocal guarantee of possession and mutual aid: collective security, the old thesis of William Pitt. Metternich was in favor of it, and even Lord Castlereagh, but their principals were not; much less the Russians and the

Prussians. For hardly was the Napoleonic danger over before the great lesson was forgotten, and the powers were as fearful as ever of "foreign entanglements." Besides, a few of them secretly regarded the territorial arrangements that had just been completed as not the most favorable to themselves, and not final.

Well, perhaps "perpetual peace" was an ideal that had better not be snatched at in fumbling immediacy. Perhaps peace would be served most effectually by pursuing a sound, realistic, and temperate policy. The millennium, wrote Gentz, vindicating the Congress in his capacity as a journalist, was unjustly demanded of the statesmen at Vienna. But they had to reckon with given conditions, and were not permitted to bring any one single principle to realization. Had they earnestly tried to reconcile the laws of force with the precepts of reason and wisdom? Had they produced something that, even though it completely satisfied none among a multiplicity of diverse wishes, nevertheless took most of them partly into account? Would the situation that they had created be permanent? Could it be changed without catastrophic results?

These were the questions that any impartial observer would ask, perforce, in respect to the achievements of the Congress, and that Gentz undertook to answer in the affirmative.

To bring a single principle to realization: in earlier years he would no doubt have made such a demand, first as a revolutionary and then, for a moment, as a Royalist. But such facile idealism could not hold out against that prolonged study of the world and of power to which he had devoted himself.

XIII

PARIS, 1815

UNDER the date June 18, 1815, Gentz wrote: "Stadion, Palffy, Wessenberg, Humboldt, and others had dinner with me at Weinhaus. Worked until eleven. I am beginning to get up early and go to bed early." In the charming villa that he had rented, its wide plate-glass windows looking out over the garden in the twilight, he was chatting gaily with his guests at the very moment when Napoleon was asking his adjutant on the battlefield at Waterloo what was moving over there on the horizon. The adjutant took the telescope and answered: Prussian flags. Whereupon the Emperor merely shook his head, and turned as white as chalk.

Hardened by long familiarity with momentous happenings, they heard of the battle seven days later in Vienna without much emotion. No one had seriously doubted the issue of this belated but bloody epilogue.

For a few weeks more that summer Gentz idled in the country, content with his work and his income. Then he was called to Paris to take part in the renewed peace negotiations. His party left in two traveling carriages with six horses: Leopold, the valet; Bastien, the cook; and Charles. In his handbag were a copy of the *Edinburgh Review* and some volumes of Voltaire and old Johannes von Müller. In Nuremberg he visited Campe, the bookseller; in Frankfort, Bethmann, the banker; in Cologne, hated the Prussians; exchanged written courtesies in Coblenz with Goerres; in Mons, met Baron vom Stein, who also was on his way to Paris; and arrived at the capital after a journey of fifteen days. Because of the many soldiers abroad, the insecurity, and the turmoil, detours had been found advisable.

The city that had held his spirit in thrall for five and twenty years he now saw for the first time and, almost a stranger to external impressions, he was bewildered. At first he lived in the Rue Richepanse, near the Place Louis Quinze; then in the mansion of the Duc de Dalberg, in the Rue Anjou. He visited the *quais*, the shops in the Palais Royal, and the fountains at Versailles with Charles; the Comédie Française, the opera, the famous restaurants—Robert, Massinot,

Rocher de Cancale—with Metternich. But he who had formerly thought himself a confirmed metropolitan was no longer in the mood to enjoy the pleasures of a great city. "Here one only exists in a whirl, and does not really live. One must be a resolute pavement-trotter, and strong and healthy besides, in order to enjoy this monstrous city." Sometimes he was overcome by uncanny associations: there, in the house of Louis, the Minister of Finance, had lived Calonne and Necker, subjects of his youthful studies; in the palace of the King: "A curious sensation seized me as I walked through the great halls of the Tuileries, and thought of all that had happened there in the past eight and twenty years." Louis XVI, threatened by the mob, putting on the red revolutionary cap; the deserted palace, with the guillotine underneath its windows; the court of the young and exuberant First Consul; and the Emperor as he returned from Elba, his heart filled with delight and doubt, springing up the familiar steps not five months since. Truly, one had lived through an extraordinary era.

Joseph Fouché, Minister of the Interior in the new royal government, drew a vivid picture of the recent past for the secretary of the allies. In particular, the last days of Napoleon had been really awful this time. He seemed no more than a bankrupt adventurer, an unwelcome ghost. Those who were endeavoring to repair the disaster that he had wrought treated him with brutal disdain. No more help was to be expected now from the Bourbons, no more moderation and elaborate fictions from the allies. Nearer and nearer came the hostile armies, at their head the most threatening, General Blücher's Prussians. The rich were for capitulation, but the poor, and some of the soldiers, were in favor of fighting it out to the very end. The dethroned Emperor, still brooding in the Palais de l'Élysée, offered himself to them as a general, and he who had so thoroughly despised the people appeared on the terrace, his hand on his heart, tossing coins to the proletariat as they passed by. It had required the greatest diplomacy to get this impossible man out of the city, and start him on the journey that ended with his imprisonment.

As for Louis XVIII, an overwhelming majority of the people, at least in the capital, would have none of him. The Parliament had proclaimed Napoleon's son Emperor, but Lord Wellington explained to its delegates in plain language that this was out of the question, and that the allies would hear of no one but the legitimate King. Under the protection of the foreign armies Louis made his second dismal entrance; a confederate dissatisfied with the temperate joy over the outcome of the battle of Waterloo. Without the King and his followers, asked Talleyrand, would a single battle lost have laid the whole country open and defenseless before the victor? There was, for all that, some sort of collective responsibility on the part of one nation in its dealings with other nations; an identity of representative and nation. Louis XVIII was to blame for the Hundred Days, because he was French and represented guilty France. During the first years of the Revolution clever émigrés had tried to convince Europe that there was a difference between the French people and the Jacobin regime; now, conversely, one was supposed to discriminate between a corrupted people and a respectable government.

A little subtle, all these distinctions, at least for General Blücher's troops, who camped out in the courtyard of the Tuileries and enjoyed disturbing the King in his asthmatic slumbers. They were inclined to think that they had won the battle of Waterloo against the inhabitant of the palace, no matter who this might be, and despite his having called it "a superb battle."

Although Napoleon was now a prisoner, the allied armies pushed on without mercy into the interior of France. Already there were a million foreign soldiers in the country, still more than in the year preceding and of much more evil intent. The King realized, and admitted, that he would not be able to maintain his position without the protection of the alien troops, but these very protectors made him to the French a ridiculous and hated figure.

That a man of natural dignity could long for, and choose, such a position appears inconceivable. Although he announced that he had returned to stand by the French in their extremity like a father, one will hardly credit Louis XVIII with a consuming love for his native land. Why, then, did he not prefer his long-accustomed exile to presiding over privy councils whose members he did not know, but upon whom he was dependent because they understood the country whose current condition he did not know either? A "philosopher" in the prerevolutionary sense of the word, passing formerly as a scornful opponent of the brother who had been executed, Louis was still not skeptical enough to have any doubts respecting the divine right of his house. His house and France appeared to him as one: no happiness for the Bourbons except on the throne; no happiness for France without the Bourbons. As is the case with decayed nobility, the high intelligence that shone from his eyes, and even his smiling tolerance, were but an inversion of his arrogance. His brother, the sillier and more credulous Comte d'Artois, was friendly with the people. Louis, on the contrary, was so haughty that whenever he fell down he would lie flat until someone of appropriately high rank came to help him. He was prevented from getting up alone by his corpulence and the weakness consequent upon his gout. He wore red velvet boots, an old-fashioned blue civilian's coat with red epaulets, and a ridiculous little hat; and as he floated rather than waddled along, supported by two adjutants, he looked infinitely tired and old; yet crafty, too, and in a certain way majestic. Gentz, who was vouchsafed a long private audience, during which he was even honored with a seat, found him far superior to his paralyzed environment.

AMONG the allies there were two opposing views as to the best way of treating the restored King. One proceeded on the assumption that subjects and their rulers, France and Europe, must now be reconciled; that degrading peace terms meant a hopeless round of wars and revolutions, and that with an apparently friendly government it would therefore be best to deal mildly and considerately. The Czar and his group were of this mind, as were Castlereagh and Wellington. Against them the Prussian Germans, spurred on by voices from their fatherland, contended that this time the enemy must really have a lesson that never would be forgotten.

Baron vom Stein insisted that no reliance could be placed upon the Bourbons; as for the French people, to turn away from the vanquished leader after the battle of Waterloo did not require much courage. At the beginning of the adventure there had been an attempt to differentiate between Napoleon and the people, to be sure, but the people themselves had not admitted such a distinction. Furthermore, as soon as the foreign troops had been withdrawn civil war would inevitably break out in France. Hence it would be better to leave her to her terrible fate, but to secure for themselves meanwhile the safest possible military frontiers by seizing Alsace, Lorraine, the Vauban fortifications, and Flanders. A patriot from the Baron's neighborhood, sojourning in France, formulated the aim of this policy with praiseworthy frankness. As the desirable was impossible, wrote this truly logical man, namely, the complete destruction and partition of France, one was limited to seizing as much of her territory as might be. "The objection will be raised that this must inevitably lead to new wars. Of course it will, for there is no such thing as lasting peace. But should the worst come to the worst, it will be well for us if France has to fight for a few hundred years, as in the past, before she reaches the Rhine again. . . ."

IN HIS attitude toward the nation the King found himself face to face with the same difficult choice: to avoid the mistakes of the past and conciliate through reason; or this time no mercy! In so far as his arrogance allowed decisions, he himself was inclined toward moderation though without much enthusiasm. So was the Ministry that the British had forced upon him, in which, next to Talleyrand, the aging Fouché played the principal role. But his family and his intimate circle were ruthless. "Make an end to clemency," was the battle cry. An enraged mob of Royalists echoed it in the southern provinces, and Gentz read with horror of bloody scenes such as had not been witnessed since the days of the ill-fated Foullon and the Princess de Lamballe. A White Terror is generally worse than a Red. While a million alien soldiers ravaged the land it was given over besides to the fury of civil war. Famine raged.

Both dilemmas, that of the allies and that of the King, were in reality one and the same. Only a humane, a European, peace treaty would have allowed a liberal internal policy. On the other hand, the ultraroyalists showed themselves, according to Gentz's expression, the most "voluble" in accepting stringent peace terms, if only they were allowed to be harsh toward Jacobins and supporters of Napoleon. Without hesitation Gentz accordingly chose peace abroad with neither victor nor vanquished, and constitutional government at home. As always when he faced a real crisis romanticism and its opposite, cynicism, vanished into thin air. There had been time for these in the tepid and luxurious atmosphere of the Congress, but now the ground was red hot, and the comparison with a volcano to be taken almost literally. Once more this ringing prophecy of evil went forth to the world. "The King's authority does not extend now to more than twenty-seven departments. . . . Besides the aliens who are ruining him with their friendship, and a Ministry that is not only powerless but divided against itself, this unhappy man has no support but a negligible party of so-called Royalists; an ignorant, incompetent lot who understand no method of government save bloodshed and who, in their desperation, curse all the rest of the French (every day, as I hear) and are cursed by them in turn." "When one listens to this set the last hope of a brighter future for France disappears. Moreover, the well to do are already looking about for havens to which they can flee, and as the King will never be resolute enough to evade the influence exerted by the real originators of all his troubles, it is impossible to see how this unnatural situation can end otherwise than in the most frightful explosion. At the same time, the external pressure is great beyond all imagining, the misery of the country alarming, the disruption of its finances abysmal, and there is a rising fear that famine impends. The wild, extravagant doings in Paris throw a veil over all these hardships and dangers. . . ."

Then, more hopefully, and with more lenient peace conditions in mind: "Certainly Louis XVIII is not tottering so precariously on his throne as a thousand signs and symptoms might lead one to suspect, and it will depend wholly and solely on the decisions of the allied cabinets whether they will make his position permanently secure; that is, for the rest of his life (since for the continuance of his august line I would not give one single heller)."

Then, pessimistically once more: "The King is surely lost, and lost before very long, if he does not send his whole family into exile."

The only exception that Gentz made was Louis Philippe, Duke of Orleans, who thirteen years before had whispered to him in the British Lower House: "This means trouble." He had little better to say now. Grown gray, and enormously fat, he was still the shrewd, penetrating man by whom Gentz had been so impressed during his stay in England. He read Gentz an alarming memorandum on the condition of the kingdom, and was off again in a trice for London. What else these two discussed has not come down to us, but when Gentz occasionally intimated that the older line of the Bourbons would never under any circumstances be capable of ruling again, it is clear that by the younger line he meant none other than the liberal head of the House of Orleans.

The politicians of the capital, those in office and those in opposition, acquainted Gentz with all their troubles, glad to have found someone who, though he had influence, would listen to them understandingly. He dined with the Ministers, Baron Louis, Pasquier, and Fouché; and with the celebrated liberals, Madame de Staël and Benjamin Constant. Five months previously Constant had sketched out a parliamentary system of government for Napoleon, under the illusion that he could bring about through the Emperor what apparently he could not through the King, and had had some very dramatic conversations with him. Gentz nodded affirmatively as he listened to the account of the famous ideologist. Yes, it would have been better to try fair dealing with the returned Dictator in March. "But what could you expect, my dear man? If only you knew all our follies. . . ." At night reactionaries and progressives, native and foreign, gathered in the salon of Talleyrand, the Chief of the Cabinet. Russians and Prussians were there also, of course, but kept to themselves and were insolent to the French; the British and the Austrians showed greater tact and cordiality. Napoleon's last days were eagerly discussed. If a foreigner suggested that after all the fallen man had been estimable enough in his way, his former subjects would fly into a rage: "Not at all! Not at all!" Nevertheless, they thought it magnificent that in surrendering he had proved himself to his enemies a "second Themistocles," whereupon the British would burst into peals of laughter.

Scornful and gloating, the victors commented among themselves on the flattery that they received from their humiliated hosts. "Has there ever been such a nation . . . ?" Thus inevitably began the conversations whose aftercourse everyone knew in advance. The host, blasé and tired, relying on the automatic influence, so to speak, of his cleverness and his reputation, sat and played for money with old ladies. Fouché drew representatives of all parties aside into a window niche. He made the deepest impression upon Gentz, and, indeed, he was admired by common consent as "the most infamous and useful man that the King could find." The military men, administrators, and scientists from Napoleon's circle weighed more heavily than the ideologists, who now were struggling for power. The Minister of Police was a questionable gentleman, but born for his calling.

He was a new type in the long line of curious politicians with whom Gentz had been connected. There were William Pitt, the British Roman, great orator and economist, who was ruined by the turmoil on the Continent; Lombard, the wily bureaucrat and cultured wit; Stein, the Germanic reformer and aristocratic democrat; the fastidious, serene archdiplomat and cosmopolitan, Metternich; the secretive attendant on so many ephemeral heroes and governments that were no more, Talleyrand; and now the petty bourgeois, hungry for power, gray, with his piercing eyes devoid of lashes and his quick, supple movements, Fouché: a tender husband and father, an amusing comrade who was always ready to help, blameless in his private life, innocent of hatred or vindictiveness, but capable of out-and-out villainy when his own welfare, or what he conceived to be the welfare of the country, demanded. "The Jacobins were not in jest where power was concerned," Gentz had written twenty years previously, and now the most notorious representative of that gang sat smirking at him from across the room. He had triumphed in so many situations where others had gone down, and Gentz would have died of fear! Twenty years before he had taken the liveliest part in the downfall of Robespierre, and only two months ago in the overwhelming of Napoleon. Talleyrand was cowardly; this ill-favored graybeard had courage, the gloomy courage of the skeptic. Fouché no longer had faith or illusions, and apart from force, or moderation if need be, he believed in nothing.

It was customary to represent the Jacobins as men who pursued one single, logical principle with blind fanaticism, but at the bare mention of principles Fouché had only a dismal sneer to offer, and it is curious that Gentz appears to have seen in just this widely experienced opportunism and pessimism of the police official the true spirit of Jacobinism and of the Revolution. Later he summed up his opinion of Fouché as "one of the worst scoundrels that ever lived, but a *highly* practical man, and the most consistent revolutionist that I have ever met. . . . Moreover, if Bonaparte had followed *this* Minister, he would still be reigning today. . . ."

The most consistent revolutionist. Because literally he held nothing sacred? Because he had even forced Louis XVIII to appoint him Minister; him, who had voted for the death of the royal brother; him, the blood-bespattered member of the National Convention? The police, technical aids of power, with whom even idealists cannot dispense, are often taken over together with power itself. He was the most consistent revolutionist, perhaps, because he did not fear the people. The conservatives had been afraid of the masses ever since 1789, when they had suddenly become so formidable, but Fouché, himself sprung from the people, understood his own kind. He knew that if they were met openly, boldly, and jovially they were much easier to manage than ambitious men. He admitted their leaders to his office, joked boisterously with them, and sent his agents to them in the Faubourg St. Antoine. Street gatherings of the proletariat did not impress him, because he himself was master of the art of staging and dispersing them. It was not two months since that mournful-looking men of the lower classes in disquieting number had filed by the residence of the deposed Emperor, crying: "Bread, or Napoleon." "But the Duke of Otranto" [Fouché], so run the memoirs of an eyewitness, "was much too experienced a politician not to estimate this gesture at its true worth."

Fouché sent Napoleon away from Paris; Napoleon submitted, and disappeared in silence.

The second restoration was not Fouché's work. If amidst the dark turmoil that followed Waterloo he forced the abdication of Napoleon, and had himself chosen as head of a provisional government, it was only to keep in his own hands the decision as to how the country was to be governed in the future, and to place at its head a figure who should be acceptable to the nation; another Bonaparte, or the Duke of Orleans. He wanted to protect "the gains of the Revolution"; the laws; the great, new fortunes; and the men incriminated: himself, for example. But he realized only too soon what remained hidden from the crowd of chattering deputies: that the iron will of a united Europe would permit no choice other than Louis XVIII.

As Fouché now felt his way along the course that he saw to be unavoidable; as he led Paris to believe that he was fighting for Napoleon II when actually he had long been negotiating with the Bourbons; wrung the highest commission from the Jacobins as their savior from a terrible reaction by the nobility, and from the Royalists as their savior from the wrath of the people; as he presented himself to the allies and to the King in the guise of the great physician, the brain of France, and retained his post as Minister in spite of the restoration; he was completing the masterpiece of his long career. It was the most difficult political game of which Gentz had any knowledge. And with what cynical intelligence, with what acute perception, move after move had been made!

In conducting this second difficult transition from Napoleon to the Bourbons, Fouché had spared the country much pain and bloodshed. During the Hundred Days he had saved certain adherents of the King, and now, under the Bourbons, some followers of Napoleon. He would have preferred to save them all. It is true that, as Minister of the King, he drew up a list of fifty-seven persons to be proscribed, among them some with whom, as Minister of the Emperor, he had only just been on the best of terms. But he excused himself on the score that he had to remain in power to prevent worse from happening; that in order to continue as Minister he had to grant the Royalists a certain minimum of victims; and that had it not been for him the proscription list would have included not fifty-seven, but several thousand distinguished names. Force never leaves him untainted who makes it his occupation, nor does it leave him free to change his trade. If now Fouché retired under protest, it was no peaceful and comfortable private life that beckoned.

He fell despite the superior skill of his maneuvers. Once in the saddle, the King and his supporters bethought themselves of decent principles again, and now it occurred to them how abominably the ministry of a regicide distorted the beautiful picture. The Countess of Angoulême fell in a faint when she saw the murderer of her father, in silken hose, his three-cornered hat and portfolio under his arm, stealing into the council chamber of the King, where he could not help appearing nervous and abstracted. Even the tolerant Louis found his face repulsive.

Fouché told Gentz that he had had enough, and meant to retire shortly, though he could think upon the consequences of his departure only with the deepest concern; for he was the mediator between a despairing people and a regime that did not understand them. In truth, and naturally enough, he fought like a tiger for his position. He harassed his British patrons, employed publicity in the most perfidious way, and published a memorandum that painted the condition of France in the darkest colors to alarm the allies, prove his own indispensability, and no doubt injure the Bourbons as well.

All to no avail. His hour came. It was just these last steps in his defense that ruined him. He was given to understand that he no longer enjoyed the confidence of the King. Whether from patriotism, or whether because he felt his power waning, Fouché staged no more street demonstrations. The great artist in popularity disappeared in his turn, and three months after the fall of the Emperor against whom he had intrigued with such superior skill, and not without disdain, this confirmed politician, too, came to the end of his rope. Less than a year later he was in exile. Gentz insisted that sensible people of all classes lamented his going, except "those contemptible men who wanted to see France returned at any cost to the seventeenth century." He had been wholly fascinated by Fouché, as an anxious tourist in the mountains is fascinated by the smooth and effortless pace of his guide.

If Gentz had long since begun to turn away from politics as a science and a religion, to politics as an art of the moment, his sojourn in Paris was a milestone on the road. Never before had he been so struck by the truth of his simile, coined years before, of the practical, unprejudiced physician who alone can cure, where the philosopher and theorist inevitably fails. There were dreadful wounds to be healed. Chaos could not be resolved by rigid moral distinctions or by stringent penal codes, but only by letting bygones be bygones. Expert knowledge! Experience! Tolerance of opposition! All these he now exhibited toward his younger friends with paternal superiority. "Farewell! And throw aside all political speculation. Human affairs have become so unaccountable that one must know an immeasurable amount before one can understand how little one knows. A smile (of sympathy) comes over my face when I read the guileless fancies in your letters. . . ." "I think you much too prudent and modest to imagine that you know more about this subject than *Fouché*, who probably understands the soul of France better than any man alive. . . . With your notions, my dear friend, though they might have been mine ten years ago (which, however, I admit only with considerable reservation) the world cannot and should not be governed any longer; all will be lost beyond redemption should it even be tried. Furthermore, those who could try are all so weak that it would be doubly wicked to set them on the wrong road. . . ."

Young Pilat, to whom this letter was addressed, was an enthusiastic advocate of Legitimism, and of revenge on the slayers of Louis XVI.

The counsel of moderation advanced by foreigners had but little effect at the moment. The Parliament, elected by the rich, clumsily imitating the procedures of the British, and not knowing what to make of it all, was united only in hatred of the new times. Even Talleyrand, Chief of the Cabinet, who had tried to save himself by the deposition of Fouché, succumbed a few days later to the reactionaries.

The real purpose of Gentz's visit, the conclusion of another peace between France and Europe, was more happily achieved. Even though the sentimentalities of the preceding year had been left far behind, the Czar, Lord Castlereagh, and Gentz triumphed over the demands of the Prussian Nationalists. Only such inconsiderable gains of the Revolution as had been left untouched a year before were demanded. An allied army was to keep order in the conquered country for five years. To meet the costs of the last war an indemnity of seven hundred million francs was to be paid; a large sum, yet not intolerably large. The art treasures of Europe that Napoleon had assembled in Paris, and whose value was set at astronomical figures, were to be returned to their rightful owners.

Gentz went so far that even here he would have preferred not to disturb a situation that had existed for years, and described the Prussian eagerness to recover their own as vandalism. There were columns whose removal would necessarily be followed by the collapse of whole edifices; statuary that the Parisians would see disappear "only with tears and curses." "If you knew how all friends of order, all friends of present and future peace, regard these events you would be surprised. It costs us dear that we did not stand out in good time and more firmly against the folly and insanity of the world." Not less vigorously did he oppose Humboldt's attempt "to wring from this unfortunate government the cost of all that Napoleon has ever done to Europe, down to the very last heller." To exact more than the country could pay would be politically fatal, would be economic madness.

The alliance of the four great powers was renewed. For reasons of discretion the King of France was not allowed to join because it was directed, if not against France, at least against a return of the Prisoner and a recurrence of French unrest; for such a federation seemed to require some sort of hostile object. Periodic congresses to exorcise still unknown dangers were expressly provided for.

Talleyrand, who was made nervous by the very word "alliance," had once suggested that a permanent European secretariat be established at Vienna, and that Gentz be entrusted with its management. The various governments were to contribute equally to cover its cost, and the salary of the secretary was to correspond with the dignity of his high office. Gentz's eyes grew big when this proposal was submitted to him by the Prince during one of his social evenings; but Humboldt smiled scornfully, and even Metternich preferred to regard the whole matter as a joke.

Instead of this there was the Holy Alliance: the suggestions of the Czar could not be pushed aside so easily as those of a mere Minister who, besides, was in danger of being overthrown. Alexander was much given to prayer, under the influence of a formerly hedonistic noblewoman, now no longer young, who combined a clear appreciation of the benefits of class distinctions with a fashionable piety, and a Christian charity that reached down to embrace even the common people. This mundane mystic had bewitched the fond monarch, and in her vision of a community of states founded on the precepts of Christianity—devout and contented subjects on the one hand, fatherly rulers united in God on the other—he recognized the need of his times. He felt that the era demanded something, that after all things could not go on simply as they had in the past; and others felt this, too. But he and his Baroness brought about only a feeble pledge that was supposed to settle affairs by magic, whereas these could have been controlled only by a courageous and radical change.

There was much laughing and shrugging of shoulders among the diplomats. "The so-called Holy Alliance," wrote Gentz, "is what one calls a political nullity, without real substance, without real sense: a theatrical setting conceived by a mistaken, or at least an unfortunately expressed, piety if not by common vanity. . . . If it should contribute in any way at all toward securing peace, as a few who must be considered sincere think it will, it may prove despite everything to have been more valuable than so many other farces of our time that have brought forth nothing but disaster. In any case it will soon be forgotten, and will embellish the diplomatic archives of the nineteenth century only as a monument to human and royal eccentricity."

With delightful humor he sketched the character of Madame de Krüdener, the little hours of prayer that she held with the Czar, the embarrassment of the other monarchs, and described how even the British Prince Regent had endorsed the holy covenant "frivolously, in order merely to do his august ally a favor or else to poke fun at him. I believe the latter to be more probable, especially since the signature of a British sovereign is null and void without the countersignature of the minister." As a matter of fact, the Prince Regent could do no more than write a letter of assent.

The realism of the statesmen finished off the chimera. They would have nothing to do with it; and a good thing, too, for in politics chimeras cause nothing but trouble.

Had Gentz published his criticism of the restoration he could have been called its opponent. Unfortunately he derided and deplored only in detail what, as crown publicist, he appeared nevertheless to defend as a whole; yet if pressed he probably would have denied that there was a whole. Both he and Metternich were scandalized at the praise that young Pilat bestowed in his journal on the Spanish tyrant, Ferdinand VII; the more so since the party strife in Spain did not concern Austria. "In your zeal for Legitimism you do not seem to have heard that there is serious thought of locking up this legitimate King in a lunatic asylum; incontestably the only throne for which he is fitted." But it was the whole system, the new order in Europe, surely, in whose train Ferdinand had come to power, and so this monster should have been a matter of concern to the Secretary of Europe, to Castlereagh, to Metternich, and to all the other distinguished men of the Congress.

In order that he might quietly observe the development of events for a while longer, Gentz remained in Paris after the others had left. He recapitulated his impressions as follows in a letter to Nesselrode, the Russian Foreign Minister. "If the King continues to heed the madmen who have led him hitherto; if the government does not find means of suppressing the spirit of reaction and frenzy by which the active minority in both Chambers is possessed; either a new revolution must inevitably follow or, if this can be put down by the army of occupation, as I believe it can be, there will arise such a disgraceful, such an atrocious situation that the allied powers should be really ashamed to lend their strength in maintaining it." "As long as the alliance of the four great powers endures there will be neither war nor revolution in Europe. . . . Nevertheless, the present condition of France is contrary to nature; an exact antithesis to all that nineteen twentieths of the nation feel and wish; an exact antithesis to the eternal laws of social progress. Royalty, upheld by foreign power and by fear, will never emerge from the atmosphere of unrest, peril, hate, and intrigue while this condition lasts. This will be so three years from now, five years from now, and always, as long as error is not ruthlessly nipped in the bud. Those who believed in 1814 that they could simply restore the old regime have done France as much harm as Robespierre and Bonaparte. But the logic of events is stronger than man. The French Revolution must complete its course as did the English revolution of the seventeenth century. . . . Absolutism restored will stand the test as poorly as it did in England. A solution like that of the year 1688 is the only one that logically can conclude the Revolution of our own era. Absolute monarchy, once overthrown, never reëstablishes itself. The old Bourbons cannot and should not continue to reign. . . ."

How could the writer of this letter, being what he was, help despising a public opinion that abused him as a blindly passionate reactionary and henchman of princes?

His sojourn in Paris over, the Secretary of Europe made his way slowly back to Vienna. Before him he saw only tedium, or at the best a condition out of which he could make no sense, either in respect to his own activities or to those of the several nations. For even in the absence of Napoleon one must surely want and do something. "Despite my horror of war, universal peace seems a curious thing when one has lived most of his life from one catastrophe to the next."

Nor were there lacking those who, younger, more animated, and more stupid, asked him in threatening tones: "What next?" The Teutomaniacs, who had cursed the doings of the Congress, cursed the Second Treaty of Paris even more savagely. In their characteristic mood, half a rummaging in the past and half an eagerness for destruction, they had discovered that great portions of France had belonged to the German Empire in days long gone by. Now, they cried, they wanted these back again. They wanted what was not, and what could not be, for their main purpose was to dispute the present order and keep the fires of unrest burning. To a certain extent they acquired merit thereby in the eyes of God and man, for present attainments never satisfy. They talked much of a "third war" to come, whether because they felt that the Vienna settlement did not promise to hold good universally and permanently, or merely because the number three signified for them some mystic consummation.

They were fortunate in having the forceful Goerres as their spokesman in his *Rheinischer Mercur*. *Directed at Vienna* was the title of one of his pamphlets, in which he openly attacked Gentz. He called the European peace a swindle. "Let no one suppose that such a gigantic fraud will ever become historical and achieve validity in God's sight, or that dead words can live again. Nothing will last unless based on the fundamentals of justice and truth, and everything that is not done right must be done over again from the beginning. All this has happened before, and it reflects the nature of our own era, which is not willing to relinquish its practices but insists on holding fast to them until everything has been done in conformity with its aims. . . ." According to Goerres, it was not the concern of a German statesman to secure world peace, or internal order in France, or the welfare of mankind. An adequate *Lebensraum*, expansion, and satisfaction in German nationality were his objectives. "This considerate, tender policy, that besides the rebirth of Africa so assiduously attends to that of Germany's neighbor who, as far as she is concerned, might better not have been born, has never even asked whether the rebirth of its own fatherland would be possible since Russia in Poland and Britain in Hanover and Belgium have driven a sharp wedge into Germany. Rather it has deserted us without a backward glance and, after having done as little as it could, has thrust anarchy upon us instead of providing a system of government. . . . But let that considerate policy have no concern. If it persists in restoring the old, aimless way of life, as it has shown a strong disposition to do, the golden century will not be half over before these reborn French, at whose delivery it has officiated as such a compassionate and efficient midwife, will rise once more on the near and far sides of the Rhine and betake themselves to Vienna. . . ."

In the *Oesterreichischer Beobachter*, the journal that was now his medium, Gentz answered the raging publicist. Germany, he wrote, was not alone in the world. A theory according to which there were no law save that of actual force, no prescriptive rights, and no binding tradition could lead only to bloody chaos. "If what has been surrendered by the most sacred treaties, whose loss is sanctioned by the custom of centuries, is still to be regarded permanently as our property, then no title to possession, no security of possession on legal grounds, has the slightest validity any longer. According to such a view there is not a state in Europe today that would not have to consider a part, and often more than half, of its lands as forfeited. . . ." Alsace and Lorraine had long since entered the French commonwealth. If now they were to be torn away they would be estranged anew from Europe, from their monarchy, and from one another. That was not the wish of the allied courts. "They strove for perpetual peace. Only that which could guarantee it was welcome to them, and anything that would undermine it, that sooner or later was certain to destroy it, was an obstacle that they wished to avoid. They had not come to annihilate or dismember France, but to reconcile her wholeheartedly with Europe. The former would have been simple and easy and, indeed, would have required neither great skill nor extraordinary courage; the latter could be achieved only through self-control, renunciation of apparent advantage, and a mature and well-considered course of action." "The restoration of permanent order in the interior of the country: this alone is what we mean by the rebirth of France; an aim that the *Rheinischer Mercur* has treated with jests as bitter as they are inopportune. Not from any false tenderness toward France, but from obvious self-interest, from solicitude for the common welfare of Europe, we must all strive for this rebirth. . . ."

Now, continued Austria's spokesman with suppressed emotion, has "a political author the right—we do not mean the legal right, which in no case should we like to think restricted—but the moral right, the spiritual right, to propagate a wholly false view of a situation by deliberately intermixing and confusing ideas; from which can come only discontent with the present, exaggerated demands on the future, disparagement of whatever is undertaken and actually accomplished for the common good, and a hostile attitude toward everything about us"? Was freedom of the press possible in the absence of self-control, of some sense of responsibility for one's acts and their consequences?

A dramatic discussion! Nationalism, the awakened cult of national unity and independence, has seldom attained such heights as with Goerres and his circle. The more clearly, therefore, did this first encounter between the two great writers indicate the problems of the future.

Never since the Middle Ages had the Germans, as a nation, exerted all their weight against other nations; partly because they had been paralyzed by unfamiliar diplomatic wiles, partly because their own rulers tended toward moderation. It was the second, not the first, upon which Gentz insisted. In his view a German politician should be at the same time a European politician, responsible for the freedom of Europe from all, even from German, oppression. He himself was such, by character and conviction. In his education, even in his speech, German and Western elements combined. But suppose the Germans were now suddenly to take as high treason the moderation that holds nationalism in check? Suppose they were to become as "German" as Louis XIV had been French, and with a better chance of success begin to do to Europe what Napoleon had done to them? Suppose a savage enthusiasm for what they themselves were should replace their Europeanism? Nay, more, suppose they should camouflage their attack on the existing order with the cause of democracy, with the right of the people to self-determination?

As Gentz sat writing his reply to Goerres he realized pretty well by what problems the epilogue of his political life would be dominated.

PART THREE

GENTZ IN AUSTRIA

XIV

AT HOME

IN THE little village of Weinhaus, near Vienna," the *Archivrat* von Klinkowström wrote down about 1870 in his reminiscences, "there stood in the late 1820's a villa that everyone stopped to admire for the abundance of flowers by which it was set off. In the courtyard peacocks, guinea fowls, turkeys, and other exotic birds strutted about, to the delight of inquisitive youth in the neighborhood. . . . Every afternoon between four and five o'clock came a moment that precipitately banished us curious lads from before the green trellised gateway. At about that time two milk-white horses would approach at a smart trot, bringing home in his elegant equipage the occupant of the villa; none other than the statesman Friedrich von Gentz, then highly honored and rewarded by all the courts of Europe. . . ."

He was returning from the city, from Metternich's council chamber, where every day a meeting of the Chancellor's intimate advisers was held, and the "very secret and confidential" dispatches that had arrived from abroad were studied, and distributed for reply. Our old bachelor generally spent the evenings at home, busy with his writing and reading, and enjoying the stillness of the rural night. In the garden there stood a hothouse, in which the rarest of blossoms were raised during the winter months. He filled his house with flowers, and sent them to his friends.

His homes—for he had one in town also—were painstakingly furnished with an eye to comfort, and even luxury. "The floor of the reception room," says the poet Grillparzer, "was covered with padded rugs, so that with every step one sunk as though in a marsh, and experienced a kind of seasickness. On every table and chest of drawers stood glass jars filled with preserved fruits for instant nibbling by the sybaritic master of the house. At last I came upon him in his bedroom, in a gray silk dressing gown, lying on a snow-white bed. Inventions and conveniences all about. There were movable arms that brought nearer his pen and ink when they were wanted, a writing desk that slid back and forth by itself, and I verily believe that in case of need even the chamber pot would present itself for use, no doubt at the pressure of a spring. Gentz received me coolly, but politely. . . ."

But from the diary of the man so maliciously sketched here it appears that he was suffering from "bilious fever" when Grillparzer called, which may excuse the silk dressing gown. Gentz was often ill during the 1820's, especially with gout, as befitted his age and station; hence the descriptions of his appearance are widely at variance. He seemed invigorated and triumphant when he returned from the mineral baths at Gastein or Ischl in the fall; during the winter he lost sleep, and was inclined to fits of depression. "As for his posture," wrote a German diplomat, describing him in 1823, "he bent forward, and his progress was shuffling and uncertain; his head was covered by a reddish wig, and his apparel not wholly in accord with the latest style. His face expressed sagacity, yet his glance was shy. He was seldom seen on foot, but generally in a fiacre, or carried in a sedan chair. . . . A pair of great black spectacles before his eyes served to keep him in countenance as well as to inspect whoever was present. . . ."

Since the days of the great Congress Gentz had avoided more and more the social life of the capital; as he liked to have it believed, on account of his health. "But the real truth is that I have withdrawn from all worldly frivolities not from any feeling of illness or of age, but from a simple loathing for men and affairs. When one is able to work twelve hours every day without noticing the least fatigue one surely has no cause to complain." "Nevertheless, I have become anything but unsociable or misanthropic. Those whom I like to see still come often to my house."

He experienced the joys of family life in so far as his servants invited him to participate in theirs. He liked to frolic with their children, and occasionally, as is brazenly indicated in his diary, with their wives as well. For his love making still savored of the commonplace, and this distinguished man was not above an ephemeral attachment for the rejected flame of his secretary. As his sensuality receded with age, his liking for handsome young people became stronger again. Until 1819 Charles, the soldier, lived in his home; a soldier no more but long since a young man informed by frequent journeys with his patron, whom Gentz finally sent to England for a year of study and afterward palmed off on Prince Metternich for a government courier. He was active in arranging that Charles should have the choicest assignments: to London, to Lisbon, and even to Brazil. In the end, however, he came to lament bitterly the ingratitude of the young scalawag who owed him a living and a well-ordered existence. Charles's successor was Franzel, the son of a valet, with whom of late years Gentz sat at table, and, indeed, even traveled. But that he did with other children of his servants, too, and on one occasion was accompanied actually by a retinue of eleven persons in three carriages.

He had a family of his own besides, but of them there is not much to relate. Peppi, the son of his earlier "Cattel," the "girl of low station," he sent on trips to the mountains with his favorites, and he took over the responsibility of the boy's education. There seems to have been a daughter as well. "Went for a drive about ten o'clock, and at the house of Krüger, the actor, called on Madame Spengler (my daughter). Pleasant end to an interview that I had greatly dreaded."

He was no less dismayed at the prospect of meeting his sisters, who were living a quaint, unmarried life in Berlin; so much so, indeed, that at the last moment he sought to avoid a reunion after long, long years, and the pious Adam Müller had to reproach him gravely for his weakness: this horror of everyone from out his own past. In the end he met both ladies at Teplitz in spite of it, and "after a little embarrassment the meeting turned out to be even cheerful, and gratifying on both sides." He was notified of the death of his last surviving brother, Ludwig, after not having seen him for twenty-five years. "The dissimilarity of our characters always kept us at a certain distance from one another. . . . Thus his death could not make a vivid impression on me. But, depressed as I now am, this event makes me feel as though the voice of death had summoned me too." Later he was visited by the son of this brother—"It was a curious sensation, to see this relative for the first time; so close to me, and yet so utterly strange"—and was highly pleased that his young nephew found general approbation.

Gentz carried on a sporadic correspondence with the scattered friends of his youth. The old adventurer had known the storms of life too well not to realize that loyalty is essential, though he did not particularly relish looking either forward or backward. Far, far removed from his starting point, and facing himself as he had appeared in the past with chilling discontent, he had retained enough imagination, nevertheless, enough of his original, earlier self, to feel his life as a coherent whole and often to review it with disconcerting clearness. "I am an old child," he wrote, meaning that he had always remained the same. Moreover, as his memory flagged—"through my head and through my life there have passed too many things, too many situations, events, ideas, combinations, labors, men, destinies: the past only floats now before my eyes"—the first memoirs appeared, in which past events took shape and the revolutionary epoch seemed complete and comprehensible at a glance.

"Yesterday I read with great pleasure the little book of de Pradt. I think it the best thing that he has published for a long time. Furthermore, with a few exceptions it is entirely true, even including what he says about me. For though it was not exactly Pitt's strongbox—with which I did not become acquainted for ten years after I had entered upon a literary career—but my fate and my inclination that led me to this sort of activity, it is widely recognized, nevertheless, that writers who devote themselves to current events, especially in the service of an established power and for the sake of a lost cause, cannot count upon enduring fame. I did not need de Pradt to tell me that. . . ."

In respect to a number of the *Westminster Review* he wrote: "In the opinion of these radicals, who have but a very superficial acquaintance with our situation, to be sure, Gentz is the real inventor of a certain artful obscurantism, by dint of which Prince Metternich has attracted talented men from various parts of Germany to defend or disguise the shocking despotism of his court. . . . The diatribes, excessively crude, are amusing enough to read for all that. . . ."

His studious mind could absorb untold amounts. It is true that in the period immediately following the great Congress he thought that he had had more than enough of diplomacy, politics, and even history, and that he would be able to breathe freely again only in the open air. The thought drove him to the mountains, and in twelve- and fifteen-hour tramps with Charles and an adventurous Englishman he climbed the fabulous, snow-capped summits, and sent back ecstatic and classically beautiful descriptions to his friends below. Even later, when illness interfered with his walking, he insisted upon being carried in a chair to vantage points whence the most magnificent views could be enjoyed, and there he would sit alone with a telescope through whole long afternoons. The love of nature in her wildest, most primitive forms, as it springs from the secret recesses of our being; the love for the clear, cold air of the mountains; of guardian shadows; of verdure, and snow, and the sunlight on the hills—the fear of nature transformed into a passionate longing, remained with him.

But politics and history, the other pole of his being, shortly reasserted their rights.

Into the "Oriental question," which dominated politically the 1820's, Gentz plunged as into the study of a new discipline. His excerpts from the history of the Greeks, the Turks, the Serbs, and the Rumanians grew into great piles, and his literary executors could not understand where he, allegedly so frivolous and absorbed in the tasks of the day, had ever found the time for so much profound research. In his spare moments he returned again and again to the great masters: to the *Critique of Pure Reason;* to Burke; and to Gibbon. "A singularly pleasant sensation, after so much ephemeral scribbling, to come once more upon a classical writer, upon a solid and finished performance." Then there were Goethe's continually appearing reminiscences and essays, which he never denied himself. "We shall understand one another completely if only you are not bewitched by a passion for Lord Byron as is your old Goethe (whose often rather insipid fragments I always read anyway with real emotion). . . ." Occasionally we catch him over a new novel, of which, however, he is ashamed. "I read the famous romance, *Fragoletta*, that rare new fruit of the intellectual excesses of our time, with more interest than it actually deserves, and, to tell the truth, with real avidity. . . ." Looking through the newspapers every day was one side, and the most disagreeable one, of his post as head censor and chief publicist.

Did he enjoy life? And to what purpose did he live? There were moments when he seriously asked himself these questions. "I ponder much, it may be too much, on my condition; but I cannot do otherwise. Although not actually in pain, I am pursued by an exhaustion, an ennui, an inertia that is not to be overcome. Nothing is easy for me. Incessantly I ask myself: What is the use of this or that? And immediately all reading, all work, becomes obnoxious to me. . . ." As one who lived much alone, never returning at night to the shelter of a family or a group of intimate friends, coming back to a home where only effete luxury awaited him, he could not do otherwise than concentrate on his feelings, his state of mind, and review the fortunes of each day. "This day ratified the conviction that my lucky star has not yet entirely deserted me." His lucky star meant new commissions, congresses, fame; but above all, money, which was always a matter of concern to him. Here the historical and the personal were intimately blended. When the Greeks began fomenting unrest in the Balkans the Prince-Hospodar stopped sending money from Bucharest; when George Canning came to an understanding with Russia no more was received from the British Ambassador. Thus he was interested materially also, and only too deeply, in the victory of a party to which he had devoted himself. "Courier from London and Paris. Read for three hours. The horizon grows constantly darker. An indescribable feeling of increasing vexation and danger possesses my spirit more and more strongly." Wessenberg, a friend of his, thought that the constant pursuit of money, not to save but to squander with childish openhandedness, embittered, even shortened, his life.

In the long run, certainly, luck never forsook him. New sources opened as old ones dried up, and between 1818 and 1822 the great European Congresses at Aachen, Carlsbad, Troppau, Laibach, and Verona more than compensated for what he had formerly received from Great Britain.

In connection with these gatherings he made the acquaintance of wealthy bankers, to whom he knew how to make himself indispensable by looking after the interests of the outcast Jewish people, by providing the baronial title, and by exchanging secret political news. And they returned his confidences "in an interesting way." He became more and more intimate with the Rothschilds in particular, who rose during the 1820's to be the leading bankers of Europe, and in their politics leaned toward Metternich's conservatism. Baron Solomon, the Vienna representative of this affluent firm, often appeared at Gentz's villa, casually handed over to him his "share in the proceeds of a speculation" (though in reality Gentz had not speculated), and wept before him when there were losses to be mourned on the exchange. Solomon Rothschild later maintained, indeed, that Gentz had only to indicate on a slip of paper the sum that he needed in order to receive it instantly. Prince Metternich sanctioned, and even encouraged, this relationship. Gentz was the first prominent man to break through the social prejudice and sit down beside Jews at table without reddening. As for the Rothschilds, they were drawn to the conservatives. True, they were Liberals in London; Legitimists in Paris, then Orleanists, according to circumstances; but deep in their hearts they were devoted to the old, haughty, aristocratic regimes, who understood nothing of money and with whom the most profitable business could be transacted. Moreover, in his struggle with Teutomania, Metternich tried hard to combat the rabid antisemitism of these young people that was one of its salient features.

In short, money always appeared when Gentz needed it most desperately: 1,000 ducats, 300 pounds, or "an agreeable communication," which for a few weeks relieved the poor spendthrift again of every care. What would happen after that, he never inquired.

Yet he was hardly happy. Gratification had to replace happiness, creation, and the pleasure of give and take. Thus did he indulge himself when, sitting alone in his villa of an evening at his desk, he would put aside his pen, saying: "Come, you have written quite enough in your life," and reach for a volume of Gibbon. Sometimes he enjoyed a trip through the northern Alps. "After luncheon, about four o'clock, I decided to return, seated myself in my comfortable carriage, and on a beautiful evening drove with great satisfaction through the magnificent Piesting Valley as far as Salenau, where I stayed overnight." He was still able to take pleasure also in his occupation, his studies, or the dictating of beautifully fluent memoranda, to the extent that, even after having been deeply troubled and seeking sleep and death, life suddenly seemed too short again. "Greatest intellectual activity. . . . So much reading, so much study, so many alluring pursuits besides so many practical affairs—and this furiously rapid passage of the hours!"

He enjoyed his fame, too, and laughed happily when he was flattered by kings and ministers at conferences of the Holy Alliance. Nevertheless, he spoke of the "illusions of his career." Ideas and visions remain; political triumphs vanish like shadows. In this vein he had written twenty years before to the long-since-defunct Johannes von Müller: "I do not deny that more than once, in a moment of irritation, I would have forcgone any further active share in the whole illusory business, and that a sort of remorse steals over me when I think that I have passed the best years of my life with it. How imposing and fortunate you seem to me because, equipped with all that could be demanded of a statesman, as well as of an author, you still acquired in good time wisdom enough to undertake a work that will endure in lasting independence of all the confusion of our era."

Even now he still thought at times that it would have been better to remain an author than to become a diplomat. The friends of his youth who had remained true to philosophy he gladly forgave when they were no longer so deeply interested in the questions that now absorbed him: German students, Italian conspiracies, and even the Turko-Greek problem. But once overboard in these waters, one had to swim and swim until one went under.

A feeling of the most profound irresolution, of fear and loneliness, sometimes overcame the aging politician, even amidst all his indulgence. He expressed such experiences in an eerie verse from Lucretius, his favorite poet:

> The spring of pleasure exhales a bitter scent
> That, rising from beneath its flowers, affrights us.

So, too, he was tormented by bad dreams; by one single and periodically recurring dream. To the physician this is the most telling evidence of secret guilt, which looms in many aspects of his life: his distinction between sensual and spiritual love—joys bought and paid for on the one hand, intellectual women and attractive young men on the other; disdain for the graphic arts; the increasingly biased obstinacy of his political convictions. Once upon a time, in early life, he must have shrunk back in alarm from some task, must have been untrue to himself: and so his whole life long. The unrealized, the betrayed possibilities, social, moral, human above all, haunted him as they haunt every one of us.

XV

DIPLOMACY OF THE HIGHWAY

In very early youth he had been called upon to deal with the gigantic questions that laid their mighty weight upon European statesmen at the fall of Napoleon. The natural effect of this close contact with the vast and formidable problems of 1814–15 was to make him regard the state-system then founded as a structure on which only reckless or criminal unwisdom would dare to lay a finger. John Morley, *Life of Gladstone.*

TO HAVE survived the French Revolution; to have freed themselves of Napoleon; and then to have established a state system that gave promise of durability: this was as much as could be expected of any one political generation. In the eyes of that generation, at any rate, it was enough. Nor was intellectual Europe any stranger to the feeling that dominated the statesmen; they had done their duty and should now enjoy peace. Poets and philosophers lived in a world of "afterward." The dramatic events of the past twenty years, so suddenly followed by calm, tempted to historical studies and to meditation on the philosophy of history. The monstrous expenditure of energy that had distinguished the Napoleonic Wars had left skeptical and sophisticated thinkers behind, and in place of the optimism, veracity, and straightforward objectivity of the eighteenth century romantic distortion, metaphysical trifling, yearning, and pessimism could now be promised an eager audience.

At the University of Berlin there arose a teacher who had eked out an obscure and miserable existence as editor and schoolmaster in Napoleon's day, but meanwhile had meditated deeply; and as now there were no more bulletins from the front, and no more coups d'état, his philosophy was passionately seized upon. It was Professor Hegel's thesis that the era of great substantial deeds was over, and that nothing remained but to ponder on the colossal events of the recent past and try to understand them. The present era had brought history to a stop. It was the end, fruitful only by reason of its contemplative grasp of all that had gone before. Future there was none. "When philosophy paints in her gray monotone," wrote the dejected scholar, "a whole civilization has grown old, and cannot be rejuvenated by speculation alone, but merely conceived. . . ." The disseminator of these gloomy views was much in vogue.

Still, no epoch can be adequately summed up by one single intellectual trend. In spite of all bloodshed life soon reëstablishes itself, and every "afterward" is at the same time a "before." Inevitably those who did not wish to live in a postwar world without present or future, mostly the young, wanted to be heard. "Such terrible storms have not passed over Europe," wrote Joseph Goerres, "in order that even while their thunder still mutters on the far horizon the clouds of mediocrity that they drove asunder may gather again: a nebulous realm, in which every force is considered a discord, every aptitude a dangerous power, every idea a plague, and every enthusiasm and inspiration is treated as sinister folly."

This aspect of the situation, here expressed with Teutonic turgidity, is more or less the dominant motif of Stendhal's novels: the fate of Julien Sorel, possessed by the Napoleonic legend, gifted, wild, curbed, and poor, who made his lonely and tortuous way through the restricted domain of disillusioned aristocrats and old men; the fate of young Fabrice, who was present at the battle of Waterloo, and frittered away his life between the imperial and ducal boundary posts of north Italy.

The rule of Napoleon had eventually become vicious and intolerable. Yet it had always been active, and held out hope for the future, since the great Opportunist had not feared the new era. Hence, after they had overcome him, his opponents were confronted with the difficult task of ordering things in a manner entirely different from his, while also remaining unafraid of the new era and at the same time promoting a democratic future. But for this they lacked creative courage. Their denial of the dynamic principle in the defective form given it by the Jacobins and by Napoleon became for them a denial of the dynamic, that is to say the progressive, in general. They defended the system that they had established in 1814 against everybody and everything, convinced as they were that the whole edifice would collapse and the old dragon of chaos break out again if even one stone should be replaced. States that wanted to become more powerful than they were, colonies that wanted to become states, nationalities that wanted to become nations, members of the middle class who were wearied, and factory workers who were hungry, all had this in common: that they were dissatisfied with the existing state of things. In the opinion of Prince Clemens Metternich they threatened the "system of Europe," and were preparing for revolution; a congress should be called, therefore, to decide upon concerted action against them.

To handle these different problems conjointly, to treat them as one and the same problem: this is the key to Metternich's system. Its merits for the future lay in the first of the two proposals; the reason for its failure is evident in the second. Not to discriminate is the death of all good politics. There are always many and varied antagonisms at work in the struggle of historical forces, which for this reason would be more justly compared with a parliament of innumerable factions, all pulling in different directions, now combining and now separating again, than with the classical two-party system. A great orator may appear and, for a brief time, split his listeners into two compact groups, one of which follows him blindly whereas the other hates him. But soon there will be schisms in each of the two, and astonishing ties between them, and great confusion, and suddenly two new leading parties again.

The French Revolution was such a phenomenon, and it turned the whole world at first into one single acquiescent party. But later it and Napoleon were so strong and domineering that opposition arose, and up to the year 1814 there were only two groups in Europe, an assenting and a dissenting. What Prince Metternich and Hofrat von Gentz sought was preservation of this world-wide two-party system after the downfall of Napoleon; a situation that would have been highly advantageous to them since their party, the conservatives, prevailing by virtue of their slogans, "old Europe," and "peace," were in power and should be able to remain so indefinitely; and since Austria, the state that they represented, must have anticipated isolation and ruin from a division of any other sort.

Austria was the European state par excellence. She engaged in diplomatic relations even with her own provinces, and to her domestic and foreign politics were all one. A revolution in the Kingdom of Naples, unrest in the Balkans, or nationalistic agitation in Germany affected her directly, for she herself was part Italy, part Balkans, and part Germany. What Gentz had been teaching for twenty-five years, that in politics there really is no "foreign country," that what our neighbor does may very well affect us, and that the principle of sovereignty must be tempered by that of joint intervention, was nowhere so true as in the case of Austria: in serving the cause of a conservative, interventional, European partnership she was serving her own interests.

For other countries it was different. To be sure, everyone seemed bowed down by the terrible example of the French internal Revolution and its repercussions in "foreign countries" everywhere; but such profound experiences are often susceptible of two different interpretations. One suggested the desirability of intervention, of neglecting entirely the distinction between domestic and foreign; the other, in view of the dire results attending the combined Austrian and Prussian crusade against revolutionary France in 1792, suggested the direct opposite. At the Congress of Verona (1822) Lord Wellington availed himself of the negative argument, drawn from the experience of the recent past, to advise against interference in the Spanish disorders; for Great Britain had little to fear from democratic revolutions on the Continent. Conversely, the Russians adopted a reactionary and interventional attitude toward the Spaniards as well as toward the Poles, whose state they had engulfed, but a revolutionary attitude toward Turkey, which they thought to inherit. Other countries—other interests, pretexts, and principles. Only in the Austrian monarchy did the essentially European, or interventional, principle coincide throughout with the interests of the state. Hence the Russian and British policy must have seemed to Prince Metternich like the rankest treason toward the "European cause."

He loved Austria. "Believe me," he wrote to his mistress, "here all is admirable. Nowhere are we really understood. Ours is the government that most highly respects the rights and liberties of everyone. . . ." He loved old Europe. He knew how each, old Europe and old Austria, depended upon the other, and believed that he served his larger homeland in shamelessly vindicating the smaller.

With courteously smiling eyes under raised brows, he looked about him like an attentive watchman; flirtatious and sociable, yet intimately familiar with all the secret state interests; peremptory; practical; pitiless, even, when occasion required. His handling of affairs, which appeared pliant simply, was in reality hard, and for the preservation of "peace" he had no hesitation in ordering armies to march. "We shall turn against wrong the very moment that it begins to threaten us; we shall beat back the foe who tries to take the initiative, and would make slaves of us in our own house; we protest against every unjustifiable usurpation, and shall put an end to it if we are able. An eye for an eye, a tooth for a tooth is our motto. We recognize no other. It is as old as the world, and as valid for states as for individuals. . . ."

Never would this generation cease to hear those somber, defensive accents, familiar for so many years.

THE allies conferred whenever a difficulty arose that touched them all. There were almost constant traveling, meetings en route to congresses during sundry overnight halts, consultations in carriages as they rolled along the highways, and arguments on how this or that disturbance could best be overcome, peace secured once more, and a definitive settlement achieved. Feelers were secretly put out, there were great conferences, parades, entertainments, and a final protocol in which the brilliant assemblage rarely failed "to express to Hofrat von Gentz its warmest appreciation of the material support that it had enjoyed through his distinguished labors, stamped as they were with his great talent." "I am the link between five cabinets assembled here," he boasted. He had become indispensable for, unlike them, he really had "Europe" in mind, and was unhampered by any patriotic egoism. In addition, there was his gift of triumphing over purely verbal difficulties with an appropriate expression, or of veiling actual contradictions with the trickery of words.

When Lord Castlereagh presented a statement that arrogantly pushed British interests into the foreground, it was Gentz's mollifying French that made it endurable to the allies. When Count Capo d'Istria, the impetuous Greek-Russian, wanted a too-interventional plan incorporated as a statute, it was the "pruning knife of Chevalier Gentz"—the phrase is the British Ambassador's—that reduced the motion to inoffensive moderation. And if the representatives of Great Britain and France, say, definitely refused to commit themselves by signing a joint protocol, Gentz would sign it alone, so that his name actually did become a link between five assembled cabinets.

Ducats and decorations were further proof of European recognition. Whereupon, far from dissatisfied with himself and with the world, he returned again to Vienna. He called the politics of those years "diplomacy of the highway."

They were not the invention of Metternich, but rather a consequence of recognition by the states that there was a main interest common to all. They were a reverberation of the great revolutionary uproar that grew more and more faint until it finally died away. Never before had the rulers of the Old World lived together in such intimacy as during the coalition that ruined Napoleon; and since the alliance was to be preserved during peace times nothing was more natural than to stimulate the cordial good-fellowship of its founders from time to time. If one insists upon attributing this system of periodic congresses to one man alone the credit should go to Lord Castlereagh, who introduced into the Treaty of Alliance of November 20, 1815, the following noteworthy article:

"To facilitate and to secure the execution of the present Treaty, and to consolidate the connections which at the present moment so closely unite the Four Sovereigns for the happiness of the world, the High Contracting Parties have agreed to renew their meetings at fixed periods . . . for the purpose of consulting upon their common needs, interests, and for the consideration of the measures which at each of these periods shall be considered most salutary for the repose and prosperity of Nations, and for the maintenance of the Peace of Europe."

It speaks for the wise intention of this system that Great Britain, the constitutional and the least "reactionary" power, formally made provision for it. And when the gods met again, at Aachen, in 1818, three years after Waterloo, it was virtually in pursuance of this admirable plan. It was decided to withdraw the allied armies of occupation from France before the time originally set, and to free the conquered state from the custody of Europe. Disputes between smaller states were adjusted, war on the infamous slave trade was declared, and, in addition to such questions as these, bagatelles like the treatment of the imprisoned Bonaparte came up for discussion. The Congress of Aachen was fortunate in its subjects and in its results.

Thereafter the alliance began to degenerate. Its original purposes accomplished, all memory of the need that had brought it into being faded away. The capricious course of events introduced disturbances that never could have been anticipated in 1814, and for whose settlement the congress system was not intended. It became apparent that a league of European states required a common object of hostility for its continuance, and at the hands of the conservative statesmen this common object became vexatious in the extreme, as well as wholly inadequate. It was one thing to hold together against Napoleon, but quite another to do so in favor of degenerate and pygmy despots. Furthermore, even the states most satiated for the moment had wider interests than mere conservation, and as each of them used the alliance to enlarge its own scope at the expense of others, there remained of the common cause in the end nothing but the name. Ten years after the downfall of Napoleon the states had gone their own ways, each one for itself, united in partnership only for some occasional and ruthless end.

The world problem, which Gentz and Metternich wanted to treat as everywhere one and the same, occupied the allies successively in the following forms: a struggle between nationalistic youth and the conservative governments in Germany; a strife between dynasts and liberals in Spain and Italy; a movement for independence by the Latin-American colonies; and a national rebellion of the Greeks against the Sultan. All these conflagrations were connected to a certain extent, though each of them had its own wholly individual nature, too. Gentz and Metternich realized the first of these facts, but overlooked the second. The issues that most nearly concerned Austria, the German and the Italian, they succeeded in settling, for the moment at least, after their own interest; over the Spanish situation they had but little influence; in the Balkans, none at all.

DIMLY conscious of their untried powers, looking ahead into a blind alley, thoroughly dissatisfied with a dull civic order and a life of comfortable complacency that was devoid of historical events, the youth of Germany did not want what their governments wanted. They wanted one single empire of all Germans: Christian, medieval, yet revolutionary, too, at the same time; not easy to describe, but wholly and entirely German, at any rate, and severely hostile to the French.

Goerres, who was closely connected with these enthusiasts, sought to explain their activities to the French people as follows: "In Germany it is not the Third Estate that is responsible for the revolution; the governments started it, under the protection of a foreign power [Napoleon's]. . . . In our country the advocates of despotism employ Jacobinic forms and practices, whereas the friends of freedom, on the contrary, uphold in part the principles of the French ultrareactionaries. This is the complication that presents such an obscure riddle at first to the foreign observer. . . ."

It is the complication that always arises when subjects of political strife in different countries or in different eras are compared, but characteristic of Germany in particular, for nowhere as there have ideas been allowed to transform themselves into their opposites; nowhere as there has there been such intellectual confusion as a consequence of inaccurate thinking and boundless enthusiasm.

We shall not attempt to decide how Gentz would have reacted had he seen a pure and vigorous liberalism of British type in operation. But this he did not see. He saw instead what he hated most in all the world: intellectual chaos, and an aggressive mood that was a menace to civilization. He heard of orgies in which the liberal Code Napoléon was burned, as well as the books of absolutism. He read pamphlets that raged against the German dynasties, not so much because these governed despotically as because they represented a Western and supernational civilization. He looked into the heart of a revolutionary tendency that was based not upon unification of the world through a community of friendly liberal states, but upon nationalistic discrimination, disruption, and conquest. He realized that the rulers, those of south Germany and even Prince Metternich himself, were nearer to the Anglo-Saxons than these alleged "liberals," these fanatical advocates of *Volkstum* [a combination of nationality and folkways], of book burning, and of Francophobia. Had not Burke prophesied thirty years before that the gravest, and for the rest of the world most dangerous, consequences of the French Revolution, the real French Revolution, would occur not in France, but in Germany?

Now Gentz warned: "The *allgemeine deutsche Studentenbund* [German Students' General Union], as its statutes show, is based expressly and essentially on the unification of Germany; and not merely on an ideal, or academic, or literary unification but on a physical and political unification. Thus it is revolutionary in the most extreme and dangerous sense of this term. For think what one may, theoretically or historically, of the present organization of the German states, the unification toward which these true and consummate Jacobins have been striving for six years cannot be achieved without the most violent revolutions, without the overthrow of Europe."

On a visit to the University of Heidelberg this man of the eighteenth century saw some representatives of the movement. "All that mars the picture are the grotesque and repulsive figures in filthy ancient German costumes, their books under their arms, abominations before God and man, on their way to absorb the false wisdom of their infamous professors. Five hundred such students would really disgust one with Paradise." Once, indeed, when three of these "horrors," with full beards and shirts open at the neck, called on him at his hotel in Gastein he could hardly overcome his fear and detestation, expecting every moment to see these rough hikers draw pistols or daggers from their haversacks.

A foolish political assassination brought the German youth movement to a climax, for in those days Germany was a law-abiding country, and political murder unknown. "I do not like assassination in the name of a love for humanity," declared Metternich. "I do not like farces and follies of any sort whatsoever, and still less of the sort that would kill decent men sitting peacefully in their homes." He ordered the ministers of the German Confederation to Carlsbad for a confidential discussion.

The conference at Carlsbad (1819) concerned only the Germans, and had nothing to do formally with the great alliance. It is not true, however, that the practical and liberal Britons disapproved of its resolutions. On the contrary, Lord Castlereagh expressly agreed with them, and when their wording is carefully examined today one can only recall sadly and enviously the time when such decrees passed for the most monstrous example of despotism and reaction. It was Gentz who really inspired them. Letters threatening the fate of Kotzebue had driven him to fear and rage, and at Carlsbad he was in his most reactionary mood. But what was it that he advised?

"The appointment of a curator for every single university, who shall be a distinguished man of pleasing and benevolent manner, familiar with world affairs and not unacquainted with the sciences (though not necessarily a scholar), who shall be responsible for the whole university and consequently must dwell in its neighborhood." "A purge of the professorial group, undertaken without stir or passion, if need be by the removal of objectionable professors to other posts in civil life where they can do no harm." Periodicals, but not books of more than twenty pages, were to undergo preliminary government censorship throughout the German Confederation. Gentz defended this decree ex officio on the ground that the progress of the sciences and everything relating to it certainly could not be impeded by police regulations. "Entirely different stars preside over this progress. So far there has been no instance where works of definite and permanent value have been held back by censorship or press laws. Good writers will never be muzzled; the indifferent and the bad cannot be muzzled soon enough."

The public mind can be effectively restricted only by forcing a positive doctrine upon it and suppressing everything that conflicts with this, but Metternich and Gentz felt that such coercion was contrary to good taste. They themselves believed in no dogma. Moderation, reason, standards belonged in the realm of manners, self-control, and education, not in that of magisterial compulsion. The young reproached these leaders precisely because they had no dogma to offer; nothing great, no inspiring urge; only mocking reproof.

Thus it could be more justly said of Gentz that he defended intellectual freedom, for he felt very strongly that the German Nationalists aimed at restraint, at exclusiveness, and the extermination of dissenters. He contested their right to freedom whose doctrine, if it triumphed, would inevitably mean the end of intellectual freedom in a much more real and terrible sense.

His position is even less paradoxical when it is recalled that already he had interpreted his struggle against the French Revolution as a struggle for freedom and individuality against Jacobinic equalitarianism. After all, "freedom" is a word to which the most dissimilar and wrangling parties can lay claim. Freedom from what? Freedom for what? Whose freedom?

It must be added that the decisions of Carlsbad and Vienna proved to be wholly abortive. For a few years they brought the smaller German states under Austrian influence, and meanwhile apparent calm reigned in Germany. But not for long. The censorship, laxly administered with a guilty conscience, silenced neither good writers nor bad, and on the whole there was nothing so extreme or so silly that it could not be printed somewhere. Over this situation "entirely different stars" presided in very truth. Freedom does not perish through press restriction, and least of all through men like Gentz. Where it is lost the chances are a hundred to one that the fault is its own. It is destroyed because it knows not what to do.

Gentz's position on the German problem determined his actions and sympathies in the south European question, though here the consequence was in itself inconsequent: succor extended by this liberal and rational man to fanatical priests and to alarmed and bloodthirsty dynasts.

In Spain, where the partisans of an ultrademocratic and highly impractical form of government were at odds with a monstrous King, the Austrians had wished to exert nothing more than "moral pressure," but when the Spanish unrest spread to Italy they were forced to act. A glance at the political map will show clearly that the supporters of the Austrian monarchy could tolerate no revolution in Italy; whence it followed, unfortunately, that they had to hurry to the aid of the reinstated rulers, the sovereign of the antiquated pontifical state and the ignoble King of Naples. The one necessity flowed from the other. If the supernational monarchy of the Hapsburgs, which had great advantages in addition to its serious defects, were to be preserved neither Germany nor Italy must be allowed to become national republics. The opposition against the restored rulers in Italy was moving toward a republican national state. What other course was left open to an Austrian statesman?

The advocate of Gentz can plead further in his defense that he suffered under the evil alliances forced upon him by the caprice of history. He may cite the fact that the campaign by which Austria returned the King of Naples to his absolutism was of operetta-like character, and that even the British Ambassador, a kindly man who helped the revolutionists to escape by furnishing them with false passports, said that he was disgusted by the capriciousness of the Neapolitans. Furthermore, Metternich's critics themselves admit that after this scandalously cheap victory he did all that he possibly could to repair the situation in Naples in a reasonable way. Nevertheless, this period remains the darkest in Gentz's life. Unproductive at a time that called desperately for new concepts, he was the captive of forces that he despised.

He defended himself. He showed that ideal governments hatched out by radical professors were not really suited to the south European countries. He insisted that the majority of Italians did not want a national state, and that they would be incapable of administering one. He impugned the principle of the centralized national state in general, for Italy as well as for Germany. "That a people, or peoples, speaking one and the same language—for similarity of origin, of religion, of single traits of character, and so on are partly uncertain, partly vague criteria—acquire thereby a permanent right to form a political whole: this proposition is unknown so far in constitutional law. Whether so-called natural law would demand it, let those find out who still concede to this monstrosity a place in their system. History has decided against it. If one large group of closely related peoples have gradually consolidated to a political whole through similarity (not identity) of fortunes, customs, needs, and dialects, as happened in France, against this one ten other examples could be cited where dispersed races that unquestionably sprang from the same root have always remained separate from one another in respect to politics. . . . Nor will an impartial observer of world conditions find anything unnatural in this; otherwise nothing would be more contrary to nature, surely, than the union of manifestly German lands with France. The principle alleged is as foreign to nature as it is to law. The laws by which self-contained states grow in the world of reality have little or nothing to do with relationships between speech, customs, or beliefs; they are not the outcome of man's free choice, but facts and combinations of facts that we have to acknowledge and to which, willingly or unwillingly, we must bow. . . ."

But what if the majority of the inhabitants in a country will not submit to them? The statesman is only secondarily a jurist; he will hardly insist upon positive law when that which contradicts it is more promising, is desired after mature consideration by most of those concerned, and is at least tolerable to the community of civilized states. In such a case the wise statesman will press for a change in the positive law then in force, and after a time the new facts will become as legitimate and as historic as were the old.

The European community, thus objected its Secretary, had more harm than good to anticipate from a national revolution in Italy. Moreover, a resolve by the majority of all Italians hardly entered into the question. A mature resolve by illiterate peasants? What we should really have to fear if events in Italy were allowed to take their course is not a national state, but chaos: chaos on the borders of our frail and venerable Austrian Empire. This we experienced once in our youth; now that we are old we do not wish to go through it again.

The answer came to him from Great Britain, from a man who at one time had been "rather a believer in Gentz"; from Canning, the successor of Castlereagh. Its import was essentially this:

That your state edifice is shaken by every disturbance anywhere on the Continent is your misfortune. In our country it is different. We do not fear disorders in foreign lands, and shall know well how to settle the new problems here in our own islands. Where our real interests dictate we interfere, but we shall not defend everywhere an order that has suffered internal decay for the mere reason that after its collapse there is nothing to be expected at first but turmoil. We have no illusions. We know that King and radical in Spain are equally bad. There is no denying, either, that the Greeks are a most rascally set, and we have no intention of helping them. Every nation for itself, and God over all. The old will die, the new will mature. Public life will always be more highly developed and liberal in our country than elsewhere. Let nature take its course. . . .

To THE historian the dissolution of the post-Napoleonic unity of Europe is recognizable and real as far in advance as was the dissolution of its Napoleonic unity. In 1815 Gentz had written: "We see the most diverse interests, the most antagonistic enterprises, the most contradictory philosophies and secret desires disregarded for the moment and squeezed into an amalgam that in its real nature is only a coalition for specific purposes. . . ." Three years later, at the Congress of Aachen, he had to help Lord Castlereagh formulate a decision that clearly indicated even then Great Britain's disavowal of the interventionism of the Continental statesmen. "Nothing could be more immoral, and more prejudicial to the honor of the governments, than a principle according to which we should have to give support at any time to established powers, without troubling ourselves in the least as to the degree in which they were right or wrong. . . ."

The thoroughly conservative and European-minded Castlereagh expressed himself still more unequivocally in 1820 on the Spanish question. The alliance, he said in his admirable *State Paper*, was directed against revolution, of course; not, however, against democracy in general, but only against the special military and aggressive form given it by Bonaparte. In no case was it "intended as an union for the government of the world or for the superintendence of the affairs of other states." "Great Britain has perhaps equal power with any other state to oppose herself to a practical and intelligible danger capable of being brought home to the national feeling. When the territorial Balance of Europe is disturbed, she can interfere with effect, but she is the last Government in Europe which can be expected or can venture to commit herself on any question of an abstract character." "We shall be found in our place when actual danger menaces the system of Europe; but this country cannot and will not act upon abstract and speculative principles of precaution."

Hence Pitt, now dead and gone, had not been so far wrong in ignoring the French Revolution as long as it did not pass beyond the borders of France.

What then, asked Gentz bitterly, remained of the great lesson of the recent past?

Inconsistently, as matters stood, Great Britain did not deny that Austria had the right to intervene in Italy, but she herself wanted nothing to do with this intervention; thus at the Congresses of Troppau (1820) and Laibach (1821), which were concerned with the Neapolitan revolution, she and France were represented by observers only, and Metternich, eager for universal ratification of his undertaking, had to accommodate himself to intimate coöperation with the Czar. On the other hand, dissolution of the Ottoman Empire on the pattern of Polish partition and establishment of the Russians in the Balkans was as intolerable to Great Britain as to Austria. If in respect to the Italian question there was something like an alliance of Austria, Russia, and Prussia, so in the Balkan question Austria and Great Britain appeared to find a mutual and legitimate interest in the problem of Turkey.

The Congress of Verona (1822) was the most inclusive and magnificent since that of Vienna. The autocrats of the East appeared in person, and the constitutional powers of the West were represented by imposing delegations. Lord Castlereagh was to have led the British group, but shortly before the Congress opened he had put an end to his life with a razor: one more whose nerve power had been early consumed by the great crisis. Wellington appeared in Castlereagh's place. The King of France was represented by Chateaubriand, the poet; not a handsome, romantic figure, as Gentz had expected, but a humpbacked and misshapen, upon whom a truly ludicrous effect was conferred by a wide sash and a Saracen sword. In the Roman amphitheater Rossini conducted by starlight before the most distinguished audience in the world.

By day, in the hotels of the ministers, discussion centered on the fact that Turks and Greeks were crucifying, impaling, and throwing one another into the sea by the thousand; on the status of the former—and, in the opinion of the Legitimists, still—Spanish colonies in America; on the awkward position of Ferdinand of Spain, held more and more in check by a radical parliament while civil war raged in the interior of his country; and on the unrest everywhere when men were bound by laws in which they no longer believed.

Faced with this unrest, the great alliance failed. The differences were too wide to be bridged now, even by Gentz's verbal cunning. No longer was there a "common cause." True, the Russians wanted to intervene in Spain to restore the authority of the King, but at the same time they wanted to meddle in the bloody Balkan quarrel in order to destroy the authority of the Sultan. The interest of official France was concentrated on Spain, with a view to proving that she was a power still capable of war and to restoring her former influence in the Iberian Peninsula, under the subterfuge of antirevolutionary necessity. For social and political reasons Austria would have liked to see the evil Ferdinand reëstablished, but did not want French preponderance in Spain; she did not desire Latin-American independence, yet saw no possibility of preventing it; above all she wanted to obstruct Russia's expansion at the expense of Turkey, thought that she needed Russia in the Spanish-South American question, utterly condemned Great Britain's position here, and needed Great Britain in order to save Turkey. George Canning thought to legitimatize the independence of South America with the help of the United States, did not wish to let Russia inherit Turkey, and looked with hatred and contempt on the intervention in Spain for which France was preparing. Though he was unable to prevent it, it was the last of its kind.

So, too, was the Congress of Verona the last of the European congresses. The conservative accord among the powers was already on the way to complete dissolution when President James Monroe delivered the message in which he alluded to the difference between the political systems of America and Europe, and emphasized in threatening tones that the one had no concern with the sphere of the other.

Gentz, having read the message, expressed his opinion of it as follows:

"The speech of the President of the United States is an official document that will mark an epoch in the history of our times. Its every line deserves to be weighed with the most serious attention. Not alone the present attitude toward Europe of this federation that has become so great and formidable, but the relation of the whole American Continent to the Old World is here expressed with a clearness and precision that puts an end to all doubt and equivocation. The separation between America and Europe is completed, and irrevocably completed. If the reconquest of the colonies on the American Continent or their voluntary return to the mother country had not already become impossible, this opposition by the North American public, long silently brewing and now openly declared, would suffice to remove every thought of it. At the moment the islands do not come into question. The United States herself feels that she does not yet dare to carry presumption to this extreme, and probably foresees that even without her interference the dominion of Europeans over Cuba, Jamaica, Martinique, and the rest will not continue much longer. . . ." He called Monroe's message a document of "thoroughgoing abomination and unexampled effrontery." "But the immediate practical result is, unfortunately, that on the whole the situation actually is thus. . . ."

Not that Monroe's message had contributed anything decisive to the question that it directly concerned. The separation of the colonies from Spain was virtually complete, and save for their powerless motherland none of the European states had any intention of correcting the situation. Gentz's neglected advice had been from the first that the King of Spain might as well relinquish his American empire voluntarily and generously, so that at least the dignity of Europe should remain unimpaired. It was Monroe's defiance of the Old World that the inveterate European resented so bitterly.

Among diplomats the message was not taken very seriously. It was not in keeping with the available military resources of the United States, and altered nothing in a situation that had already been settled by British policy. Only a philosophical politician like Gentz could appreciate all its potentialities for the future.

Gentz's "Europe" was thought to be the "world": a partnership of the Christian, or "civilized" states. Until then, indeed, there had been no power outside Europe that could have been dangerous to any of her states. Hence "perpetual peace," whose establishment Kant had projected thirty years before, was assumed to be at once a European and a world peace; for Kant took it as a matter of course that the whole world would gradually become "European." Gentz, too, his pupil, was occupied with universal, not Continental, politics; to him Europe was the center of the world, not one continent among others.

The old Kant and the young Gentz had both greeted the founding of the United States with jubilation as a republican, Christian, that is to say, "European," undertaking; Europe on the American Continent had shown the way to her brothers at home, and the Old World would soon imitate what the New had so successfully tried.

In the universality of the eighteenth century, a republican, optimistic universality, the United States, too, might perhaps have shared. But the Revolution that had succeeded so admirably in America miscarried in Europe. During the next twenty-five years the Old World itself had split asunder, and the new was in hostile array against the old. A conservative, anxious, and interventional mood had gained the ascendancy: Interventionism was a false interpretation of universality. The American system was different from this, and had to proclaim itself different. Accordingly it might be said that Metternich and his group were more to blame for the momentous separation of the two hemispheres than Monroe and Adams. With equal truth it could be said that Great Britain had contributed more than the conservatives toward preserving contact between the Old and the New Worlds just by leaving Spain, or "Europe," in the lurch respecting the South American question. George Canning, the Foreign Minister, did not fear the new times as Gentz feared them. A strong personal and national self-assurance led him to challenge difficulties as they arose. Looking back, he said: "The great danger of the time, a danger which the policy of the European system would have fostered, was a division of the world into European and American, Republican and Monarchical: a league of worn-out governments on the one hand, and of youthful and strong Nations, with the U.S. at their head, on the other." That Gentz should have recognized immediately the "doctrine" in Monroe's message does him credit. But it was really his gloomy defensive attitude that divided the world in two, while Great Britain's liberal politicians and businessmen held it together.

IN THE Greek question Austria and Great Britain found their interests at first in accord. The Ottoman Empire must not be allowed to disintegrate. The Russians must not be allowed to reach Greece, much less Constantinople. The Greeks must find out for themselves how to escape from a situation for which they alone were responsible. The Turks, who were deaf to counsel, were to be advised to make concessions to the spirit of the times and to the Czar of Russia. But the deplorable military situation of the revolutionists, the gruesome details that were on everyone's lips, and the growing enthusiasm for Greece, in England and on the Continent, made such a course more and more difficult.

Gentz was accounted one of the most unfeeling opponents of the Greek cause. An enemy to German and Italian nationalism, he was all too consistently an enemy to the nationalism of the Balkan peoples as well. Of the Serbian revolution he had already written: "I should not like to see the advancement of the Serbs purchased at the exorbitant price of a new encroachment on the fundamental structure of an Empire that, wholly apart from this, is already rocking on its foundations, and you really must forgive me if I am unable to rise to these heights of philanthropy. . . ." His lack of sympathy with the Serbs might have been forgiven, for the Serbs were not very interesting. But when he announced himself wholly unmoved by the magic name of Greece he stood out before all the world as a cold-hearted old villain. Nothing alienated him more from his time than this antagonism. The more furious became the enthusiasm for Greece the more did he retire into the role of the cool expert, and the higher rose his contempt for the literati. He laughed at the English intellectuals who donned Plato's purple robe, and found Byron theatrical and without style. He maintained that the modern Greeks had nothing in common with those of antiquity save an arrogated name; he, the politician, knew better than the literary loudmouths that the Greeks had raised impudence in piracy to unexampled heights, that their financiers were corrupt thieves, and that they yielded nothing to the Turks in the matter of refined cruelty.

Once more his advocate may be allowed a few words in his defense. He did not see the Greek problem as essentially a social one. He did not accuse the Greeks of being Jacobins. What he feared was not domestic revolution but foreign war; destruction of the balance of power; a Russian Napoleon. This theme of a Russian peril was an old one, and even during the Napoleonic upheaval it had never been entirely lost to view. If Russia were to realize her whole inconceivably strong potentiality through modern means, the remainder of Europe would become a sort of Russian appendage. Perhaps, wrote Gentz in 1815, we shall come to view the epoch of the Revolution not as that of the ephemeral French, but rather as that of the final Russian, advance.

"Napoleon's downfall was a pure and unqualified advantage for Russia; for the rest of Europe, and especially for the states bordering on Russia, it was largely balanced by the increased strength that she secured for herself at the expense of the general equilibrium. . . . For this great power there is virtually no further real danger; if she attacks her neighbors her greatest risk is merely that she may fail in her purpose and have to postpone her venture to a more favorable time. The difficulty of penetrating to Russia's interior is now so generally recognized that nothing but lunacy and despair could any longer prompt an attempt to conquer this great Empire. Finland, the only country from which at least one of her vital centers could be reached and a fraction of her power paralyzed, is now under her domination. While the other states of Europe exhausted themselves in the struggle against Napoleon, Russia, who allied herself with him, understood well how to extract the most solid benefits from the ephemeral union. It would be easy for her to fall upon her neighbors, for she has so many greedy and ambitious reasons for trying it, and, if the expression be allowed, such substantially centrifugal habits, that war, which others regard as a necessary evil, will always be to the Russians a matter of choice, of emotion, and of speculation. . . ."

But whosoever attacks Turkey attacks Russia. "The end of the Turkish monarchy could be survived by the Austrian for but a short time."

Historians know how exactly this latter thesis was verified a hundred years later. Amazed at the prophetic insight of the veteran politician, they ask once more whether in the Turko-Greek question, too, Gentz was not acting under a tragic compulsion that is recognizable in all the conclusions of his later years. Did not even Great Britain subsequently come under such a compulsion and have to make war on Russia in the middle of the century for the defense of Turkish despotism?

But only impotently governed states, only tired and flagging spirits, let themselves be driven into situations where there is no choice except that between two evils. The passive, the defensive character chooses, if an option still remains; the active contemplates remote possibilities and does not choose, but invents. The dilemma whether to leave the Balkans and the Dardanelles to Russia, or be forced into opposing liberation of the Greeks from the Turkish yoke, when superficially examined, might have been Great Britain's as well as Austria's. Canning did not acknowledge it. With creative audacity he combined Great Britain's political interests with the moral and the popular. The Turks ought to lose their important position in the Mediterranean; the Russians must not gain a foothold there; the friends of Greek freedom should have their way. Courageously, as when he offered to join the United States in the South American question, he now forced his coöperation upon Russia, roused public opinion through the press, kept British ships running, and finally achieved what he had in mind: a sovereign Greece, under British protection alone. A war between Russia and Turkey followed, nevertheless, but it did not have the disastrous results that Gentz had anticipated.

THEREAFTER one spoke no more of "Europe." No consciousness of a common cause survived in the minds of those who sought to consummate the British and Russian will to power. The idea, an outcome of the struggle against Napoleon, disappeared in the air like a rocket. The Austrian Europeans, upon whom its light had shone for an instant, withdrew into passivity, haughty and grieved. Twelve years after Napoleon's fall Gentz decided that his own life had been dedicated to a "lost cause."

XVI

VICTA CATONI

DEFEAT and defense in such exasperating repetition cease to be stimulating. More than anyone else Gentz had upheld the concept and common cause of "Europe" since 1814 and now, under his very eyes, it had become a melancholy cult of the defunct or the just barely extant, a feeble pledge that no one longer wished to keep. But how could such a proud and abundant spirit go so far astray?

The Anglo-Saxon mind, confident of the future and represented in the 1820's by Monroe and Canning, will always have difficulty in understanding the fear that never left informed European intellectuals after the French Revolution. The British were protected by their traditions, their religion, their political skill, their world-wide holdings. The Americans had their continent to themselves, where the energies of the nineteenth century, intrinsically democratic energies, could freely take shape and grow; spread unhindered through the country and organize it. In Europe there was fear that these energies would arise all at once in many long-established centers, and would not find the space that they needed for their development. They would turn furiously on one another, and they would destroy; especially as there was so much there that could be destroyed. They would lend a new and evil strength to the old powers and greeds, and steam engines and propaganda would serve the Middle Ages.

This is really what Gentz feared, for his long experience showed him the cul-de-sac toward which the Old World had been moving since the downfall of Napoleon. He would have liked to arrest this progress, and if only he could do so was willing to put up with the offenses of the Sultan and the infamous King of Naples; but he realized only too well that it could not be stayed.

IN EUROPE, the conservative theory, to which the shock of the French Revolution first gave rise, followed two directions in the main: that of Edmund Burke, and that of Joseph de Maistre. The former was English; Protestant, realistic, and coördinated: "A disposition to preserve and an ability to improve, taken together, would be my standard of a statesman." The latter was French; Catholic, rationalistic, and highly impractical: "It is absolutely necessary to kill the spirit of the eighteenth century." In his later years Gentz wavered between the two, realized the inadequacy of both, sought for a third, and found rest nowhere.

He was drawn to Burke by his early education; by his youthful belief in the progress, the lofty mission of the human race; by his sense of the substantial, the practical, the real; by his hatred of extremes and his deep, inborn feeling for balance in thought and deed. To a true reactionary, his old friend Adam Müller, he could occasionally explain himself:

"An author whom you will not reject says: 'A rationalistic training, when too biased, and pushed beyond its proper limits, requires its traditional complement as much as a traditional training, conversely, requires rationalistic vitalizing when it has grown rigid and foreign to the nature of mankind.' This is the quintessence of my philosophy, which has now come to maturity. From which of the two sides equilibrium may be threatened at any given time is a question concerning which doubt and dissension may occasionally prevail. When I entered the political arena there was a real tendency to suppress the traditional element completely and give undivided sway to the rationalistic. I took the field against this mistaken endeavor, and though in the heat of battle I may sometimes have gone too far, perhaps, I cannot well be taxed with ever having closed my eyes entirely to Charybdis in my fear of Scylla. . . . In the revolutionary movement of the period I never disapproved of the natural and excusable wish to rise from a bad condition to a better, but I did abhor the narrow and arrogant proposal to begin the world anew. Now when you, equally narrow, arrogant, and sarcastic, preach counterrevolution and banish with bitter disdain all the endeavors and all the products of our time, which certainly I am not inclined to overrate, bluntly demanding a return to the church system, the feudal system, the financial system, and the commercial system of past centuries . . . how shall I do such violence to my ideas as to sanction yours?"

Here we have the system of checks and balances, that wise conjunction of opposites; unprejudiced decision according to circumstances: British tradition. But Burke and Canning had the British Government, the British constitution, and British history behind them. The equilibrium that they taught was not derived from a rational principle but rather from historical reality. What had poor

Gentz behind him? Nothing but his intellect, an impressionable medium susceptible to the most diverse ideas. For him the German past was not the fertile soil of British history. With differences in degree, what he had said of France in 1814 was true of the Continent in general: a land "where, for five and twenty years, first the all-leveling scythe of a people's wrath and then the policy of a military and despotic regime have obliterated every trace of legal rights; where there are no longer any social distinctions, any organized trades, any privileges, any methods of orderly procedure save only those that the present government has created. . . ."

The absolutism of the rulers had had the same effect as the Revolution; it had cut the roots that connected past and present, or had let them rot away in its evil keeping. This had become very clear in respect to the new parliaments, or "constitutions." Gentz did not believe that these systems would be permanent, established as they were merely on paper. "A document," he wrote, "is not yet a real constitution; time alone can create one." He would have liked to see a revival of something that had already been created by time: the former estates, which into the seventeenth century had mediated between rulers and their subjects everywhere in Germany. It was from these that the modern British Parliament had really developed. Undeniably; but on the Continent they had either died out or been killed off, and the dead do not return to life. It was all very well to speak of coördinated development in Burke's lofty sense; here there was nothing capable of development.

Conservatism on the Continent, therefore, was just as unrestricted, just as rationalistic and theoretical, as liberalism, and a great deal more paradoxical; there was no corresponding reality with which it might have been tempered. Joseph de Maistre was its most consistent advocate: Voltaire in the service of Catholic dogma; a man of unruly intelligence that raged against itself; devout, pessimistic, and truculent. Gentz read his forceful prose with enjoyment, and indeed there had been a time when de Maistre's sparkling paradoxes had exerted a definite influence on him; this was during the period of the great congresses especially, from 1818 to 1822. Then, like de Maistre, he wanted to see "revolution and counterrevolution drawn up against each other in battle array"; then he wanted to see the spirit of the age "vanquished with cannon." "Any feudalism, even one that was very poorly organized, would be welcome to me if only it delivers us from the power of the mob, of counterfeit scholars, of students, and of journalists especially." "My suggestion still holds good: to guard against abuse of the press . . . nothing whatsoever should be printed for years. The enforcement of this rule with the rarest exceptions, these to be determined by a tribunal of recognized supremacy, would lead us back within a short time to truth and to God." "You are entirely right. All is lost unless religion be reëstablished, not only as faith but as law. I go even further: religion will never be reëstablished as faith unless first it be reëstablished as law." And the confirmed Protestant even ventured to accuse Luther's Reformation of having initiated the revolutionary principle. "Protestantism is the original, true, and only source of all the monstrous evil under which we sink today. If it had only remained within theoretical bounds it could and must have been tolerated, since it relieves a profound urge in human nature. But when governments acquiesced in making Protestantism a recognized religion, a form of Christianity; in accepting it as one of the rights of man; when they conformed to it, gave it a position in the state next to the true and established Church, if not, indeed, on the ruins of this; the religious, moral, and political world order was instantly dissolved. . . . The whole French Revolution and the still worse one that is imminent in Germany have the same common origin."

The resourceful, harassed mind that ponders on the causes of current events will discover much; even this thesis appears not wholly without foundation. Was not the Prussian state, so deeply feared by Gentz, essentially Protestant? Had not Luther already split Europe's Catholicism asunder with his Protestant national rebellion? Had not this schism of the nations been widened by the French Revolution? Would the "still worse one that is imminent in Germany" complete, perhaps, her Protestant-nationalistic desertion from the cultural unity of the nations? A labyrinth of thought, from which a return to the shelter of Rome was not, however, the right egress.

De Maistre was by nature an arch-Catholic, and forced his powerful intellect into conformity with the law of the Church. Gentz demanded of others, and even scornfully, that they conform, but was wholly unable to subordinate himself to any dogma. De Maistre's criticism of the Revolution was not so unrealistic, but abstract dreams were his only remedy. Gentz was no dreamer. He could not forget that the Pope, over the political supremacy of whose sacred office de Maistre was so enthusiastic, was really an infirm old man and head of a state that was obsolete to the point of repugnance. The empirical conservatism of the British, deeply as he admired it, was not suited to the more unhappy conditions on the Continent; but the rational conservatism of the French was not suited to anything whatsoever.

The Germans contributed their philosophy of history, according to which everything is right for its own time, one thing develops from another, and each at last must end deservedly on the junk pile of history. This conception of the historical, of rising and setting, could lead to a philosophy that encouraged change and believed in the future just as easily as to a philosophy of conservatism; nothing was determined in advance.

Professor Hegel, for example, in Berlin, a historical thinker if ever there was one, aroused in some of his pupils thoughts that were dangerous to the state. But however diverse the notions that history may support, the true historical temperament will always be inclined to turn to the past and the present, which is a stratification of pasts, rather than to the future, which rolls toward us shrouded in mystery. A feeling was abroad, too, against which even Hegel, master of history, was unable to defend himself. The new era that was approaching, and of which the French Revolution had been but a preface and a foretaste, would bring with it changes of such frightful character that even history itself, epitome of permanence in the midst of change, would pale before them, everything rooted in the past would be destroyed, and all recollection blotted out. The moment at which historiography reached its highest perfection was at the same time the moment when one began to descry on the far horizon the first faint signs of its dissolution.

It is to be emphasized that Gentz accepted in all its essentials the historical concept of the revolutionaries. Both he and the Revolution were children of the eighteenth century, the century in which the future was joyfully anticipated as never before and never afterward. He had not abandoned the idea of the future as the beginning of something fundamentally new; it was only that his joy in it had perceptibly diminished. Nevertheless, he could still view it in his more cheerful moments with a certain amount of optimism. At such times he thought that "progress" should not come about too violently, and that it should be guided by wise statesmen.

When he was in a more gloomy mood he doubted that the great change would be beneficial in any way, but never denied its inevitability. In such a humor, he saw nothing ahead of him that held any promise of security. The so-called middle class was not a real class at all, not a caste as the nobility had been, and no lasting pattern of life was to be expected from it. The liberalism of the professors, upright, well-disposed, and optimistic men, was a straw that could not stand for a moment against the advancing storm. Parliaments, with their property qualifications and rhetoricians, were short-lived farces; wishful and childish nonsense. The easy optimism of the revolutionaries he despised. In Anglo-Saxon lands the democratic and religious movements were closely related; on the Continent the Left was nonreligious or antireligious, and in this respect essentially frivolous. That a compelling faith could not be reëstablished by decree Gentz was only too well aware; yet he saw in atheism, the rationalism that led down even to anarchy, no definite assurance of human happiness. Nor did he find inherent in such elevating forces or abstractions as "people," "nation," and "liberty" any implicit guarantee of good. The people, he noted, spoke incessantly of revolution, and when it came thought that it must comply with their expectations and proceed wholly in accord with their notions.

"With the best intentions in the world they plunge their fatherland into ruin, and if France is to be given over once more to all the horrors of anarchy she will be the first to cry out over the 'violation of principles,' the first to be amazed because her fantastic systems have brought forth nothing but disorder and ruin." Mankind could not be governed by rational means alone. Once the old magic lines had been overstepped, and all the venerated safeguards against unbridled license destroyed, new and more oppressive and degrading ones would soon be established.

What remained? Fear. Knowledge that led to no definite conclusion. At such times Gentz could not read history without being attacked by the tormenting thought: Everything was bound to happen as it did. It all began with the eighteenth century. No, with the Reformation. No more irrefrangible law, no more unifying faith, no world order more. This was the fundamental problem; this, and not the menace of the "dangerous classes," whom the rich citizens of Paris were now beginning to fear. It is true that occasionally Gentz, too, saw the "possibility of a rising by the lower classes against the upper, by the poor against the rich"; but he thought that this danger could always be controlled with a little common sense. "For it remains an eternal truth that not the preponderance of the masses, not their untrained force, but organized power and the superiority of the mind rule the world."

Genuine conservatives (of whom there were not many on the Continent, to be sure) do not belong to any one definite class, and are not opposed to any one definite class. Thus Gentz was without a class, as much as he was without a fatherland. The war between the capitalists and the proletariat, which the French were now consciously beginning to wage and which reached its climax twenty years later, was not his concern. The revolution by which he felt himself being swept away against his will sprang from deeper sources, and the economic was only one side of it at the most. Not the factory workers, but nationalistic students, liberal professors, journalists, and parliamentary speakers were its supporters, and it was they who interested him.

The more profound, the more intellectual this revolution, the more ineluctable it was also. Whosoever recognized its inevitability and still remained opposed to it would have to seek consolation as a knight who does not desert his post, though all hope be past. When his cousin, Ancillon, the Prussian Foreign Minister, the friend of his youth, published a book: *On the Reconciliation of Opposing Opinions*, Gentz wrote to him: "It is precisely the mediation proposed by you that is my despair today. I am familiar with these difficult antitheses. I have examined them all, and have now reached a point where I can endure only a definite and determined standpoint. . . . Even the time for honorable capitulation seems to me past; moderation will no longer save us; let us therefore employ the remainder of our powers in preserving what we desire and always have desired. The cause that we defend will be lost; I know it well and I know, too, why. . . ."

Was this enough? Could a fraction of the public, even the smallest fraction, be inspired by such writing? In his day success was impossible without the support of public opinion, and with his friend, Adam Müller, Gentz once discussed the chances of a journal like the one that he, with the unconscious courage of youth, had published twenty-five years previously in Berlin. The plan came to nought because he could find no one to share his views, because Müller seemed to him too unrealistic and too overbearing, but principally because no manuscripts satisfactory to him were submitted. Again, in such a journal one must express one's intentions, say what one contemplates for the future and help in some degree to shape it. But what had he in mind for the future? What demands could be made when the new was rushing in so overwhelmingly from all sides and he could think only of defense?

"The bare struggle for the maintenance of established authority and against revolutionary endeavors has in it something unsatisfying, something oppressive, something narrow, and so on. On the other hand, it is extremely hazardous at a time like this to estimate with any precision just what will intervene between the old, which badly needs fresh support and substantial modification, and the new, which is wholly objectionable. It is hard to answer this question even in theory, for mere perfunctory return to an earlier phase of any sort is obviously impossible. . . . But when it comes to methods and their execution, what dangers on all sides! . . . I wished that all political polemics might be limited for the present to the following: 1. Refutation of all false data, false teachings, and wretched scribblers. 2. Familiarization of our contemporaries, even the more advanced among them, with the idea of postponing all innovations, if only for a few years, and merely preserving authority from collapse. 3. Laying down certain principles for the reform of the states in the future.

"Note carefully: I *wished* limitation to this range of activities, which still would permit wide latitude. Whether this would be practicable, whether this insipid, negative, resigned course is fitted even to those who may be expected to work for us and with us, I prefer to leave to your own judgment. . . ."

The journal did not materialize.

The desire to evade the merely negative, to escape from the labyrinth of thought, leads to exaltation of the practical. In so far as it involves decision the practical is always biased. "We little people," wrote Gentz to Metternich, "though often we think that by persistent study we can penetrate more deeply into affairs, are disturbed nevertheless by each changing situation and frequently doubt and subtilize, therefore, when we should act." "You, on the contrary, have imperturbably gone your way once you had sketched out a course, one that corresponded essentially with the facts, to be sure, and have always acted in conformity with it."

In comparison with any theory the practical is more rounded, more real, more three dimensional, and we have often seen Gentz, in a life replete with crises, flee to the practical: to Metternich, to Fouché, to the British. As a part of this phase he discarded in his later years, more completely than ever before, all interpretations that had to do with natural law, and even wished to see the right of conquest maintained. As a part of this phase, again, he sought university reform, above all in the sense of a greater emphasis on the natural sciences. "It has long been my belief . . . that the superiority of the natural sciences over the philosophical and critical must be explicitly vindicated. Herein lies one of the best means of re-establishing the preponderance of authority over license. For anyone can philosophize and criticize (and mysterize and poetize) to his heart's content, but the natural sciences must be studied; and if only youth will resolve again on real application it will at the same time become susceptible once more of that intellectual subordination without which all academic life is but a prelude to the unrestrained anarchy where all political activity wanders about today."

From a practical point of view he rejected the idea of a league of nations as a purely legal fiction; peace among states would not be assured by abstract law, but by a higher morality alone. "The only imaginable way of putting the relations among states on a par with those among their individual citizens would be subjection of the whole world to one and the same supreme lawmaking will—a notion as rash and impractical as it is repulsive, and wholly and atrociously opposed to other higher aims of mankind. All remaining proposals are inadequate. . . . Neither in autocracy nor in polyarchy is there to be found a means for setting up a general and legal system of government among the states.

"When reason demands that an effort be made nevertheless to approach such a system as nearly as possible, what course still remains open? The road to this goal must be sought where it lies. Treaties alone are the means of coöperation among states, and there is no higher legal sanction for them, since states are no longer independent if they recognize a superior authority. In any case, the only sanction for treaties among states is reciprocal morality. Accordingly this must be cultivated; must be more and more firmly established. The states, their rulers and their citizens, must learn justice. *Discite justitiam!* In this way alone is to be sought, if not perpetual peace, at least an abatement of war. All other endeavors are either pernicious or fantastic. . . ."

Often it is as though, tormented whenever he looked into the distant past or future by recollections, possibilities, speculations, he held his hand before his eyes and confined himself to the here and now. "I will explain to you in a few words what attitudes of mind I do not like, and my reasons therefor:

"1. All lamentations over the past, the present, and the future. Over the past, because they are utterly useless; over the present, because everything concerning it has long since been said; and over the future (I do not mean what is imminent within a month or so), because they only confuse and enfeeble the mind and project me into an era that I cannot control and of which I can form no sort of reliable estimate.

"2. All ideal wishes and plans, no matter how captivating they may seem, because they are wholly incompatible with the harsh, perverse, and stubborn nature of the present evil.

"3. And not least, even such proposals as are in themselves feasible, in themselves highly desirable, but too slow, and incapable of realization in time to meet the pressing need. . . . I have become, if you will, *ultrapractical*. . . ."

But the practical can be achieved only where skill is, where power is. Power, and those who used it wisely, had attracted this inveterate controversialist from the first. Thus, like Goethe, he clung to Prince Metternich; thus he confessed that sometimes he even missed Bonaparte. When he pondered Roman history he concentrated his scorn on Brutus and Cassius, murderers from ideology; his admiration on Caesar, who would have had the power to heal. And so he acknowledged: "The difference between us seems to me to lie in this; that in general your mind inclines more toward independence (though of course not exclusively), mine more toward regulation; sometimes, indeed (and here I impeach myself), with a certain depreciation of and scorn for freedom. I like power."

Not to have power, yet to enjoy it and attach oneself to the powerful—a writer in this situation must of necessity lay himself open to talk. When Gentz's old-fashioned sedan chair rocked across the court of the Chancery, the writers of Vienna clenched their fists behind his back. Franz Grillparzer viewed his lodgings with hatred. Friedrich Hebbel referred to his "habitual shamelessness." Though the bare idea that the conduct of a "friend of the people" might occasionally be governed by motives that were not wholly altruistic was tantamount to blasphemy, it was taken for granted that this Gentz had sold himself to the rulers for a jingling reward; against his better judgment, as was shown by a product of his youth: his epistle to the King of Prussia. In 1820, as a joke, enemies of the dreaded Chief Censor republished this composition, in which Gentz had demanded of the King freedom of the press; prefacing it with a derisive introduction: "Then and Now."

On the cover of the unwelcome little book Hofrat Gentz reproved himself in pencil as follows: "This pamphlet cannot be defended as a youthful indiscretion. The author was over thirty years of age when he wrote it. . . . Ignorance and conceit were the real parents of the abortion. Fortunate indeed is he who can be reproached with no greater sin than this during the course of his political life! Yet I feel that it is serious enough, and I must regard as a well-deserved chastisement the annoyance of seeing this product of frivolous loquacity and offensive presumption now brought up against me by my enemies. . . . As for the arguments against censorship, they were such that these revolutionary cutpurses would have been ashamed to renew them, supposing them still capable of shame." Of course: for he had advised the King to grant freedom of the press out of his disdain for base journalists, who otherwise would only have been raised to cheap martyrdom.

Gentz suffered under what he called the "unfriendly opinions" that were current against him. We are so ready with criticism of an opponent! Hardly anyone knew how lonesomely and conscientiously he picked his way, how carefully he examined all aspects of a question, and what storms raged within him before he made up his mind to take sides. Even such an evident fact as that he could have gathered more riches and much higher titles had he not been so rigidly meticulous in refusing to become a Catholic was unknown to most of his critics. Thus he was inordinately happy when from time to time even a liberal spoke of him as he thought he deserved: "For what he says to my credit contradicts in the strongest terms the opinion of the rabble (who see in me only the blind tool of power)."

GENTZ was a man never to be forgotten by anyone who ever had touched his life, and he himself kept faith wherever he was able. Well into his later years, and particularly then, the figures of his youth kept appearing with reproaches, forgiveness, or gratitude. Thus it was when, in 1827, he heard for the first time in five and twenty years from Amalie von Imhoff, the maid of honor at Weimar, from whose soft eyes he had once drawn the impulse toward a purer and a steadier life. She was now a sedate widow in straitened circumstances; a writer who enthusiastically supported the cause of Greece, and her letter was full of reproaches against him who was accounted the most determined enemy of Greek freedom. It affected the elderly Hofrat deeply, this word from a woman to whom his tenderest recollections had clung in secret for decades, and whom he thought the purest being that he had ever known. For a few days he went pensively about, reviewing old times and recalling old associations. Then he sat him down and wrote:

"I have never been a hypocrite, and have now reached a stage in life when nothing but truth has any influence over me. Thus what I am about to say to you comes from the heart. Throughout all the tumult of an active, stirring, sometimes radiant, and not always happy life your image has been constantly before me like that of a saint. I recall the feeling that you aroused in me as the highest and noblest ever to gladden my heart, and if I have never spoken to you of this memory it was only because I did not dare imagine that my homage could hold the slightest value for you.

"It has pleased you to combine your friendly remembrance with a serious theme, and instead of recalling to me the happy side of our past to announce the continuance of your friendship in a sort of challenge. . . . You refer to my own suspicion over the ultimate fate of my opinions; that is to say, over the ultimate triumph of those that are opposed to them. I might put this suspicion down to my own credit, for it shows at least that through all my activity in deed and effort the impartial view of reality essential to a practical life has not been lacking. But in so doing I should still not have answered the question how and why the anticipated failure of my endeavor was no reason for me to abandon it.

"History is an endless transition from old to new. In this constant succession of events all things destroy themselves, and the fruit that has ripened detaches itself from the tree that brought it forth. But should these recurring changes not lead to the rapid destruction of everything that exists, including all that is good and right, there must necessarily remain, besides the large and finally predominant number of those who labor for the new, a smaller number who, by insisting on moderation, strive to preserve the old, and who, even though they cannot halt the stream of time, wish at least to limit it to a prescribed bed. In periods of violent upheaval such as ours the struggle between these groups assumes a passionate, overwrought, and often angry and destructive character; but the principle always remains the same, and clearer heads on both sides know how to guard themselves from the blunders and follies of their confederates.

"I made my choice in my twenty-fifth year. Fascinated before that by the new German philosophy and also, no doubt, by some supposedly new disclosures in the field of political science, which in those days, however, was still very unfamiliar to me, I recognized my mission clearly and distinctly with the outbreak of the French Revolution. At first I felt, and later knew, that by virtue of the talents and abilities that nature had reposed in me I had been called as a champion of the established, and a foe to innovations. Neither my station in life, my circumstances and expectations at the time, my manner of living, nor any sort of inborn or acquired prejudice, nor any worldly interest had determined this choice. All my earlier political articles were written at a time when, wholly confined to reading and study, I had not the slightest connection with any important political figure, either within or without the country where I lived. That some of these articles should have made my name familiar in higher circles was only natural. My establishment in Vienna as a consequence had a decisive influence upon the further development of my mind, of course, as well as upon my material existence. But even here I remained wholly a volunteer for a longer time, perhaps, than you would believe. With a simple account of my history I could convince you that, although in 1805, 1806, and 1809 I wrote war manifestoes against Napoleon, my real occupation with politics and what I call, in a very modest sense of the term, the period of my political activities did not begin until the close of the year 1812.

"From this time on certain duties connected me with the cause for which I had previously labored only by reason of an inner drive. I became engaged in the most important transactions of a state whose system silly ranters thought to disparage by giving it the honorable name of stability system. I became the confidant of a Minister against whom the liberal party in all countries had sworn deadly hatred, whereas his clear mind and serene and amiable character kept him from becoming a bitter foe to any man. Because of my position at the imperial court a still higher one was occasionally assigned to me, which I may perhaps venture to call European. It has been my rare lot to act as secretary for six sovereigns' and two ministerial congresses: at Vienna, Paris, Aachen, Carlsbad, Troppau, Laibach, and Verona. As all these gatherings were devoted to the preservation or strengthening of domestic and foreign peace they must have been an abomination to the great majority of those to whom peace as such was odious, and who dreamed of nothing but progress, agitation, and overturn. And as I was often credited with a more important share in the decisions than I actually had, I was cursed by a thousand tongues, of course, as one of the most active tools of despotism.

"Those who know me better will acquit me of this charge, nor will they refuse to testify that my character and my way of thinking have always remained the same, and that I have never descended to partisanship, or fought with unfair weapons, or esteemed my opponents lightly. I have always been conscious that despite the majesty and power of my superiors, despite all the single victories that we achieved, the spirit of the age would prove mightier in the end than we; that thoroughly as I have despised the press for its extravagancies it will not lose its formidable ascendancy over all our wisdom; and that guile will be no more able than force to stay the great wheel of time, as you have written with equal truth and beauty. But that was no reason for me not to carry out the task faithfully and persistently, once it had fallen to me; only an unworthy soldier deserts his flag when fate seems unfriendly, and I have enough pride to say to myself in darker moments: Victrix causa diis placuit, sed victa Catoni. . . ." *

His letter was not the product of a momentarily solemn mood. More than twenty-five years previously Gentz had described the task assigned him by fate in almost the same words.

As for Cato's proud solace, it is worthy of note that long years afterward a romantic politician once tried to convert the Junker, Otto von Bismarck, to his side with this quotation. Whereupon Bismarck replied that he knew nothing of such heroism; he would rather be among the victors.

* The victorious cause was pleasing to the gods, but the vanquished one to Cato.

XVII

JULY

Jetzt fühlet schon mein Leib die Näherung des Nichts;
Des Lebens lange Last erdrückt die müden Glieder;
Die Freude fliegt von mir mit flatterndem Gefieder
Der sorgenfreien Jugend zu.
Mein Ekel, der sich mehrt, verstellt den Reiz des Lichts
Und streuet auf die Welt den hoffnungslosen Schatten;
Ich fühle meinen Geist in jeder Zeil' ermatten
*Und keinen Trieb als nach der Ruh.**

THE aging Gentz often recalled this verse, by a celebrated poet of his youth. He was tired of his long balancing on a tightrope. Others had gone before, among them Adam Müller, his friend of years. "My life grows sadder day by day," he lamented. Watching little Franzel, the son of his valet, at play he called his belated and only pleasure.

But his life, at once stunted and blessed, was not to end without rising once more to a crescendo of activity and adventure. Several surprises were still in store for him.

The first of these was that in his middle sixties he was in sound health again. The newly discovered baths at Ischl, it appears, were responsible, and everyone was surprised to find him looking younger by decades. No happiness, no life, without health. The old bohemian felt a renewed zest for living, ventured once more into society, to which he had had an aversion for years, and was found as inspiring and as witty as ever. Anticipation was there, so happiness was not wanting. He went to the theater: *The Unhappy Marriage, Herr Joseph and Frau Waberl, Julerl the Milliner;* and to the ballet: *Orpheus and Eurydice, The Swiss Milkmaid, The Fairy and the*

* Already I await oblivion's coming night;
Life's everlasting burden to weary frame still clings;
And happiness departs, a bird on fluttering wings,
To seek youth's glad release.
Satiety's dark cloud obscures the smiling light,
Drawing across the world its shadow cold and drear;
I feel my heart grow faint, my passions disappear,
And long for nought but peace.

Knight. Here, on November 25, 1829, he leveled his opera glass at Fanny Elssler, the ballerina.

He was entranced. He saw her again ten days later in *The Mountain Sprite,* once more after eight days, and confessed that he had eyes only for her. From then on he went to the ballet as often as he possibly could. He wanted to meet her face to face; to speak with her. The Intendant of the theater, Count Gallenberg, though a little surprised, yielded to his entreaties and invited him and Demoiselle Elssler to supper. The evening saddened him, for in the presence of her employer the girl lost all her enchantment, and appeared plebeian. But no sooner had he seen her on the stage again than he was in love once more, and deeper than ever.

What was to be done? Fanny was nineteen; brunette, and slim, and pale, and beautiful. Her fame was growing rapidly, and had she wished for a "friend" from the world in which Gentz was at home she could easily have had one much more imposing than he, the gray-haired, bohemian diplomat and habitual debtor. As for her heart, there was no lack of gay young men in Vienna, so that nothing remained for Gentz save the joy of resignation; save heartache and bitterness. But just because of his renunciation he felt himself doubly worthy to receive; and slowly and more strongly, month by month, the warming hope was confirmed that in the end he might still achieve the impossible.

He wrote to her on her saint's day: "I could not make up my mind to greet you today with fresh flowers, for they are far too sad a reminder of decay. Among those that I do send, one or another at least will still win an approving glance from you weeks or months later, and perhaps arouse a fleeting thought of me. If only a hundredth part of the wishes that I consecrate to you should be fulfilled, yours will be the happiest lot that ever opened out before a mortal. Your beauty and your talent assure you of many worshipers; I can count myself only among the silent and the unselfish. But of one thing I am proud: How you can be loved, and how you should be loved, by those who wish (with better rights than mine) to deserve your love in return, all who are to come near you may learn to your future happiness, my dearest Fanny, from your faithful admirer, Gentz."

A new friendship, begun at this time, gave him courage. Major Prokesch, a capable young officer, had just returned from a trip of investigation in the Near East, whence he had sent home some admirable reports. He was of modest origin, more scholar than sol-

FANNY ELSSLER (1810–1884)

dier, and a writer and romantic poet as well. Since he was eminently qualified, and at least halfway in agreement with the government, Prince Metternich saw no reason against letting him embark on a career. In Vienna Prokesch made two friends: the Duke of Reichstadt, Napoleon's son, whose restless spirit, confused by an irresistible temptation to achieve something of significance, he tried to steady; and Gentz, whom he met at exactly the right moment. The thawing heart of the inveterate rationalist was refreshed by the friendship of the accomplished soldier. Gentz instructed him, who stood on the threshold of political life, in all its difficulties and anxieties, while Prokesch advised Gentz in his belated adventure and wrote sonnets for him, which were sent to the beloved.

A memorial tablet in Vienna calls Fanny Elssler "the smile of her century." Her father had been Joseph Haydn's copyist, in the service of Prince Esterházy; her family was in modest circumstances, Austrian to the core, Catholic, and fond of life and the arts. Her great talent and her popular appeal, together with her kindness, must have made the charm of this little person complete. She was sensitive and intelligent, but certainly quite inexperienced, and Gentz appeared to her as Faust to Gretchen. He invited her to his luxurious villa in Weinhaus, and showed her his gold dinner service; all his diamond-studded orders in their beautiful cases; his letters, from the rulers of Europe; and pointed with smiling face to his books, of whose contents, God be praised, she understood nothing. In the voice that had charmed so many others before her, he read from his political writings, and especially the celebrated *Preface* of 1806, his masterpiece. No doubt the good Fanny was impressed by all this. But she felt, too, that she was desired for reasons other than mere sensuality; that here was someone who really meant well; and that the salvation of a man who was lonely despite the opulence of his surroundings was at stake.

She yielded, and Gentz was happier than ever he had been before in all his sixty-five years. That which he had always craved amidst his excesses, love combined with a pure, guiding tenderness, now attained a completion beside which his whole former experience with life and with people paled into nothingness.

"I must confess to you," he wrote to his old friend Rahel, "that all the emotions that ever boiled in my breast—and for the past twenty years I had believed myself free of them forever—were mere child's play compared to that which this girl has kindled in me. . . . I had neither looks, nor youth, nor riches, nor anything else to offer that might win a young girl over, much less one who belonged to the stage. The enlightened among the common herd think, and say, that I won her only with my so-called eloquence. That would be remarkable enough, but it is still far from the truth. I won her solely and alone with the magic of my love. When first she met me she did not know, she did not dream, that such a love could be; and she has confessed to me a hundred times that the way in which I treated her from the beginning had opened a new world to her.

"Here alone is the key to the whole matter. Of course I never made the foolish pretense of expecting a response (in the narrower sense of the term), nor ever fancied that she could fall in love with me (for amidst even the most violent transports my common sense never deserted me). I was content to inspire her with a feeling that hovered between friendship, gratitude, and love, and I actually succeeded—as one succeeds in everything toward which one strives with real perseverance and with all one's energy—in establishing and strengthening this feeling to such an extent that gradually it filled her whole soul; until today, unless I am sorely deceived, it could be supplanted or overpowered only with difficulty by any other." "I teach her French, and educate her like a dearly loved child. This is the one occupation that has retained any charm for me, and only in her company am I sometimes able to forget sorrow, age, and death. I look upon her as a gift from Heaven, as a spring flower blooming for me amidst icy wastes and sepulchers."

To Fanny herself: "I cannot end this day without telling you of the feelings with which it closes. It is more, even, than love that inspires me; it is an elation of the soul that comes near to devotion. . . ." "One thing I am sure of is that no length of time, no eternity, can extinguish the feeling that you have aroused in my heart. Even the noble word, fidelity, is not strong enough to express it. I live only in you, and to die has no other meaning for me henceforth than to leave a world where you still live and breathe. . . ."

In his diary he wrote on one occasion, in childlike ecstasy and with red ink: "This evening, which came to an end at half past eleven, can be expressed only in rose-colored strokes. I shall never forget the happiness that fell to my lot today." "We employ ourselves in reading. These calm, sweet hours contrast in the happiest way with the bitter thoughts by which I am consumed. Fanny is, and will remain, my only stay."

Less reserved entries are not lacking, for which he used a special notebook.

Unhappiness is guilt. Since the elderly egotist did encounter this belated joy it must be that he deserved to leave the world a more contented, a more happy, and thus a more innocent man. He was as good to Fanny as he could possibly be.

When travel separated the two there was no end to their longing. So it was during Fanny's appearance in Berlin as a star, to which Gentz acceded, since on no account would he permit anything to interrupt her career; and in July, 1830, when he had to accompany Prince Metternich to Bohemia, and thought only of his love while threatening clouds gathered on the horizon. At such times he received consoling letters like this:

"When I imagine that Gentz is with me, which unfortunately he cannot be, I lose all wish to enjoy myself. When I imagine how you long for me when I read your letters I assure you that I am really sorry for you, that you of all persons, who are so good, should be so heavily punished by fate, only courage my dear Gentz, God still lives and we two still live, and as long as that is so we must not despair. Happier days will come again, that will make up to us for the manny empty and unhappy days only have courage my dear Gentz. I cannot keep from you that it grieves me that in every one of your letters You always say to me that your letters will make me tirred, or even that I have to puzzle over them, do you think that I cannot read your letters? Or do you think perhaps that they annoy me? Oh no you are wrong my dear friend. . . ."

Or: "Good day dear Gentz you are really to astonish that I rite to you in French are you not you see how I follow your advices . . . adieu dear Gentz I kiss you in German and remain your German Fanny."

Among the poets of the day that he read because she would be pleased, and read aloud to her, there was one in particular, a Jew from the Rhineland and a protégé of Rahel, named Heine. Gentz declared himself enthusiastic over him. In the *Book of Songs* there were many in which he saw himself. Strong sensuality, combined or not combined with the highest intelligence; joy in love, barely concealing loneliness, uncertainty, and derision; the playful melancholy, gay impudence, and exuberant virtuosity of the style; and then a sudden breaking through of the genuine, the shining countenance of a human being, sad and pensive, and torn by the struggle of living and thinking—in this portrait of the Rhenish Jew the

Huguenot recognized his own. "I still comfort myself with the *Book of Songs*," he confessed to Rahel. "There is only one man in Vienna that wholly shares my feelings about these poems: Major Prokesch. Varnhagen must certainly know him. I bathe with him by the hour in these sweetly sad waters. . . ."

Society dropped its long-cherished darling. The scandal made its way even into the French papers. The Viennese were amused; that the carriage of Metternich's bosom friend, the graying high priest of "principles," should stand every evening before Fanny's modest dwelling seemed to these easily entertained and quizzical folk like a farce by Raimund come true. How much of the serious, how much of the sad lies concealed in such a farce when one is himself the derided, gray-haired lover, only Gentz knew. The Emperor Franz sniffed, angered in particular because Metternich had compelled him to double the salary of his Protestant Hofrat.

It was all one to Gentz. He went no more to gatherings of the idle aristocracy, but passed his evenings at home with Fanny, and read the latest works of Heine and Börne—revolutionary Jews both.

During this period Prokesch brought him into contact with his other friend, who was even more depressed and unhappy: the son of Napoleon. This association, and that with Fanny Elssler, have been connected and all sorts of stories and operettas have been written on the subject, in which there is but little truth. The philanthropic Gentz merely tried to fulfill the wish of the Duke, that Prokesch be appointed his adjutant; but the attempt was thwarted by Metternich. Prokesch and Reichstadt together, said the Chancellor, would turn the world upside down.

It was early in August, 1830, and Metternich's intimate circle were gathered at his castle in Bohemia, when the news arrived of a reactionary coup d'état by the King of France. Charles X, it was said, had sent the Parliament home, suspended freedom of the press, and restricted the right of suffrage to a few great landholders. Gentz realized immediately that this sudden move would not succeed. After fifteen years spent in developing a system of government that had been gratifying on the whole, and worthy of imitation, France could not return to absolute monarchy. If the impossible old man tried it now his fate was certain.

Less certain was the fate of Europe.

Through couriers from the banking house of the Rothschilds those in the chateau at Königswart learned almost immediately of all that followed: of the uprising of students and workingmen, the street fighting behind barricades, the flight of the last of the three royal brothers so strangely treated by fate, and the timely arrival in Paris of Louis Philippe, Duke of Orleans, whom Gentz knew so well.

Here was the collapse for which everyone had been constantly prepared during the first years of the restoration. Logically it meant war, and the more so because the great Alliance of 1815 was still in effect. That is to say, it surely would have meant war fifteen years previously. But the treaties were old and events were new, and there was no concealing the fact that the treaties were no longer entirely applicable to them. For example, it was wholly unthinkable that the British should make war on France for the sake of restoring Charles X. For the moment there was nothing to do but confer with other European cabinets, delay recognition of the new King, and see what he would do in his turn.

Gentz exerted all his influence in favor of a cautiously empirical and discreet solution of the problem. Had he not, many years before, roamed the woods about Twickenham with the young Duke of Orleans and admired his shrewd, worldly-wise observations? Had he not later, in 1815, desired and prophesied reign by the "younger line"? Had not constitutional monarchy and the "golden mean" been the dream of his youth?

Metternich had no such reminiscences. He declared the golden mean impossible of attainment. He did not believe that the capitalists, the ambitious journalists, the glib professors who were now striving for power in France would be able to provide the country with a stable political pattern; and in the long run perhaps he was not so far wrong. But this crisis was no time for the long view. Gentz besieged the Chancellor with the argument that the influential citizens of Paris had succeeded in halting the revolution through the bulky, bourgeois figure of Louis Philippe, whereas a second world war after only fifteen years would of necessity result in much more dangerous upheavals and social collapse. "Right," he insisted, "is arrayed against wrong; prudence against urgency. A revolution is never right, but once necessity has brought it about its decrees must be accepted. . . . I should become an adherent of Louis Philippe. If he is a scoundrel he will fall. The period will tolerate one as little as a Nero or a Caligula. . . ."

Metternich objected that it was not yet entirely clear what this new French revolution really meant. Events in Paris were obscure and equivocal, and the new rulers took advantage of this ambiguity. Louis Philippe could represent himself to the world as a legitimate monarch, or at least as an almost legitimate monarch; but also as a man of the sovereign people, of national insurrection, of revolutionary brotherhood. Once he had entered upon the dangerous game of power he had to keep both alternatives in mind, to make use of either one according to the way in which old Europe received him. What lay behind the resurrection of such ghosts of the past as Lafayette? What were the plans of the aged Talleyrand, now hurrying to London as the Ambassador of the new King?

In one respect the July Revolution was a triumph for Metternich's interventionism; it proved that Europe was really controlled by one social nervous system, and that when revolution broke out in one country it would soon spread to all the others. It was just this that formerly, in 1789, no one had understood, and that had had to be learned by years of agony.

In August the Belgians rose against the bureaucratic regime of the King of the Netherlands; in November, the Poles against Russian rule; in February, the Romans against their antiquated sovereign. The arrangements effected at Vienna, which statesmen had been trying for fifteen years to confirm and make permanent, seemed to be on the point of dissolution everywhere. The revolutionary wave that had brought him to the top might force the King of the French to help the Poles; that would mean world war. Or to annul the great peace treaties and annex Belgium; this, too, would mean world war or, more accurately put, world-wide civil war. For if the penetrating Heinrich Heine were to be believed, there were no longer any nations in Europe, but only two main parties; and it was a question whether war would not tear asunder any state that entered upon it.

Such were the dangers by which the elders, who had experienced the great Revolution to the full, now saw themselves faced after fifteen fairly peaceful years. Some of them, Professor Hegel, for example, were seized by deep horror and a feeling that the world was falling into ruin. Others, who had profited but little by experience, confused the periods and thought that now they could accomplish and enjoy that in which they had failed forty years previously. A horde of exultant regicides invaded the councils of the Bourgeois King, very old gentlemen all, who had been made barons or princes and considered themselves representatives of the future because they had tried to usher it in four decades since;

but they were merely laughed out of court by the younger people. And still others, more mature, felt called upon to save the world from a repetition of the bloody folly of those days. Among these was Gentz, and he was entirely unmoved when sophists reproached him with inconsistency and change of heart.

To reconcile Europe to Louis Philippe the confirmed mediator regarded as the last task to be laid upon him. In this he counted particularly on the House of Rothschild, who were rumored to have lost seventeen million gulden on the exchange, and were determined to lose no more. His letters were addressed to Baron James Rothschild, in Paris, who employed them in his dealings with the Chief of the Cabinet, Périer, also a banker by occupation, and with the King himself.

The text of the man who had thundered for war against the Revolution thirty-five years previously was now: no war between ideologies! "An idea prevails among the masses, and even among many persons of understanding, that may do more than any other toward paving the way to war, unless the governments resolutely close their ears to it. This is, that in Europe today and, indeed, throughout the civilized world, there are two diametrically opposed systems of thought (generally called Legitimism, and sovereignty of the people) and that sooner or later, preferably sooner, the supremacy of one or the other must be determined by force of arms." Gentz believed this idea to be as false as it was dangerous. It was not true that the two systems could not exist side by side. "In the abstract they are sharply opposed to one another, it is true; but in practice the difference is appreciably lost. . . . When we seek counsel in history we find that Great Britain, a constitutional monarchy, has lived for a hundred years in friendship and close association with purely monarchical states. We find, which is still more remarkable, that Catholicism and Protestantism, thought to be as far asunder as the two poles, can live peacefully together after a hundred years of bloody strife, not only on the same continent but in the same country, and in the same town. . . ."

But in order to counteract the poison in this conflict of systems, continued the tardy advocate of peace in all the wisdom of his years, the forces whose senseless accumulation threatens an explosion must be neutralized, and excessive armaments reduced. Without disarmament there could be neither confidence nor any assurance of peace. Reciprocal disarmament: this was the expression, this the last idea, that the Secretary of Europe drew from his overspent mind; this the course against which Heine subsequently wrote his famous warning to the French ministers. Metternich, interested in a general way, thought that disarmament should be not only material but above all moral, though in view of the activities of the French radicals, the Polish war, and the Italian revolts encouraged by France there was little hope of this.

However, the great crisis ebbed slowly away, about in the manner that Gentz had advocated. Because various and contradictory solutions were entertained in various localities, no ideo-political front cut across the Continent. That Austria acquiesced, willy-nilly, in the division of the artificially created Kingdom of the Netherlands and the establishment of Belgium as an independent kingdom Metternich accounted the worst blot on his career. But Gentz praised this solution as the supreme triumph of wisdom. Long wars had been fought over Belgium in the past.

The most vexatious problem was the eternal Polish question, flaring up ever anew; the curse that pursued an evil deed of sixty years before. "The most important thing of all," wrote Metternich to his Ambassador in Paris, in June, 1831, "is to end the Polish matter; it causes the most appalling confusion in every mind. A nation that defends itself bravely and selflessly will always stir public feeling."

Metternich was not a hard man, and he, too, would have liked to see Poland restored in 1814; but since it was impossible that he could do anything for the insurgents under the circumstances, he saw no desideratum other than a prompt termination of the affair. Not so Gentz. For fifty years, ever since, as a youth, he had first opened his eyes to the doings of politics, he had loathed the wrongs that had been visited on the Poles, and for twenty, at least, had suspected the machinations of Russia on the frontiers of Europe. Now he ventured to say openly that he wished for the victory of the Poles. Was it not true, he asked, that only the miracle of Polish opposition had kept the Czar Nicholas from pushing westward in the interests of the Legitimism of the Bourbons or the House of Orange? Here he showed once again that he was not an Austrian at heart, but a politician without a fatherland; a political free lance. He encouraged the French ministry to mediation "in a spirit of justice." Indeed, he went as far as to hint at an armed threat to Russia, which was almost tantamount to a betrayal of Austrian policy. Not, of course, with a great army; that would be useless against the Czar. A naval demonstration, advised this expert on contemporary history and the map of Europe; a naval demonstration before St. Petersburg and Odessa, would lend the necessary weight to the voice of reason. Why not do for the Poles what shortly before, and in concert with Russia, had been done for the Greeks?

But King Louis Philippe was only too eager to prove to the world that he was no revolutionary, and Polish independence was of as little concern to his bankers as once it had been to Napoleon. Could not Thiers remind the Chamber that the revolutionary Emperor himself had said the absorption of Poland by Russia was predestined by history, and inevitable? Warsaw fell, but before it fell there were horrible murders; betrayed by Europe, faced by certain defeat, the more temperate leaders withdrew and the blind rage of a lost people turned against themselves. It was more convenient, of course, to construe the matter in an opposite sense: the Poles were defeated because the radicals had espoused their cause. With this interpretation did conservative Europe console itself.

The Belgians obtained their rights, but the Poles did not. In Germany there were new parliaments, and even deposed rulers. In Italy the old regimes were sustained by the Austrian Army and a conference of ambassadors, which, however, strongly advised the Pope to try a little modernism. War between the old order and the new did not break out.

Discussing the function of the smaller German states in the *Allgemeine Zeitung*, Gentz wrote: "True to their contractual obligations toward the allied governments, they will be no less true to the pledges given their peoples to foster the development of lawful freedom. . . . In conformity with the spirit of order, and also with the spirit of the century, they will stake their honor on proving to the world that methodical progress is not necessarily incompatible with conservatism; rather, that harmonious union between them is possible; that the real strength of these states lies precisely in such a union; and that this conciliation of antagonistic forces must win them a high place in the republic of Europe. . . ."

They were his last published words. After having wavered his whole life long between the Anglo-Saxon principle of compromise and the Continental principle of intransigence in taking sides, he came to rest on compromise. Once again, as in 1797 and 1815, he was called a Jacobin. In the last year of his life Gentz moved away from Metternich, who, as a diplomat, had once been disposed to adapt himself to Napoleon, but who now stood like a rock of conservatism, like a rigid column, in the ever-widening road along which the century was advancing with constantly increasing speed. The old companions in arms could no longer do without one another, and were sometimes nearly suffocated by laughter as together they read Heine's malicious reports from Paris; but generally they met only to quarrel.

"I like to hear them talking together," noted the Princess, "for despite all his whimseys Gentz retains a gift for inspiring others that never deserts him." "Clemens still found time to quarrel with Gentz, who always ends up by irritating him." "Gentz was absorbed by an article in the *Allgemeine Zeitung*, and Clemens allowed himself to be drawn into an argument with him that terrified me." And so it went on. In the words of this aristocratic lady, they quarreled usually over the "agonizing death struggle of this sad world," the Prince defending intransigence and attack whereas the old and deserted Hofrat was for flexibility and understanding. A thing like the Carlsbad decrees can be attempted but once, Gentz would say, familiar with history and deluded by no romanticism. If it fails, it fails. You think that if you were to act even more harshly now than you did eleven years ago the results would be better. No! They would only be worse. Your Highness cannot contend against the spirit of the age. . . .

The man who spoke thus was even now half detached from this world. His eyes roamed about over the elegance of Metternich's breakfast room, and suddenly he thought: "How easy it all is for many in this world, and how surrounded they are by pomp and glory, while others have only pain, and toil, and sorrow, and must bear the blame besides."

How violently, amidst the great European crisis and at the height of his love for the ballerina, there burst forth again his old sense for the historical and his dormant sympathy for the progress of "reason"; how he did not wish to appear before his Maker as an enemy of his own epoch, so to speak, is shown most clearly in the conversations that were taken down by Major Prokesch. The young officer could still count on thirty or forty more years of life; should they be years of defense, of misery, of defeat? The problems of the day, Gentz said to him, could no longer be solved by force. Metternich's "arch lie" was that he traced all revolutions to secret societies; in other words, to something that could be disposed of easily and neatly. "I shall stand or fall with Metternich; but nowadays he is a fool. If I were to write the history of the past fifteen years it would be one long indictment of Metternich." "Gentz agreed with me that the Prince has not kept abreast of the times." "Long explanations by the Prince of the impracticability of the golden mean. This the reason for Gentz's irritable condition. In the evening he prophesied to me the utter failure of all the Prince's measures against representative government and freedom of the press." Finally, even this: "Gentz admitted to me that the overthrowing of Napoleon was a misfortune for Europe, and the most serious blunder of Austrian policy."

Prokesch left Vienna for Italy, as a diplomatic agent, in the spring of 1832. There, in Rome, he received news of the death of both his friends: the old political sage, and the young revolutionary Duke of Reichstadt. Whereupon he paid Letizia Bonaparte a visit that has become famous.

GENTZ died on June 9, 1832, in his Teinfaltstrasse lodgings in Vienna. He who had feared death for so long, who had shunned all funerals, and had been dizzied by fear at the very sound of *Dies irae, dies illa,* died easily; in despondency, or say, rather, of despondency. He died because he no longer feared death, or because he no longer valued life. During the preceding winter he had put his papers in order, "so that no stain might cling to his memory." On New Year's Eve he had abandoned himself once more to buoyant hopes. Since April, without being really ill, he had felt himself facing oblivion. Cholera, which was raging at the time, had taken its dreadful toll, snatching even at the great: at Professor Hegel; at Périer, Chief of the French Cabinet. In March Goethe had died, and we are told that Gentz was shaken to the core by the news.

The surest sign of his approaching end was that he could no longer feel any affection for his ballerina. Of late he had been living only for her; for her, not for politics, which he now viewed with weary and apathetic clarity. "The feeling that binds me to you is the only one that still survives in me." It wasted away. "The poor child," he said, "tries her hardest to cheer me, but here," pointing to his heart, "her image has become dim."

Toward the end of May he took to his bed. In vain was he besought to take stimulating remedies. "The physician who is treating Gentz," wrote Princess Metternich, "a Doctor Frank, called on us. He complained that the sick man will no longer take the medicines prescribed by his physicians, and added that he would stake his life on the recovery of our old friend if only he would follow directions." But Gentz would not. He would not "commit the infamy of becoming old." And his fate, which had pampered him all his life, remained true to him in death.

Auctions followed. His friend Prokesch, who returned from Rome, acquired some art glassware and a watch. "The man whom I esteemed most highly in life," he set down in his private diary, "was full of weaknesses: Gentz. He was so thoroughly *human!* I can think of nothing better to say of him."

The same thought was expressed in a beautiful and touching letter written by his old friend, Rahel von Varnhagen, nee Lewin. "His perfidies—and he practiced them against me to the full—were different from those of others. He glided, as though borne on Fortune's sledge, along a road that he traveled alone, and no one is to be compared with him. . . . We are bound to praise many persons for all that they are and do, yet they never creep into our hearts; there are a few with whom we can find serious fault, yet they open our hearts to love. Gentz did that for me, and for me he will never die."

Rahel herself followed a year later.

When Fanny Elssler met Prokesch for the first time after her loss, she threw herself upon him in tears, but she did not delay overlong in rendering her youth its due. Her fame, which soon shone throughout the world, helped her to forget the curious fate of her early years and the name with which hers had been linked. From a North American tour she brought back a fortune, far more than her elderly admirer had ever possessed. She died in 1884.

Prince Clemens Metternich, eight years younger than Gentz, outlived him by twenty-seven years, during sixteen of which he continued valiantly to defend the old order against the new; against the monstrous and anarchistic. He was convinced that a long, long chaos would intervene between the old era and the definite establishment of the new, and that only those born after 1900 would be able once more to achieve anything of historical permanence.

How, the good man did not say.

With the death of the eccentric character whose acquaintance he had made as a young diplomat in 1802, in Dresden, and under conditions so grave and trying—gay, too, let it be confessed—Metternich entered upon loneliness and old age. "What would Gentz have said to all this?" he murmured to himself as, in March, 1848, in variously disguised coaches and then on the railway he fled through Bohemia and Prussia to England. There he met old King Louis Philippe, who forty-six years previously had said to Gentz in the House of Commons: "This means trouble." There, too, he met Disraeli, who got on famously with him, but who would have been even more congenial to Gentz.

What would Gentz have said? Gentz, who had gone before, since there was nothing further that he wished to say to all this? He had mistrusted the new era, the era of nations and national wars, of captains of industry, petty bourgeois, and factory workers; the era when man might be no longer interested in history; might even cease to number the centuries. Had they not, in his own youth, and still childlike, begun their count with the Year One? He conceded that this new era would be suited to its sons; but not to him, so proudly and anxiously linked with the past; not to him, great-grandson of the Electoral Court Historian and judge over all the French in Brandenburg. Furthermore, he would have found but little pleasure in going on, especially as his financial returns would have become increasingly exiguous and inadequate.

How much safer it was in the grave, under the stone designed by Fanny's loving hand!

At the age of sixty-eight Gentz had achieved no more than the average expectation of life, and many among his famous contemporaries outlived him by years. The Emperor Franz, who had once so ungraciously given him office, still reigned; the young King of Prussia, too, though now snarling and old, whom Gentz had so impudently advised upon his accession to the throne. Thus if he had experienced so much, so incredibly much, it was not through the tale of his years. He was born one year after the Seven Years' War, at a time when Voltaire, a seigneur of the eighteenth century, stood at the height of his fame. When Gentz died, Napoleon was a wholly discredited myth. Steamships plowed the ocean, carrying artists and businessmen who hoped to do better in America, a state that did not even exist in his youth, than they could have done in the Old World. The last imperial figure, Franz Joseph of Austria, was a child. Otto von Bismarck, who later visited Prince Metternich from a mixture of courtesy, curiosity, sadism, and sympathy, was still a youth. Young, also, were Charles Darwin, Karl Marx, Walt Whitman, and Richard Wagner.

The generations blend marvelously one with another, and not only in the halls of death do men of widely different periods meet and take counsel together.

EPILOGUE

THE hero of our story fared but ill after his death. The usual measure of a politician is his achievements, and none of Gentz's outlasted him. Those who shared his beliefs, in part at least, died off and left no followers, and the factions that came more and more to occupy the political arena were united in regarding him as their enemy; the Nationalists, ostensibly conservatives, hated the cosmopolitan, and the democrats and socialists together damned the reactionary.

Both parties were rooted in the great crisis with which we have been concerned. Napoleon's autocracy had shown the nations what it meant to be deprived of self-government, and the wars of liberation taught the people what they were and what they could claim. Nationalism and democracy grew up together in Europe as brothers, until one killed the other and was itself destroyed in consequence.

The belief that progress comes about automatically was supported by two exponents: nation and class. But great historical forces are never so wholly good as the nineteenth century believed. The German theory of class warfare and revolution destroyed the high hopes that many were building on the Fourth Estate, as the proletariat were then called. German nationalism poisoned the self-realization of nations; indeed, it finally engulfed class warfare and brought forth in 1933 a revolution compared with which Jacobinism and Napoleonism were high-minded moderation. This awful revolution, though born in the hearts of a muddled people, has called in question the very concept "revolution" itself. In the presence of the blindly raging confusion that it caused there must be developed a type of thinking as precise, as individual, and as fresh as that of a few during the great crisis that marked the close of the eighteenth century.

Among those few was Gentz. His portrait can therefore be drawn more accurately today than at the time when they who believed in nationalism and in the people were so sure of their cause.

GENTZ occupies a unique position in modern political history. In comparing himself with Burke, and Burke's career with his own, he deplored the lack of any public life in the German countries;

yet it is doubtful whether his talents could have developed under such surroundings, and whether his eloquence, so brilliantly displayed in salons and conference rooms, would have flourished in the robust and hostile atmosphere of political democracy. He can be thought of only under the conditions in which he actually lived, and in this his milieu he was incomparable.

His real achievement was his life. He was no creative political economist, for example; but his knowledge of British economic theories and British economic conditions was profound and, in Germany, unique. Neither did he exert any influence on the literature of his day; his style was no better than that of the best writers, at a time when everyone wrote well. He was original, however, in raising the composition of political essays and newspaper commentaries to an art, and in polishing a memoir as though it were a poem; so that British, and even French, statesmen gladly availed themselves of the lucid eloquence of this German. Nothing vexed him more than to have those outside his fatherland hold "German" and "obscure" synonymous. It is this love of form, of clarity, that above all is characteristic of him; that distinguished him among his compatriots and set him apart from them.

Finally, Gentz was creative neither as statesman nor as political thinker; most of what he said and thought had been derived from academic tradition and from the past, and even a "stuffy" and visionary man like Adam Müller had more ideas than ever Gentz had. But his intense intellectual awareness as he moved along the path of his thought without ever sacrificing honor or independence; choosing, rejecting, hesitating, alone despite all his sociability, deciding on what was necessary at the moment in accordance with theory, or in the absence of theory, or in defiance of theory—*that* was original. Such a man can be fully represented neither by what he taught nor by what he accomplished. One must try to recapture his personality.

Among practical politicians Gentz was regarded as a scholar; he demanded of statesmanship a maximum of learning, of morality. Among professional thinkers he necessarily ranked as an eclectic and opportunist. He who shared the convictions, untainted by any dialectic view of history, of the early British economists, who praised the emergence of large states as one of the achievements of the Revolution, was at the same time a conservative, and "liked power." He defended positive law, yet would never give up his faith in "natural" law, or justice. He was conservative, but in his youth at any rate, and in effect always, a believer in progress; a rationalist, yet wanted to retain the old solid bulwarks upon which he relied to protect against the irruption of forces that were ostensibly more reasonable, although actually no less irrational.

Thus he thought the thoughts of his time; the contradictions that Hegel's great, imaginative mind had forced together into apparent harmony, into a system, and that here did but feed the energy of his intellect; so that thanks to his philosophical education, or often in the absence of any philosophy, or even in defiance of it, he arrived at decisions that were pragmatically correct. In truth, he was no more rationalist than romanticist; only a shrewd man sworn to clarity. Hence despite all his contradictions there is nothing in his thinking that would mystify. His background was Prussian, Germanic; yet the Western world accepted him gladly, and the commoner from Breslau and Berlin rose to be "Secretary of Europe."

Gentz did much that was good. Good, or at least logical and farsighted, was his early rejection of the *methods* of revolution; the more so because, in his homeland, he was working toward democracy in the sense of a peaceful evolution. Penetrating and brave was his criticism of Prussian neutrality, and in his struggle against Bonaparte, his alarms, his warnings, his rallying cries, he had a touch of greatness, and even of genius. Here he was the European Demosthenes, and this was his real hour. Later, when he wished to save the vanquished and outmoded Emperor, and spare the Continent all the agonies of a war to the finish, the motive at least was good. It is proof of an admirable flexibility of mind that in 1814 he advised against the belated restoration, and in 1815 did his utmost to prevent a vindictive peace that was pregnant with fresh folly. Accurate, amazingly accurate, was his judgment of Prussia after 1813. In the end he won great credit during the crisis of 1830, though in sad contrast with his early beliefs; it was his interpretation of events that saved Europe then from a second world war. In a life devoted to diplomacy, that is sufficient; it indicates an uncommonly large number of accurate judgments in this sphere of perplexity and failure. Whether things would have gone much differently without him, and how effective he actually was, can never be decided, for direct action was never permitted him. Enough that he was one of the guiding spirits of his era.

But Gentz did much, too, that was not good. Here we are not thinking of his campaign against German nationalism—as temperate as it was hopeless. He had ventured to attack a superior opponent that was secretly aware of its own future power, and that always reacted with shameless self-pity; hence he could not escape censure. Nor do we refer to the self-chosen course of his thoughts and deeds, concerned as they were with the state, with society, with *Kultur* rather than with the self-realization of nations. His premises must be accepted as they were, and no doubt there were times when it was more difficult to vindicate them than it is today.

Though always on his guard against a mistaken and too rigid consistency, he did not always avoid what turned out to be the wrong corollaries of his premises. His aversion to the Greek struggle for freedom and his involvement in the Italian disorders were inexcusable. Whether he liked it or not, he was closely implicated in maintaining a fool on the throne of Naples, and in supporting the antiquated pontifical state with Austrian soldiers and Rothschild money. One might argue that this is of comparatively slight importance; that he who has to deal with world affairs and does even a little good under such difficult conditions, has done his duty. But Gentz's faults are too instructive to be passed over in silence.

He was attracted by power; by the old, fragile, skillfully managed power of the Bourbons and the Hapsburgs; of Great Britain, even, because by dexterity and conciliation she had come to own, and painfully defended, possessions that were out of all proportion to her size. But he hated cowardly and inept countries, countries that had not achieved as much as they could in accordance with their populations and prospects; countries that fed on the incalculable strength of their peoples: Russia, and Prussian Germany. He hated the injustice of natural predominance, but was a friend to the unjustifiable power of the weak, superior only through long-established skill and saturated with culture.

Had he been a man of restricted outlook like his friend Metternich, there would be no cause for reproach. But he was not. He was modern, skeptical, and replete with historical understanding. He knew the power of the nations, the power of industry, the power of the press and of all public utterances, and foresaw all the coming events that sooner or later were to effect the ruin of his state, of his society, and of his whole fastidious world. What was his expedient? An assumed division of labor. He justified his activities in behalf of conservatism on the score that thousands of others were fostering progress in one way or another, and that to him, and to him alone, had been entrusted the defense of a "lost cause." He understood his era thoroughly, but instead of pondering deeply over it and reaching a positive, solid, and unassailable position he was content with a biased and evasive one.

Herein lies his fault, lies the betrayal of himself as thinker and statesman; if he had been a mere diplomat it would have sufficed that he secured a long peace for the Continent through the policies that he advocated.

He was a thinker who believed that because he had forced himself into politics he must force himself into one-sidedness, and so was driven into guilt; the more so because he made use of his politics in greedily pursuing the pleasures of life.

This is the advantage possessed by Heinrich Heine, for example, over Gentz. One was a conservative with a weakness for revolution, the other a revolutionary with a weakness for conservatism. Their mistrust of themselves sprang from profound historical misgivings, but especially from their knowledge of the people, to whom they both had the misfortune to belong. They suspected that Germany was as little fitted for revolution, in the Western sense, as for conservatism, and that she was only aping both principles, or serving them deceitfully, while secretly planning a third and more evil one. Burdened with a knowledge that was all too full, all too subtle and discriminating, they liked to console themselves with the idea of the soldier who holds out to the end at a lost post:

> I fought, devoid of hope that I should conquer,
> Knowing unwounded I could not return.

Gifted writers, both won world-wide recognition for German thought and German word; in return they received no thanks from their compatriots, but were repelled and cast aside. For their part, they lived half in Germany and half in France and western Europe, and their national consciousness was blended with criticism and enmity. By virtue of intellectual talent they raised themselves from the middle to the ruling class of aristocrats and bankers, where they strutted as admired prodigies though consumed in secret by financial worries.

Both started in Rahel Lewin's salon, Gentz thirty years before Heine; both crossed the path of the Rothschilds; both were friends, connoisseurs, and jovial critics of Jewry. Both hated Prussia. Both had the passion for moderation, the scorn, the derision, the inclination to laugh that distinguish superior intelligence; hatred for the opponent who would destroy them because they did not think as he did; intellectual vitality; and a sense of dignity and of freedom.

They despised stupidity, success, terrorism, and every form of dictatorship; not only that which they feared would more and more dominate the future. Both had—but Heine, some thirty years younger, more strongly in proportion—the historical sense that later animated Nietzsche: The sensitive feeling for hidden connections that is combined with literary virtuosity, with protest against the Germanic and love for the Western, the Latin, countries. The divine spark of his poetic genius permitted Heine to leave all questions open, and content himself with a serene and finished statement of problems and contradictions. Gentz had to resort to more study and discipline; he became a partisan, made himself useful, and narrowed his scope in order to fit himself for a calling. Only in his letters does he show a sort of kinship with, a friendliness for, the poet whose political articles he mercilessly censored in his official capacity. Heine, it appears, understood this well, for Gentz was long since gone and he himself marked for death when he complained one day that he was so tired of Paris, and would like above all things to go to Austria, "if only Gentz were still living."

Heine's fame was secure in liberal Germany and, indeed, throughout the whole world. The Secretary of Europe was forgotten. An occasional word of praise is to be found in old volumes of English and French journals, but hardly in German periodicals; here the few voices raised in his favor are heard only by scholars. Naturally enough, posterity cares but little for publicists who simply express for their times the anxieties of their times. But Gentz was more than a publicist. If he deserves oblivion and reproach it is because he went no further than to fear the future and the masses, instead of exerting himself to educate the people; because he withdrew into the convenience of mere opposition.

Nevertheless, his struggle against Napoleon's Empire, his enlightened sense of freedom and of the necessity for a voluntary union of the nations, make him worthy of remembrance.

INDEX